ISBN 978-1-333-92669-4
PIBN 10605114

FROM A PHOTOGRAPH BY ELLIOTT & FRY

General Sir William R. Robertson G.C.B. K.C.V.O.

ONTARIO.

# THE GREAT WORLD WAR

## A HISTORY

*General Editor:*
FRANK A. MUMBY F.R.Hist.S.

*Contributors*
THE EDITOR: DAVID HANNAY
C. GRAHAME-WHITE: HARRY HARPER
EDWIN SHARPE GREW & OTHERS

VOLUME VI

THE GRESHAM PUBLISHING COMPANY LTD
34 SOUTHAMPTON STREET STRAND LONDON
1917

# NOTE

The chapters or sections are initialled by the several contributors, namely:—

F. A. M. **Frank A. Mumby.**

E. S. G. **Edwin Sharpe Grew.**

(Vol. VI)

# CONTENTS

## VOLUME VI

# LIST OF PLATES

## VOLUME VI

### PHOTOGRAVURES



### COLOURED MAPS

# THE GREAT WORLD WAR

## VOLUME VI

---

## CHAPTER I

## THE FALL OF KUT

Kut's Fate in the Balance—Fresh Start of the Relief Force under General Gorringe—Capture of the Hannah Position—Racing the Floods—Failure to force the Sanna-i-Yat Position—Overflowing of the Suwekie Marsh—Critical Position of Gorringe's Force—Another Repulse at Sanna-i-Yat—Heartbreaking Weather Conditions—General Keary's Advance along the Southern Bank—Turks flooded out—The Highlanders' Opportunity—Keary's Brief Triumph at Beit Aiessa—Turks' Crushing Counter-attack—Vital Positions Lost—Third Failure at Sanna-i-Yat—Townshend's Vanishing Hopes—Life in the Beleaguered Garrison—Death of Field-Marshal von der Goltz—The *Julnar's* Desperate Venture—A Gallant but Unavailing Attempt—Relief Force exhausted—Garrison starving—The Inevitable End—Last Messages from Kut—The Capitulation—Reception of the News at Home and Abroad—King George's Message—Townshend's Chivalrous Treatment—The Empire's Determination—Honours for the Kut Garrison.

THE veil which concealed from the public at home the critical condition of the heroic garrison at Kut was drawn down over the whole Tigris campaign for some weeks after the repulse at Es Sinn on March 9, 1916. Hopes were raised that the promising Russian advance in Armenia and Persia towards the Tigris basin[1] might link up with the British in time to save the situation, but Kut had fallen before a force of Cossacks, after an adventurous ride from the Persian border, succeeded in effecting the first Russian junction with General Gorringe on the Tigris. The capture of Erzerum by the Grand Duke Nicholas early in the year had failed to shake the hold of the Turks in Mesopotamia. Now that the Gallipoli campaign had released the pick of their troops, they were able to strengthen their grip on their Bagdad outposts, besides resisting the Russians in the Erzerum theatre of war. At all costs, Field-Marshal von der Goltz, commanding the Turco-German operations in the Bagdad region, was determined to capture the British garrison at Kut, little dreaming, after the final defeat of General Aylmer, that he himself would not live to witness a triumph

[1] Described in Vol. V, p. 213.

# THE GREAT WORLD WAR

## VOLUME VI

## CHAPTER I

### THE FALL OF KUT

Kut's Fate in the Balance—Fresh Start of the Relief Force under General Gorringe—Capture of the Hannah Position—Racing the Floods—Failure to force the Sanna-i-Yat Position—Overflowing of the Suwekie Marsh—Critical Position of Gorringe's Force—Another Repulse at Sanna-i-Yat—Heartbreaking Weather Conditions—General Keary's Advance along the Southern Bank—Turks flooded out—The Highlanders' Opportunity—Keary's Brief Triumph at Beit Aiessa—Turks' Crushing Counter-attack—Vital Positions Lost—Third Failure at Sanna-i-Yat—Townshend's Vanishing Hopes—Life in the Beleaguered Garrison—Death of Field-Marshal von der Goltz—The *Julnar's* Desperate Venture—A Gallant but Unavailing Attempt—Relief Force exhausted—Garrison starving—The Inevitable End—Last Messages from Kut—The Capitulation—Reception of the News at Home and Abroad—King George's Message—Townshend's Chivalrous Treatment—The Empire's Determination—Honours for the Kut Garrison.

THE veil which concealed from the public at home the critical condition of the heroic garrison at Kut was drawn down over the whole Tigris campaign for some weeks after the repulse at Es Sinn on March 9, 1916. Hopes were raised that the promising Russian advance in Armenia and Persia towards the Tigris basin[1] might link up with the British in time to save the situation, but Kut had fallen before a force of Cossacks, after an adventurous ride from the Persian border, succeeded in effecting the first Russian junction with General Gorringe on the Tigris. The capture of Erzerum by the Grand Duke Nicholas early in the year had failed to shake the hold of the Turks in Mesopotamia. Now that the Gallipoli campaign had released the pick of their troops, they were able to strengthen their grip on their Bagdad outposts, besides resisting the Russians in the Erzerum theatre of war. At all costs, Field-Marshal von der Goltz, commanding the Turco-German operations in the Bagdad region, was determined to capture the British garrison at Kut, little dreaming, after the final defeat of General Aylmer, that he himself would not live to witness a triumph

[1] Described in Vol. V, p. 213.

which he felt could not much longer be delayed.

The flood season on the Tigris always lasts until May, and Sir Percy Lake, the British Commander-in-Chief, well knew that any further attempt to save General Townshend and his garrison must be made before then, or be too late. Major-General Sir G. F. Gorringe, who succeeded General Aylmer on March 12, 1916, was one of Kitchener's men—he had acted as his aide-de-camp after distinguishing himself in the Khartoum expedition and superintending the reconstruction of Gordon's recaptured citadel—and could be depended upon to do all that was humanly possible in the circumstances. Fresh troops had arrived since the repulse at Es Sinn, and as soon as this reinforcement was complete it was decided to make a fresh start. Unfortunately it was no longer feasible to advance on Kut by the route across the right or southern bank of the Tigris, careful investigations showing that the whole of this area could be inundated, as explained in the preceding chapter, by the breaking of the river bunds, which were under Turkish control. Preparations were accordingly made for an attack on the Hannah position, some 20 miles to the east of Kut, which had defied General Aylmer's attempt to force it in January, and then, if successful, to advance thence along the left or northern bank.

Major-General Sir G. F. Gorringe, who succeeded General Aylmer in command of the Kut Relief Force

Notwithstanding the floods, and the heavy fire from the Turks, the 7th Division had been preparing for this new move during the second half of March by steadily sapping towards the enemy's trenches. Before the end of the month their sap-heads were not more than 150 yards from the Turkish front line. On April 1, the 7th Division were relieved in the front trenches by the 13th Division, who had moved up from Sheikh Saad preparatory to the assault. Both on this day, however, and the following day the rain fell in torrents; some of our troops on the right bank were flooded out of their positions; and the operations had to be postponed. It was not until the evening of the 4th that the ground again became passable, final arrangements being thereupon made to deliver the blow on the following morning.

This attack, which, as Sir Percy Lake testifies, had been prepared with the greatest care, was brilliantly executed by General Maude and the 13th

Division. The enemy held a bottle-neck position at Hannah of formidable strength, as General Aylmer had found to his cost months before. It was now a maze of deep trenches occupying a frontage of only 1300 yards between the Suwekie Marsh and the Tigris, affording no room for manœuvring, and extending for 2600 yards from front to rear. So great was its strength that the Turks thought it could be held with only a few companies and some machine-guns. They were soon undeceived when the attack began at daybreak on April 5, for the 13th Division, jumping out of their trenches, rushed the Turkish first and second lines in rapid succession. Our artillery and machine-guns promptly opened on the third and other lines in rear, and by 7 a.m. the whole position was in our hands. Aeroplane reconnaissance then reported that the enemy was strongly reinforcing his entrenchments at Felahieh and Sanna-i-Yat, 3 and 6 miles respectively from the front trenches just captured by the 13th Division at Hannah. As these positions could only be approached over open ground entirely destitute of cover, General Gorringe ordered the newly-won positions to be consolidated, and further attack to be deferred until the evening.

Lieutenant-General Sir Percy Lake, who succeeded Sir John Nixon in supreme command in Mesopotamia
(From a photograph by Elliott & Fry)

Meantime the 3rd Division under General Keary had been gaining ground on the right bank. The 8th Infantry Brigade, led by the Manchesters, who had fought their way into the Dujailah Redoubt in the forlorn hope at Es Sinn a month before, captured the enemy's position on Abu Roman mounds in the morning, and a strong Turkish attempt to retake it during the afternoon with infantry and cavalry, supported by guns, was repulsed.

During the day the river, swollen with the rains, as well as with the melting of the snows from the Armenian highlands, rose considerably and again proved the dominating factor of the situation. It was obvious that a fresh flood was coming down, and that the only safe course to pursue would be to capture the Felahieh and Sanna-i-Yat positions before the rising tide should enable the Turks to inundate the country between us by opening the bunds. After nightfall, therefore, General Gorringe continued his forward movement along the left bank, where, following upon a heavy bombardment of the Turkish trenches from 7.15 to 7.30 p.m., the 13th Division assaulted and carried a series of deep trenches in several of the Felahieh lines. The Warwicks and Worcesters were singled out for special mention for the gallant part they played in this assault. By 9.30 the whole position, after being stubbornly

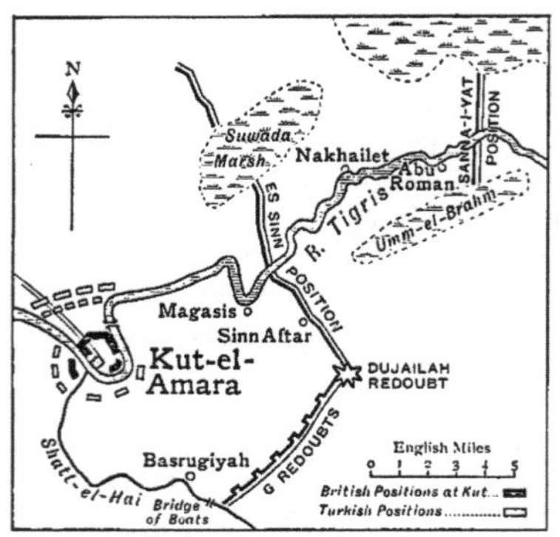


Map showing the Turkish Positions in the Last Actions before the Fall of Kut

defended by three battalions of Turks, was captured and consolidated. "High praise", writes Sir Percy Lake, "is due to Major-General Maude, his brigade commanders, and all under their command for this successful night attack." The casualties suffered by the 13th Division during the day amounted to some 300.

It was now the turn of the 7th Division, which, hitherto held in support, moved forward during the night, and passing through the 13th Division took up a position about 2 miles east of Sanna-i-Yat, ready to attack the northern portion of these entrenchments at dawn on the following morning (April 6). The costly failure which ensued appears to have been largely due to insufficient knowledge of the ground. "Previous reconnaissance of the terrain to be traversed", writes the Commander-in-Chief, "had of course been impossible during daylight, as it was then still occupied by the Turks." The line of direction was to have been maintained by moving with the left flank along a communication trench which joined the Felahieh and Sanna-i-Yat positions, but the passage of numerous and deep cross-trenches so hampered the advance that dawn, when the attack was timed to take place, found the troops still some 2300 yards from the enemy's position. With the ground perfectly flat, and without a vestige of cover, this delay was fatal to success. Sir Percy Lake himself declares that "in these circumstances it would have been wiser to have postponed the attack at the last moment". With the floods still rising, however, and time running so short, it was decided to continue the advance in the face of the deadly fire from the Turkish trenches. Perhaps it was remembered, also, that delay in delivering the attack had been the undoing of General Aylmer's abortive attempt on Es Sinn in the previous month. Whatever the reasoning it was soon apparent that the Turkish fire, both from heavy artillery and machine-guns, was too accurate and destructive to allow any troops to cover the whole of that exposed ground. Though pushing the advance with the utmost gallantry, and reaching within 700 yards of the Turkish trenches, our thinned ranks eventually fell back on to the supporting line, about 1000 yards from the enemy, where they dug themselves in. The operations were hampered by the overflowing of the Suwekie Marsh, which approaches or recedes from the river according to changes of wind. Thus the troops had to fight the floods as well as the Turks, for the river, which had been rising steadily all night and throughout the morning, reached at midday the highest level of the year. What this meant to the troops is shown in the following passage from the official dispatch:—

"The wind changed to the north, and blew the water of the Suwekie Marsh southwards across the right of the 7th Division; protective bunds along both the Tigris and the edge of the marsh had then to be constructed under the enemy's fire. Our guns were surrounded by floods, and for some time the position was extremely critical. The marsh continued to encroach so much on the ground occupied by the 7th Division that all efforts had to be devoted to securing from the floods the positions already gained."

The Turks were probably in similar plight, or they would have taken advantage of a crisis which placed the relief force almost at their mercy. The situation was hardly less serious on the right or southern bank, where the inundations not only rendered communication increasingly difficult, but even threatened to cut off General Keary and the 3rd Division altogether. Fortunately a new bridge, in face of many difficulties, was completed over the river at Felahieh two days later, and safe communication was restored.

The Battle-fields of the Tigris: scene in the swampy desert, intersected by canals, through which the troops had to advance

In the early hours of the following morning (April 9) another attempt was made to carry Sanna-i-Yat by storm, this time by the 13th Division, who had taken the place of the 7th Division in the trenches during the night. The 13th were destined to meet with little better luck than their predecessors. Advancing to the assault at 4.20 a.m. they were discovered when within 300 yards of the enemy's trenches, where Very lights and flares were at once sent up as on the Western front in Europe, and a heavy rifle and gun fire was opened. In the fearless charge which followed, some detachments of the King's Own Royal Lancaster Regiment, Welsh Fusiliers, Loyal North Lancashires, and Wiltshire Regiment fought their way into the centre of the Turkish front-line trench, and victory might have been theirs had supports but reached them in time. But in the glare of the lights the second line appear to have lost direction and wavered, falling back on the third and fourth lines. "Support thus failed to reach the front line at the critical moment," writes Sir Percy Lake, "in spite of the most gallant and energetic attempts of officers concerned to remedy matters."

Somewhere in Mesopotamia: British troops going on picket duty

Another splendid effort had thus been rendered useless, and another repulse registered in the chequered history of the Mesopotamian campaign. The unsupported troops in the enemy's trenches, heavily counter-attacked by vastly superior numbers, were eventually forced back to from 300 to 500 yards from the Turkish line, where the brigades dug themselves in. Though the repulse was serious enough, our losses were grossly exaggerated in the Turkish *communiqués*, in which the enemy declared that 3000 of our dead had been counted in front of his trenches. On being questioned regarding this statement Sir Percy Lake, as the Lord Chamberlain informed the House of Lords on April 13, reported that our total casualties, including both killed and wounded, were much below that figure. He added that the weather was still very bad. There was a hurricane on the 12th, accompanied by torrents of rain, and the floods on both banks were increasing. Some further details of these heartbreaking conditions are given by Mr. Edmund Candler, the representative of the British Press with the Expeditionary Force:—

> "On the night of April 11 we were visited by a thunderstorm of extraordinary violence, and on the following afternoon we had a waterspout, a hailstorm, and a hurricane. The spray was leaping 4 feet high in the Tigris, and on our left and on our right the Suwekie Marsh threatened to come in and join the river and flood our camp. At about sunset it broke into our forward trenches and the Turkish position facing them, a wave of water coming over the bund like a wall, swamping kit, rations, and entrenching tools. Some of the brigade on our right had to swim. . . . These violent disturbances are normal here, as it is a country of excess. The weather is seldom moderate. A storm may be followed by a day of tropical heat, so that there is a difference sometimes of 40 degrees between the day temperature and that of the night."

Sir Percy Lake had been at Wadi in close touch with General Gorringe since April 6, and after this last failure to force the Sanna-i-Yat position the Commander-in-Chief and Corps Commander discussed the situation together in detail.

> "While", writes the Commander-in-Chief, "it was clearly very desirable to secure the Sanna-i-Yat position with its obvious advantages, yet we had to bear in mind how very short the time at our disposal was if Kut was to be relieved, and the delay which a systematic approach by sapping right up to the position must involve. It was therefore decided that another attempt to force the enemy's right about the Sinn Aftar Redoubt offered prospects of speedier success."

This was no easy matter, however, with flooded areas to traverse over which no such thing as a road existed. Some sort of permanent track above flood level, along which transport could work, was essential, in order to supply the troops with food and ammunition when they should have succeeded in crossing the inundations; and arrangements to this end, as well as to secure the control of the river bunds which were covered by the enemy's advanced position at Beit Aiessa, were put in hand at once. On the afternoon of April 12 the 3rd Division under General Keary, holding this southern bank of the river, advanced across the flooded area until they forced back the enemy's pickets east of Beit Aiessa, crossing as they did so inundated belts intersected by deep cuts from 500 to 1200 yards wide, extending from the Tigris to the Umm-el-Brahm Marsh. Some of our troops, after bivouacking in the mud, had to attack waist-deep in water. Having occupied the enemy's advanced line they consolidated the position during the night.

While this advance was in progress the 7th Division, who had again taken over the advance on the northern bank, pushed forward the trench work in front of Sanna-i-Yat as far as the floods and atrocious weather would permit. Friend and foe were handicapped alike at this point, where the water from the marshes was driven by the north-west gale into some of the enemy's trenches, with the result that the Turks, forced to seek refuge in new positions, were severely punished in the process.

> "This temporary target", wrote Mr. Candler, "was a chance not to be neglected. Highlanders got their machine-guns on to them, and mowed down some 200. They were delighted to see the Turks driven into the open at last in the light of day. The enemy's casualties must have been heavy."

The hurricane continued throughout April 14, but died down during the night, and on the two following days the 3rd Division was able to make further progress on the southern bank, capturing the enemy's advanced trenches, which the Turks endeavoured in vain to retake. Many Turkish dead and a considerable number of prisoners were left in the captured trenches on the 16th. That night the guns were moved forward and final preparations made for the culminating assault on the main Beit Aiessa position on the following morning (April 17).

The attack began at 6.45 a.m., when the 7th and 9th Infantry Brigades advanced, under cover of an intense bombardment, with such dash that they actually reached the Turkish positions before our artillery fire lifted. As soon as the bombardment ceased they leapt into the trenches, and a short, sharp, hand-to-hand fight left the Beit Aiessa position in their hands, together with 180 prisoners—including eight officers—two field guns and five machine-guns. The enemy also left from 200 to 300 dead in the trenches. It was a victory, as Sir Percy Lake records, which reflected great credit on Major-General Keary and the troops under his command. Day after day, in the face of appalling conditions, they had made steady and consistent progress, often with a shortage of rations, due to the unavoidable difficulties of transport. The pity of it was that they were so soon to be robbed of the fruits of a triumph which had revived our hopes of winning through to Kut after all. Orders were issued for the 13th Division to move up in relief of the victorious 3rd at nightfall, preparatory to further operations next day, but before these orders could be carried out the foe had forestalled us with a series of counter-attacks which, though they failed to recapture the whole of the position, dashed our new-born hopes to the ground.

Apparently the Turks were able to launch the first of these attacks with some 10,000 men, comprising the whole of one division and portions of two others. So confident were they of their strength that surprise does not appear to have entered into their calculations. This formidable force was seen about sunset approaching from the direction of Es Sinn, and two hours later it launched its attack in dense formations after a bombardment in which the enemy's guns, besides concentrating on Belt Aiessa, established a barrage in rear of the 3rd Division, sweeping the passage through the swamps along which lay their communications. Our own artillery took up the challenge, but the Turks succeeded in pressing home their attack against the 9th Infantry Brigade, a double company from which had been pushed forward to guard the two captured field guns, which could not be brought in during daylight without heavy losses. Unfortunately this double company, retiring before the crushing mass of advancing Turks, masked the fire of its main body. The whole of the 9th in turn was soon hard pressed, and presently gave ground, exposing the left of the 7th Infantry Brigade, which was also forced back. The retreating troops rallied on the 8th Infantry Brigade, which was holding its ground firmly on the left of the line, as well as on a portion of the 7th Brigade. That was the extent of the enemy's gain, though the first assault was only the prelude to a series of others of equal violence, lasting throughout the night, several of which were led by German officers. The 8th Brigade, on the left, repelled as many as six such attacks. Our shrapnel found the advancing foe in spite of the darkness, and as the bursting shells lit up the shadowy battle-field, revealing them advancing or lying prone under the artillery fire, our infantry poured in a deadly fusillade at ground level. Mr. Candler tells us that over 2000 dead were counted next morning at a point opposite this one brigade alone. With their masses of troops, however, the Turks got back their guns, and some bodies of them broke through a gap between two of our battalions. "But our line held firm," wrote the Commander-in-Chief, "and the enemy retreated at dawn, having suffered losses estimated at 4000 to 5000 men." Some Germans were among the killed. Our own losses were not light, but, including killed, wounded, and missing, they were considerably less than the number of Turkish dead. Connaught Rangers, South and East Lancashires, Wiltshires, Punjabis, and Sikhs were among the units mentioned for particularly distinguishing themselves by their steadiness and bravery throughout this stern ordeal, as well as two batteries of the Royal Field Artillery, and a mountain battery which expended all its ammunition and did great execution at close range.

The net result of this memorable battle was that though the enemy had paid dearly for his counter-attacks, and had failed to obtain any success after his initial rush, he had effectually checked our advance, regaining the vital part of Beit Aiessa nearest the river which included the bunds controlling the inundations. The recapture of this portion, as Sir Percy Lake pointed out, was essential. Although some progress in this direction was made during the succeeding days by trench-fighting and by consolidating positions pushed out towards Sinn Aftar, every advance had to be made under the most unpromising conditions, with the flood season at its worst and the whole terrain a sea of swampy mud, where not actually under water. "The boggy nature of the ground", we are officially told, "made movement difficult, and many of the troops were worn out with fatigue."

In the same trying conditions the 7th Division, some 4 or 5 miles behind on the opposite bank of the river, were meantime struggling forward with saps whenever the floods abated. Then came signs of a weakening of the enemy's forces facing them at Sanna-i-Yat, and it seemed that the time had arrived to make another bid for that fiercely contested stronghold. The 7th Division was accordingly ordered to prepare for an assault on April 20, supported by troops on the southern bank, but on the eve of the attack the swollen waters of the marsh again flooded their trenches and the ground in front of them. So the new adventure had to be postponed until the morning of the 22nd, the Sanna-i-Yat position in the meanwhile being systematically bombarded. When at length, however, the 7th Division advanced, after a final bombardment, it was found that the floods made it possible for one brigade only to attack, the extreme width of passable ground being reduced to some 300 yards. The leading troops of this brigade—the 19th, consisting of a British composite battalion—advanced with grim determination under cover of our artillery on both banks, as well as massed machine-guns on the southern bank, and carried the enemy's first and second

Drawn by Douglas Macpherson

**The Navy's Share in the Mesopotamian Campaign: river gunboats on the Tigris supporting infantry columns on the river banks**

The bridge and gun-positions, as well as other vital parts of the vessels, were protected by piles of sandbags. Besides an observing-station improvised on the forward mast of the gunboats, giving a wide range of vision over the desert on either side, other look-out stations were erected on the barges, and covered with greenery, as shown in the illustration, to confuse the Turkish gunners.

lines in their immediate front, fighting their way in spite of bog and flooded trenches. A few men even penetrated the third line. But the Turks, now heavily reinforced, counter-attacked in superior strength, and though their first assault was bloodily repulsed the unsupported British troops were unable to maintain themselves against the next attack. Many of them, unable to use their rifles, which had become choked with mud in crossing the flooded trenches, were powerless to reply to the enemy's fire; and other brigades, pushed up to right and left to reinforce them, had failed to reach their objective across that swampy wilderness under the withering fire from the Turkish machine-guns. Thus the day was lost by 8.40 a.m., and our exhausted survivors were back in their own trenches. Both sides suffered heavily, our casualties amounting to about 1300. Those of the Turks could only be estimated from the significant fact that they were evacuating their wounded until nightfall. By mutual consent, it should be added, parties went out on this occasion to collect their respective wounded under the Red Cross and Red Crescent flags.

With this costly failure disappeared the last hope of saving Townshend and Kut, unless supplies could be rushed through to enable that hard-pressed garrison to hold out until the relief force could gather fresh strength for a further attempt. Communication with Kut had been maintained by wireless throughout the operations, and it was known that at the outside not more than six days' reduced supplies remained to the garrison. Yet the humiliating acknowledgment had to be made, after these persistent but unsuccessful attempts on both banks, that it was now physically impossible for the relief force to win through in that time.

"General Gorringe's troops", writes Sir Percy Lake, "were nearly worn out. The same troops had advanced time and again to assault positions strong by art and held by a determined enemy. For eighteen consecutive days they had done all that men could do to overcome, not only the enemy, but also exceptional climatic and physical obstacles—and this on a scale of rations which was far from being sufficient, in view of the exertions they had undergone, but which the shortage of river transport had made it impossible to augment. The need for rest was imperative."

Meantime, in Kut itself, the garrison was weak with hunger, and, after more than four months of close investment, very near the end of its resources. So weak were the troops that they had not sufficient strength towards the end of their long ordeal to carry their kit. The different units saw little of one another during this closing phase, save in the liquorice factory on the southern bank, where the two battalions holding that post could supplement their rations with fish, and life generally was more tolerable than in the garrison itself. Here neither officers nor men had much strength left for unnecessary walking, and during the last fortnight of the siege the force was so exhausted that the regiments holding the front line remained there throughout that time without being relieved. Mr. Candler, who was able to furnish the first particulars of these privations from wounded officers afterwards exchanged, states that the daily death-rate during the last days of the siege averaged 8 British and 21 Indians. On April 21, the day before the last failure of General Gorringe to force the impenetrable barrier of the Sanna-i-Yat, the 4-oz. grain ration gave out. From the 22nd to the 25th the garrison lived on the two days' reserve ration issued in January; and from the 25th to the 29th on supplies dropped by aeroplane.

The rations had been gradually reduced with each succeeding week as one disappointment followed another in the news of the relief force. Some Arabs who succeeded in escaping down the river spoke of the continued cheerfulness of the garrison, in spite of their privations, and of their confidence that the place would even yet be relieved. It was added that the respect of the Kut inhabitants for General Townshend, based on his personality and the achievements of the troops under his command, was not far short of idolatry. The stores dropped by aeroplane at this stage consisted chiefly of salt atta, flour, and tea.

> "Previously", according to Mr. Candler, "aeroplanes had been employed for dropping light articles into the camp, such as rifle-cleaners, spare parts for wireless, nets for fishing, and at one time cigarettes and tobacco, but, as it was impossible to supply all, General Townshend ruled out these luxuries as introducing a form of privilege. He himself shared every privation with his troops."

The dearth of tobacco was a great hardship throughout. As much as 8*d.* was paid for a single cigarette towards the end. One box of Egyptian cigarettes realized £8, and a single tin of condensed milk £2, 5*s.* English tobacco was worth nearly 10*s.* an ounce even in January, and when that was exhausted every kind of substitute was tried to satisfy the smokers' craving. All the animals found their way into the larder before the end, save a few irreplaceable pets like General Townshend's fox-terrier Spot, which was among the first members of the Kut garrison to return to Basra, bearing an inscription in his master's handwriting setting forth his record of service from the battle of Kurnah, in December, 1914, to the siege of Kut. The story is told of a favourite mule whose life was saved almost to the very last. It wore round its neck the ribbons for three campaigns on the Indian frontier, and when sent at last to go the way of all dumb creation in Kut was twice returned by the supply and transport butcher, who had not the heart to kill it. In the end, however, it had to be sacrificed like the rest of the artillery, cavalry, and transport animals. A new unit, known as the "Kut Foot", was formed by the drivers of the field batteries when the artillery horses had gone to replenish the larder.

Hostile aeroplanes added considerably to the hardships and perils of the garrison, especially during February and March, when more damage was done by aviators' bombs than from shell-fire. One bomb, on March 18, fell on the hospital, killing and mortally wounding 10 British soldiers and wounding 22 others. On the previous day a number of bombs fell near head-quarters, killing many Arab women and children, after which the aviator sank one of our boats, which carried a 4.7-inch gun. Thenceforward the enemy appeared to be reserving both their bombs and their shells for the relief force, restricting their artillery fire to the evening bombardment, which generally took place between 4 and 6 o'clock.

With General Townshend at Kut: view within the lines of the beleaguered camp

"Their shelling", to quote from Mr. Candler's dispatches, "was mostly confined to the town and fort, where the Union Jack and observation post offered a good target with a battery of 5-inch guns, and head-quarters adjacent. They had some naval guns, but the majority were 40-pounders. On the right bank they had a species of trench mortar, christened by our soldiers "Petulant Fanny". She fired very noisy 15-inch bronze shell, always in the same place, but never hit anybody."

On April 19, 133 days after General Townshend's arrival in Kut, and three days before the final repulse of the relief force at Sanna-i-Yat, Field-Marshal von der Goltz, according to a Berlin official telegram, died of spotted fever in the head-quarters of his Turkish army. Sinister rumours were afterwards heard as to the real nature of his death, but whatever the cause his disappearance heightened the tragedy of an event which undoubtedly crowned his many years of work as the reorganizer of the Turkish army. When he died our only hope of staving off the impending disaster at Kut was the introduction of such additional supplies into the beleaguered camp as would enable it to hold out for a still longer period. In the hope of prolonging the resistance even for a day or two, aeroplanes both from the Royal Flying Corps and the Royal Naval Air Service dropped emergency supplies amounting between April 16 and April 29 approximately to eight tons, besides fishing nets, medicines, and specie. Although these supplies, as Sir Percy Lake pointed out, could not materially alter the course of the siege, the performance merited high praise, involving a great strain on the pilots, who were subject at the same time to attacks by enemy air-craft of superior speed and fighting capacity. One of our machines was shot down in the course of these operations and another damaged, but this last, with great skill, was brought safely home.

There now remained but one faint chance of reaching Kut with sufficient supplies to enable it to hold out until relief arrived, and that was by river. It was a poor chance, but the Royal Navy was ready to make the attempt, and accordingly prepared the *Julnar*, one of the fastest steamers on the Tigris, to run the enemy's blockade. With a picked crew under Lieutenant H. O. B. Firman, R.N., and Lieutenant-Commander C. H. Cowley, R.N.V.R., the gallant *Julnar*, carrying 270 tons of supplies, left Felahieh on her hazardous mission at 8 p.m. on April 24. Lieutenant Firman, who held the Persian Gulf and Somaliland medals, had been selected to command a river gunboat on the Tigris at the beginning of the year, and Lieutenant-Commander Cowley, in the Commander-in-Chief's own words, "held a magnificent record of service throughout the campaign in command of the *Mejidieh*". Both officers cheerfully volunteered for a duty which they knew to be, at the best, a very forlorn hope.

The British Head-quarters at Kut: view showing the wireless installation on the roof

"All the gallant officers and men who manned that vessel for the occasion", wrote the Commander-in-Chief, "were volunteers, among them Engineer Sub-Lieutenant Lewis Reed, the regular chief engineer of the vessel." Though the Tigris was then at its highest level owing to the floods, the darkness and the ever-shifting shoals would have made the venture risky enough with friends on either side; but in an enemy's country, with a gauntlet of guns to be run for some 25 miles by river, and unknown obstacles to be navigated in the shape of mines, booms, and the like, the odds were 100 to 1 against the *Julnar's* success. In the hope of distracting the enemy's attention her departure was covered by all the artillery and machine-gun fire that could be brought to bear by the relief force, but the Turks were too alert to be caught napping in this way. The *Julnar* was discovered and shelled. The astonishing thing is that she succeeded in running this gauntlet until she was well beyond the Turkish main position at Es Sinn, two-thirds of the way towards her destination, when she ran aground and fell into the enemy's hands. General Townshend, well aware that the attempt was being made, reported at 1 a.m. on the 25th that she had not arrived, but that at midnight a burst of heavy firing had been heard at Magasis, about 8½ miles from Kut by river. The firing had suddenly ceased, and there could be little doubt that the daring enterprise had failed. This was confirmed all too clearly next day by our aeroplanes, which reported the *Julnar* aground and in the hands of the Turks at the point indicated by General Townshend. Both officers on board—Lieutenant Firman and Lieutenant-Commander Cowley—were afterwards reported by the enemy to have been killed, and the remainder of the gallant crew, including five wounded, to be prisoners of war.

The fall of Kut was now only a question of days. There was no further hope of extending the food limit of the garrison, for the amount that could be dropped by air-craft was negligible. "Everything that was possible with the means to hand", wrote Sir Percy Lake on behalf of the relief force, "had been attempted. The troops only desisted from their efforts when, through battle, losses, sickness, and exhaustion, the limit of human endurance had been reached." It was perfectly true. When every allowance has been made for the mistakes which marred the advance of the relieving force in certain of its stages, there can be no doubt that the valour of our troops would have carried them through to their comrades but for the inconceivable physical difficulties which faced them at every turn.

To General Townshend and his devoted garrison the now inevitable end, after a defence which will rank high among the great deeds of the British and Indian armies, must have been harder to face than all the hordes of besieging Turks. Britons and Indians alike, they had endured to the uttermost. They had held their post for 143 days, and would have died there had there been any hope thereby of saving Kut for the relief force. But this, as they learnt from the Commander-in-Chief, was impossible. They had, they were assured, already done their duty fully, and having no strength left for a fight which could only mean annihilation, they were ordered by the Commander-in-Chief of the army of which General Townshend's division formed a part, to negotiate for surrender. Proof of this is contained in General Townshend's *communiqué* to his force on April 28, printed below, explaining how, their limit of endurance having been reached and the relief force finding itself unable to reach them in time, there was nothing for it but capitulation. "Not by arms," as one of the garrison put it with justifiable pride in a letter home, "but by starvation. . . . It was a bitter blow, but there, that was all there was to be said." Negotiations were opened with the Turkish Commander-in-Chief, Khalil Pasha, on the 27th by General Townshend himself. Something of his anguish of mind as well as bodily illness is revealed in his *communiqué* of the following day, expressing his hope that his personal interview would secure for his men exceptional terms. His message was as follows:—

"It became clear after General Gorringe's second repulse on April 22 at Sanna-i-yat, of which I was informed by the Army Commander by wire, that the relief force could not win its way through in anything like time to relieve us, our limit of resistance as regards food being April 29. It is hard to believe that the large forces comprising the relief force now could not fight their way to Kut, but there is the fact staring us in the face. I was then ordered to open negotiations for the surrender of Kut, in the words of the Army Commander's telegram.

"'The onus not lying on yourself. You are in the position of having conducted a gallant and successful defence, and you will be in a position to get better terms than any emissary of ours. The Admiral, who has been in consultation with the Army Commander, considers that you with your prestige are likely to get the best terms—we can, of course, supply food as you may arrange.'

"These considerations alone—viz. that I can help my comrades of all ranks to the end—have decided me to overcome my bodily illness and the anguish of mind which I am suffering now, and I interviewed the Turkish General-in-Chief yesterday, who is full of admiration of 'an heroic defence of five months', as he put it. Negotiations are still in progress, but I hope to be able to announce your departure for India on parole not to serve against the Turks, since the Turkish Commander-in-Chief says he thinks it will be allowed, and has wired to Constantinople to ask for this."[1]

These terms, however, were refused by the Higher Command at Constantinople, the Turkish report of the proceedings stating that their reply was that there was no other issue than unconditional surrender. As will presently be seen, however, the sick and wounded were afterwards exchanged. The curtain fell on the closing act of the drama at Kut on April 29, 1916, when the gallant commander, bowing to the inevitable, sent word to Khalil Pasha that he was ready to surrender. The last wire-

[1] *Times*, December 13, 1916.

In one of the Streets of Beleaguered Kut

Employed by the British at Kut: two Arab policemen

less messages from General Townshend to British Head-quarters were received that day in the following order:—

Have destroyed my guns, and most of my munitions are being destroyed, and officers have gone to Khalil, who is at Madug, to say am ready to surrender. I must have some food here, and cannot hold on any more. Khalil has been told to-day, and a deputation of officers has gone on a launch to bring some food from *Julnar*. [The ship sent on the night of April 24 to carry supplies to Kut.]

II

I have hoisted the white flag over Kut fort and town, and the guards will be taken over by a Turkish regiment which is approaching. I shall shortly destroy wireless. The troops go at 2 p.m. to camp near Shamran.

III

We are pleased to know we have done our duty, and recognize that our situation is one of the fortunes of war. We thank you and General Gorringe and all ranks of the Tigris force for the great efforts you have made to save us.

This last message was read in the House of Lords a few days later by Lord Kitchener, who paid a warm tribute on that occasion to General Townshend and his troops, "whose dogged determination and splendid courage have earned for them so honourable a record".

"It is well known", he added, "how, after a series of brilliantly-fought engagements, General Townshend decided to hold the strategically important position at Kut-el-Amara, and it will not be forgotten that his dispositions for the defences of that place were so excellent and so complete that the enemy, notwithstanding large numerical superiority, was wholly unable to penetrate his lines. Noble lords will not fail to realize how tense was the strain borne by those troops who, for more than twenty weeks, held to their posts under conditions of abnormal climatic difficulty, and on rations calculated for protraction to the furthest possible period until, as it proved, imminent starvation itself compelled the capitulation of this gallant garrison, which consisted of 2970 British and some 6000 Indian troops, including followers.

"General Townshend and his troops, in their honourable captivity, will have the satisfaction of knowing that, in the opinion of their comrades, which I think I may say this House and the country fully share, they did all that was humanly possible to resist to the last, and that their surrender reflects no discredit on themselves or on the record of the British and Indian armies."

The first announcement to the British public, issued on the Saturday evening of April 29—within a few hours of the hoisting of the white flag over Kut fort—was probably a harder task to write than any message that Lord Kitchener ever had to issue from the War Office. "After a resistance protracted for 143 days," it began, "and conducted with a gallantry and fortitude that will be for ever memorable, General Townshend has been compelled by the final exhaustion of his supplies to surrender." He added that before doing so General Townshend had destroyed his guns and munitions, and quoted the figures already given as to the strength of the garrison at the capitulation. Though the news was not unexpected, it was received throughout the Empire with something of a personal shock, and, with the recent withdrawal from Gallipoli, was undoubtedly a heavy blow to British pride. It was naturally felt with the most painful keenness by the relief force. "I need not enlarge upon the bitter disappointment felt by all ranks on the Tigris line", wrote Sir Percy Lake, "at the failure of their attempt to relieve their comrades at Kut." This was mitigated by their Sovereign in a gracious message on May 7, 1916, in which His Majesty telegraphed to General Gorringe through the Commander-in-Chief to the following effect:—

"Although your brave troops have not had the satisfaction of relieving their beleaguered comrades in Kut, they have, under the able leadership of yourself and subordinate commanders, fought with great gallantry and determination under most trying conditions.

"The achievement of relief was denied you by floods and bad weather and not by the enemy, whom you have resolutely pressed back.

"I have watched your efforts with admiration, and am satisfied that you have done all that was humanly possible, and will continue to do so in future encounters with the enemy.

"GEORGE, R.I."

There was something of the old chivalry of war in the circumstances surrounding the surrender of Kut to the Turks. As General Townshend informed his garrison in his *communiqué* of the 27th, the heroic nature of the defence had already been acknowledged by the Turkish Commander-in-Chief, who now accorded him the honours of war by allowing him to retain his sword. Khalil Pasha was also anxious, he said, not only that the garrison should be well and promptly rationed, but that General Townshend should receive every possible comfort after the privations he had so gallantly endured. His one regret was that the supplies at his command were not more plentiful. Permission was accordingly obtained for the dispatch of stores from the British relief force, two barges loaded with day-and-half "iron rations" being sent in due course from General Gorringe's camp. By the courtesy of the same Pasha Sir Percy Lake was able to arrange on April 30 and the following days that all the more serious cases among the sick and wounded of the surrendered garrison should be handed over to the relieving force for an equivalent number of Turkish prisoners. Hospital and other ships were sent up at once to begin the evacuation of the sufferers, and by May 8 a total of 1136 sick and wounded had been safely brought down stream. Some 80 per cent of the sick were Indians. Mr. Candler mentioned that among the points discussed in the negotiations was the safety of the civil population of Kut, who, it was explained, had been retained there by *force majeure.* The Pasha said in reply that he contemplated no reprisals, but that the treatment of the inhabitants would depend on their future behaviour. He could give no pledge, but he did not intend to hang or persecute.

Thus ended a defence which, in spite of its unhappy ending, had created universal admiration. Our Russian Allies pointed out that, far from having served no useful purpose, General Townshend's force had attracted to itself two Turkish Army Corps, which were thus prevented from operating either against Salonika or Egypt, or against the Russians on the Caucasian front. General Joffre voiced the admiration of the French Army in a message of sincerest sympathy, while the French press described the resistance of such a handful of men to 60,000 soldiers for 143 days as a feat redounding to the honour of British arms, and adding a fresh page of glory to a history which was already full of such deeds. Perhaps the most inspiring message of all came from the Commonwealth of Australia, in which the Governor-General, expressing on behalf of the Government and people "their profound sorrow and sympathy in the loss of the gallant garrison of Kut-el-Amara", added that the disaster would but strengthen Australia's determination to do her part in hastening the overthrow of Britain's enemies. All India, as Lord

With the Red Cross in Mesopotamia: a halt on the march

Chelmsford, the new Viceroy, said in reply to the Commonwealth's message, was stirred by the Australian message. "The war", he truthfully added, "has created bonds of common sympathy and purpose through which all failures will be retrieved."

In a supplement to the *London Gazette* published nearly six months after the fall of Kut, a list was published of rewards and honours conferred by the King on members of General Townshend's garrison for operations before the siege began. All the officers included being prisoners of war, an explanatory note was issued to the following effect: "These officers are excepted from the rule that prisoners of war cannot be considered for reward, on the ground that had not unavoidable delay occurred in transmitting the recommendations, the awards would have been gazetted before the date on which the officers became prisoners". Major-General Townshend, C.B., became a military K.C.B.; Lieutenant-Colonel Frederick A. Wilson, R.E., and Lieutenant-Colonel Walter H. Brown, Mahratta Light Infantry, military C.B.'s; and Lieutenant-Colonel William B. Powell, Gurkha Rifles, and Lieutenant-Colonel E. A. E. Lethbridge, D.S.O., Oxford and Bucks Light Infantry, C.M.G.'s. Fifteen officers received the D.S.O., and eighteen, including two chaplains, the Military Cross. The complete list is given below. F. A. M.

---

DISTINGUISHED SERVICE ORDER

Major Ernest Vaughan Aylen, M.B., R.A.M.C.
Lieutenant-Colonel Hubert Oliver Browne Browne-Mason, R.A.M.C.
Major Thomas Roger Massie Carlisle, R.F.A.
Captain Reginald Charles Clifford, Indian Medical Service.
Major Harold Charles Hill, Mahratta Light Infantry.
Captain Charles Molyneux Sandys Manners, Rifles.
Lieutenant Alec Bryan Matthews, R.E.
Captain (temp. Major) James Charles M'Kenna, Rajputs.
Captain Leo Murphy, R.A.M.C.
Captain Basil Gerard Peel, Pioneers.
Captain and Brevet-Major Hugh Lambert Reilly, Punjabis and R.F.C.
Captain Gerard van Rossum Reyne, Punjabis.
Lieutenant-Colonel Henry Broke Smith, R.F.A.
Lieutenant Roy Thornhill Sweet, Gurkha Rifles.
Major Herbert Guy Thomson, R.F.A.

MILITARY CROSS

Captain David Arthur, M.B., Indian Medical Service.
Lieutenant William Barton, Dorset Regiment.
Captain Francis Ivan Oscar Brickmann, Infantry.
Qr.-Mr. and Hon. Capt. Alexander Brown, Dorset Regiment.
Lieut. (temp. Capt.) Ernest Wyndham Burdett, Pioneers.
Lieutenant Thomas Campbell, Norfolk Regiment.
Captain Henry Spencer Cardew, Garhwal Rifles.
Second-Lieutenant William Devereux, R.F.A.
Lt. (temp. Capt.) Arthur Henry Norman Gatherer, Punjabis.
Lieut. William Sydney Halliley, R. of O. (attd. Rajputs).
Sec.-Lt. Edward Claude Le Patourel, R. of O. (attd. Infantry).
Captain Albert Thomas James M'Creery, M.B., R.A.M.C.
Captain Kalyan Kumar Mukerji, Indian Medical Service.
The Rev. Father John Mullan, Ecclesiastical Establishment.
Lieut. (temp. Capt.) Cyril Arthur Raynor, Pioneers.
Captain Edward Warren Caulfield Sandes, R.E.
Captain Charles Hugh Stockley, Punjabis.
Junior Chaplain the Rev. Harold Spooner, Ecclesiastical Establishment.

# CHAPTER II

## THE RUSSIAN CAMPAIGN OF 1916

Russia's Deceptive Immobility—German Line and Commands North of the Pinsk Marshes—Austrian Armies and Commanders South of the Pripet—The Austrian Defences—The Russian Soldier—General Brussilov's Strategical Plan—Kaledine's Thrust and the Lutsk Salient—Scherbatcheff's Attack on Bothmer—Lechitzky's Demolition of Pflanzer-Baltin—Position at end of First Week of Operations—Linsingen's Counter-attack on the Stokhod against Kaledine—Lesh's New Outflanking Manœuvre—Sakharoff's Repulse of Linsingen—The Spreading Nature of the Russian Attack towards Brody and towards Kolomea farther South—German Reorganization of the Austrian Commands—Lechitzky's Capture of Stanislau—Bothmer's Retreat to the Zlota-Lipa—Summing-up of the Summer Campaign.

IN the winter of 1915–16 the Russian army had gathered fresh strength, putting forth in the spring a tentative paw here and there; and in March, when the Germans in the West had committed themselves to the attack on Verdun, had shown signs of an ability, or a willingness, to make a thrust forward again in the neighbourhood of Vilna. It was at the Vilna salient that the German attack the year before had, in Lord Kitchener's phrase, shot its bolt; and Vilna, with its strategic value as a nodal point of railway and other communications, represented the high-water mark of the German tide of invasion. It was also, to change the metaphor and adopt one which the Germans had applied to Verdun, the eastern portal for an invasion of Germany. Needless to say, therefore, that the Germans held it strongly, in men and in fortifications. The Russian assault in such a sector was therefore no more than a demonstration, and could have been interpreted in no other sense by the strategists of the German Higher Command, which nevertheless affected to regard it as a serious attempt to break through their lines, and magnified its repulse accordingly. Whether this was done to influence public opinion in Germany or elsewhere it is impossible to say; but, having thus asserted that the Russian "recovery" after the winter recuperation was ineffectual in enabling Russia to undertake the offensive, the German Head-quarters Staff appears to have hypnotized itself into this belief, and to have come to the conclusion that Russia was a negligible quantity.

It was in this belief that the long-prepared attack on Verdun was pursued through April and May after the first attempt at surprise had failed; it was because nothing occurred during the first half of the year to disturb the German confidence in Russia's immobility that Berlin sanctioned the Austrian attack on the Italian flank in the Trentino, and permitted the Austrian Higher Command to withdraw divisions and guns from the Austrian front which was facing the Russians south of the Pinsk marshes. It does not seem likely that this grandiose attack on Italy was conceived in the minds of the Austrian command at all. On the contrary, it bears the trade-mark of German origin. Russia's capacity to strike was not fully known even to her friends. Lord Kitchener's ill-fated journey to Russia was in part undertaken to ascertain what was the exact condition of Russian preparedness. It is no exaggeration to say that when it was revealed it astounded Russia's allies almost as much as the common enemy.

In the months from March to June, 1916, the part of the line on the Austro-German front which was most strongly held was that north of the Pripet and the Pinsk marshes. This was held by German troops; the general disposition of the German and Austrian forces being that the Germans held the front from the Gulf of Riga to the Pinsk marshes, a distance of 450 miles, and the Austrians continued the line from the marshes and the Pripet to the borders of Roumania, a distance about 100 miles less. A few troops of each power stood in the line of the other, but only one Austrian army corps was in the northern German section, while the German contingent with the Austrians was limited to a few divisions. The German chief command was under Marshal von Hindenburg, whose head-quarters were at Kovno. The most northerly section of his front, facing north-north-east, and covering Riga and the Dvina as far as Friedrichstadt and Jakobstadt, was held by the Mitau army detachment. Next in order, facing north-east, was von Scholtz, with the Eighth Army, covering Dvinsk and the front as far as Lake Drisviaty. From Lake Dris-

Russia's "Recovery" after the Campaign of 1915: one of her machine-gun sections in action

The Archduke Joseph Ferdinand, commanding the Fourth Austrian Army

viaty to Lake Narotch, the region of the lakes, was a shorter and strongly held sector held by von Eichhorn and the Tenth Army. General von Fabeck and General von Woyrsch, facing due east, held the line with the Twelfth and Ninth Armies respectively from Smorgen to Lipsk and the beginning of the Oginski Canal. The Ninth Army included the 12th Austro-Hungarian Army Corps. From the point where the Oginski Canal turns due north and south to the Pripet and to the angular salient of Pinsk was held by an army detachment under the amiable Prince Leopold of Bavaria. It was estimated that along this part of the front forty-eight German divisions were strung, an average of about 1300 men to a mile—not a very strong holding, but distributed with its masses at vulnerable points.

South of the Pripet the chief command was held by the Austrian Archduke Frederick, a portly but quite incompetent general. His command divided itself topographically into two parts. The more northerly one was in Volhynia, the southerly one in Galicia and Bukovina. The Volhynian district was held by General Pulhallo von Brlog with the Third Austro-Hungarian Army covering the district from the marshes to Tchartoryisk, and by the Archduke Joseph Ferdinand with the Fourth Army from Lutsk to Dubno, facing Rovno. But with these two armies was merged another, which was never mentioned till the Austrian debacle began, under the German von Linsingen. It is probable that von Linsingen, who had had a considerable share in the German advance of the preceding year, provided the staff and framework for a force which was filled out with Austrian troops. Adjoining these armies was the Second Austro-Hungarian Army under General von Boehm-Ermolli, which stretched from a point south of Dubno to the railway line which joins Lemberg to Tarnopol. The rest of the Austro-Hungarian front was held by the two armies of Count Bothmer and General von Pflanzer-Baltin, who joined one another at Bucacz.

In the spring of 1916 these Austro-Hungarian forces amounted in the aggregate to about twenty Austrian and two German divisions. They were depleted for the great adventure in the Trentino, but the largest withdrawals did not come from the front line but from the reserves. The German Higher Command did not believe that the Russians were capable of breaking through even an Austrian front—or else they did not think an attack would be projected there—and German Head-quarters accordingly countenanced a lateral thinning of the line which exposed the Austrian armies to very great danger if it ever should be pierced. Their confidence found an expression in the elaborate character of the trenches and dug-outs which the Russian attack subsequently disclosed in the Austrian lines. They were as elaborate as, if less scientific than, the maze of trenches on the Somme, and were even more luxurious. Mr. Stanley Washburn, the *Times* correspondent, who afterwards visited some districts behind the Austrian front in Volhynia, speaks of beer gardens and neatly whitewashed villages; of army sausage factories and soap works. Every detachment had its own vegetable garden, and this patriarchal picture was completed by the droves of pigs and herds of cattle which the army fattened for the use of its soldiers.

On the other side of this Volhynian Eden the Russians may be pictured grimly planning an entrance to it. It was no easy enterprise. Every device had been adopted to make the front Russian-proof. In most sectors there were five consecutive lines of trenches; the dug-outs were made on the pattern of the Western front; the communications behind the trench lines were scientifically efficient; field railways were continually being extended; on the roads enforced labour had been lavished. In the marshy regions of Volhynia corduroy roads of logs had been laid, and breastworks raised to take the place of trenches. Against all this engineering, ingenuity, and forethought the Russians had to set their wits, their numbers, and the unsurpassed fighting quality of the Russian soldiers, which never deterio-

The Tsar and Tsarevitch in the Uniform of a Caucasian Cossack Regiment

rated. In the last-named asset the Russian commanders held always a master-card. A German general once said that the nation with the strongest nerves would win. The Russian soldier had precisely these attributes of stolidity, obedience, and want of nervous apprehension which entitled him to the character of having no nerves

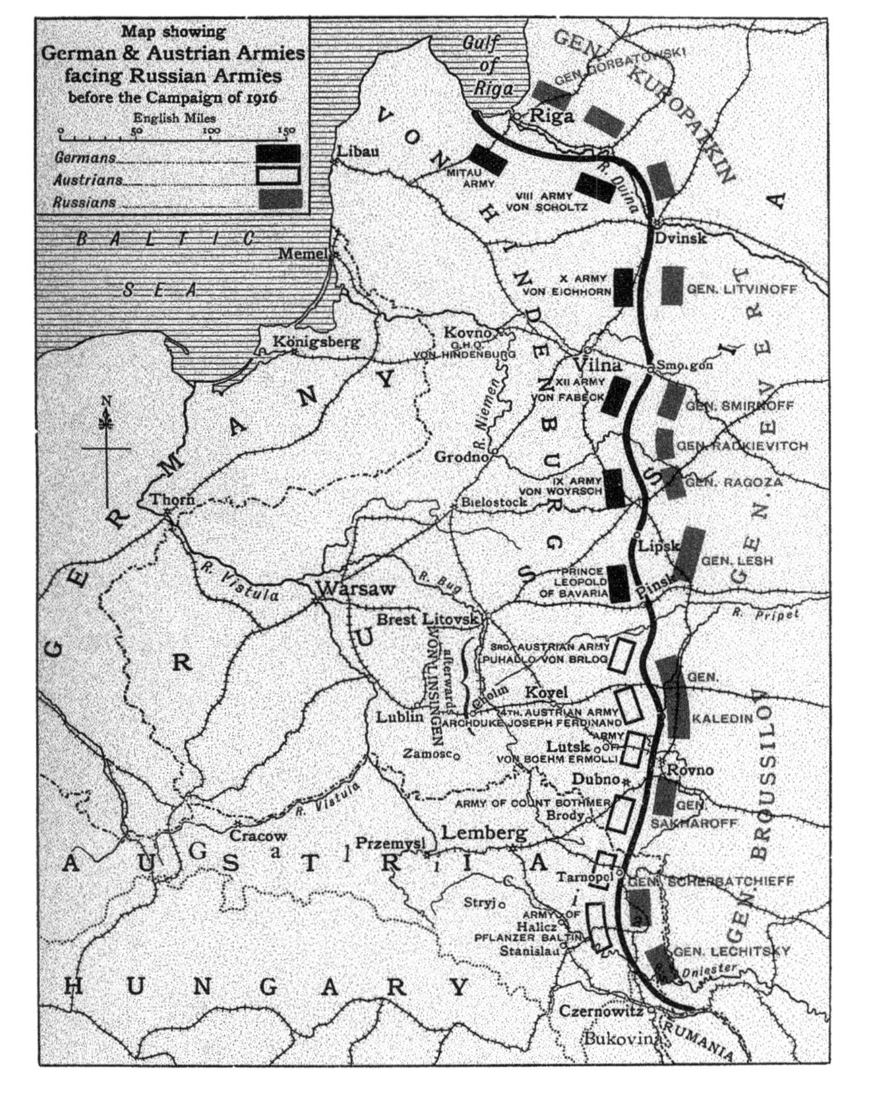

Map showing
German & Austrian Armies
facing Russian Armies
before the Campaign of 1916
English Miles
0 50 100 150
Germans
Austrians
Russians
BALTIC
SEA
Gulf of Riga
Riga
Libau
Memel
Königsberg
Kovno
G.H.Q. VON HINDENBURG
Vilna
Grodno
Bielostock
Thorn
Warsaw
Brest Litovsk
Kovel
Lublin
Zamosc
Lutsk
Dubno
Rovno
Brody
Lemberg
Przemysl
Cracow
Tarnopol
Stryj
Halicz
Stanislau
Czernowitz
Bukovina
RUMANIA
Dvinsk
Smorgon
Lipsk
Pinsk
MITAU ARMY
VIII ARMY VON SCHOLTZ
X ARMY VON EICHHORN
XII ARMY VON FABECK
IX ARMY VON WOYRSCH
PRINCE LEOPOLD OF BAVARIA
3RD AUSTRIAN ARMY PUHALLO VON BRLOG
4TH AUSTRIAN ARMY ARCHDUKE JOSEPH FERDINAND
ARMY OF VON BOEHM ERMOLLI
ARMY OF COUNT BOTHMER
ARMY OF PFLANZER BALTIN
VON LINSINGEN
GEN. GORBATOWSKI
GEN. KUROPATKIN
GEN. LITVINOFF
GEN. SMIRNOFF
GEN. RADKIEVITCH
GEN. RAGOZA
GEN. LESH
GEN. KALEDIN
GEN. SAKHAROFF
GEN. SCHERBATCHIEFF
GEN. LECHITSKY
GEN. EVERT
GEN. BROUSSILOV
VON HINDENBURG
GERMANY
AUSTRIA
HUNGARY
R. Duina
R. Niemen
R. Vistula
R. Bug
R. Pripet
R. Dniester

to be harassed. Give him weapons and reasonable artillery support and he would march anywhere and through anything. By June, 1916, his commanders were able to give him adequate artillery support, and though he never had the big-gun power behind him which the Austro-German had in their great advance of the year before, what he had sufficed; while owing to the withdrawal of a good deal of the enemy heavy artillery to the Trentino front he was no longer hopelessly outgunned.

The Russian Armies of the North which were charged with the duty of holding von Hindenburg were under the command of General Kuropatkin and General Evert. The supreme command was vested in the Tsar, with General Alexeiff as his Chief of Staff and virtual Commander-in-Chief. Under General Kuropatkin, who held the section Riga to Dvinsk, were the Twelfth Army (General Garbatowski), the Fifth Army and the First Army (General Litvinoff). General Evert, who had handled his retreat so magnificently in the last days of September, 1915, when von Hindenburg strove to close the Vilna salient, still held the Vilna sector with the Second Army (General Smirnoff), the Tenth Army (General Radkievitch), the Fourth Army (General Rogoza), and the Third Army which, under General Lesk, was on the outskirts of the Pripet marshes. The Russian Higher Command have naturally offered no estimate of the strength of these armies. The Germans overestimated them at between 40 and 50 infantry divisions and 8½ cavalry divisions.

It is the southern group of Russian armies which faced the Austrian lines on which interest concentrates. After the German wave had spent itself in a line drawn across the Pinsk and Pripet marshes, General Ivanoff, who had so stubbornly resisted the advance of von Linsingen in the plain of the Dniester, had assumed general command of these armies; but in April he had gone to General Head-quarters to act as military adviser, and his place at the front had been taken by General Brussilov, who had previously commanded one of the armies of Galicia, and had played a great part in the enforced retreat which followed von Mackensen's break through General Radko Dimitrieff's adjoining front on the Dunajec. Brussilov's army had ended its retreat in September, 1916, by a fine counter-attack in Volhynia, which for a few days placed him in possession of Lutsk, and secured a Russian footing firmly in front of Rovno. When General Ivanoff went on to the Head-quarter Staff, General Brussilov took command of the Russian southern group of armies. His subordinates were General Kaledine, who took over the command of Brussilov's old army at Rovno; General Sakharoff with the Eleventh Army on the borders of Volhynia and Podolic; General Scherbatcheff in Eastern Galicia; and General Lechitzky on the Dniester where the Russian line touched the Bukovina. The Germans gave to this group a strength slightly less in infantry but greater in mounted troops than the northern armies.

The coloured map shows the problem which the Russian commanders were set. The great retreat had left the opposing armies facing one another in an 800-mile line, which began with a hook at the Gulf of Riga, but from which all great inequalities had been smoothed out all the way from the Dvina to the Dniester and the Pruth. There were small salients here and there, slight advantages of position which one commander or another had seized or improved, but there was no one place which advertised itself as a weakness at which a resolute attack gave promise of immediate results. A German commander surveying the problem of an advance farther into Russia might have solved it by the Mackensen method of an immense concentration of heavy guns with which to blast a way through for infantry on a wide front. A Russian commander had no such resources at his disposal. He was everywhere committed to a frontal attack with no preponderant mass of artillery to expedite it or render it easier. From his point of view the problem could be solved only by an attack along a very wide front indeed, a front so wide that the enemy should be unable to swing reinforcements from one threatened point to another, and so might fail at some sector to withstand the attack. The plan was the obverse of the German method. Instead of applying an irresistible pressure at one sector, it spread a very heavy pressure over a number simultaneously. Such was Brussilov's design. It owed its success to the complete co-ordination of all the armies involved, and the carefully-planned harmony with which the various branches of the service supported each other. "On an entire front", General Brussilov told the *Times* correspondent, "the attack began at the same hour, and it was impossible for the enemy to shift his troops from one quarter to another, as our attacks were being pressed equally at all points."

The first news that the Russian plan had been launched came from Austrian sources. On Friday, June 2, 1916, the Austrian *communiqué* spoke of a bombardment beginning at the extreme south, where the Russians on the borders of Roumania were threatening Czernowitz. Next day the bombardment was ominously spreading. It reached all the way from the Dniester to the Pripet; it increased in violence. On June 4, the unexpected, the unprecedented, happened. The lethargic Russian armies, which their enemies had declared to be immobilized, began to move; and they began to move all at once over a front of 200 miles—a line as far as from London to York.

General Kaledine, who held the most northerly command south of the Pripet, and the largest, pushed forward in three directions: on the right his columns moved parallel to the railway which runs from Rovno to Kovel towards the River Styr; his centre took the road to Vladimir Volynsk; his left marched parallel to the Rovno-Dubno-Brody railway. The three advances were roughly shaped like the right half of a six-pointed star <. This might be compared to a triple attack starting from a line drawn through Lincoln and aiming at York, Sheffield, and Leicester respectively. He fell fiercely on the army of the Archduke Joseph Ferdinand, cut it up, and thrust it behind the Styr. Kaledine's troops occupied Lutsk on June 7, and forced a passage over the Styr next day. His central thrust then went on through Lutsk, and ten days later was at a point within 12 miles of Vladimir Volynsk (June 17). His right wing fought its way to the Svidniki on the River Stokhod in a day less. That was 20 miles from Kovel. His left wing reached a point 7 miles from Brody on the same day. Thus was created the great dent in the Austrian lines which came to be called the Lutsk salient. In creating it, General Kaledine had handled the Archduke's troops severely. In twelve days he captured 70,000 prisoners—of whom 1309 were officers—with 83 guns, 23 machine-guns, and an immense aggregation of the war material of all kinds assembled behind the quintuple lines.

The Holy War in Russia: soldiers of the Tsar receiving the blessing of their priest before going into action

General Scherbatcheff's action front was on a line from Kozlov (just below the railway from Tarnopol to Lemberg) to the Dniester. This section would be comparable to the stretch from Leicester to Luton. Scherbatcheff was faced by Count Bothmer, who proved a very tough nut to crack. Bothmer's outposts were driven in, his first-line trenches smothered. His adversary got to the River Strypa (running north and south), and crossed it at several points, and 17,000 of Bothmer's troops with 29 guns and 34 machine-guns were the reward of Scherbatcheff's advance in the first week. But Bothmer rallied his men and held fast to the Tarnopol-Lemberg railway, though he could not prevent the Russians from capturing Bucacz.

On the lowest section, from Zaleszczyki to the Bukovina, between the two rivers the Dniester and the Pruth, General Lechitzky struck fiercely and swiftly at General Pflanzer-Baltin. His hope was to surround that part of the Austrian army on the Roumanian frontier. He seized the bridgehead at Zaleszczyki on the Dniester, and sent his Cossacks flying across the plain between the two rivers to cut the railway which led from Czernowitz to Kolomea. The cavalry did what he asked of them, and occupied Sniatyn on the railway by the 13th. Czernowitz was thus isolated and threatened from three sides, and Pflanzer-Baltin, to save his army, had to evacuate the capital of the Bukovina—where the celebrations of the establishment of a new university under German-Austrian patronage had just been held! The Russians burst through the detachments left to fight delaying rear-guard actions, and, wading the river, captured the town, which Lechitzky entered on the 17th. His army crossed the Pruth at many points, and pressed hot on the heels of the demoralized Austrians. Lechitzky's week's work captured 754 officers and 38,000 men with 49 guns and 120 machine-guns. His success was second only to that of Kaledine's, and it reflected the less capable generalship of Pflanzer-Baltin when compared with Bothmer.

General Lechitzky, commanding the Russian Army on the Dniester

The three simultaneous attacks of Generals Kaledine, Scherbatcheff, and Lechitzky had each been productive. The success common to them all may have taken even their chief commander, General Brussilov, by surprise; for he may have believed that, though one might cut through, the others would be held up, and would play the part of preventing the Austrians from reinforcing the damaged portion of their line. But only one had failed to make considerable headway, and that was the army faced by Bothmer. If that had given completely, General Brussilov would have had three lines of subsequent attack. On the north he might press forward to Kovel, which if attained would give him the command of the most important junction of railways south of the Pripet, and would enable him to sever the direct railway communications between the German armies of the north and the Austrian armies of the south.

In the mid portion of his line he might attain to Vladimir Volhynsk, a railway junction less important but very valuable; or he might strike for Lemberg, the capital of Galicia, with all its stores as well as its value as a railway junction and a political asset. In his sector farthest south he might aim successively at the railway and road junctions of Kolomea, Stanislau, and Halicz. Each of these was valuable as giving him command of the plain of the Dniester, and as hampering the Austrian movements whether of retreat, of rallying, or of counter-attack. The advantage of arriving at any of the points that have been mentioned increased in geometrical ratio, according to the speed at which they could be reached. Thus stood the position at the end of the first stage of the operations.

General Lesh, commanding the new Russian Army which crossed the Stokhod in July, 1916

To the Germans the need for propping up their shaken allies was imperative. As soon as their General Staff realized the danger in which Kovel lay, if Kaledine's victorious army were permitted to push forward uninterruptedly, they sent reinforcements to Linsingen with instructions to counter-attack. Linsingen's attack was well devised. If the salient which the Russians had created about Lutsk be denoted by a reversed ɑ, the plan of Linsingen was not to strike at the curve of the ɑ but at the point where it joins the upright at the top. If the blow was hard enough it would break Kaledine where he was weakest and cut his communications. The point thus selected for attack was the River Stokhod. Linsingen had some success at first, and the Russians had to fall back before his vigorous blows, abandoning the bridgehead at Svidniki on the Stokhod; and during the last ten days of June both sides went at one another hammer-and-tongs without marked advantage to either. Then General Brussilov adopted a new device. He brought up a new army which was put under the command of General Lesh (a vigorous commander in the Russo-Japanese War), and of which the tactics were to outflank the outflankers by crossing the Stokhod farther to the north, where it falls into the Pripet. Lesh began as satisfactorily as the other Russian commanders. His attack developed on July 4, when he captured the railway station of Manievitchi on the Kovel-Chartorysk railway, and eventually succeeded in cap-turning all the German positions on this part of the Stokhod as far as the Pripet. He took 12,000 prisoners while doing so. Meanwhile Kaledine had returned to the attack on the upper Stokhod, recapturing the Svidniki bridgehead, and thus a firm hold was secured on the eastern bank of the Stokhod along its entire length.

Linsingen, however, had done his share in delaying the dreaded advance to Kovel, and reorganized the defensive positions on the opposite bank. It was now his turn to attempt a counter-attack, and towards the middle of July he used his reinforcements and the guns which he was now accumulating to try an attack on the lower part of the [illegible], or on that part of the Lutsk salient which was nearest Brody. Here, however, he found General Sakharoff—who was now in command of the Russian forces on this southern face of the Lutsk salient—only too ready for him. Sakharoff not only checked the German eastward thrust, but, counter-attacking, drove the enemy out of Russia into Galicia over the Lipa. He took 13,000 prisoners and 30 guns.

This attack opened up a new phase of the operations. It had become fairly evident that the railways, radiating and lateral, by which Kovel was reached from the German side were sufficient to enable the Germans to protect it by always reinforcing any sector threatened by the Russian advance. Linsingen could always throw a "mass of manœuvre" on any avenue of approach, and so maintain his defence, though he was unable to make headway in attack. On the other

General Sakharoff, commanding the Russian Forces in the South of the Lutsk Salient

hand, the Russian superiority in numbers, their careful preparations, and admirable transport enabled them, even if they could not move so swiftly or with such economy of means as the Germans, to select continually new places for attack. Thus they now began to threaten the Austro-German line on two sectors farther south. Their pressure towards Brody began to make General Bothmer's position on the right bank of the Strypa precarious, and when his resistance stiffened, the Russian effort was diverted still farther south, to what may not improbably have been throughout their chief objective—the knot of railways and roads about Kolomea, Stanislau, and Halicz. It was because they had never thoroughly held this region in 1914–15 that their Carpathian campaign had been so unproductive. If they could conquer it now they would establish themselves on solid rock; they would continually threaten the Austrian communications with their main Hungarian bases, and they would have a base themselves for subsequent combined operations with Roumania.

The operations began with those of General Lechitzky. On the night of June 18 his cavalry reached the Sereth, driving Pflanzer-Baltin's demoralized Austrians towards the Carpathian passes, some of them escaping up the Pruth towards Kolomea, others up the Sereth valley to Kuty, the bulk of them going along the Roumanian border to Kimpolung and Dorna Watra. The Russian cavalry occupied Kimpolung, and began to feel their way to the Kirlibaba Pass, which they had not seen since the beginning of 1915. But while these subsidiary operations were being pursued in the Bukovina, the bulk of Lechitzky's army pushed on towards Kolomea and the Jablonitza Pass. Kolomea, the first important railway junction in this region, was occupied on June 30; on July 4 the advance cavalry was across the pass railway; and on the 8th Delatyn was captured.

The Crown Prince of Austria, Nominal Commander of the Armies of Köevess and Bothmer, who succeeded to the Throne on the Death of the Emperor Francis Joseph in November, 1916

But the position was now too serious for the Germans to allow any consideration for Austrian feelings to interfere with an attempt to stop the rot. General Pflanzer-Baltin, minus most of his army, followed them into retirement; and the Archduke Joseph Ferdinand returned to the bosom of his family. General Hömann (German) and General Köevess (Austrian) took over what was left of Pflanzer-Baltin's army; and the Crown Prince of Austria, who was putting up a resistance in the Kirlibaba Pass region, was made nominal commander of the armies of Köevess and Bothmer. When the Crown Prince Charles succeeded to the throne of Austria on the death of the Emperor Francis Joseph, this command was transferred to the Archduke Joseph, who had been nominal commander of the Fourth Austrian Army. Otherwise the whole 800-mile front was embraced under the general command of von Hindenburg. South of the Pripet he had under him the army of Prince Leopold of Bavaria, which was opposite General Lesh, and the armies of Linsingen and Boehm-Ermolli. This reorganization was not sufficient to prevent the retreat of Bothmer from the positions about Brody to which he had clung so hardily; indeed, it was probably under von Hindenburg's orders that the retirement was ordered. It was in any case imperative.

After crossing the Lipa on July 18, General Sakharoff, following up Boehm-Ermolli, kept him on the run for nearly four weeks, though the rate of progress, which was dependent on the interruptions due to hard-fought actions whenever Boehm-Ermolli's rear-guards turned about, does not suggest rapidity. Brody was occupied on July 28; the upper Sereth, where Boehm-Ermolli was defeated after a struggle, was reached on August 4; and Zalotse was occupied on the 6th. Sakharoff had captured 33,000 prisoners in the course of his operations, and, pursuing his advantages, he reached by the middle of August the railway running from Lemberg to Tarnopol.

Meantime, while these operations were imperilling Bothmer's northern flank, Lechitzky was again advancing to threaten his position on the south. After waiting for the summer floods of the Dniester to subside he fought a battle for Tlumacz on August 7, winning it and taking 7400 prisoners, half of whom were German stiffening. Thence his right wing went on to capture the bridgehead of Niznlow. Stanislau was now within sight: the railway to the south of it was cut, and one more avenue of communications through the Carpathians was in Russian hands. On August 10 Lechitzky entered Stanislau—the second important southern junction—and its occupation made Bothmer's retreat westwards from the positions he had held merely a matter of time. Meanwhile Nadvorna and Jablonitza (at the foot of the pass) were seized. On August 13 Lechitzky's cavalry entered Mariampol, where they joined hands with the left wing of General Scherbatcheff's army advancing along the northern bank of the Dniester. This column of

General Scherbatcheff, commanding the Russian Army advancing along the Northern Bank of the Dniester

Scherbatcheff's army was under the command of General Bezobrazoff, who marched in co-operation with Lechitzky's troops on the southern bank of the river, and, having crossed the Zlota Lipa, reached Mariampol on August 14.

If Bothmer had stayed much longer in his trenches he would have been in the unenviable position of having to retreat from a salient such as those which in the previous year the Russians had been forced to evacuate at Przemysl, Warsaw, and Vilna. But he was fully aware of Brussilov's intention to surround him, and with good railway and road communications running east to west behind him, his task of retreating was easier than that of

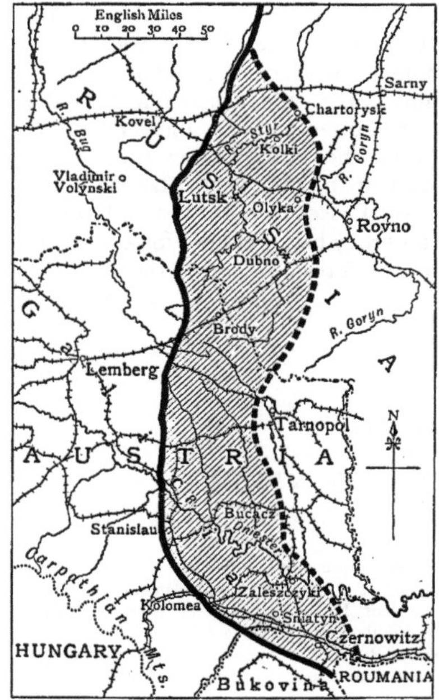


Map illustrating the extent of the Russian Recovery in the Summer Campaign of 1916

his opponents had been. He began to evacuate his positions on the upper Strypa three days (August 11) before Scherbatcheff and Lechitzky made contact at Marianpol. Scherbatcheff, whose part had been to keep contact with him, did so to the best of his ability, but there was never any doubt that, failing some paralysing blunder, Bothmer would be able to get away in time, for he was amply warned, and had far better means of retirement than his adversaries had of advance. He fell back unhastingly to the Zlota Lipa, and fought a vigorous counter-attack to protect his crossing. It was a counter-attack which, according to the Russian account, cost him dearly; but it served his purpose of allowing him to make good his defensive positions and to prepare fresh ones if they became needed on the second and superior line of defence on the Gnila Lipa.

While Bothmer, under the pressure of Sakharoff, Scherbatcheff, and Lechitzky, had been pressed back towards Lemberg, and his right wing thrown on to Halicz, the situation in Volhynia had remained nearly where Generals Lesh and Kaledine had left it in the middle of June. There was continual fierce fighting on the river line of the Stokhod. On July 27 an attack on a larger scale by Kaledine made a rent in the German first-line trenches at Swiniuchy, and captured 9000 prisouers with 46 guns. It was a considerable victory, but General Brussilov did not empower General Kaledine to follow it up. His decision was wise. The Germans knew the value of Kovel, and they had continually reinforced the lines in front of it. Kaledine's thrust was designed chiefly to prevent them from sending reinforcements to the threatened positions of Bothmer in Galicia. But there also the Germans were able to stiffen and reorganize their front, and though Halicz was continually threatened, and was often reported to be on the verge of falling, it was still standing when the autumn rains drew a drop-curtain over the summer campaign.

The Russians during these summer months had taken the utmost advantage of the strategical error which Count von Hoetzendorff, the chief of the Austrian general staff, had committed in withdrawing troops for the ill-considered adventure in the Trentino. They had pushed the attack home as far as it would go; they had destroyed the integrity of the Austro-Hungarian armies, and had compelled the Germans to repair the error which they had advised by supplying reinforcements to fill the breaches made, and to stop them from widening further. By the middle of September, 1916, Generals Kaledine, Sakharoff, Scherbatcheff, Bezobrazoff, and Lechitzky between them had captured 358,153 Austro-Hungarian rank and file, 7953 officers, 1396 machine-guns, 451 guns, and an immense aggregation of ammunition, food, and all kinds of military stores. They had rendered the whole position of the shaken line in Galicia from the Carpathians to the Pripet susceptible to further attack, and by their progress in the Carpathians from the Jablonitza and the Beskid Passes to Kirlibaba and Dorna Watra they had prepared for a junction with the forces of Roumania.

E. S. G.

---

# CHAPTER III

## THE THIRD BATTLE OF YPRES

(June, 1916)

Verdun and the German Tactics at Ypres—The Allies Approaching Advance—Enemy's Object to rob them of the Initiative—Another Blow at the Canadians—Appalling Bombardment—Generals Mercer and Williams caught in the Storm of Fire—Canadians' Battle against Overwhelming Odds—Their New Line—First Counter-attacks—Heroes of the Fight—How Lieutenant-Colonel Shaw fell—Fresh German Onslaught—Recapture by the Enemy of the Ruins of Hooge—Canadian's Triumphant Counter-attack—Squaring Accounts—Back in the Old Line—June, 1916, along the Rest of the British Front—Bantams in Action—Story of the Seaforths' Mouth-organs.

SAVE for the gruesome salient of Ypres, the British line on the Western front was comparatively quiet during the critical weeks of June, 1916. The Germans, crashing their way nearer and nearer to Verdun, utterly regardless of cost, seemed at last almost within sight of the victory which France's heroic army, still fighting there alone but undaunted, had so long denied them. Britons at home, knowing nothing of the mighty preparations then being made, in accordance with the far-sighted strategy of General Joffre himself, for the Allied Offensive which was to relieve the situation in the following month, grew restive under the enemy's calculated taunts, inspired chiefly for the benefit of our allies and neutrals, that we were deliberately leaving France to bleed to death. Some of this uneasiness was swept away by the British Prime Minister in a speech at Ladybank towards the middle of June. "The French", he declared, "have known from the first attack on Verdun that Sir Douglas Haig was not only ready to beyond Arras. Those in progress, though Mr. Asquith did not, of course, divulge the fact, were the preparations for the coming advance on the Somme.

The German Higher Command knew perfectly well that some such move was in contemplation, that the mustering in France of the vast new

Canadian Official Photograph

"Three Cheers for the King!" scene at an inspection of the Canadian troops by His Majesty

but eager to render them help whenever and wherever and in whatever shape they desired, and their illustrious commander has recognized in the most handsome terms the promptitude and zeal with which his British colleague has taken and is taking the steps which in their joint opinion are dictated by sound strategy." The chief step already taken was the relief of the French army from below Loos armies created by the organizing genius of Lord Kitchener boded them no good. They determined, therefore, to try some of their Verdun artillery tactics on the Ypres salient, and at the beginning of June scored a momentary success which probably caused some anxious moments at British Head-quarters. It was a success which seemed almost to portend another bold bid for the Channel coast, and proved, indeed, the first stage of a series of actions which came to be described at the time as the Third Battle of Ypres. But looking back with some sort of historical perspective, we can see that it was never intended by the Germans as anything more than a local offensive, designed to pin the British army to its own lines, and at all costs to upset the plans for the Allies' forthcoming advance. Their own assault on Verdun had already lasted 100 days, and a supreme effort was now being made to ensure that long-promised triumph for the Crown Prince which was to atone for all his costly sacrifices. The summit of Mort Homme had at length fallen; Fort Vaux was being battered to pieces with a storm of explosives which burst upon that devoted stronghold at the rate of 8000 shells a day; and preparations were obviously in progress for a fresh gigantic effort which was intended to seal the fate of Verdun itself. The German offensive at Ypres was part of the same plan, and designed, like the prolonged battle on the Meuse, to rob the Allies of the initiative and impress the world at large with another proof of what the enemy Press described as their "great moral and material strength".

Canadian Official Photograph

Canadian Cavalry and the King: cheering His Majesty after a royal inspection

The full force of this fresh, unexpected blow fell on the Canadians, who had but lately passed through their shattering ordeal at St. Eloi, at the southern extremity of the Ypres salient.[1] The new thrust was made against their 3rd Division, on the left of their line, after an intense German bombardment which opened at 9 a.m. on Friday, June 2, 1916, not long after Lieutenant-General the Hon. Sir Julian Byng—last heard of in Gallipoli, where he had succeeded to the command of the 9th Army Corps after the failure of the Suvla Bay landing—had taken over the command of the Canadian Corps in succession to Lieutenant-General Sir Edwin Alderson. An artillery duel had been general more or less along the whole line, but the storm of exploding metal which suddenly burst forth on that Friday morning of June 2 was heavier than any yet experienced by Canadian troops, and foretold the fiercest attack on the British front since the Battle of Loos. It continued in ever-increasing volume for four hours, tearing the Canadians' forward trenches to shapelessness, in many places obliterating them altogether. It also destroyed their wire entanglements. The Canadian official account states that the smoke and fumes of the thousands of bursting shells—high explosive, gas, and lachrymatory—hung heavily in the air, and rendered observation almost impossible.

It happened, unfortunately, that Major-General M. S. Mercer, C.B., commanding the 3rd Division, with one of his Brigadiers, General V. A. S. Williams, had arranged that morning to inspect certain of the front works. There they were caught in this storm of fire, but coolly remained to direct and encourage the men. The attack extended roughly from the heap of ruins which once was the village of Hooge to just north of Hill 60—some 3000 yards in all. Along the whole of this front and in the region behind, where a barrage was maintained to check reinforcements, the bombardment was described by the *Times* correspondent as "hell minute by minute and hour after hour"; and at its close, when the fire lifted to swell the barrage behind, the German infantry advanced in full kit and in regular formation, as if expecting to find the ground unoccupied save by dead bodies. Instead of that the enemy was everywhere encountered by desperate resistance, especially at certain points, where officers and men rivalled one another in furious hand-to-hand fighting. It was at one such point that Major-General Mercer met his death,

Brigadier-General V. A. S. Williams, wounded and taken prisoner, June 2, 1916
(From a photograph by Swaine)

[1] Vol. V, pp. 252-7.

fighting valiantly to the last, as a Cologne paper afterwards acknowledged.[1] Brigadier-General Williams was hit while repelling an attack, and was taken prisoner. Heroism was unavailing against such numbers as the Germans were able to launch against the surviving defenders of these battered trenches, though the enemy had to pay dearly for every captured yard. One of the storm-centres was the sardonically named Sanctuary Wood, now a hideous, shell-swept haunt of death, where the once graceful trees were reduced to mere naked stumps and skeletons of their former selves. Here some of the Princess Patricia's Own, commanded by Lieutenant-Colonel H. C. Buller, D.S.O., added fresh laurels to their battle honours by a magnificent stand against tremendous odds. Some battalions of the Royal Canadian Regiment, the Canadian Mounted Rifles—long since dismounted—and Canadian Infantry were also singled out for special mention for unforgettable feats of bravery and endurance.

Before three o'clock, however, in spite of all the Canadians' courage and self-sacrifice, the Germans—Würtemberg regiments, according to the German official version of the operations—were in possession of our front trenches over an area of about a mile, the Canadians stubbornly falling back to a new line running south-west of the village of Hooge through the southern portion of Sanctuary Wood towards Hill 60. From their treeless slopes of Hill 60 and the ridges above Zwartelen sloping down towards Zillebeke the Germans had narrowed still further the narrow salient round Ypres. The struggle swayed backwards and forwards throughout the afternoon, British and Canadian guns taking up the artillery challenge in ever-increasing volume, and Canadian reinforcements boldly pushing through the German barrage of fire to go to their comrades' assistance. During the night the hostile infantry, who were counted nine or ten battalions strong, pushed through to a depth of some 700 yards in the direction of Zillebeke, most of our troops having now fallen back about 1000 yards in the rear of their original line in order to prepare an organized counter-attack.

Some of the lost ground had already been wrested from the Germans before nightfall, but the position was considerably improved as a result of the counter-attack delivered at 7 o'clock the next morning. In order to take part in this operation some of the Canadian battalions were obliged to move across the open under heavy shell-fire, and through intense barrages. "Nowhere", writes the official Canadian representative, "did the line waver. Each battalion advanced and carried through its appointed task with splendid dash and unflinching determination." But as they dashed for-

[1] The body of the Divisional Commander was subsequently recovered from a demolished dug-out. All the buttons and decorations of his tunic had been cut off, but rank badges had not been touched. The remains were carried back and buried in a military cemetery close to Poperinghe, General Byng and all the Divisional-Commander's staff attending the ceremony. Major-General Mercer came over with the First Canadian contingent in September, 1914, as Lieutenant-Colonel commanding the First Canadian Infantry Brigade, and in all their hardest fighting had proved himself one of the Canadians' greatest soldiers. He was gazetted temporary Major-General in November, 1915, and also made a Companion of the Order of the Bath.

ward many of the attackers were taken in rear by machine-gun fire, and those who reached our old first-line trenches were not in sufficient strength to hold them. In places, however, the Germans were pushed back for a distance of a quarter of a mile, and the new line of defence was consolidated. This brought

Lieutenant-Colonel H. C. Buller, D.S.O., commanding the Patricias, killed on June 2, 1916
(From a photograph by Lafayette)

to a close the first phase of the Third Battle of Ypres, "the splendid gallantry with which the counter-attack was delivered and the lost ground recovered", to quote from Sir Robert Borden's message, "maintaining the glorious record established by the 1st Canadian Division in April of 1915". Canada, however, had again to mourn the loss of many of her bravest and best, for the casualties on both sides were of necessity very heavy. Grim stories are told of the fearful losses inflicted at the onset of the enemy attack by the machine-guns of the Royal Canadians and Princess Patricia's, between whom was a gap through which the exultant Germans streamed in triumph, only to be mown down in scores by the unexpected fire from both flanks. There were many compensating deeds of such unshaken valour on that day of disaster.

Colonel Buller, of the "Patricias", who was aide-de-camp at Government House when the war broke out, was among the commanding officers killed, while Major A. Hamilton Gault, D.S.O., who raised the same gallant regiment, was seriously wounded. Three battalions of the Canadian Mounted Rifles lost their commanding officers in the thick of the hand-to-hand fighting—Lieutenant-Colonels A. E. Shaw and G. H. Baker, both of whom were killed, and Lieutenant-Colonel J. F. H. Ussher, who was wounded and taken prisoner. Lieutenant-Colonel Baker was the member for Brome in the Canadian Parliament and the first Canadian member of Parliament to fall in action. How the Canadian Mounted Rifles fought and died was described to a Canadian correspondent by the only survivor of one of their companies, whose trenches, by two o'clock on Friday afternoon, were battered into nothing but shell-holes. Then, he said, the enemy exploded three mines, with the result that all the company's machine-guns and trench-mortars were blown to pieces, most of their ammunition was buried, and the air was so full of dust and smoke that it was hard to tell friend from foe. "Those men who were still alive and in fighting condition had only about 150 rounds of ammunition apiece, but they fired away till their last cartridge was spent, and then held on till they were killed or completely surrounded."

It was in such a last stand that Lieutenant-Colonel Shaw, rallying round him some eighty of these Canadian Mounted Rifles, held on to his shattered earthworks until only a few survived, and the colonel himself was killed. The few survivors fought their way out: two got home. High praise was bestowed on the supporting battalions which faced the enemy's barrage unflinchingly in their eagerness to help their stricken comrades. Their steadiness and courage were described as magnificent beyond words. Among the striking stories of the battle is that told by Mr. Beckles Willson, one of the Canadian correspondents at the front. It relates to a parson from Medicine Hat, on the Bow River, who at the outbreak of war flung aside his surplice and enlisted as a private.

"He came to England with his battalion, where his talent for ministration and good works could not be concealed, and he was promptly, when a vacancy occurred, appointed chaplain. When the battalion arrived in France he felt it his duty to strike a blow of a sterner sort for his country, and returned to the combatant ranks. He, on this day in Sanctuary Wood, wielded a rifle with accuracy and effect as long as his ammunition lasted, and then went after the Germans with a bayonet. After one particularly fierce thrust the weapon broke. Whereupon this officer bared his fists and flew at one brawny Boche with his fists, and the last seen of him he was lying prone and overpowered."[1]

[1] *Daily Express.*

When these opening attacks and counter-attacks had worn themselves out, an ominous lull ensued in the infantry operations, though our artillery did its best to prevent the Germans from consolidating the ground they had won. The enemy fully expected that the Canadians would not allow their set-back to go unavenged; nor was he mistaken, for the one consuming desire of the whole Canadian Corps was for a speedy day of reckoning. That day was only postponed by a fresh series of attacks launched by the Germans on June 6, beginning at midday with a violent bombardment both to the north of Hooge, where the British troops joined up with the Canadians, and to the south, as well as towards the Ypres-Comines Canal. In the afternoon came a series of mine explosions directly under the Canadians at Hooge, where their front-line systems passed through the ruined village. The troops holding this section suffered cruelly, and the remnants had no chance against the hordes of German infantry who rushed over immediately afterwards to complete the horrible work. Thus the fatal line through Hooge, which had changed hands so often, changed hands once more. The enemy failed, however, to make any further progress at this point, every fresh attempt to advance being defeated by the Canadians' machine-gun and rifle fire from their support trenches. Other efforts to push forward farther to the south were similarly dealt with.

Then came another lull, save for the daily artillery duels and the everyday warfare of the trenches; and it lasted so long that some of the Germans persuaded themselves that Canada was in no mood to square accounts. The weather, throughout, was abominable, with incessant rains which churned the Flanders soil into worse mud than ever. But the time was not wasted. It was spent in bringing up such a concentration of British and Canadian guns of heavy calibre as would teach the foe that he now had to reckon with artillery equal to if not better than his own. He learnt this wholesome lesson fully on the night of June 12–13, 1916, when for many hours on end he was made to undergo just such an annihilating ordeal as that to which he had subjected the Canadians on June 2. The turn of the Canadian infantry came between one and two o'clock on the morning of June 13, when our guns lifted, and established a heavy barrage on the enemy's support trenches. Brigadier-General Lipsett, who had been appointed to succeed General Mercer in command of the 3rd Canadian Division, deferred taking up his new post in order to lead his old brigade into action on this occasion.

It was still pouring with rain, but the men advanced in the highest spirits at the prospect of avenging their comrades. One officer of the Canadian Scottish who took part in the attack describes the condition of the disputed ground—battered out of all recognition by mines and shells of

Canadian Official Photograph

The Blight of Battle: Sanctuary Wood, the scene of some of the fiercest fighting in the Ypres salient in June, 1916

Canadian Official Photograph

Canada's Great Counter-attack: one of the trenches from which the Dominion troops charged on June 13, 1916

every description—as liquid mud which reached above their knees. Yet they charged up the slope until the whole of the objective attacked—the lost ridge along a front of over 1500 yards extending from the southern portion of Sanctuary Wood to a point about 1000 yards north of Hill 60—was again in Canadian hands, finally entrenching themselves in the approximate line of the original front trenches.

Here and there the defenders put up a stout fight, as the Canadians worked downwards and southwards into their old positions. One group of some forty Germans held their post until they were killed almost to a man, fighting as bravely—as the Canadians themselves were generous enough to admit—as Colonel Shaw and the dismounted Riflemen who fell with him on June 2. But for the major part the Germans who were found in possession, thoroughly demoralized by our devastating bombardment, were in no mood for resistance. One officer, who, according to Mr. Philip Gibbs's account in the *Daily Telegraph*, surrendered with 113 men, was frankly glad to escape from a battle to which he had resigned himself when our guns began in earnest. "I knew how it would be," he said. "We had orders to take this ground, and took it; but we knew you would come back again. You had to do it. So here I am." Parts of the reconquered line, writes the same correspondent, were found deserted, save by the dead.

"In one place the stores which had been buried by the Canadians before they left were still there, untouched by the enemy.

It was quite clear that our bombardment—the continual fire of our guns since the enemy's attack on June 2—had made it impossible for his troops to consolidate their position and to hold the line effectually. They had just taken cover in the old bits of trench, in shell-holes and craters, and behind scattered sandbags, and had been pounded there terribly."

Nearly 200 prisoners were taken, all told, including 5 officers, besides 12 complete machine-guns, considerable quantities of small-arm ammunition, and hand-grenades. For the Canadians the sternest ordeal came, as in most attacks of the kind, not only in holding on in the face of the inevitable storm of German shells, but also in hazardous patrol work and clearing out of enemy "pockets" in all directions. On their left one Ontario battalion bombed its way to the Canadians' original front line in the face of considerable opposition, but the upper part of Sanctuary Wood and the wreckage of Hooge remained in German hands. For the rest, the Canadians had so effectively settled accounts with the enemy that, although he made an occasional demonstration, as if in preparation for another attack along this front, he left the Canadians, comparatively speaking, in undisputed possession of their reconquered line for the rest of the summer. The prompt and vigorous retaliation of our artillery whenever the volume and concentration of German shell-fire suggested a repetition of the enemy's offensive checked any undue energy in that direction. Nor were our guns content merely to re-

Canadian Official Photograph

After the Canadian Counter-attack: emplacements of two sacrificed guns in Sanctuary Wood which were lost and recovered

ply to hostile artillery-fire. On many other occasions, we learn from the official Canadian Representative at the Front, our artillery shelled the German lines, machine-gun emplacements, observation-posts, and strong points being damaged and in some instances destroyed.

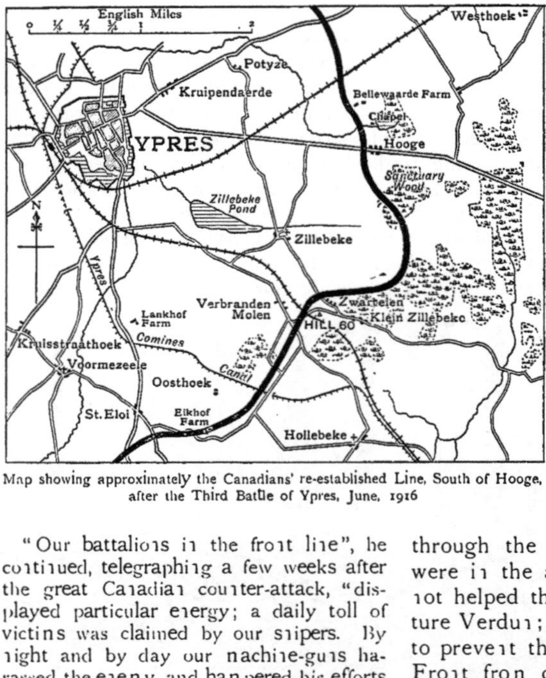

Map showing approximately the Canadians' re-established Line, South of Hooge, after the Third Battle of Ypres, June, 1916

"Our battalions in the front line", he continued, telegraphing a few weeks after the great Canadian counter-attack, "displayed particular energy; a daily toll of victims was claimed by our snipers. By night and by day our machine-guns harassed the enemy, and hampered his efforts to strengthen his defences. The size and number of our patrols were increased, and an unquestionable ascendancy established over No Man's Land."

Meantime the recaptured positions, wrecked, shapeless, and often deep in water, were gradually reconstructed, and a new and stronger defensive system built. It was arduous work in ground so wet and heavy as to be little more than a swamp in the worst places, and a deadly ordeal under the enemy's harassing fire; but the Canadians stuck to their task with fine courage and endurance until they had completely reorganized the whole of their original front line from the southern end of Sanctuary Wood to a point about 1000 yards north of Hill 60, including all the dominating ground between those two points. With this triumphant turning of the tables on the enemy the Third Battle of Ypres came to a close. The result must have been trebly disappointing to the Germans. It had brought them no nearer to breaking through the Ypres front than they were in the autumn of 1914; it had not helped the Crown Prince to capture Verdun; and it failed completely to prevent the Allies on the Western Front from delivering, a few weeks later, their long-planned joint-offensive.

For the rest of the month of June, 1916, along the British front there were not many outstanding events before the guns began the overture to the mighty drama on the Somme,

Drawn by Christopher Clark

Crater Warfare on the Western Front: British troops, after the explosion of a large enemy mine under their lines, repelling the German infantry attacks

The development of raiding on both sides had already led to fiercer warfare, with their sudden onslaughts in the dead of night, their grim work with bomb and bayonet, and their quick withdrawal according to time schedule. The advantage still rested with the British, to whose daring initiative and sporting spirit these night forays were more peculiarly adapted than to the enemy, who was more inclined to indulge in local attacks after preparing the way with a mine explosion and putting up a heavy barrage fire behind the particular sector of the British line selected for assault. Such an experience fell to the Welsh Fusiliers at Givenchy in the early hours of June 22, when the enemy exploded an immense mine in front of their trenches. It was incomparably the most powerful mine ever employed in that part of the line, and must have consumed many tons of explosives. Measured afterwards, the deep pit which formed the crater was found to be some 120 feet across, while the vast mound of soil, sandbags, and more gruesome wreckage, which rose high in the air after the terrific explosion, was scattered over an area of nearly 350 feet square. Even this awful experience, with its accompanying bombardment, failed to demoralize those of the Welsh Fusiliers who, escaping the explosion, grasped rifle and bayonet to defend their sundered trenches. The Germans, rushing forward immediately afterwards in three formidable columns, found them ready with a Berserker rage which brought all their patient planning and elaborate mining to naught. Within a quarter of an hour the Welshmen had not only beaten them off in some of the most ferocious hand-to-hand fighting of the war, but had driven them into the crater and out over the other side to their own lines—those of them, that is to say, who survived the onslaught and the machine-gun and artillery-fire which followed them into their lairs. One of their greatest surprises in the course of that ill-starred adventure was the sudden appearance on the scene of a detachment of a Pioneer battalion working close by, who, hearing how things were going with the infantry, rushed over with their spades and lent them a helping hand. British spades and British bayonets, as well as British fists, proved more than a match for German daggers, bludgeons, and pistols—the usual weapons of the enemy on these nocturnal exploits.

Earlier in June, 1916, came honourable mention—though by no means for the first time—of the Bantam Division, one battalion of which, at Neuve Chapelle, proved themselves as good as the tallest Guardsmen in raiding the German trenches. The Bantam Division was one of Kitchener's ideas. It came to him one day in Chester, according to Mr. Philip Gibbs, who saw the first drafts landing in France, and afterwards visited the division at the front with the general who had trained them since they were first assembled. "They were all wee chaps, standing no more than 5 feet 1 inch above their boots, and, for the most part, less than that." Lord Kitchener, apparently, had been struck by the number of small men who were below the standard of military height:

"Why not enrol them in a separate unit of their own? I can get you 3000 of them, sir," said the Mayor of Chester, "and they are very keen to go." Before long there were 12,000 of them, recruited from Cheshire and Lancashire, Warwickshire and Gloucestershire, and beyond the Tweed; and now a whole division are in the fighting-line, and doing jolly well."[1]

That was in June, 1916, not long after the Bantams' raid at Neuve Chapelle, where the fire-steps were raised for them, and where they climbed over to wipe out a nest of towering Prussians, not only carrying back their own wounded, but also bringing home, in proof of their victory, a captured Maxim gun. One little stalwart, hearing the cry of a wounded comrade, turned back, and then carried the helpless Bantam alone for 80 yards, until he himself collapsed. This was but one of many deeds of daring and devotion for which Bantams were decorated during the summer campaign of 1916.

Such incidents were common along the whole British front. Sometimes there would be as many as half a dozen raids into the enemy's trenches in one night. And this primitive fighting, while it added to the ferocity of the struggle, broke up much of the old monotony of trench warfare even before the Allied Offensive began on the Somme. It is fairer to generalize where regiments from every part of the Empire distinguished themselves at this period, but one dramatic incident calls for mention as being probably unique in military history. The incident is recorded in the *London Gazette* of June 21, 1916, where it is related of Company-Quartermaster-Sergeant Beech and Lance-Corporal Vickery, both of the Seaforth Highlanders, who were awarded the Distinguished Conduct Medal, that "at a critical moment they steadied the men by getting up on the parapet and playing tunes on mouth-organs, although exposed to heavy fire". Bald as it is, the official record needs no garnishing, and the episode itself deserves to rank with the famous bagpipe exploits of the gallant Highlanders. Possibly it had some connection with the fund raised some months before by Sir Frederick Bridge, the organist of Westminster Abbey, and other well-known musicians, who, hearing that mouth-organs were in great demand at the front, ransacked the shops for them, and sent them out by the hundred. The Seaforths proved that the part played in the war by these humble instruments was by no means to be despised.

F. A. M.

[1] *Daily Telegraph*, June 19, 1916.

# CHAPTER IV

## ITALY'S CAMPAIGNS IN 1916

Winter and Spring in the Trentino—Falkenhayn and the Austrian Spring Campaign against Italy—Austrian Strength in the Trentino—The Assembled Forces—Italian Line between Val Lagarina and Val Sugana—The Trentino Roads—Defects of the Italian Forward Lines—Attack of May 14—Italian Enforced Retirement—Cadorna's Re-arrangement of the Italian Defences—Austrian Thrust at the West of Pasubio—Defence of Pasubio—Arsiero and Asiago Ridge—The Italian Fifth Army in Position—Last Austrian Attempt on the Italian Right—Cadorna's Counter-offensive—Preparations for the New Italian Attack on Gorizia—The Gorizia Defences—Feint Attack on the Monfalcone Sector—Assault on Mts. Sabotino and San Michele—The Artillery Preparation—Capture of the Dominating Austrian Positions and of Gorizia—Difficulties of Advance on the Carso—The Vallone Crossed—Consolidation of Italian Gains.

THROUGH the prolonged winter and the inclement spring of 1916 the Italian armies of the mountains and the plain marked time. In that unpretending phrase is embraced an amount of toil, of endurance, of ingenuity, and of heroism which was surpassed on no other front. It was only when, after long waiting and severe trial, the Italians stood, in the autumn of 1916, east of Gorizia and masters of the Carso that the extent of their ordeal and the nature of their achievement were rightly appreciated. No one who did not know the peaks of the Tyrol could ever understand what the Italian engineers and the regiments of Alpinists did on these heights; and even those who do know them—in peace time—could scarcely believe the feats which were accomplished in fortifying them and in dragging up heavy guns and emplacing them above the clouds upon the heights. Everywhere the trowel-like wedge of the Trentino favoured an Austrian assault on Italian territory. It was a monstrous salient, of which the Austrians held the interior lines; in which even the force of three Austrian divisions, with which it was at first defended, was sufficient to prevent an Italian advance on the heart of it at Trent; and with regard to which the Italians could hope for little better than to push the Austrians back on positions from which their emergence would be fenced with greater difficulties than if they were nearer the plains. To the Austrians, on the other hand, the Trentino always offered a portal by which they might hope, if they gathered there enough men and enough heavy guns, to burst their way into the Italian plains and take the Italian army facing Gorizia in flank and rear.

It was to prevent this that all the Italian energy and genius for mountain-conquest was brought to bear. In any estimate of the Italian campaigns it is well to keep one thing in mind. In the 420-mile line held against the Austrians by Italy, a bare 130 meant hill-fighting. The rest was Alpine work. The men who did it were climbers born. They worked on the edge of avalanches. Glaciers were their manœuvring-grounds; peaks above the snow-line their redoubts.

Photograph by Brocherel

War on the Roof of Armageddon: an Italian 305-mm. siege-gun bombarding a Trentino mountain fort on a distant peak

High-angle fire was practically the only effective means of destroying the Austrian forts placed on inaccessible crags in the Trentino, whence they could command the valley passes below. For this purpose the Italians used their heaviest siege-guns, firing huge projectiles with a trajectory curve hundreds of feet overhead, often over intervening ridges, out of sight of the forts attacked, but in touch with airmen directing the gunners' aim.

Their supplies were brought to them on steel cables—by *telerifica*, the name of the device, which resembles one of those cash-carriers used in some large shops, except that it will carry half a ton or more. Their guns were dragged on sledges with incredible labour. Their fighting was often done with the thermometer below zero. In these conditions, on the roof of Armageddon, the Italians, by their bravery and engineering skill, constructed a defence and fought a fight which was the Verdun of the Alps, and was second only to that immortal conflict in wrecking the plans of the German and Austrian Higher Commands in 1916.

In the Central Empires, as among the Allies, there were Easterners and Westerners; that is to say, soldiers who believed that the opportunities for decisive actions should be sought principally on the eastern or on the western fronts. Von Falkenhayn, the Chief of the German Great Headquarters Staff, was pre-eminently a Westerner—as von Hindenburg is said to have been an Easterner—and it was his brain which devised the double offensive of Verdun and the Trentino, the first to be undertaken by the pick of the Prussian and Bavarian troops, supported by the greatest concentration of artillery which up to that time the war had recorded, the second to be entrusted to Austrian troops gathered from elsewhere on the Austrian fronts, and aided by almost as much and as great artillery as had been collected before Verdun. It may be assumed that this plan was fiercely criticized by von Hindenburg, who saw the Austrian line facing the Russians from the Pripet to the Carpathians very much weakened by these withdrawals, and who plainly perceived that even if the Russians were unable to take advantage of this weakening, nevertheless his opportunities of launching another great attack on them in 1916 were by this plan of campaign definitely put aside. From the point of view of Austria and of Conrad von Hotzendorff, the Chief of the Austrian General Staff, an attack from the Trentino on Italy would paralyse the attack which, as he and they presumed, General Cadorna was preparing to make on Gorizia. The two attacks had the same motive, that on Verdun of anticipating the Franco-British offensive, that on the Italian flank the thrust which Italy would certainly make towards Trieste.

The Trentino had fundamental advantages as a base of attack on the Italian armies; though these were set off by the persistence and industry with which the Italians had striven to reduce them. The Austro-Italian frontier, chosen by the Austrians in 1866, had been made from year to year wellnigh impregnable by an elaborate system of fortifications armed by a powerful artillery, which, sweeping the approaches and dominating the possible artillery positions within range, made it almost impracticable for the Italians to gain such a superiority of gun-fire by which to batter the defences and support infantry attacks. The Austrians were thus not only secure against attack, but also were in firm possession of avenues of approach to the Italian plains, which were thus exposed to invasion by forces which could be assembled in comparative secrecy in the mountains. If once an Austrian force, bursting the artificial barriers interposed by the Italian military engineers and by the Italian forces, could reach the plain of Venetia from the Trentino, they would be within 50 miles of the sea, and would threaten at once the two lines of railway, via Vicenza and Padua respectively, on which the Italian army on the Isonzo relied for its supplies. On the northern line Vicenza is only 25 miles, and Verona only 17 miles, from the frontier. Padua, on the southern line, is within 40 miles of the frontier, and is approached by the easy route of the Brenta or Val Sugana.

As against these advantages the Trentino had several marked disadvantages as a base from which to launch an offensive on a large scale. It was remote from the rest of the territory of Austria-Hungary; its military geography was unfavourable for rapid movement of large masses of men; it was distant from the other Austrian front on the Isonzo, and impracticably distant from the Balkan or Russian fronts should any need arise for the rapid transfer of troops; and, finally, the large army which the Austrians proposed to collect could be served by two railway lines only, one by the Brenner Pass, the other by the Puster Thal. These two lines merged into one at Franzenfeste, and had a double track only as far as Trent. The Austrians, spurred by the Germans, believed that all these obstacles could be overcome by their "efficiency" and "organization", and they hoped to be able to place in a commanding position in the Trentino a mass of troops, amply provided, which would roll like an avalanche over the Italian opposition.

Units began to assemble in the second half of March, 1916, some from the Russian front, some from the Balkans—where there was no further prospect of reducing Salonika—some from other points on the Italian front. A number of units were re-cast, Landsturm, irregular troops, and second-class troops from inland districts all being pressed in to swell the aggregate of the force. By the middle of May the Austrians had in the Trentino eighteen divisions of first-class fighting material, men trained to mountain warfare—the hammer-head of the force—and about 400,000 men in all. This army was supplied with no fewer than 2000 guns, half of them of not less than medium calibre; and to this armament was added twenty batteries of 12-inch guns, two to a battery, four 15-inch guns, and two of the monster 16.5-inch. It has sometimes been assumed that, considerable as this force and its armament were, neither von Falkenhayn nor von Hotzendorff supposed that it would suffice for an invasion of the Italian plains, but they did believe that it would frighten Cadorna out of his proposed attack on the Gorizia sector. The assumption is credible; but, on the other hand, if no more than a threat was intended, then the act of locking up so many men and so many guns in the blind alley of the Trentino appears to have been as great a miscalculation as the attack on Verdun or the uncovering of the Russian front.

At the beginning of May the Italian position cut across the V-shaped Trention in a concave loop ◡, except that the right-hand side of the loop was very much bent up towards the north-east. The left side of the loop began on Lake Garda; but for convenience one may suppose that the left-hand point of the loop ◡ rested on the Val Lagarina, and the right-hand on the Val Sugana. The fighting took place between the limits of these two valleys, the Val Lagarina and the Val Sugana, which were main avenues to the plains. The Austrians could not, without very great loss of men and time, possibly force their way along these main valleys; their effort was directed, first, at pressing the middle of the loop backwards so as to make it sag more; and secondly, at cutting through the loop where either on the right or on the left it rested on the Val Lagarina or the Val Sugana, and so threatening to take the forces defending these valleys in the rear.

The Italian line may be described with closer local detail as follows:—From south of Rovereto, in the Val Lagarina, it ran eastwards along the Val Terragnolo north of the big mountain mass of Pasubio; thence it turned a little north-eastwards, skirting the Folgaria plateau where the Austrian lines were. From Mt. Soglio d'Aspio it went east by north to the Cima Manderioto, across the Brenta valley sharply north to Monte Collo, above Borgo.

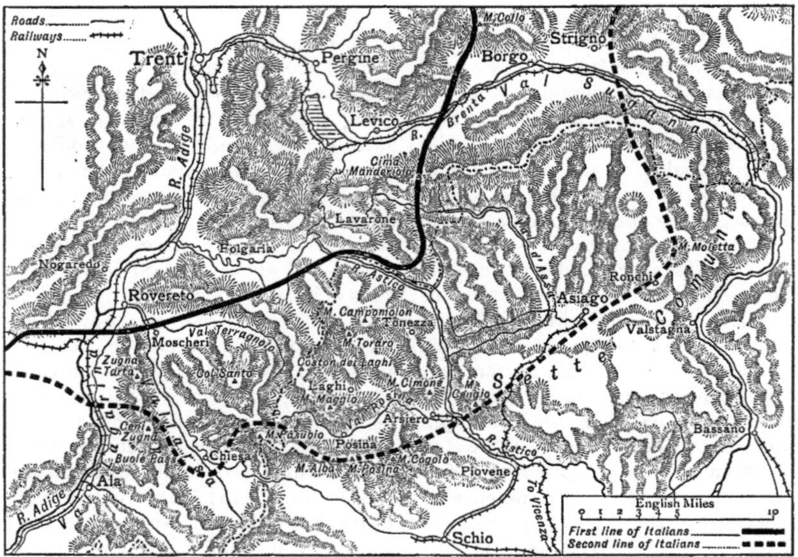

Map illustrating the Austrian Attack in the Trentino, May, 1916

On the extreme left, the Rovereto end of the line, the Italians were strung across the Zugna Torta ridge, which was difficult to hold under the converging fire that the Austrians could pour upon it; and this weakness was not uncharacteristic of the whole of the Italian first line, which had really been pushed forward in advance of its strength in order to maintain close contact with the Austrians. The real Italian line of defence lay behind this, running from the southern part of the Zugna ridge to the Pasubio group, along the hills north of the Val Posina to the Upper Astico, over the plateau of the Seven Communes (the Setti Communi), and reaching the Val Sugana east of Borgo.

The Austrians had three good roads on which to move men and guns. The left-hand one was the best, and ran through Rovereto and the Vallarsa valley to Chiese, and then on to Schio. Next eastward was the road from the Folgaria plateau down the Astico valley to Arsiero. The next eastward to that fell from the Lavarone plateau down the Val d'Assa to Asiago. Schio, Arsiero, and Asiago were connected by light railways with the main line through Vicenza. Asiago was only 8 miles from Valstagna, in the valley of the lower Brenta (Val Sugana). A force which, holding Asiago, could get through the loop ⌣ to Valstagna would cut the Val Sugana and be behind the forces defending it. Arsiero and Asiago might prove within the Austrian reach, but when they had been seized there remained the greater task of seizing the ridges or plateau to the south of them in order to be able to *march on a wide front* into the plains. That was the ultimate problem on the east of the loop ⌣. On the west of it the Austrians must carry Pasubio in order to command the Schio road.

The forward lines of the Italians were not well placed, and the Italian forces were very much under-gunned. In May, 1916, none of the Allies was within reach of the superiority in artillery enjoyed by the Central Powers. Italy was very far from being on an equality; and by the requirements of General Cadorna's strategy the Trentino would have to give way to the Gorizia front. General Brusati, who was in command of the 1st Army holding the Trentino, was aware of the Austrian concentration of men, but had not appreciated the weight of gunfire which, as in other Austro-German "drives", would be brought to bear on him. Cadorna, who had a juster perception of the probabilities, replaced Brusati by Pecori-Giraldi, and in concert with him greatly strengthened the two flanks of the Val Lagarina and the Val Sugana; but before the centre could be strengthened in correspondence with the flanks, the Austrian attack was under way.

It began with the bombardment of May 14. Over a front of 30 miles the 2000 guns deluged the Italian front line, while the 15-inch and 16½-inch monsters threw their missiles far behind on to the communications, and even into Asiago. The Italian line under this compulsion at once moved back at its centre, but on the strengthened flanks resisted fiercely at Zugna and Borgo. On May 15 and 16 the fight ing increased in intensity at Zugna, where the ridge could not be held, and the Italians had to seek positions on the Coni-Zugna crest to the south. Next day the whole of the middle section of the loop ⌣ from Monte Maggio to Soglio d'Aspio had to be brought back, and the day after that (19th) the pushing back of the centre along the Astico valley continued, so that Monte Toraro, Monte Campolon, and Tonezza had all to be abandoned.

Towards Borgo the right wing was holding on manfully, but the crumpling of the mid section meant that the Arsiero plateau on which it rested must be given up. The line (May 19) ran from the Coni Zugna over Pasubio, and then, rather shaken and confused, went north of the Val Posina and the tableland of the Setti Communi to the Val Sugana. Next day the strategic surgeon Cadorna stepped in and decided that the weak part of this position must at once be cut away. He brought the centre of the line right back to the ridge south of Posina, where the original loop ⌣ was so deeply indented that it was south of Asiago, and had indeed been now split into two loops, ⌣ ⌣, a little one and a larger one, with Pasubio in between. The right-hand loop tipped up northwards after crossing the Val d'Assa till it reached the Val Sugana. This retreat was conducted slowly over four days' fighting, in which the losses in wounded and prisoners were heavy, but in which the Austrian attackers were also severely handled.

May 25 was one of the critical days. The centre had sunk back; the Austrians made one of the first of their wing attacks on the double loop ⌣ **P** ⌣, where **P** stands for Pasubio. They had attacked on the Italian left at Coni Zugna and Pasubio, and had pushed up the road from Rovereto to Schio so far into the smaller loop that they took Chiese, which is just below the Buole Pass. If they got on much farther they would take Pasubio in the rear and Pasubio would fall. If they got through the Buole Pass then Coni Zugna must go. The left Italian flank would then be cut off, and a gap opened in the left-hand loop by which the Austrians could pour into the plains. Cadorna had already summed up the situation, and did not underrate it. He had called up the Fifth Army—intended for his own attack on Gorizia—but it could not get up in fewer than ten days. The First Army must hold on till it came. Meanwhile, though its far right wing in the Val Sugana had withdrawn steadily to a position which was a stronger one lower down the Val Sugana, the sector next to this, the right centre, on the Setti Communi tableland, was enduring a very fierce period. On the 25th, 26th, 27th, 28th it was steadily outranged and driven back, till on the last of these days the Austrians commanded Asiago.

The critical moment on the left was meanwhile approaching, and the critical point was the Buole Pass. It was here that the triple struggle, for the Pass, for Pasubio, and for the Coni Zugna, culminated. Not one of them fell. Each successive attack by the Austrians was beaten back, and on May 30 the Austrians flung away 7000 men in a costly failure at the Buole Pass. It was their last attempt to burst their way through by weight of numbers as well as by weight of guns: but they had not shot their bolt. They still swarmed on three sides of Pasubio endeavouring to reduce it, and for three weeks the Italians, heavily outnumbered, and shelled unceasingly, clung tooth and nail to their

In the Rock-made Trenches on the Italian Front: Italian cavalrymen doing work as infantry

improvised trenches, and at the end were still in possession of them. The middle sector of the Italian line was almost as hard put to it, and on less debatable ground was forced still farther back. Their positions were divisible into two sections: the left section from Pasubio to and along the Posina stream; the right section across the Setti Communi tableland.

On the same day as the attack on the Buole Pass the Austrians took Mount Cimone, which dominates Arsiero; on the 28th they had forced the Italians back to the defence of the lower rim above the tableland. It is the last ridge between the hills and the plains. They had not even then been stopped or held. They laid hands on the ridge itself on May 30. Arsiero and Asiago had gone; and at Asiago the Austrians were only 8 miles from Valstagna. If they had got to Valstagna they would have been in the rear, and would have cut the communications of the Italians holding the Val Sugana. On June 1 an Austrian Army Order proclaimed that but one mountain intervened between their troops and the Venetian Plain—and still their advance had not been arrested. But the Fifth Army which Cadorna had called up was now in position to arrest it; and Cadorna knew it. At a later date the Italian Supreme Command issued a summary of the territorial gains of the Austrians in this offensive. They were comprised in the limits which were reached on June 3:

"The zone abandoned by us was entirely mountainous, rugged, and wooded. The inhabited centres, which were all of modest importance, were only four—Tonezza, Arsiero, Asiago, and Borgo. In the Val Lagarina and Val Sugana we always remained on conquered territory. In the Astico valley and in the Setti Communi we withdrew from a narrow strip of territory within the old frontier. In order to obtain this limited success an army of 400,000 men with 2000 guns had to fight a series of difficult and sanguinary battles lasting over thirty days. They sustained losses of certainly more than 100,000 men killed and wounded."

While the Fifth Italian Army was preparing its counter-attack a continuous struggle went on at the Italian centre and right centre, above Posina and on the Setti Communi tableland.

Drawn by H. W. Koekkoek

Italy's Counter-stroke to the Austrian Offensive: Italian infantry fording the River Posina at Ponte Rotto, July, 1916

The Austrians had tried to cut through to the Val Lagarina by way of the Buole Pass and had failed; they had tried the second-best way of getting behind Pasubio by way of the road which leads from Rovereto to Schio and again failed. They tried on the other side of Pasubio to cross the Posina torrent and ridge so as to strike the same road, and the points selected for their attack were Monte Alba, Monte Posina, and Monte Cogolo respectively. For days together these three names appeared in the *communiqués*, but they never passed definitively into Austrian possession. Towards the end of their attempt, as it began to falter and fail, they made their efforts at Monte Cogolo between Asiago and Monte Cengio; and they made a great attempt (and a still greater claim) on a point which they called a Maletta height. This indicated an attempt to break through the rim of the ridged tableland north-east of Asiago along the avenue of the Val Frenzela which leads to Valstagna—below the Italian right flank. From June 4 to 13, points on the ridge which is the upper lip between the tableland

and the plain were searched with all the guns the Austrians could command, in the hope of finding a weak place to break through. But the infantry attacks which followed could never be pushed home against the Italian battalions, which held on though sometimes reduced to a third of their strength. On June 15, 16, and 17 the last Austrian attack on the southern rim of the Setti Communi tableland was delivered, and flickered out. The gunners thenceforward were the only combatants, and Cadorna, a week later, sent his troops forward to the counter-attack. In the official review of the operations which the Italian Supreme Command afterwards published, it was asserted that while General Cadorna had perceived the possibility that the Austrians might break through to the plains at some point, he had early made preparations (the moving up of the Fifth Army) to deal with any such penetration as soon as the Austrians attempted to debouch; but that on June 2 he had come to the certain conclusion that the enemy would be unable to cross the mountain barrier.

Cadorna's own counter-offensive, preparations for which began on that day, was arranged so as to deliver two vigorous attacks against the enemy's wings, supported by energetic pressure along the entire front. This counter-offensive began on June 16, though its effects were not perceptible until a week later, when the Austrians began sullenly to withdraw, evacuating Arsiero and Asiago—in flames—and being able through the nature of their positions to get their larger-calibre guns safely away. If their only intention had been to delay General Cadorna's preparations for his own offensive, even that intention had only succeeded at a great cost. The cost had been considerable to the defenders, but greater to the attackers; and while, as after events showed, Cadorna's attack was delayed only for a brief period, the Austrians, by locking up their crowded men and guns in a deep salient with few roads and fewer railways, had undermined the whole of their strategic position on the Eastern front, and had given Brussilov, the Russian General, a hope and a success of which he could hardly have dared to dream.

The expectations of distant onlookers may have been disappointed when, during the latter half of June and in the month of July, the Italians, though apparently pressing on a rebuffed Austrian army, had little to show in the way of captures of men or guns, and showed no great persistence in pushing for positions in Trentino. What was in fact happening was that General Cadorna, though making a great display of activity there, was quietly withdrawing men and guns to supplement the effort which he had from the first projected on the Isonzo. By the first week in August, 1916, he was ready to strike here.

The position of the bridge-head of Gorizia has been described in a former chapter.[1] Its capture was an essential preliminary to any attack on Austrian territory, or on the Austrian forces, which could be undertaken at anything like a cost commensurate with the advantages to be obtained. It was

[1] Vol. V, pp. 5-6.

Drawn by H. W. Koekkoek

Cadorna's Counter-stroke in the Trentino: Italian troops driving the Austrians from the burning streets of Asiago, where the enemy had emulated German vandalism in Belgium by setting fire to the Italian houses

deeply wedged in behind mountain positions which had been strengthened by every device of rock trenching and tunnelling, and by every calibre of fortress gun which the Austrians had at their command. The buttresses of its defence were Mt. Sabotino on the hither side of the Isonzo river, with ridges running south from Mt. Sabotino to Oslavia and the Podgora plateau; on the farther side of the river was the rock position of San Marco, and farther south the great bastion of the Carso, jutting out into Mt. San Michele and cleft by the long ravine of the Vallone.

The Austrian front was defended by the Fifth Austrian Army under General Boroviec, whose command extended from the sea up to Tolmino, 25 miles north of Gorizia, where he was joined by the Tenth Austrian Army under General Rohr. It was on General Boroviec's front that Cadorna's attack, supported by 100,000 men in line, was launched. The first assault made by the Italians was not the principal one, but was a feint attack delivered ten miles south of Gorizia on those Austrian positions at Monfalcone which lie in front of one of the southern buttresses of Carso. The inference which Cadorna wished the enemy to draw was that here he proposed to undertake a movement to turn the great mountain-block which lies on this side of the Carso and is separated from it by the Vallone. Plenty of fire was put into this subsidiary assault, and about 150 Austrian prisoners were taken. The attack fulfilled its object of drawing Austrian forces to the threatened point and of provoking a strong counter-attack. August 5 was an artillery day only. On August 6 the Italian batteries began in earnest, and this time neglected the Monfalcone sector for the points selected for the real attack—the Sabotino block and the San Michele height which forms the northern boundary of the Gorizian Carso.

The work of the batteries and trench howitzers was a classic example of the concentration of fire against fortified lines. It had long been carefully prepared; the ground carefully examined by patrols, photographed by aviators, and the ranges marked to the yard. The tempest of fire wrecked the Austrian first lines, demolishing the shelters, destroying the observation posts, cutting the communications. Then the infantry advanced on the model taught by the experience of the Western fronts, one artillery curtain going in front of the infantry advancing in column, and spreading fanwise; another curtain barring the way against enemy reinforcements. The infantry went forward with Italian fire. They flowed over every obstacle on the rampart between Sabotino and the Gorizia bridge-head. On the heights which protected the town from the west a column under Colonel Badoglio took by assault the defences of Oslavia, and the whole position of the Sabotino followed. In the open country below Oslavia the infantry broke through the entanglements and the trench network constructed by the enemy between the southern spurs of Podgora and the Isonzo, and got well down to the bank of the river. On the Gorizian Carso the strong lines on Mt. San Michele

Fruits of Victory at Gorizia: Italian troops going into action passing some of the 15,000 Austrian prisoners on their way to internment

Official Italian Photograph

The Italians' Triumph at Gorizia: the entry of General Cadorna's troops into the captured town on August 10, 1916

which had broken so many Italian assaults in the past were in their turn broken, and a long line of trenches was carried thence southwards to San Martino. Finally, towards Monfalcone the attack begun two days before was renewed by a battalion of Bersaglieri cyclists, who, after a desperate fight, took one of the key positions and held it.

With Sabotino and San Michele in their hands the Italians had now to turn the keys in the lock, and to sweep the ridge which lay between them immediately west of the town. Three days of bloody clearance followed among the deep-sunk trenches, the fortified and armoured parts, the mutually supporting lesser heights which formed the last defences of Gorizia. But with the help of the artillery, and the confidence born of success, the work was done. On August 8 all the heights on the west bank of the Isonzo were Italian, and on the 10th the Duke of Aosta entered Gorizia at the head of the 3rd Army, which he commanded. The fighting had been too close and continuous for the capture of many Austrian guns, but 10,000 prisoners testified to the completeness of the victory.

The taking of Gorizia was one of the great feats of the war; it was one of the greatest in Italian military history. To Italy it was the turning of the tide, the assurance that, after what at one time seemed like the threat of disaster in the Trentino, their feet were now set on the steps to victory and on the pathway to Trieste. General Cadorna deserved the congratulations showered on him. From the beginning of the war he had played a waiting game, often hampered by the malign influences which in every country are due to underground German intrigue, but watching always for every opportunity, missing none that was offered, and husbanding the precious lives of his men for the moment that was bound to come.

He lost no time in following up his success. During the days between August 6 and 10 the Austrians had made frantic efforts to recover Monte San Michele. They did not succeed, and they also lost Baschini. Cadorna, as soon as his engineers had repaired the bridges, sent his cavalry into the wedge of the plain, and forced the Austrians back to their positions on the hills east of the Isonzo. Here, however, they had strong positions long prepared, stretching from Monte Gabriele, which is *vis-à-vis* to Monte Sabotino, across the river, down to the bulk of San Marco, which is east and south of Gorizia. This position was protected by flanking batteries on the Bainsizza plateau, and the plateau itself was very strongly fortified, as the Italians had found when they had tried months before to push their advantage from Plava. Simultaneously with the movement in the plain the Italians began to work their way across the Carso. It was a task for supermen. The surface is undulating, and honeycombed with holes and caves of which the Austrians had made the fullest use for purposes of defence, linking them up with concrete and steel-lined trenches, and converting the natural features into modern fortifications. They thought it impregnable; it might have been, had the Italian attack been less scientifically furious or the surprise less effective. On August 10 Rubbini followed Boschini, and the whole of the Gorizian plateau at

Gorizia and the Carso: map illustrating the Italian advance towards Trieste in 1916

its northern end was secured as far as the deep gash of the Vallone. On the 11th the Italians crossed the Vallone and occupied the village of Oppaechiasella. Next day, irresistibly pressing on, they carried further heights, and stormed the position of Nad Logem (Hill 212), where they took 1600 prisoners. On the subsequent days, down to the 15th, they prosecuted their success with the same vigour, carrying their lines past Debeli and Nad Logem up to Monte Pecinka. Then they settled down to reorganize their lines and positions for the next push. In the course of their operations from August 4 to 15 they took 18,758 prisoners, of whom 393 were officers, 30 big guns, 63 bomb throwers, 92 machine-guns, 12,225 rifles, 5,000,000 cartridges, 3000 shells, 60,000 bombs, and other war material.

Drawn by H. W. Koekkoek

**Masking the Italian Approach to Gorizia: General Cadorna's infantry resting on a road sheltered from the enemy by means of screens**

In preparation for the final advance on Gorizia the Italians screened off stretches of the approach-roads wherever gaps appeared among the natural "mask" of fringing trees, thus preventing the Austrians from learning how many and what troops were advancing. The screens were made of straw matting suspended on ropes on the telegraph and other poles.

During the next two months the Italians steadily consolidated their gains. Much that had fallen to them had been the fruits of surprise and of swiftly-seized opportunity. The Austrians still had numerous valuable and patiently fortified positions, and had every incentive to prevent the Italians from debouching from these that had fallen to them. Between mid-August and mid-September, nevertheless, the Italians took the San Grado position north-east of Nad Logem, so securing the northern angle of the Carso completely, and removing the damaging effect of the Austrian fire based on that point. Progress was necessarily slow on the Carso, the difficulties of supply were very great, and on that parched, desert-like plateau water was lacking. But the capture of the San Grado position enabled the Italians to steal down in the plain along the Vipacco river, and so to turn some of the Austrian lines so obstinately held on the higher ground. On October 10 a surprise attack was successfully driven into the Austrian positions north and south of the Vipacco river, and conformably with this success the Italian line on the Carso pushed forward by about a mile. In the two days' fighting, 7000 Austrian prisoners were taken.

This was the prelude to a still more important advance on the northern Carso at the beginning of November. It was made along the northernmost ridge, which commands the Vipacco valley, as well as on the mid-Carso, and on the Carso's chief road, which cuts across it from Doberdo to Comen. From the Vallone ravine (November 2) the assault began by scaling the rocky ascent which rises in successive terraces towards the east, and from there was pressed over a 3½-mile front till it had won a depth of over 2 miles from the Vallone. It captured the two Austrian defensive lines of Nad Logem-Oppacchiasella, and the line running through the village of Lokvica, with the roads radiating from Castagnevizza. Two days of incessant fighting did not exhaust the momentum of the advance. The 11th Italian Army Corps succeeded on November 3 in driving a wedge through the two Austrian lines until Monte Faiti was reached and occupied. On November 3, pivoting on that height, the Army Corps moved in echelon southwards and eastwards till the whole enemy salient was cleared, and the new Italian line ran from Monte Faiti (Faitihrib) to Castagnevizza (Kostanjevica). Farther north all the minor heights, where the northern brow of the Carso slopes down to the Vipacco river, were carried by assault as far as Hill 126. The whole advance covered a tract of ground more than 2 miles deep, and the total number of prisoners taken in three days amounted to 9000 men, including 259 officers, and ten 4-inch guns. It was another step on the way to Comen and Trieste.

E. S. G.

# CHAPTER V

## THE SECOND YEAR OF THE WAR

The Lion and her Cubs at Bay—Lord Kitchener's Death—Closing Scenes in his Career—The Tragedy off the Orkneys—French and German Losses in Military Leaders—Lord Derby and his Group System—King George's Appeal—"Single Men First"—Close of the Test Campaign—First Step in Compulsion—Increasing Need for Men—Position of Conscientious Objectors—Secret Session of House of Commons—A Still-born Service Bill—The New Act of 1916—Close of the Voluntary System in Great Britain—What Conscription Meant—His Majesty's Message—Crisis in Ireland—Germany's Opportunity—Roger Casement and his Conspiracy—Changes in the Coalition Government—The Growth of Munitions—Women's Splendid War Work—The Sinews of War—Britain's Economic Situation—Increased Cost of Living—Imports and Exports—Entering the Third Year of War—The Allies' Unshaken Confidence.

BEFORE the scene shifts to the Somme, which was to remain the dominating factor of the Western front for the remainder of the year 1916, it is advisable to review the world drama as a whole in a survey bringing the record down to the second anniversary of the war. One of the apocryphal sayings attributed to Lord Kitchener was that Britain would not really begin the war for two years; and Germany, who believed in the story but laughed it to scorn in its early days, confident that she would have won the war long before the Old Contemptibles could give place to a British army on a Continental scale, now began to realize that the impossible had come to pass. The beginning of the third year of the war found not only the British lion but all her cubs at bay on the Western front, smashing a path through mile after mile of elaborate

How the Lion's Cubs answered the Call: scene outside a recruiting office at Ottawa, Canada

trenches, which the enemy had boasted as impregnable, capturing many thousands of German prisoners, besides hundreds of German guns, and indirectly helping the French to save Verdun. Kitchener's New Army, with the heroic remnants of the Old, as well as the veteran divisions of the Territorial Forces and the gallant armies from Overseas, had at length come into its own.

The tragedy of it was that Lord Kitchener himself, who had organized the whole as no one else could have done, was not destined to hear how magnificently it stood this supreme test on the banks of the Somme. Probably no more staggering piece of news ever flashed round the Empire than Sir John Jellicoe's message of June 6, 1916, to the effect that H.M.S. *Hampshire*, with Lord Kitchener on board, had foundered off the Orkney Islands on its way to Russia. The general public had no idea that Lord Kitchener had even left London, and received the news first with stupefaction and then with a sense of having lost a sheet-anchor in a storm. Many long clung to the hope that it might even yet prove untrue, and eagerly snatched at rumours and legends asserting his survival. It seemed impossible, as the Prime Minister afterwards said at Ladybank in describing Lord Kitchener's farewell to him, "to connect that imposing figure, that embodiment of virile force, with any sense of mortality. Yet," added Mr. Asquith, "in the plenitude of his powers he was going forward straight to his doom—a fine, and in many ways an enviable end". The King's Army Order on the day following the tragedy removed the last lingering doubt from most people's minds as to the War Minister's fate:—

"The King has learnt with profound regret of the disaster by which the Secretary of State for War has lost his life while proceeding on a special mission to the Emperor of Russia.

"Field-Marshal Lord Kitchener gave forty-five years of distinguished service to the State, and it is largely due to his administrative genius and unwearying energy that the country has been able to create and place in the field the armies which are to-day upholding the traditional glories of our Empire."

Happily for the Empire the task which he had set himself at the very outset of the war, and he alone, with his clear vision and quick grasp of essentials, had seen to be imperative—the transformation of our small standing army into a military power of the first order—was finished. The whole Empire was organized for war. The mighty host which he had created could now meet the most formidable army in the world on equal terms, and go on increasing from strength to strength until final victory had been won. Perhaps Lord Kitchener as conscious of this as the waters closed round him off the desolate coast of the Orkneys on that fatal Monday evening of June 5, 1916. His last days at home had been cheered by the success of his historic meeting with his critics in the House of Commons. Every one knew, though the meeting had been private, that it had proved a complete triumph for Lord Kitchener, who referred to it on the eve of his departure for Russia, in Mr. Asquith's phrase, "almost with the gaiety of a schoolboy".

A critical stage had been reached in the conduct of the war both by land and sea. Only a few days before, the British Grand Fleet had fought the German High Seas Fleet off Jutland, and scored a victory which, though robbed of an annihilating blow by the North Sea fog, which enabled von Scheer to steal back to cover with his crippled armada, had left our naval supremacy more firmly established than ever. On land we had mustered on the Western front, in June, 1916, the most powerful army that we had ever placed in the field, and the hour would soon strike when it would be put to the test. Farther afield the outlook was less promising. Kut had gone the way of Gallipoli, falling back into Turkish hands; and the Balkan campaign, with both Serbia and Montenegro wholly seized by the Central Powers, and Greece hopelessly obdurate, was merely marking time, awaiting eventualities. Austria, with her partner Germany making a frenzied effort to crown the appalling sacrifices at Verdun with success, was delivering her thrust at the Trentino. That thrust proved ill-advised, but it seemed like upsetting the Italian campaign for the rest of the year. Only on the Russian front were the Allies' arms progressing with something like a real advance, and General Broussilov's brilliant operations doubtless had not a little to do with the "special mission" to the Tsar with which Lord Kitchener was charged by King George when he started on his last journey.

It was not his only mission abroad since, at the close of the first year of war, we briefly described his first visit to the Western front. That visit had been succeeded by another, this time on the invitation of the French Government, when General Joffre seized the opportunity to present the British Field Marshal with the black-and-green ribbon for his services as a volunteer with Chanzy's army in the Franco-Prussian War. Memories were then revived of those old campaigning days, as well as of the more dramatic episode at Fashoda, twenty-eight years later, when his love for France and early associations with her army helped to avert the irreparable catastrophe of a conflict between the two nations destined to fight shoulder to shoulder in the years to come for Liberty, Truth, and Justice. At the end of the same year (1915), after the costly advance which marked the Allied offensive in Artois and Champagne, and the failure of the Gallipoli campaign—the scene of which he personally visited before deciding upon the evacuation of the peninsula—he visited the King of Greece at Athens during a critical phase of the Balkan campaign, and concluded a memorable tour of the Eastern theatre of war with a visit to King Victor Emmanuel and the Italian front on the Isonzo. This mission, concluding, as it began, in Paris, helped materially towards the closer co-ordination of the Allies' plans, and incidentally cleared the air of certain noxious rumours regarding his position at home. The visit to Russia six months later promised to complete his personal knowledge of all the main fighting fronts of Europe, and the victorious opening of Broussilov's bold move at the beginning of June filled him with the highest hopes as he set out on the journey which in a few short hours was to end so disastrously.

The facts relating to the tragedy itself are extremely meagre. Travelling from London to the north of Scotland by the night express on June 4, the War Minister, on arriving at his destination, paid a visit to Sir John Jellicoe, who was one of the last to speak to him ashore. After bidding the admiral good-bye, he embarked with his staff on board H.M.S. *Hampshire* (Captain Herbert J. Savill), which only a few days before had played her part in the battle of Jutland[1]. He was accompanied, among others, by Sir Frederick Donaldson, Chief Technical Adviser to the Ministry of Munitions, Brigadier-General Wilfred Ellershaw, of the War Office Staff, Mr. O'Beirne, of the Diplomatic Service, who had spent nine years in the embassy at Petrograd, and Lieutenant-Colonel O. A. FitzGerald, Lord Kitchener's personal military secretary and devoted friend.

Lord Kitchener's Last Voyage: Admiral Jellicoe's farewell to the War Minister and Staff before their embarkation in H.M.S. *Hampshire* for Russia

Lord Kitchener is the third figure from the right, in a military overcoat. He is introducing Mr. O'Beirne, of the Foreign Office, to Admiral Jellicoe. Behind Mr. O'Beirne, on the gangway, is Lieutenant-Colonel FitzGerald, Lord Kitchener's personal military secretary, who also perished with him.

It was blowing hard as the *Hamp-*

[1] "It was hard luck", said one of the *Hampshire's* survivors, "to come to such an end after going through the Horn Reef battle unscathed. In that battle we led the *Iron Duke* into action, and our shells sank a German light cruiser and two submarines. We did not have a single casualty in our ship, although big shells fairly rained into the water all around us."—*Times*.

departure for Russia, in Mr. Asquith's phrase, "almost with the gaiety of a schoolboy".

A critical stage had been reached in the conduct of the war both by land and sea. Only a few days before, the British Grand Fleet had fought the German High Seas Fleet off Jutland, and scored a victory which, though robbed of an annihilating blow by the North Sea fog, which enabled von Scheer to steal back to cover with his crippled armada, had left our naval supremacy more firmly established than ever. On land we had mustered on the Western front, in June, 1916, the most powerful army that we had ever placed in the field, and the hour would soon strike when it would be put to the test. Farther afield the outlook was less promising. Kut had gone the way of Gallipoli, falling back into Turkish hands; and the Balkan campaign, with both Serbia and Montenegro wholly seized by the Central Powers, and Greece hopelessly obdurate, was merely marking time, awaiting eventualities. Austria, with her partner Germany making a frenzied effort to crown the appalling sacrifices at Verdun with success, was delivering her thrust at the Trentino. That thrust proved ill-advised, but it seemed like upsetting the Italian campaign for the rest of the year. Only on the Russian front were the Allies' arms progressing with something like a real advance, and General Broussilov's brilliant operations doubtless had not a little to do with the "special mission" to the Tsar with which Lord Kitchener was charged by King George when he started on his last journey.

It was not his only mission abroad since, at the close of the first year of war, we briefly described his first visit to the Western front. That visit had been succeeded by another, this time on the invitation of the French Government, when General Joffre seized the opportunity to present the British Field Marshal with the black-and-green ribbon for his services as a volunteer with Chanzy's army in the Franco-Prussian War. Memories were then revived of those old campaigning days, as well as of the more dramatic episode at Fashoda, twenty-eight years later, when his love for France and early associations with her army helped to avert the irreparable catastrophe of a conflict between the two nations destined to fight shoulder to shoulder in the years to come for Liberty, Truth, and Justice. At the end of the same year (1915), after the costly advance which marked the Allied offensive in Artois and Champagne, and the failure of the Gallipoli campaign—the scene of which he personally visited before deciding upon the evacuation of the peninsula—he visited the King of Greece at Athens during a critical phase of the Balkan campaign, and concluded a memorable tour of the Eastern theatre of war with a visit to King Victor Emmanuel and the Italian front on the Isonzo. This missio[n] concluding, as it began, in Paris, help[ed] materially towards the closer co-[ordi]nation of the Allies' plans, and in[cidentally] cleared the air of certain [...] rumours regarding his position. The visit to Russia six mo[nths] promised to complete his knowledge of all the mai[n]

victorious
move at
im with
on the
hours

ragedy
Travel-

part in the battle of Jutland[1]. He was acconpa1ied, a1o1g o1ers, by Sir Frederic< Do1aldso1, Chie Tech1ical Adviser to the Mi1istry of Munitions, Brigadier-Ge1eral Wilfred Ellershaw, of the War Office Staff, Mı O'Beirne, of the Diplomatic Service who had spent nine years in the e1bassy at

d Derby said i1 his
e i1 the House of
aid a heavy toll to the
ılar security, but . . .
exacted a heavier toll
rd Kitche1er, coffined
n-of-war, passed to the

ınworthy exit fron the
ıich he had played so
part. Lord Kitche1er
great tas< was aecon-
he had forged a nighty
ı his successors could be
o <eep i1 good wor<i1g
he had said good-bye
, 1ot o1ly to the Gover1-
e Gra1d Fleet, but also
hin self, as well as to his
ome. His good-bye to
ıas bee1 so con plete as
uggest son e prenoıitio1
oachi1g e1d. This idea is
y his frie1d Lord Derby;
owever, that it really seen ed
ide1ce i1 its wisdon had
to give hin the rest which
ever have give1 hin self.
n orial service at St. Paul's
atte1ded by the Ki1g a1d
y Quee1 Alexa1dra a1d
ıbers of the Royal Fan ily,
f the Navy a1d Arn y, as
f every part of the En pire
y bra1ch of 1atio1al life,
with represe1tatives of all
es a1d na1y 1eutral States,
of the nost novi1g cere-
of the <i1d ever held i1 this
; a1d it had its cou1terpart
other cathedrals a1d parish
s throughout the British Isles.
Kitche1er had falle1, but the

*shire*, accompanied by two destroyers, started on her journey about five o'clock on that Monday night of June 5. The wind increased until it blew a gale from the north-north-west. About seven o'clock the seas were so heavy as the cruiser took her westerly course round the northern island of the Orkneys that Captain Savill was obliged to order the escort of destroyers to detach themselves, the *Hampshire* thence battling her way alone along that inhospitable coast. What happened thereafter is only known in a confused and fragmentary way. Heavy seas broke over the ship as she ploughed her path through them, so that she had to be partially battened down. According to the Admiralty account she struck a mine between 7.30 and 7.45 p.m., and immediately after the explosion began to settle by the bows. Within about fifteen minutes the ship, with all on board save a handful of men, foundered, and neither Lord Kitchener nor any of his staff survived. Several boats, according to people ashore, were seen to get safely away from the sinking cruiser, only to be dashed to pieces on the rocks, but according to the few survivors what had seemed to be boats were really rafts[1]. The only boats that could be got ready in the time were either smashed at once or foundered with the ship, which, sinking by the head, turned a complete somersault forward, carrying her boats and all in them with her. From the rafts which reached the shore only twelve exhausted men survived, and it was from their evidence that the story was pieced together at the subsequent naval enquiry.

It transpired that immediately after the explosion, which extinguished all the lights, Captain Savill gave orders for all hands to go to their appointed stations to abandon ship. The discipline was splendid, though it must have been obvious from the first that the ship was doomed, and that few, if any, of those on board were likely to survive. "As the men", to quote from the official report of the subsequent enquiry, "were moving up one of the hatchways to their stations, Lord Kitchener, accompanied by a naval officer, appeared; the latter called out: 'Make way for Lord Kitchener,' and they both went up on to the quarter-deck, and subsequently four military officers were seen on the quarter-deck walking aft on the port side." Lord Kitchener watched the last preparations unperturbed, quietly pacing the deck as he did so, one of the officers accompanying him apparently being Colonel FitzGerald.

Presently the captain's gig was lowered, and Captain Savill called to Lord Kitchener to get into it, but whether he failed to hear this amid the turmoil of storm and disaster, or decided that all such attempts to escape were futile, it is impossible to say. No one among the survivors saw him attempt to enter any of the boats. The only one who remembered seeing him on deck—Leading Seaman

[1] These circular rafts, with from fifty to seventy men on each of them, got clear of the ship, but few lived through the awful seas to reach the shore. All the survivors reported that men gradually dropped off and even died on board the rafts from exposure, exhaustion, and cold. Some of the crew perished on the rocks; others died after landing. Of some seventy men on one raft only six survived.

Rogerson—declared emphatically, in a personal narrative published in the *Times*, that he went down with the ship. By this survivor, who escaped in one of the rafts, he was last seen still standing on the starboard side of the quarter-deck talking to his officers.

"I won't say", declared Rogerson, "that he did not feel the strain of the perilous situation like the rest of us, but he gave no outward sign of nervousness, and from the little time that elapsed between my leaving the ship and her sinking I feel certain that Lord Kitchener went down with her, standing on deck at the time."

No sooner was the dreadful news flashed to Sir John Jellicoe that night than destroyers and patrol-boats were rushed to the scene of disaster in the faint hope of picking up survivors, while search-parties ashore worked their way along the coast. It was all in vain. "As the whole coast has been searched from the seaward", Sir John Jellicoe was forced to acknowledge on the following day, "I greatly fear that there is little hope of further survivors." In forwarding the report of the subsequent enquiry, the Commander-in-Chief voiced the feeling of the whole of the Royal Navy when he wrote:—

"I cannot adequately express the sorrow felt by me personally and by the officers and men of the Grand Fleet generally at the fact that so distinguished a soldier and so great a man should have lost his life whilst under the care of the Fleet."

Colonel FitzGerald's body was washed ashore on the Orkney coast, and buried at Eastbourne, but that of his chief was never recovered. "We in these islands from time immemorial", as Lord Derby said in his eloquent tribute in the House of Lords, "have paid a heavy toll to the sea for our insular security, but . . . the sea never exacted a heavier toll than when Lord Kitchener, coffined in a British man-of-war, passed to the great beyond."

It was no unworthy exit from the stage upon which he had played so illustrious a part. Lord Kitchener knew that his great task was accomplished; that he had forged a mighty weapon which his successors could be relied upon to keep in good working order; and he had said good-bye before leaving, not only to the Government and the Grand Fleet, but also to the King himself, as well as to his beloved Broome. His good-bye to the nation has been so complete as almost to suggest some premonition of the approaching end. This idea is dismissed by his friend Lord Derby, who said, however, that it really seemed as if Providence in its wisdom had determined to give him the rest which he would never have given himself.

The memorial service at St. Paul's Cathedral, attended by the King and Queen, by Queen Alexandra and other members of the Royal Family, leaders of the Navy and Army, as well as of every part of the Empire and every branch of national life, together with representatives of all the Allies and many neutral States, was one of the most moving ceremonies of the kind ever held in this country; and it had its counterpart in many other cathedrals and parish churches throughout the British Isles.

Lord Kitchener had fallen, but the

A French Hero of the Great War: the late General Gallieni, Minister of War, inspecting French Boy Scouts while Military Governor of Paris

tide of battle still rolled on. It was for those who remained—as Mr. Bonar Law said in his tribute to his memory in the House of Commons—to close their ranks with a single eye to securing the victory, the ultimate attainment of which the late War Minister had never doubted. He was not the only leading actor in the world-drama to fall at this period. Only a few weeks before he vanished in the northern seas, Germany lost her distinguished organizer of the Turkish army, Field-Marshal von der Goltz, whose death at Bagdad, on the eve of the fall of Kut, remained shrouded in mystery, though officially attributed to spotted fever. While attending the memorial service in his honour in the Reichstag in the following month—only a few days after the Kitchener memorial service in St. Paul's—Germany lost another of her war lords in General von Moltke, who died of heart failure during the ceremony. A nephew of the famous organizer of victory in the Franco-Prussian War, in which he himself served as a subaltern, General von Moltke, at one time a great favourite with the Kaiser, was the Chief of Staff who was credited with formulating the plan of campaign in the West with which Germany embarked on the Great War. With the failure of that plan and the German retreat from the Marne the favourite was discarded, and, stripped of his power and position, henceforth became little more than the mere mouthpiece of the Imperial War Council.

France also lost one of her leading soldiers in General Gallieni, who died shortly after resigning as French Minister of War in the spring of 1916. Before becoming Minister of War General Gallieni had served as Military Governor of Paris during those critical days when the guns of the advancing Germans could be distinctly heard in the threatened capital; and all through he had played a great part in the work of national defence. In his scheme for the military organization of Paris he had included the Boy Scouts, and may be seen in the accompanying illustration reviewing some of these ardent spirits among the rising generation of his race—"Bwa-Skoo", in the Parisian pronunciation. General Gallieni will always be remembered, however, for his share in the victory of the Marne. On that critical morning of September, 1914, when flying scouts brought word into Paris that von Kluck had suddenly swerved eastward—apparently neglecting Paris just when the capital seemed almost within the hollow of the enemy's hand—Gallieni, as well as Joffre, saw the opportunity, and seized it in a flash. He it was who rushed the Paris Sixth Army together under General Maunoury, formed of all the troops available, and sent it out, in taxi-cabs and every other possible conveyance, to fall like a bolt from the blue on von Kluck's right flank. The whole Allied army had its share in the triumph which followed, but in that unexpected blow lay the germ of a victory which helped to shape the destiny of the world. General Gallieni was succeeded by General Roques, and Lord Kitchener by Mr. Lloyd George, who had relieved him of his most criticized department just a year before by exchanging the Chancellorship of the Exchequer for the newly created Ministry of Munitions, the work of which will presently come under review.

Only a few days before Lord Kitchener—to resume the main thread of our story—left these shores on his fatal journey he had witnessed the passing of an Act which, in regard to national service, had at length brought this country into line with all the other belligerent Powers. We had wrought wonders with our traditional principle of voluntaryism, mustering an army of Continental dimensions and glorious courage of which the whole Empire had reason to be proud, but in the special circumstances of this unparalled struggle it had long ceased

The Recruiting Campaign in the Winter of 1915-16: the raw material and the finished article—home from the trenches in France—greeting each other outside a recruiting office

to meet the increasing needs of the situation. Compulsion was essential to the maintenance of an army capable of securing the only victory which could ensure a lasting peace.

Lord Derby, though in favour of compulsion at the time, made a last effort to save the voluntary system when, on October 11, 1915, he became

Director-General of Recruiting, and formulated what became known as the Derby Scheme. He took up office at the personal request of his friend—"the greatest friend I ever had", as Lord Derby feelingly acknowledged at the time of the War Minister's death, little dreaming that the day would come, before the year was out, when he would fill the same exalted office at Whitehall. Lord Kitchener had always hoped that the principle which had done so well at first, and furnished such splendid material in the field, would prove equal to the task of fighting the war to a successful issue. It had already produced three millions of volunteers, and was to yield two millions more before the stress of circumstances forced it to give place to conscription—"results", as Lord Kitchener said, "far greater than most of us would have dared to predict, and certainly beyond anything that our enemies contemplated". Yet Lord Kitchener did not disguise the fact from the public that, failing volunteers, conscription would have to be resorted to. The primary object of the National Register, as he told his Guildhall audience in the summer of 1915, was "to note the men between the ages of nineteen and forty not required for munition or other necessary work, and therefore available, if physically fit, for the fighting-line"; and four months later, in the same historic hall, he declared: "I shall want more men and still more till the enemy is crushed."

This was shortly after the inauguration of Lord Derby's Group System, which its author described as the last effort on behalf of voluntary service. With the aid of the National Register a canvass was conducted of all men between eighteen and forty who had not been starred as munition workers or other indispensables, and who were divided into forty-six groups, according to age, as follows:—

| Unmarried. | | Married. | |
|---|---|---|---|
| Age. | Group. | Age. | Group. |
| 18–19[1] | 1 | 18–19[1] | 24 |
| 19–20 | 2 | 19–20 | 25 |
| 20–21 | 3 | 20–21 | 26 |
| 21–22 | 4 | 21–22 | 27 |
| 22–23 | 5 | 22–23 | 28 |
| 23–24 | 6 | 23–24 | 29 |
| 24–25 | 7 | 24–25 | 30 |
| 25–26 | 8 | 25–26 | 31 |
| 26–27 | 9 | 26–27 | 32 |
| 27–28 | 10 | 27–28 | 33 |
| 28–29 | 11 | 28–29 | 34 |
| 29–30 | 12 | 29–30 | 35 |
| 30–31 | 13 | 30–31 | 36 |
| 31–32 | 14 | 31–32 | 37 |
| 32–33 | 15 | 32–33 | 38 |
| 33–34 | 16 | 33–34 | 39 |
| 34–35 | 17 | 34–35 | 40 |
| 35–36 | 18 | 35–36 | 41 |
| 36–37 | 19 | 36–37 | 42 |
| 37–38 | 20 | 37–38 | 43 |
| 38–39 | 21 | 38–39 | 44 |
| 39–40 | 22 | 39–40 | 45 |
| 40–41 | 23 | 40–41 | 46 |

The plan was to induce men to "attest" their willingness to serve—receiving khaki armlets, bearing the Royal Crown, to be worn in proof that they had offered themselves—and then to await their turn to be called up as they were required. The King himself inaugurated the campaign with the following appeal:—

[1] No man in these groups was to be called up until he had reached the age of 19.

"BUCKINGHAM PALACE.

"TO MY PEOPLE

"At this grave moment in the struggle between my people and a highly-organized enemy, who has transgressed the laws of nations and changed the ordinance that binds civilized Europe together, I appeal to you.

"I rejoice in my Empire's effort, and I feel pride in the voluntary response from my subjects all over the world who have sacrificed home, fortune, and life itself, in order that another may not inherit the free Empire which their ancestors and mine have built.

"I ask you to make good these sacrifices.

"The end is not in sight. More men and yet more are wanted to keep my armies in the field, and through them to secure victory and enduring peace.

"In ancient days the darkest moment has ever produced in men of our race the sternest resolve.

"I ask you, men of all classes, to come forward voluntarily, and take your share in the fight.

"In freely responding to my appeal you will be giving your support to our brothers who, for long months, have nobly upheld Britain's past traditions and the glory of her arms.

"GEORGE R.I."

With this, and a personal letter from Lord Derby — a copy of which was sent to every eligible man—the new recruiting scheme made a promising start. It was not long, however, before the question of the married man threw a blight on its prospects. Lord Kitchener had stated in his Guildhall speech, on July 9, 1915, that single men, "as far as may be", were to be preferred before married men; and Mr. Asquith in the House of Commons at the beginning of the following November gave it as his opinion that the obligation of the married men to enlist ought not to be enforced, or held to be binding on them, unless and until the unmarried men had been dealt with. "Single men first" now became a watchword. Not because of any lack of patriotism, but because the country as a whole expected that the single man should present himself first. Under the old voluntary system the married men had responded nobly to the call—a fact acknowledged by the Prime Minister in a speech in which he noted that in any time of great national crisis it is probable that a larger proportion of married than single men will always enlist under a voluntary system, "for the reason that the added sense of responsibility which a man has undertaken by the mere fact of starting a home is likely to make him think more seriously of his duty to his country". At all events, the feeling on the subject became so strong that when, a week or so later, Mr. Asquith uttered words which raised doubts as to the sincerity of his pledge, the scheme received a blow from which it never recovered, though Lord Derby did his best to mend matters by a personal assurance that the married men should not be called up until the great majority of the single men had enlisted, and that if a great majority did not enlist—or there was any "general shirking" of unmarried men, in Mr. Bonar Law's words—then methods would be used to compel them to join.

It was originally intended that the test campaign should come to a close on November 30, but the date was eventually extended to December 11,

Drawn by Christopher Clark

The Army of "Armleteers"

Upwards of 2,800,000 men in Great Britain offered themselves in the closing months of 1915 under Lord Derby's group system. Armlets of dark khaki-coloured cloth, bearing a crown cut out of scarlet cloth, were served out to all who attested.

the sudden rush of recruits during the last few days being impossible to cope with. This overwhelming stream raised a new hope that conscription might not after all become necessary; and, indeed, the total response to Lord Derby's appeal proved, numerically, enormously large. Upwards of 2,800,000 men offered themselves, this in itself being a fine tribute to the old voluntary system. But when the figures came to be analysed, and the men themselves to be examined, the total number available for service was disappointing. Our national task involved far more than the maintenance of new armies in all parts of the world. There was the navy — the greatest navy the world had ever known — and there were munitions not only for ourselves but also for our Allies. There was also the vital need to sustain food-supplies and national credit, as well, also, to a large extent, the credit of the Allied Powers: and all this hinged largely on the export trade from this country, which demanded a vast amount of industrial labour. Hence the need for exemptions and the establishment of tribunals all over the country to consider the appeals both of masters and men. Women came to the rescue by the hundred thousand, and proved excellent workers; but even when this fact and the help of all other kinds of unskilled labour were taken into account, it was impossible in a complex society like ours, with its world-wide responsibilities, to put all our able-bodied men into the fighting services.

The very number and scale of the exempted men made conscription inevitable. The man in the street, where so much was held from his knowledge in a war over which the veil of secrecy was drawn more tightly every month, sometimes had cause to complain of the inequality in the treatment of individuals. Parents and relations especially, as Lord Derby

The Earl of Derby, P.C., G.C.V.O.
(From a photograph by Russell & Sons)

pointed out in his report, could not understand why their sons, husbands, or brothers should join while other young men held back and secured lucrative employment. Also, the system of submitting cases to tribunals was viewed with distrust from the first. It was new; it involved the disclosure of private affairs; and it led to a fear that cases might not be fairly and impartially dealt with. Conscription, therefore, could only have been a matter of time, even if the proportion of single men attested under the Derby Scheme had been sufficient to cover the Prime Minister's pledge. In point of fact it was not sufficient, a total of 651,160 unstarred single men remaining unaccounted for. This, as Lord Kitchener, Lord Derby, and the Prime Minister alike agreed, was far from being a negligible quantity, and in order to redeem the pledge it was not possible to hold married men to their attestation until the services of single men had been obtained by other means. The only remaining means was national service, which brought about something approaching equality of sacrifice, and marked a definite stage in the complete organization of the country for war. Lord Derby's canvass showed very distinctly that it was not lack of courage that was keeping some men back. Nor was there, he wrote at the close of his report on December 12, 1915, the slightest sign but that the country as a whole was as determined as ever to support the Prime Minister in the pledge which he made at the Guildhall three months after the outbreak of the war—to the effect that we would fight to the last until Germany's military power was fully destroyed.

The first definite step in compulsion was the passing of the Military Service (No. 2) Bill, introduced in January, 1916, enacting that every male British subject who, on August 15, 1915 (the date of the National Register), was between the age of eighteen and forty-one, and was either unmarried or a widower without children, should be deemed to have been duly enlisted in His Majesty's regular forces for general service with the colours, or in the reserve, for the period of the war. It was not a popular step on the road to conscription. With its schedule of exemptions and long lists of reserved trades it allowed too many loopholes for escape. It was condemned by such uncompromising opponents as Sir John Simon, the Home Secretary, who accordingly resigned; and a special Labour conference called to discuss the situation voted against the measure by a large majority, but qualified the vote by resolving not to carry the protest to the point of resistance. This last sound decision removed the only serious danger from the passage of the Bill, Ireland being excluded from its scope, the Nationalists, after supporting its opponents at the first reading as a matter of principle, abstaining from further voting.

Its real danger arose from its own inherent weakness and the insistent call for men at the front. Side by side with it, too, the Derby group system was re-opened, and the single groups were swallowed up so rapidly that the attested married men were warned that they would be required before the new Bill had actually been applied to the single men who had not come forward at all. This led to another outcry of broken faith, though the truth was that military necessity had rendered this urgent call imperative. The need for men to repair the wastage of war was shown by the following table, published at the time, showing the total British losses down to December 9, 1915:—

| | Killed. | Wounded. | Missing. | Total. |
|---|---|---|---|---|
| *Flanders and France—* | | | | |
| Officers ... | 4,829 | 9,943 | 1,699 | 16,471 |
| N.C.O.'s and men ... | 77,473 | 241,359 | 52,685 | 371,517 |
| | | | | 387,988 |
| *Dardanelles—* | | | | |
| Officers ... | 1,667 | 3,028 | 350 | 5,045 |
| N.C.O.'s and men ... | 24,535 | 72,781 | 12,194 | 109,510 |
| | | | | 114,555 |
| *Other Theatres of War—* | | | | |
| Officers ... | 871 | 694 | 100 | 1,665 |
| N.C.O.'s and men ... | 10,548 | 10,953 | 2,518 | 24,019 |
| | | | | 25,684 |
| Totals | 119,923 | 338,758 | 69,546 | 528,227 |

Already, before the end of 1915, Parliament, in response to the imperative demands from the War Office, had authorized the raising of another million men, making 4,000,000 in all, and the task of providing the necessary stream of reserves to replace the wastage, and keep the fighting divisions up to their full strength, was soon to prove beyond the power of any machinery save compulsion all round.

One of the minor difficulties was the position of the conscientious objectors, for whom a special corps was formed. This was called the Non-combatant Corps—the N.C.C. for short—and members had to satisfy the local tribunals before whom their cases were decided that they were sincere in their scruples, and not merely shirking active service through cowardice. The rates of pay of the men of this corps were the same as those laid down for the infantry of the line. Its officers and non-commissioned officers were selected from regular infantry personnel not fit for general service, but fit for service abroad on lines of communication. Companies were trained in squad drill without arms, and in the use of the various forms of tools employed in field engineering. Privates were equipped as infantry, save that they were not armed, and wore the letters N.C.C. as a cap badge and shoulder title. Needless to say, their lot in the army was not a happy one, and the concessions made to them added to the grievances of the discontented attested men. Matters moved to a crisis when the Army Council, of which Lord Kitchener was chief adviser, presented the Government with a frank statement on the subject of man-power and the army's immediate requirements.

A Secret Session of the House was held on April 25–26, 1916, to consider the situation. So drastic were the precautions taken at this memorable Secret Session that the Lords, as well as all strangers, were ruled out of the Commons, while the Press galleries in both Houses were not only cleared but also kept bolted and barred throughout, and the approaches to the doors guarded by officials. An authorized account of the proceedings was subsequently published, summarizing Mr. Asquith's speech, in which he gave particulars of the expansion of the army from the first days of the war, and of the total military effort of the Empire. It was shown that the results of recruiting, more particularly since the preceding August, when the National Registration was carried out, had fallen short of the requirements necessary to fulfil our proper military effort. This, it was stated, was not due to an overestimate of the number of men available, but to the length of time which must be occupied in sifting individual cases without impairing other essential national services or causing grave cases of hardship. To meet the situation the Government proposed to bring in an additional Military Service Bill, the main features of which were:—

1. The prolongation until the end of the war of time-expired men, whose period of service under the existing law could be extended for one year only.

2. To empower the Military Authority to transfer men enlisted for Territorial battalions to any unit where they were needed.

3. To render an exempted man liable to military service immediately on the expiry of his certificate of exemption.

4. To bring under the terms of the Military Service Act all youths under 18 on August 15, 1915, as they reached that age.

General compulsion was to follow if, at the end of four weeks ending May 27, the necessary numbers required by our military obligations had not been obtained by these means and by voluntary enlistment from among the unattested married men. It was, at the best, a forlorn hope to save the last vestiges of a voluntary system which the nation itself as a whole had long since realized as inadequate to cope with an unprecedented crisis, and it was foredoomed by the storm of condemnation which greeted the scheme even before it could be introduced by Mr. Walter Long, President of the Local Government Board, who was in charge of it. Sir Edward Carson helped as much as anyone to kill it at its birth by his scathing criticism, pointing out the injustice, for instance, of applying compulsion to men who had already served their country for the whole time for which they had enlisted, and for a year more, before compelling those to join who had never served at all. As for the second item, he objected to the breaking of the Government pledge with the Territorials, while the proposal to bring in boys of eighteen was manifestly unjust where there was no general compulsion. The last nail in the coffin of the still-born Bill was hammered home by Mr. Walsh, the miner member for the Ince Division, who, calling for fair play, not only endorsed Sir Edward Carson's protests, but also showed himself fully prepared to support conscription. "Why temporize any longer?" he demanded. "It is simply fooling with the whole business." Similar views were expressed by other members of both parties. No one, indeed, had a good word to say for the new Ministerial compromise. Mr. Asquith was quick enough to see that the measure was doomed, and "advised" the President of the Local Government Board not to press his motion for leave to introduce it. Thus the unwelcome scheme was killed at its birth, and general conscription became merely a matter of time. A week later the Government, at last taking its courage in both hands, brought in a new Bill—the Military Service Act (1916)—extending the compulsory obligation to all male British subjects, married as well as single, between the ages of eighteen and forty-one, exceptions still being made in the case of those men who came within the scope of the exempted trades. Other clauses provided for an extension during the period of the war of the service of time-expired men, and authorized the transfer of Territorials into other corps of Territorials or regular battalions.

Official Photograph

New Artillery for the New Army: a monster gun in action on the Western Front

This Bill was introduced on May 2, 1916, and, passing rapidly through Parliament with overwhelming majorities, received the royal assent on May 25. A month's grace was given to everyone to volunteer before the Bill became law, and every youth thereafter was allowed the same period on attaining the age of eighteen in order that he might have an equal opportunity of serving as a volunteer instead of as a conscript.

The Great War was destined to give a new meaning to the word conscript in British ears. We had cause to be immeasurably proud of those who rushed to the colours at the first call of King and Country, as their forefathers had done before them, stoutly maintaining that "one volunteer was worth three pressed men any day". The voluntary principle had become almost a sacred tradition with people who forgot that most of our ancient military achievements were only won by compulsory service. There was nothing derogatory in conscription. Nor was there anything inconsistent in introducing compulsion in a democratic country. Compulsion in our case simply meant, as Mr. Lloyd George assured his constituents, "the will of the majority of the people—the voluntary decision of the majority. . . . Compulsion simply means that a nation is organizing itself in an orderly, consistent, resolute fashion for war." Cromwell's "New Model" was not an army of volunteers, and only by conscription had

Lincoln eventually won the American Civil War. Thus republics, as well as empires, have been saved by compulsion before now, and by no other means were we likely to win the battle of right and freedom throughout the world. We needed to mobilize the whole of our military strength to maintain our eighty-three divisions already in the field, and those which must be added to it as the struggle increased in intensity. To realize what this meant we had only to remember that the strength of a single modern division was as much as Marlborough ever handled in his epoch-making wars; that Wellington opened his Waterloo campaign with not more than 40,000 men—less than the full strength of two of our divisions to-day; and that when we entered the Great War we possessed almost the tiniest army in Europe, smaller even than that of our gallant little ally Serbia. It was something to be proud of to have raised this tiny force, by voluntary effort, to one of the greatest, as well as one of the best-equipped armies in the world. King George paid fitting tribute to this patriotic effort on the nation's part in the following message to his people, issued on the day on which the New Military Service Act received the royal assent:—

"BUCKINGHAM PALACE, *May 25, 1916.*

"To enable our country to organize more effectively its military resources in the present great struggle for the cause of civilization, I have, acting on the advice of my Ministers, deemed it necessary to enrol every able-bodied man between the ages of eighteen and forty-one.

"I desire to take this opportunity of expressing to my people my recognition and appreciation of the splendid patriotism and self-sacrifice which they have displayed in raising by voluntary enlistment, since the commencement of the war, no less than 5,041,000 men, an effort far surpassing that of any other nation in similar circumstances recorded in history, and one which will be a lasting source of pride to future generations.

"I am confident that the magnificent spirit which has hitherto sustained my people through the trials of this terrible war will inspire them to endure the additional sacrifice now imposed upon them, and that it will, with God's help, lead us and our Allies to a victory which shall achieve the liberation of Europe.

"GEORGE R.I."

Ireland, as before, was excluded from the scheme of general compulsion. Grave events had taken place in that unhappy land during the preceding month, the first news of which was made known by Mr. Birrell, the Irish Secretary, during the Secret Session of the House of Commons. Many accounts have been written and a number of books published on the rebellious movement which came to a head in Dublin on Easter Monday morning, April 24, 1916, but all still leave unanswered the vital question as to what part it played in the plans of the German General Staff. Germany had long had her eyes on a land which from time immemorial had been used by Britain's enemies in Europe as an indispensable pawn in the great game of war. Had the British fleet failed to restrict the activities of the German navy to its own protected waters, or those within easy reach of then, there is little doubt that some such diversion would have been attempted in the early stages of the conflict as the landing of the Spanish force on the Kerry coast—which, in Great Eliza's day, led to the troublesome Desmond Rebellion — or the desperate venture of Wolfe Tone in 1798, when he brought the French fleet to Bantry Bay and Lough Swilly with similar designs to those which Roger Casement had in view when he stole ashore on the coast of Kerry from a German submarine in 1916. Exactly what connection there was between the raid of the German battle-cruiser squadron on Lowestoft at daybreak on April 25, 1916—the morning following the outbreak in Dublin—is not clear, but that such a connection existed may be taken for granted. Perhaps it was merely part of a general scheme to weaken British plans for the expected joint offensive on the Western front, and incidentally to fill to the brim the cup of bitterness which Germany knew awaited her most dangerous foe within the next few days over the fall of Kut.

Whatever the connection, it is beyond dispute that Roger Casement, in spite of the knighthood conferred upon him two years before his retirement in 1913 from the British consular service, had been plotting with the enemy ever since the war began. It is not without significance that in the winter of 1913–14 he appeared as an earnest supporter of a scheme—destined to fall through—for establishing a port of call for the Hamburg-America line at Queenstown, ostensibly for the convenience of the American mails, but possibly for future use as a base for German military operations. When war broke out he was in America, collecting funds, according to his own story, for the arming of Irish rebels. Thence, with his hot-brained schemes of revolt, he made his way to Germany as the self-styled "Irish Ambassador" to the Central Powers, arriving in Berlin via Scandinavia with a wild story to the effect that he had narrowly escaped assassination at the hands of British emissaries.

Germany welcomed with open arms the self-proclaimed ambassador, with his dreams of world-politics which fitted so neatly into her own unscrupulous schemes; collected between 2000 and 3000 Irishmen from the various prisoners' camps, concentrating them at Limburg; and gave him every opportunity of forming from among these a new Irish Brigade to fight against Britain for the freedom of Ireland. Having solemnly declared that "all the Irish at home and abroad would work to help the victory of the Central Powers, as this would mean the destruction of the British yoke in Ireland", Casement was assured by the Imperial Chancellor that under no circumstances would Germany invade Ireland with the object of conquering it, but that "should the fortunes of war ever bring German troops to Ireland's coasts they would land there solely as the forces of a government inspired only by goodwill towards a country and a people for whom Germany wishes nothing but national welfare and national freedom".

Lavish promises were held out to induce the Irish soldiers to join this renegade. Instead of remaining in the humiliating position of prisoners, argued Casement, they would become the honoured guests of Germany, "who had already practically won the war". Pamphlets and lectures on the iniquities of Great Britain and the wrongs of Ireland, together with countless conversations, yielded after more than a year of patient endeavour the grand total of 52 alleged converts out of the 2500. There was not a single officer or non-commissioned officer among them. The majority, like Private Bailey, of the Royal Irish Rifles, who became a sergeant in the new brigade, probably joined only to escape from the hardship and inactivity of prison life, and in the hope of returning by a subterfuge to the British army. The remainder treated with utter scorn Casement's endeavours to seduce them from their allegiance. More than once he was hissed out of camp, and on one occasion, when he was struck and pushed out, the German sentries had to rush to his assistance.

The next move in the melodrama was a characteristic piece of bluff on the part of Germany in the shape of a report to the effect that Casement had been arrested in the Fatherland on a charge not stated, and was awaiting trial there. The British authorities were not deceived by this clumsy manœuvre. News reached Dublin Castle, on April 18, 1916, that a ship had left Germany for Ireland some days before, accompanied by two German submarines, and was due to arrive on the 21st in time for a rising that was timed for the following day, Easter Eve. In point of fact, the rising had been planned for Easter Sunday (April 23). Casement landed on Thursday, the 20th, and was apparently before his time; but this might not have ruined the whole scheme had our navy not been ready to frustrate his gun-running tricks. That morning the patrol boat sent to watch the Kerry coast for the expected arrivals stopped and challenged a foreign steamer as it was making for Fenit Harbour, south of Banna Strand. The vessel proved to be the *Aud*—a captured Wilson liner which the Germans had converted into an innocent-looking tramp, painted with the Norwegian colours, and declared to be bound from Bergen to Genoa. Not satisfied with her declaration, the captain of the *Bluebell*, the British patrol boat, ordered her to follow him to Queenstown for further investigation. Thereupon the *Aud*, showing her true colours by hoisting the German flag, was scuttled by her crew, who, on taking to their boats, were made prisoners on board the *Bluebell*. Divers subsequently found the wreck loaded with arms and ammunition.

In the meantime the German submarine had succeeded in landing Casement on another part of the Kerry coast, sending him ashore near Ardfert with ex-Private Bailey and a certain "Captain Monteith", who had been deported from Ireland in 1914 for opposing recruiting for the British army, and had apparently worked hand and glove with Casement in his plot with Germany. Their landing was a most inglorious affair. The cockle-shell of a boat in which they had said good-bye to the German submarine, which now left them to their fate, capsized on landing, and they had to scramble ashore through the surf, loaded with revolvers and as much ammunition as they could carry.

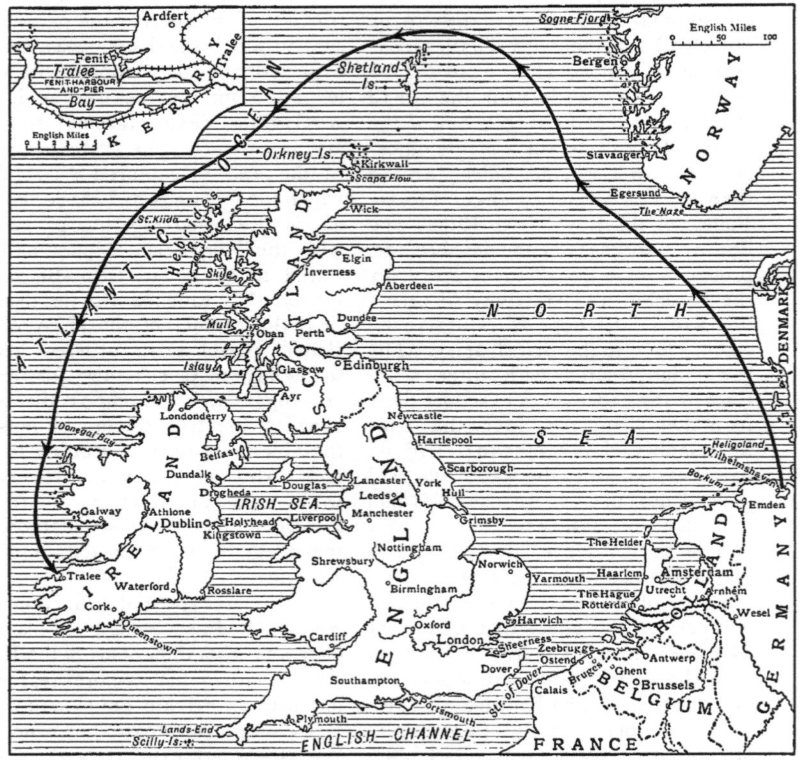


Germany and the Casement Plot: map showing approximately the course taken by the gun-runner and the submarine, with Roger Casement on board, from Germany to the coast of Kerry.

There was no one to meet them. Casement and the *Aud* were ahead of time, and before he could communicate with his confederates he was arrested, hiding in a sort of prehistoric fort, by the local police. Bailey was also rounded up,[1] though the mysterious "Captain Monteith" succeeded in eluding the police—afterwards, it was reported, escaping to America. For Roger Casement this was the end of

[1] Bailey was found "Not Guilty" when tried with Casement for high treason. He had nine years' record of good service in the British army, and stoutly maintained that he had joined Casement's Irish Brigade with one object only—to return by a subterfuge to the army and fight once more, not for but against the Germans.

the drama, save the inevitable sequel, when, after his formal degradation from knighthood—one of the rarest forms of punishment known to this country—and his four days' trial before the High Court in London, he paid the full penalty of treason with his life.

This is not the place to tell the story of the short-lived Dublin rising. That inexplicable episode came as a bolt from the blue to the majority of Irishmen themselves, whose attitude at the beginning of the Great War had been hailed by Viscount (then Sir Edward) Grey as the "one bright spot" in the whole dark situation; while in the war itself the Irish regiments, as Lord Kitchener acknowledged, had proved, as always, among the bravest of our troops in the field. Suffice it to say that Mr. Birrell, acknowledging his responsibility for the situation which had led to these deplorable results, resigned his office as Chief Secretary for Ireland, and shortly afterwards the Lord-Lieutenant, Lord Wimborne, though absolved from blame by the Royal Commission, followed suit. Lord Wimborne, however, was restored to his post later in the year, after the failure of Mr. Lloyd George's fresh proposals for settling the Irish question,[1] and the re-establishment of "Castle Government" under a modified form of martial law. A new Chief Secretary was found in Mr. Henry Edward Duke, K.C., the Unionist member for Exeter—a Devonian who at one time filled a place in the Press Gallery of the House of Commons, and had earned a high reputation as a man of broad sympathies and impartial mind.

These were not the only changes in the Coalition Cabinet, since Mr. Churchill resigned as First Lord of the Admiralty, and Sir Edward Carson as Attorney-General. The most vital change was the succession of Mr. Lloyd George to the seat of War Minister upon the death of Lord Kitchener, with Lord Derby as his Under-Secretary, Sir William Robertson remaining the indispensable Chief of the Imperial General Staff. Sir Edward Grey was at the same time raised to the dignity of a viscount, thus receiving some reward for his ten years' tenure of the Foreign Secretaryship, and also enabling Mr. Lloyd George to go to the War Office; for, by the Act of 1858, not more than four of the Chief Secretaryships of State could be held at one time by Ministers with seats in the House of Commons.[1] Other changes to be noted in the Coalition Cabinet during the second year of the war included the promotion of Mr. Herbert Samuel from the position of Postmaster-General to that of Home Secretary in succession to Sir John Simon, who, as already mentioned, had resigned as a protest against the introduction of conscription; the entry of Mr. H. J. Tennant as Secretary for Scotland; the resumption by Mr. M'Kinnon Wood of his former post of Financial Secretary to the Treasury; and the appointment of

[1] These proposals were, briefly, that the Home Rule Act should be brought into immediate operation, excluding the six Ulster counties; and that at the close of the war the future government of Ireland should be settled at an Imperial Conference.

[1] The Home, Foreign, Colonial, and Indian Secretaryships were already held by Commoners.

Women Workers and the War: drilling and assembling operations on fuses
(Copyright of the Ministry of Munitions)

Mr. Joseph A. Pease as Postmaster-General, and of Mr. E. S. Montagu as Minister of Munitions.

The last appointment brings us to one of the most remarkable developments in the history of the war. A year's work in this department had yielded phenomenal results. It had become clearer with each succeeding month that machinery and munitions, as much as, if not more than, men, were to be the deciding factors of the conflict. Never had the preponderance of machinery been so clearly established in all the histories of warfare since the world began. It was the immeasurable superiority of the enemy's equipment in this respect which alone had accounted for his early successes and our failure to drive him back over his own frontiers. Lord Kitchener's growing armies, and the increasing output of munitions under the new organization, reduced this heavy handicap until we were able at last to fight on comparatively equal terms, though not for another year could we hope to reach anything like the full limit of our world-wide resources. How much had been done in the way of munitions may be judged by comparing the situation in May, 1915, with that of July, 1916, the month which brought the second year of the war to a close. In May, 1915—as Mr. Lloyd George afterwards told the House of Commons, when there was no longer any danger in confessing our weakness at that time—while the Germans were turning out about 250,000 shells per day, the vast majority of them being high explosives, we were turning out not more than 2500 a day in high explosives and 13,000 in shrapnel. This was mentioned in our last annual survey, where the various reasons for the shortage were also given.[1] In July, 1916, we were supplying munitions, not only to our own ever-increasing armies in all parts of the world, but also to our Allies. With the improvement in equipment came improvement on the battle fronts. When Mr. Lloyd George, as the new Secretary of State for War, presided over a conference held in London in July, 1916, in the first flush of the advance on the Somme, to discuss the equipment of the Allied forces, he could point to a remarkable change in both respects. The last Munitions Conference had been held in the autumn of 1915, shortly after the Allied offensive had won its costly and indecisive victory in the West, and when the enemy in the East had pressed the Russians back some hundreds of miles, besides overrunning the Balkans. Now the Allies in the West had again wrested the initiative; Verdun was saved; the valiant soldiers of Russia had returned to the attack with a vengeance; and the irresistible advance of the Italians had changed the whole complexion of the war in the Southern Alps. The truth was that our munitions were at length proving equal to a sustained attack.

"Hundreds of thousands of men and women, hitherto unaccustomed to metal and chemical work," said Mr. Lloyd George, "have been trained for munition-making. Every month we are turning out hundreds

[1] Vol. IV, p. 23-4.

British Official Photograph

The Equipment of Britain's New Army: a heavy howitzer in action on the Western Front

of guns and howitzers, light, medium, and heavy. Our heavy guns are rolling in at a great rate, and as for ammunition, we are turning out nearly twice as much ammunition in a single week—and what is more, nearly three times as much heavy shell—as we fired in the great offensive in September, although the ammunition we expended in that battle was the result of many weary weeks of accumulation. The new factories and workshops we have set up have not yet attained one-third of their full capacity, but their output now is increasing with great rapidity. Our main difficulties in organization, construction, equipment, labour-supply, and readjustment have been solved. If officials, employers, and workmen keep at it with the same zeal and assiduity as they have hitherto employed, our supplies will soon be overwhelming."

The Somme itself was to furnish additional proof that this was a war of equipment, that only a ceaseless supply of munitions, as well as of men, could rob the most highly-organized army in the world of what Sir William Robertson described as the very great advantage of getting the upper hand at the start and winning first blood.

When Mr. Lloyd George succeeded Lord Kitchener as Minister of War he was followed at the Ministry of Munitions, as already stated, by Mr. Edwin S. Montagu, Financial Secretary to the Treasury and Chancellor of the Duchy of Lancaster. The new Minister of Munitions had been Mr. Lloyd George's right-hand man at the Treasury in the arduous duties which fell upon that department at the beginning of the war, and after entering the Cabinet at the early age of thirty-five, had retired when the Coalition Government had been formed. He now resumed his seat in the Cabinet, and a month later, shortly after the second anniversary of the war, followed the example of his predecessor at the Ministry of Munitions in rendering an early account of his stewardship. He explained how the department, which had only been in existence thirteen months, already numbered on its central staff over 5000 persons, and was growing till it promised to become one of the largest ministries of the State. Not unnaturally some criticism and suspicion had been roused by this mushroom growth, but Mr. Montagu asked the House to believe that the increasing variety, diversity, and complexity of the task had rendered this growth inevitable. They had now to control an expenditure of far more than £1,000,000 a day, and a comparison of this with the cost of the central staff showed that the cost of administration was low, amounting to less than one-sixth per cent. Some astonishing figures were given relating to the ever-increasing output of munitions, amplifying the earlier statement of Mr. Lloyd George, already quoted. The increase in two years in the shell output showed quite fantastic results when the percentages were compared with those of the first two months of the war. For example, since September, 1914, the empty-shell output from home sources had increased 170 times in the case of 18-pounders, and 2650 times in heavy natures. As this was not a true test of the activities of the Ministry of Munitions, Mr. Montagu took as his basis of comparison the average weekly production of complete rounds up to the end of June, 1915, covering the year before the new department came into existence. He showed that the rate of production during the year 1915–16 was $6\frac{1}{2}$ times that during the preceding year, and for the week ending July 1, 1916, it was $17\frac{1}{2}$ times as great as the average rate in 1914–15. The weekly average production of munition for field howitzers in 1915–16 was 8 times that for 1914–15, and in August, 1916, was 27 times as great. For medium artillery, too, the increase had grown until, by the second anniversary of the war, it was more than 34 times as great as the weekly average up to the end of June, 1915. The most striking improvement of all had been in the class of ammunition where increase was most difficult, the weekly average in the production of heavy shell in 1915–16 being 22 times as great, and by the month of August, 1916, 94 times as great as it was in 1914–15. Putting the figures even more graphically, Mr. Montagu explained that the output which in 1914–15 took twelve months to produce could now, at the close of the second year of the war, be attained from home sources in the following periods:—

For 18-pounder ammunition in three weeks;
For field-howitzer ammunition in two weeks;
For medium-sized shell in eleven days; and
For heavy shell in four days.

That is to say, we were producing every four days, in August, 1916, as much heavy howitzer ammunition as it took us a whole year to produce at the rate of output of 1914–15. If we lumped all natures of gun and howitzer ammunition together, we were now manufacturing and issuing to France every week about as much as the whole pre-war stock of land-service ammunition in the country.

British Official Photograph.

The Work of the Ministry of Munitions: a line of heavy guns in action on the Western Front during the Battle of the Somme

Similar results had been achieved in the production of guns of every calibre, to say nothing of rifles, trench mortars, and every other form of weapon for modern warfare. In August, 1916, we were turning out in a month nearly twice as many big guns as were in existence for army service when the Ministry of Munitions started. Between June, 1915, and June, 1916, the monthly output of heavy guns increased more than sixfold, and Mr. Montagu estimated that the existing rate would eventually be nearly doubled. By June, 1916, the monthly output of the 4.5-inch howitzers had become three times as great as in June, 1915. For every 100 18-pounders turned out between the outbreak of war and May 31, 1915, about 500 were turned out in the following year. These and many other equally striking figures are all the more impressive when we remember that the Royal Navy was still absorbing something like half the engineering capacity of the country; that we were sending France—robbed of nearly three-quarters of her steel-producing capacity by the loss of her northern provinces—one-third of our total production of shell steel; and that, in addition to meeting the needs of both services, we were supplying our Allies with a substantial quantity of finished munitions, immense quantities of the constituents of explosives as well as of machinery, and millions of tons of coal and coke per month.[1]

Britain's Army of Women Workers: mess room at a national projectile factory
(Copyright of the Ministry of Munitions)

No small proportion of the Munition Ministry's Staff was needed for the supervision and control of the new Government factories. Before the war there were only three national factories

[1] A footnote to an authorized pamphlet on *Britain Transformed* stated that one of the British armament firms had a factory exclusively engaged in providing a particular gun for the French Government; that Russia had been supplied with great quantities of grenades, rifle cartridges, guns, and explosives; that the Belgian and Serbian armies had been re-equipped; and that both Italy and Roumania had been supplied with most important munitions.

working for the army. Two years later there were ninety-five, one of which alone was then filling nearly twice as much gun ammunition as Woolwich, upon which had fallen during the first eighteen months of the struggle practically the whole of the burden of completing ammunition. There were at the same time no fewer than thirty-two national shell factories, managed by local boards of management under the supervision of the Ministry; and so well did they work that, though none of them had ever handled a shell before, they produced, between September, 1915, and August, 1916, an output of certain natures of shell four times greater than that during the first ten months of the war. Twelve other national factories were making heavy shell under the management of large engineering firms, also supervised by the Ministry, and though by August, 1916, they had barely developed one-half of their total capacity, they were already sending out 25 per cent of the heavy shell produced in this country. "Their daily output", said Mr. Montagu, in another of his graphic illustrations, "would fill a train one mile long composed of 400 trucks and requiring eight engines to pull it."

Of the remaining national factories twenty-two were devoted to the manufacture of explosives and their raw materials, others to the manufacture of cartridges and cartridge cases, while one made nothing but gauges, and another nothing but small tools. The whole nation owed a debt of gratitude, not only to those responsible for the establishment of these national factories, but also, as the Minister acknowledged, to the courage, faith, and perseverance of those responsible for the labour policy which rendered them effective. To which must be added the unforgettable services of the women who gladly put aside all other responsibilities and stepped into a province hitherto regarded as exclusively that of men, and often of skilled men alone. Great strides had been made in this direction since their employment was described in our last annual survey.[1] The number of women workers in munition factories increased by the summer of 1916 to 400,000: women of all grades of society, but equally willing to sacrifice their own interests in order to serve the national cause. The same response came from one end of the country to the other, women and girls alike cheerfully submitting to long hours and arduous as well as monotonous work. It was not only monotonous and often heavy work: it was not without its manifest dangers. More than one explosion took a heavy toll of victims—for the most part, as it happened, among the men; but in every case the work was resumed as soon as possible. In one case, before the end of 1916, unfortunately the victims were women, between fifty and sixty of whom were killed and injured in an explosion which took place at a national factory in the North of England. Here the great majority of the workers were women, and their behaviour earned a high tribute in the official report published at the time. "They displayed", it stated, "the greatest coolness and perfect discip-

[1] Vol. IV, pp. 20-22.

line, both in helping to remove the injured and in continuing to carry on the work of the factory in spite of the explosion." Twenty-six of the victims were killed outright, but the damage done to the factory itself was slight, and the effect of the accident on the output of munitions negligible. The courage displayed earned the rare distinction of mention in a Special Order to the Troops at the front.

The technical efficiency of the women workers, on the whole, was a revelation to most people. When the Ministry of Munitions started it seems to have been the prevailing opinion that it was physically impossible for women to manufacture heavy shell, yet before another year was out the 10,000 machine tools then at work in the new national factories were very largely operated by women, 15,000 of whom were engaged on this work alone. Mrs. Humphrey Ward, in her inspiring little book on *Britain's Effort in the Allied Cause*,[1] has painted the best picture of one of these national factories in being:—

"The large airy building with its cheerful lighting, the girls in their dark-blue caps and overalls, their long and comely lines reminding one of some processional effect in a Florentine picture; the high proportion of good looks—even of delicate beauty—among them; the upper galleries, their tables piled with glittering brass work, among which move the quick, trained hands of women: if one could have forgotten for a moment the meaning of it all, one might have applied to it Carlyle's description of a great school as 'a temple of industrious peace'. *Some day, perhaps, this 'new industry'*—as our ancestors talked of a 'new learning'—this swift, astonishing development of industrial faculty among our people, especially among our women, *will bear other and rich fruit for Britain under a cleared sky*. It is impossible that it should pass by without effect—profound effect—upon our national life. But at present, it has one meaning and one only—*war!*"

The trade unions, too, were loyally fulfilling their pledge to support the Government to the utmost of their power in the successful prosecution of the war. Now fully alive to the life-and-death nature of the national struggle, they had renounced for the period of the war their combatant code of trade-union regulations, and loyally co-operated in every innovation, which had but one aim in view—the final victory over the common enemy. When, in the first month of the mighty battle on the Somme, Sir Douglas Haig called on the workers to forgo their August Bank Holiday, as they had already forgone their Whitsuntide rest, and devote themselves instead "to maintaining and if possible increasing the supply of guns and shells, without which victory is impossible", a special conference of representatives of the principal organized trades of the country returned a message saying that they resolved to postpone all holidays, general or local, which involved interruption of production, "until such time as we are assured by you that military exigencies permit of the postponed holidays being taken". In that spirit was August Bank Holiday of 1916 kept throughout the kingdom.

It was not only in the national factories and private armament firms that the revolution in munitions was taking

[1] Published by Messrs. Smith, Elder, 1916.

place. Engineering works throughout the country were rapidly improvised into shell factories; the manufacturers of ploughshares took to making swords; works ordinarily engaged in cotton-spinning and other peaceful arts gradually found themselves producing nothing but implements of war. By the end of the second year, instead of a few private armament firms there were something like 4000 controlled establishments engaged exclusively in turning out munitions. The United Kingdom was becoming one gigantic arsenal. Tools were adapted to unskilled hands with an ingenuity that never seemed to fail. The whole metamorphosis, indeed, was a sterling proof of the skill, adaptability, and indomitable energy of British manufacturers when put to the test, and a source of especial pride to British engineering.

With the growth of armaments and the expansion of both the navy and the army, as well as British loans to Allies and Dominions, came a proportionate increase in the cost of the war. In our last survey it was shown that this already, during the first thirteen months of the conflict, had reached the unprecedented sum of £1,262,000,000. It rose during the next year until, with the vote of credit to the amount of £450,000,000, passed by the Commons towards the end of July, 1916, to cover three months' expenditure, the aggregate since the outbreak of war on twelve votes reached the colossal sum of £2,832,000,000. The published totals for the period from April 1, 1916, to July 22, 1916, show roughly how the money was divided up: Navy, army, and munitions, £379,000,000; loans to Allies and Dominions, £157,000,000; food supplies, railways, and miscellaneous items, £23,000,000. This makes a total of £559,000,000, with an average for the whole period of £4,920,000 a day. By the end of July, 1916, however, the average daily rate had risen approximately to a round £5,000,000, the army, navy, and munitions alone accounting for £3,600,000 per day. We can only realize what this increase meant when we remember that the normal daily expenditure upon the navy and army combined in peace time did not amount to more than £220,000. Deducting that sum from the total of £3,600,000, and we find the nation at the end of the second year of the war faced with an extra expenditure of more than £3,300,000 per day directly attributable to the war.

These stupendous sums were cheerfully voted by a nation pledged to spend its last shilling, if necessary, in the cause for which it had drawn the sword. Three months before it had welcomed Mr. M'Kenna's second Budget financing another year of war, though it was the most formidable statement ever presented in regard to its enormous figures of revenue and expenditure, and imposed heavier taxation on all classes. All the income-tax rates were increased, both for earned and unearned incomes. The new scale on earned incomes rose from *2s.* $1\frac{1}{5}$*d.* to *2s. 3d.* for incomes up to £500; to *2s. 6d.* for incomes up to £1000; and by successive stages until the maximum of *5s.* was reached for incomes exceed-

Drawn by W. Hatherell, R.I.

Queen Alexandra as a Christmas Fairy: Her Majesty serving soldiers at a free buffet in London

The free buffets at the great railway stations, for soldiers home on leave from the front, proved a boon throughout the war. Queen Alexandra, who was keenly interested in them, paid a surprise visit to Lady Limerick's buffet at London Bridge during the Christmas holidays of 1915, and took her turn among the voluntary workers for an hour and a half.

ing £2500. On unearned incomes the new scale began at 3*s.* for incomes not exceeding £300, rising by stages of 6*d.* to 5*s.* for incomes exceeding £2000.

The novelty of a bold Budget was the tax on amusements, rising by steps from ½*d.*, where the entrance fee was 2*d.* or under, to 1*s.* for an entrance fee of 12*s.* 6*d.* This applied to theatres, cinemas, football matches, horse-races, and similar amusements. Matches and mineral waters were also seized upon for revenue purposes, while additional duties were levied on such familiar articles of taxation as sugar, coffee and cocoa. The excess profits duty was raised from 50 per cent to 60 per cent, so that with the increased income-tax in addition to this the State reaped the benefit in many cases to the extent of something like 80 per cent.

Meantime wages continued to rise proportionately in all the principal industries. In those directly concerned with the war the earnings for the most part remained incomparably higher than in normal times, the working classes on the whole being better off in this country than ever before. It is true that they needed a larger income to cope with the continual increase in the cost of living. How this had risen was shown in an official reply to a question in the House of Commons in August, 1916, giving the following average percentage increase, as compared with July, 1914, in the retail prices of the chief articles of food in large towns in the United Kingdom at the beginning of each of the undermentioned months:—

| 1914 | Per cent. | | Per cent. |
|---|---|---|---|
| September | 11 | November | 13 |
| October | 13 | December | 17 |
| **1915** | | | |
| January | 19 | July | 35 |
| February | 23 | August | 36 |
| March | 26 | September | 37 |
| April | 26 | October | 42 |
| May | 28 | November | 43 |
| June | 35 | December | 46 |
| **1916** | | | |
| January | 48 | May | 59 |
| February | 49 | June | 62 |
| March | 51 | July | 65 |
| April | 52 | | |

The figures were based on returns collected by the Board of Trade, from retailers conducting a working-class trade, in every town in which the population at the last census exceeded 50,000. The changes of prices of the various articles of food were combined in proportions roughly corresponding to the relative expenditure on these articles by working men's families before the war.

In regard to other groups of expenditure, enquiries had not been made every month. For the months stated below, the average percentage increases since July, 1914, were:—

| | Rent. | Clothing. | Fuel and Light. | Miscellaneous Items. |
|---|---|---|---|---|
| 1915. | p.c. | p.c. | p.c. | p.c. |
| July | nil | 25 | 20 | 10 |
| September | 2 | 30 | 25 | 10 |
| December | 2 | 35 | 30 | 15 |
| 1916. | | | | |
| March | nil | 50 | 30 | 15 |
| June | nil | 55 | 40 | 30 |

Assuming no change in the standard of living, the average of increase in the cost of living, since July, 1914, in the large towns would have been approximately 25 per cent at July, 1915;

nearly 30 per cent at September; 35 per cent at December; 40 per cent at March, 1916; and between 40 and 50 per cent at June, 1916. It was pointed out, however, that since changes of prices invariably lead to some shifting of consumption from one article to another, it did not follow that the budget of the average workman's household had necessarily increased in the above proportions.

The higher prices were equivalent in regard to meat to about *6d.* per pound for the better cuts, and *5d.* per pound for the inferior cuts. Fish and eggs were, on the average, more than 80 per cent dearer than in July, 1914; while tea, bacon, cheese, bread, and butter may be grouped roundly as 50 per cent dearer at the end of the second year of war. The increase was illustrated about this time at the National Food Economy Exhibition in London, at which the existing cost of a dinner for a family of six was compared with the cost before the war. The dinner was stuffed breast of mutton, potatoes and greens, and gooseberry tart:

| | Normal Prices. | | War Prices (June, 1916). | |
|---|---|---|---|---|
| | *s.* | *d.* | *s.* | *d.* |
| 1½ lb. breast of mutton | 0 | 4½ | 1 | 0 |
| Bread-crumbs, chopped parsley, and suet ... | 0 | 1½ | 0 | 2 |
| 3 lb. potatoes ... ... | 0 | 2 | 0 | 6 |
| Cabbage ... ... | 0 | 2 | 0 | 4 |
| 1½ pt. gooseberries ... | 0 | 2¼ | 0 | 3 |
| ¼ lb. sugar ... ... | 0 | 0½ | 0 | 1¼ |
| 12 oz. flour ... ... | 0 | 1 | 0 | 2¼ |
| 4 oz. fat ... ... | 0 | 1½ | 0 | 2 |
| | 1 | 3¼ | 2 | 8½ |

In spite of all these higher prices, and the strain and stress of the war, the general condition of the country, in many respects, had never been so satisfactory. Some of the coast towns within reach of the enemy's indiscriminate attacks from the sea and air lost their holiday seasons and suffered accordingly, besides receiving more than their share of German hate, but their misfortunes were exceptional. Unemployment was practically non-existent throughout the country; pauperism had reached such a low figure that it constituted a record; and a notable decrease of drunkenness was officially recorded in the summer of 1916 as a result of the regulations of the newly-constituted Central Control Board, whose operations affected approximately two-thirds of the total population of Great Britain. The health of the country had also been wonderfully maintained, although for a period of two years there had been enormous numbers of men suddenly collected in certain areas, where, at the beginning, there was often insufficient accommodation.

The high prices prevailing in practically every department were not without their compensatory advantages from the national point of view. It was largely this factor which accounted for the steady growth in the value of British exports, this showing an increase of more than £11,600,000 for July, 1916, as compared with the total for the corresponding month of 1915. We sent abroad, for instance, a total of some 158,000 tons less coal, yet received £1,500,000 more for it, the same thing occurring in many other exports, the result being to strengthen our foreign exchange standing without

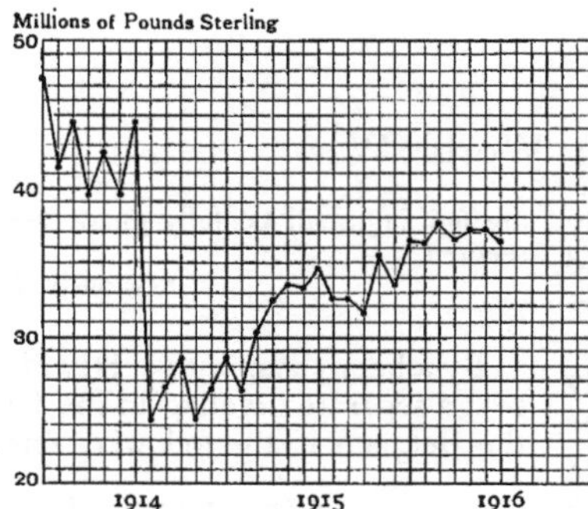


How British Exports were affected during the First Two Years of the War

proportionately depleting our stock of goods. With imports, of course, the increase in prices had the reverse effect, but the adverse balance of trade at this period showed healthy signs of contracting as a result of the Government's policy of restriction in regard to the importation of such bulky articles as paper pulp and motor cars. For the month of July, 1916, this adverse balance had dropped to 22½ millions, from the 31½ millions of the corresponding period for 1915.

With regard to British exports, the total value for July, 1916, was upwards of £46,300,000, an increase of more than £11,600,000 as compared with July, 1915, and greater by nearly £2,000,000 than that for July, 1914, the last complete month before the war. The ebb and flow of trade since the beginning of 1914 is shown in the accompanying diagrams, the dots indicating the totals in millions of pounds sterling for every month to the close of the second year of war.

It must be remembered that the Board of Trade returns, from which the diagram of exports is made, include goods bought in the United Kingdom by, or on behalf of, the Governments of the Allies, but do not include goods from Government stores or bought by His Majesty's Government and shipped in Government vessels. The diagram of imports, like that of exports, does not go beyond the second year of the war, but its upward tendency promised to leave far behind in its total for 1916 even the enormous figures for 1915, which amounted to some £853,700,000—an increase of more than £157,000,000 on 1914, and the largest annual imports on record.

In the war of endurance Great Britain, though she would need to

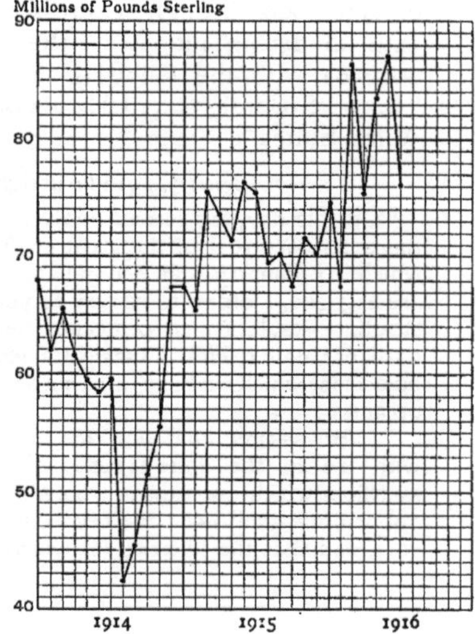


How British Imports were affected during the First Two Years of the War

husband her resources more closely before the end appeared in sight, had little fear of being outstayed by Germany, upon whose economic life the blockade policy of the Allies was slowly but surely having its effect. "The final victory may come soon, or it may come late," wrote Mr. Lloyd George to the *Glasgow Herald* on entering the third year of the war, "but as far as human foresight can perceive, it is coming with the grim tread of destiny." The King himself, who, a short time previously, had set a noble example of sacrifice in contributing to the sinews of war with a personal gift of £100,000, fittingly expressed the national determination on the same occasion with the following message "to the Sovereigns and Heads of the Allied States":—

"*August* 3, 1916 (midnight).

"On this day, the second anniversary of the commencement of the great conflict in which my country and her gallant Allies are engaged, I desire to convey to you my steadfast resolution to prosecute the war until our united efforts have attained the objects for which we have in common taken up arms.

"I feel assured that you are in accord with me in the determination that the sacrifices which our valiant troops have so nobly made shall not have been offered in vain, and that the liberties for which they are fighting shall be fully guaranteed and secured.

"GEORGE R.I."

By a happy inspiration His Majesty sent a separate greeting to the King of the Belgians to the following effect:—

"*August* 3, 1916 (midnight).

"On this second anniversary of the day on which my country took up arms to resist the violation of the neutrality of Belgium, I desire to assure Your Majesty of my confidence that the united efforts of the Allies will liberate Belgium from the oppression of her aggressors and will restore to her the full enjoyment of her national and economic independence.

"I would also desire to convey to Your Majesty my deep sympathy in the grievous trials to which Belgium has been so unjustly subjected, and which she has borne with such admirable fortitude."

"GEORGE R.I."

Thus the nation and the whole empire—for similar messages came from all parts of the King's dominions—entered upon the third year of the war full of new hope, and as determined as ever to fight on until the Allies had finally conquered, and the cause of freedom and justice been completely vindicated.

F. A. M.

# CHAPTER VI

## THE GERMAN TREATMENT OF PRISONERS

German Indifference to Prisoners' Welfare—Attitude of the German People—Breakdown of German Organization—Conditions at their Worst in the Winter of 1914-5—Intervention of Mr. Gerard, the United States Ambassador—The Question of Reprisals—Major Vandeleur's Report—Treatment of Men worse than that of Officers—French, Russian, and Belgian Official Reports on the Treatment of Prisoners—Individual Witnesses—M. André Warnod—The Typhus Epidemics—Neglect of Sick and Dying Prisoners at Schneidemühl, Güstrow, Langensalza, Niederzwehren, Stendal, Gardelegen—The Culminating Crime of Wittenberg—Captain Lauder's Indictment—Released Prisoners in Switzerland—The Murder of Captain Fryatt.

A SINGLE cause for the abominable treatment of prisoners of war by the Germans cannot be assigned. So far as one reason is discoverable it may be traced to the idea embedded in the German mind, that war to be successful must be "absolute war", waged without pity or scruple, designed to inflict the greatest amount of terror and injury on the opponent, and intended to reach beyond the actual combatant to the relatives and dependents for whom he is fighting. This idea, sown by Clausewitz and consecrated in the Franco-German war of 1870, justified to the German mind all the bombardments of open towns, the sinkings of passenger ships, the holocaust of defenceless Belgium; it more than justified a severity to prisoners which descended on occasion to callousness, neglect, and cruelty. There are subsidiary explanations. In the view of chivalrous peoples, and in the view of a good-natured people like the British, an enemy when he is captured is an unfortunate man who has done his duty, and is to be commiserated on his fate; he is therefore to be treated as kindly as circumstances will permit. We do not kick a man when he is down. But in the German view, a prisoner is a man who has committed a crime against the German nation. He is reviled for it by the German people while on the way to the prisoners' camps, and in the camps is made to suffer for it. Yet another explanation, less damning to the Germans, is that their organization for the guarding of prisoners in the present conflict completely broke down at the beginning of the war, and was the last organization to be repaired. The want of food in all the prisoners' camps was in part attributable to scarcity in Germany, joined to the German custom of feeding common soldiers poorly, and to the German conviction that when the soldiers were those of the enemy it was a detestable necessity to have to feed them at all.

The foregoing explanations cover most of the facts regarding the treatment of prisoners in Germany. The facts are hardly in dispute. Through the kindness and vigilance of Mr. Gerard, the United States Ambassador in Berlin, and of the secretaries at the Embassy, some of the abuses were removed or remedied. Mr.

Gerard reported from time to time that the food at this or that camp, though perhaps rather unpalatable or monotonous, was sufficient in quantity; or that the sleeping accommodation or the sanitary measures had improved. On the other hand, a number of witnesses, British and French, declared that the German camp commandants carefully stage-managed the camps and the food for any visit by the American Ambassador. We should be less disposed to believe this if it were not that the worst camps and the unpardonable inhumanities of Wittenberg, Schneidemühl, Güstrow, and Stendal were not the subject of reports by him, for the good reason that they were screened from his notice.[1] These were the camps at which there were serious typhus epidemies, and in which the prisoners were allowed to suffer and to die with less help and with less concern than if they had been a herd of sacred German swine. Güstrow was the camp from which the most persistent reports of German brutality and cruelty to prisoners, French as well as British, emanated. If all the stories told of these camps were literally true, then would the indictment against the jailers be as heavy as that which the crimes in Belgium have indelibly written on the German record. They

British Civilian Prisoners and their Quarters at Ruhleben

[1] Mr. Gerard did not visit Wittenberg till after the typhus epidemic. In November, 1915, the impression left on him "was even more unfavourable than I had been led to expect".

come from all sources, from French as well as from British and Russians and Belgians; for though during a great part of the war preferential treatment was extended to French prisoners, especially to officers, some of the most damaging accusations come from them; and it was the French Government which was the first to take measures to secure, by a policy of reprisals, better treatment for their soldiers. The German Government made the feeblest efforts to reply to the charges. The complaints about food they treated with a contemptuous surprise that was not wholly affected: they may have believed that the unwholesome rations which they supplied were good enough for prisoners; and since these rations were supplemented quite early in the war by parcels of food sent from the prisoners' countries, the Germans logically concluded that they need do nothing better. The food parcels, except in some of the worst-managed camps, usually arrived regularly and were methodically distributed. The complaints of ill-treatment the Germans of course denied; unhappily their denials were not to be trusted, though actual ill-treatment seems to have been peculiar to some camps rather than a rule, and was due to the spite and brutality of individuals or the incompetence of their superiors. The only answer that the Germans were ever able to make, about the infamous neglect of prisoners in the camps smitten by typhus, was that by this neglect they preserved the town or towns in the neighbourhood of the camps from the danger of infection.

It is perhaps the surest proof of the German transgression that they made no attempt to palliate it by bringing counter-accusations, as they had done when other offences were charged against them. To refute the accusation of the crimes committed in Belgium they published a White Book, which refuted nothing, and which proved nothing, except that at Dinant, Termonde, Andenne, and Aerschot they had given orders for massacre. They replied to the unassailable charges of their breaches of the rules of war by publishing charges against British and Indian soldiers which the barest investigation showed to be false; they published an even more stupid string of "outrages" committed on Germans in England, and the "outrages" turned out either to be calumnies or the outraged Germans were shown to be criminals. But they never attempted to show that the German prisoners in British or in French or in Russian hands were treated with anything but humanity and consideration. Each country is bound by convention to lodge, clothe, and feed its prisoners in a suitable manner, and to pay to officer prisoners a fixed allowance. While Germany consistently sought to lessen this payment to officers, and never at any time pretended to treat the rank and file in the matter of food, clothing, or lodging on anything better than a prison basis, the other countries, from the first, endeavoured to regard the German prisoners as soldiers first and prisoners afterwards. In Great Britain there was a disposition from the first to treat German prisoners in a manner better than the regulations prescribed, and it was only after the news of the ill-treatment and semi-starvation of British prisoners began to leak through that a cry was raised against the "luxury" in which German officers were installed at Donington Hall in Leicestershire. Even then there was never any suggestion that the food allowance of the rank and file should be lessened, or any retaliatory measures taken against them. After an official statement in the House of Commons that but for food parcels many of our prisoners in Germany would not have had enough to eat, the outcry became more vehement; but the idea of starving prisoners to strike a balance with the German scale of treatment was one that was too repugnant to the British mind ever to be seriously considered. The French people, more logical and less sentimental than ourselves, were first to secure better treatment for their prisoners by a policy of threatened reprisals. If the Germans furnished an insufficient diet, then the French threatened to reduce the dietary allowance to German prisoners to a lower scale of grammes and calories, and the scientific character of the threat appeared to influence the German mind. If the Germans reduced the money allowance to prisoner officers, the French did the same. These steps brought about some amelioration of treatment of prisoners of British, Russian, and Belgian, as well as of French nationality, and conditions slowly improved during 1916. But it was in the earlier stages of the war, when the Germans were too confident of victory to care about consequences, that the greater crimes against prisoners were committed, and these no reform could palliate nor any reprisal efface.

The worst treatment of prisoners occurred in the first year of war, though as late as November, 1915, Mr. Lithgow Osborne, of the United States Embassy, could observe of the treatment of British prisoners in the camp at Wittenberg that "instead of the Germans regarding their charges as honourable prisoners of war, it appeared to me that the men were regarded as criminals whom a regime of fear would alone suffice to keep in obedience". It was not, however, British prisoners who were the only sufferers. There was in some respects a remarkable uniformity in the methods and manners of the Germans to all their captives. The prisoners' overcoats were stolen whether they were made in Britain, France, or Russia. Belgian and French soldiers were insulted and threatened and stoned by German mobs at Aachen or other railway stations when on their way to German prisons. Russian wounded and Russian doctors were spat upon and stacked in horse trucks just as British officers and wounded were, and all were impartially called *Schweinhunde* by their captors. The experiences of Major C. B. Vandeleur, of the 1st Cameronians, who escaped from Crefeld, and gave an account of his experiences in a letter to the Foreign Office in April, 1915, might serve for those of many other officers among our Allies:—

". . . At the station we were driven into closed-in wagons from which horses had just been removed, fifty-two men being crowded into the one in which the other four officers and myself were. So tight were we packed that there was only room for some of us to sit down on the floor. This floor was covered fully three inches deep in fresh manure, and the stench was almost asphyxiating. . . . Up to this time I had managed to retain my overcoat, but it was now forcibly taken from me by an officer at a few stations farther on. . . . All along the line we were cursed by officers and men alike at the various stations."

We quote Major Vandeleur because his evidence is a British official document. But what he says has been repeated with variants by officer after officer who has been able to give evidence. Some of these officers have preferred for military reasons to remain anonymous, or have been requested to do so by their superiors. Aide-Major X—, of the French medical service, who was wounded and taken prisoner by the Germans while in charge of a field-hospital at Stenay, is one such witness; but except for the injuries he suffered, and the vile threats made to him by drunken Germans at Stenay, the latter part of his story might be substituted for that of Major Vandeleur. Captain J. Hepper, Royal Army Medical Corps, had the same experiences, and they were common to Russian officers and doctors as well as to Belgian officers, as the official reports of the Russian Imperial Commission of Enquiry and of the Belgian Official Commission testified. But the bitterest part of the evidence which officers offered was that, while after a time their treatment improved, they had reason to believe that the conditions which their men suffered became worse after reaching Germany.

The first official indictment was that of Major Vandeleur:—

"I would especially call attention to the barbarous way in which British soldiers are being treated in the various laagers of the Germans. The information which follows has been obtained from the British orderlies who came to Crefeld as servants, and also from English and French medical officers who had been in the camps. The men in all cases had their greatcoats, and in many cases their tunics as well, and their money taken from them. . . . The men state that they slept on straw which had not been changed for months, and was quite sodden and rotten. All the men who came as orderlies were crawling in vermin, and half of them were suffering from the itch. The medical officer had to isolate these men before they could be employed as servants. I was also informed that the feeding arrangements for the British soldiers were very bad indeed, and, as the men had no money to supplement their rations, they were in a half-starved condition—which their appearance corroborated."

Major Vandeleur's observations, necessarily limited, were corroborated by the Second French Official Report (March, 1915). It recorded that in many of the camps some of the prisoners were almost dying of hunger. Punishment consisted, as a rule, in being tied by the neck to a post, both hands and feet being made fast . . . it also generally involved the loss of rations.

"In one of the camps a young soldier who was almost dying of hunger begged to be given something to eat. He was beaten by a warder and then given six days' cells. At Darmstadt a corporal used to hit the prisoners over the head with his sword if they did not salute him. On another occasion he stabbed a soldier in the chest who said men ought not to work without food.

The man died next day. At Güstrow a man was struck with a bayonet because he stopped work to light his pipe. Another was killed with a bayonet for having broken a pane of glass."

The French Report commented on the insufficiency of food, on the mortality among the prisoners from bronchitis and pneumonia, and on the terrible condition of the majority of exchanged French prisoners when they reached the Swiss border.

The Russian Official Report confirms in almost exact terms the recorded experiences of British and French prisoners with regard to the privations, suffering, and insult endured on the journey to Germany, and on the abominable conditions of the prison camps.

"At Stendal about 10,000 men were interned. They were so badly fed that many died of ill-nourishment and exhaustion, while the strongest among them became so feeble that they might have been knocked down by a child. The German sentries treated the captives with the utmost rigour and cruelty. For the slightest mistake or offence they were beaten with the butt-ends of rifles, tied up to a post for several hours at a time, and attacked by the watch-dogs."

One British witness testified that the Russians were, if anything, treated more brutally than any others, and fared worse because they had less to eat; they used to beg food from British and French soldiers who had parcels, and were punished by the German jailers when caught doing so. But in other respects all prisoners, even Belgian civilians,[1] suffered equally. They were fed on the worst kind of food, they were packed together in insanitary buildings, or were insufficiently sheltered; and in many camps they were subjected to the severest punishments for trifling offences, and to the vicious spite of brutish jailers. The foregoing extracts from official reports were confirmed and amplified by many witnesses who were exchanged as permanently incapacitated prisoners of war. Their complaints are so alike as almost to be interchangeable; as, for example, may be perceived in this extract from a French prisoner, M. André Warnod:—

"Prisoners at Merseburg are dying from hunger; three men sleep on two verminous mattresses, and there are prisoners who have not been warm for a moment all the winter. After some months of wear and tear the woodwork is all warped, and the roofs let in the rain. But it is a model camp, made in Germany, and in theory there is nothing lacking."

The diet improved during his stay, but it was always meagre: the bread dark, close, damp, and pasty, and on meat days the bits of chopped meat which were added to the soup were —"such meat—udders and garbage, liver, heart, and milt". The men were largely dependent on parcels received from relatives and friends. We need quote only one more passage from M. Warnod; it relates to the men forced to work outside the camps, and who received very little better treatment:—

"Nearly all the workers made the same complaint of insufficient food, for the diet which just keeps an inactive prisoner alive

[1] Nineteenth Report of the Belgian Commission: The account of the treatment of Belgian workmen deported from Luttre.

is not much more plentiful for a wretched prisoner who has to put in ten or twelve hours of arduous and exhausting work. . . . The working parties have no more freedom than behind their camp fences. They live in the worksheds, and on Sundays, if they do not work, they are shut up all day in the worksheds where they sleep. Another

Russian Prisoners in Germany: scene in one of the internment camps

complaint is the impossibility of washing after a hard day's work in a coal mine or a brickyard."

If this had been all, though it was bad enough, if the hardships, the insults, the miserable food and worse accommodation, the random or deliberate punishments, the occasional brutal outrages and murders, if these had been the sum of German transgression against the customs of civilized peoples in the treatment of prisoners, apologists might have found some explanation if no excuse for them in the Teutonic code of war and in the German's attitude of mind towards their enemies. But for another kind of barbarity, that which the Germans practised on their prisoners stricken by epidemic disease, there is no excuse consistent with the promptings of humanity. It was evident from the first that batches of men fresh from the hardship or the anguish of the battle-field, and herded together hungry and unsheltered in insanitary refuges, were ripe for disease. In the first months of winter disease smote them hard, pneumonia, bronchitis, influenza, diphtheria took their toll, and afterwards, as insufficient food began to tell, various kidney diseases. Then appeared typhus, a disease of dirt and cold and hunger. The introduction was said to be due to a mass of unfed Russian prisoners, and in the official Russian report of the outbreak at Schneidemühl it is called hunger typhus. But typhus which can be transmitted by lice made a similar appearance in Serbia, and was imported by the Austrians. It is a likely disease—if and when the germ of typhus is present—in the conditions which the Germans imposed on their prisoners. According to Dr. Francis Léonetti, French Army Medical Service, typhus made its appearance in nearly all the prison camps, but in some it was kept under. Dr. Léonetti was transferred in turn from Güstrow in Mecklenburg, to Langensalza in Thuringia, and Niederzwehren near Cassel in Westphalia.

At Güstrow in the winter of 1914–5 there were 12,000 Russian, 4000 French, 2000 Belgian, and 1000 British prisoners. All were in tents without sufficient protection against cold and wet, and were suffering from hunger and infested by vermin. The sanitary conditions were of the very worst kind, and lice swarmed in the clothes, blankets, and mattresses. Typhus raged in the camp for five months. There were hundreds of wounded who could not be treated for lack of dressings.

At Langensalza an epidemic of typhus lasted from January till May, 1915. There was scarcely any accommodation for the patients, who in one week numbered 3000. There were no medicines. Men sickening with the disease lay on the floor in corridors during the day, and were sent back at night to their quarters, where they mixed with their comrades.

At Niederzwehren an epidemic had lasted from February till May, 1915, when Dr. Léonetti reached the camp with six other doctors; but the deaths had been attributed by the German authorities to other causes. When, however, the epidemic spread to the German sentries, thence to the Cassel garrison, and finally to the town, the Germans woke to the situation. Foreign doctors were sent for, and by the end of June there were eighty-eight in the camp. The epidemic was then got under. On Dr. Léonetti's arrival there were 6000 sick in the camp.

The reason for Dr. Léonetti's removal from camp to camp was that whenever an epidemic broke out the work of tending the sick was given to British, Russian, or French doctors (and in one camp to French abbés); the German medical attendance was either insufficient, inefficient, or cowardly, though there were honourable exceptions, and to the devotion and courage of one German specialist, Dr. Rheberg, a tribute is due. The cowardly flight of German doctors took place at Schneidemühl, where the whole work of looking after the sick was done by Russian doctors, and where during two months of the epidemic more than 4000 Russian prisoners died. It was the same at

Stendal[1]—where French and Russian doctors took charge within a barbed-wire enclosure—and at Gardelegen.

Gardelegen camp, as described in the official report[2] by the Government Committee on the treatment of British prisoners of war, covers an area of about 350 yards by 550, which is about as large as Lords Cricket Ground, divided into eight compounds each containing eight huts. In these sixty-four huts there were in February, 1915, when the typhus epidemic broke out, about 11,000 prisoners, French, Russians, Belgians, and about 260 British. Of the overcrowding Major Davy wrote:—

> "The overcrowding was such as I have never before seen or imagined. The hut contained in its breadth four rows of straw palliasses so arranged that they were touching. Here men of all nationalities were crowded together. In these huts devoid of tables and stools the men lived, slept, and fed. They sat on their palliasses to eat their meals; they walked over each other in passing in and out; they lay there sick, and later on, in many cases, died there cheek by jowl with their fellow prisoners."

The prisoners were insufficiently fed: from the beginning of April, 1915, the British, and still more the French, existed more and more on what they received from home. The Russians were not so fortunate; up to the end of June, 1915, they received very few parcels from home, and were in consequence starved. Captain Brown describes those unfortunate soldiers struggling on hands and knees, in a pit where potato peelings were thrown, to find a stray potato or a piece of rind with a little more potato than usual. All the prisoners were inadequately clothed; the heating arrangements were defective: the sanitary condition of the camp was described by Major Davy in terms which cannot properly be repeated. The natural consequence of these conditions was that by the month of February, 1915, every prisoner was infected with the body louse; lice swarmed in every garment the men wore and in every blanket they slept in.

On February 11th the Germans, evidently fearing that an epidemic of some kind was impending, brought in Major Davy and Captain Brown from Magdeburg, as well as four French medical officers and a Russian doctor, who was afterwards followed by three others. When the epidemic was subsiding Captain Scott Williams and three more French doctors were brought in. The first impressions which two of these officers received of this miserable camp have been recorded: they convey an impression of the utter misery of the camp which chills the blood as one reads. This is Captain Brown's impression:—

> "Snow was falling heavily and the cold was intense. On entering the barrack-room the shock I received was too awful for words. All windows were closed as the only means of warmth. There were about 150 of the most miserable human objects I ever beheld—British, French, and Belgians occupied this room. The men were emaciated, ill-clad, and dirty beyond description, and in most cases were engaged in killing as many lice as possible in their clothes."

The German doctor was Dr. Wenzil,

[1] At Stendal, according to the evidence of Dr. Rebadeau-Thomas, the German Government took action only when the disease began to spread among its own people.

[2] White Paper (Cd 8351), Evidence of Major P. C. T. Davy, Captain A. T. Brown, and Captain Scott Williams.

with a medical student, Boas, and a staff of German orderlies. They all fled the camp as soon as typhus declared itself. Wenzil afterwards died: his successor never once entered the camp. The whole burden of tending the camp fell on the British, French, and Russian doctors, and on the soldiers of all nationalities who heroically volunteered to act as nursing orderlies. The French Roman Catholic priests who were prisoners volunteered to work among the sick: eight of them contracted typhus, and five died. Twenty-two British were among the nursing orderlies: twenty caught typhus, but only two died. Of the sixteen doctors in the camp twelve took the fever and two died. The British doctors speak with enthusiasm of the work of their French colleagues, and of Dr. Saint Hilaire in particular. The one gleam in the inhuman story of the way in which these men were left by the German doctors and the German commandant and officers, to cope unaided with the terrible conditions at Gardelegen when the epidemic was at its height, is that a Dr. Kranski, who had been in practice in Alexandria before the war, came to the camp as a volunteer to do what he could. He succeeded in getting an increase in the number of drugs and medical necessities, such as dressings; but there was never enough. There were not enough beds even; and there was not enough food; milk was obtained in small quantities—by paying for it. The German authorities, who drew a cordon round the camp on which by their neglect and inhumanity they had brought its terrible visitation, ordained that the sick were to continue on the same rations on which they had starved before—the same soup, the same black bread, the same weekly raw herring for each. The epidemic burnt itself out by June, 1915, having caused over 300 deaths.

Released from Germany: British wounded at Château d'Oex, Switzerland

Wittenberg may be selected as the culminating example of German inhumanity, but with minor differences, its abominations were not different from those at Schneidemühl, Stendal, or Gardelegen. There as in the other camps the ground was prepared for the disease by vile and insufficient food, by the gross overcrowding of between 15,000 and 16,000 prisoners on an area of $10\frac{1}{2}$ acres, by the absence of fuel and of proper clothing, and of proper provision for cleanliness. The state of the prisoners when first seen by Major Priestley, Captain Vidal, and Captain Lauder, the three Royal Army Medical Corps officers who, having been imported into the camp during the epidemic, survived their experiences and related them on their return to England, was in Major Priestley's words deplorable—"they were gaunt, of a peculiar grey pallor, and verminous". When the epidemic broke out in December, 1914,

"the German staff, military and medical, precipitately left the camp, and thenceforth, until the month of August, 1915, with the exceptions detailed later on, no communication was held between the prisoners and their guards except by means of directions shouted from the guards or officers remaining outside the wire entanglements of the camp. All supplies for the men were pushed into the camp over chutes. The food for the hospital and medical officers was passed in on a trolley over about 20 yards of rail, worked by winches at either end so as to avoid all contact between the prisoners and the outside world. No medical attention during the whole time was provided by the German staff."[1]

Dr. Aschenbach, the German doctor, paid only one visit to the camp during the whole course of the epidemic. He came attired in a complete suit of protective clothing, including a mask and rubber gloves. His visit was brief and rapid. He received the Iron Cross.

For a full understanding of the appalling conditions of filth and disease in which Wittenberg Camp was sunk—its stricken men mingled with the uninfected, its helpless patients covered with vermin as with dust—the official report of the three surviving British doctors should be read. Originally six British Royal Army Medical Corps officers had been sent. Of these Major Fry, Captain Sutcliffe, and Captain Field died. Captain Lauder was attacked, but recovered. On him and on Major Priestley[2] and Captain Vidal, splendidly supported by English prisoners who volunteered as nurses, the task of seeing the camp through the epidemic rested. Many of these devoted prisoners caught the infection and died of the fever.

Wittenberg can never be forgotten. It should never be forgotten. Its typhus epidemic set the seal on a treatment of prisoners which from the first had been notorious for cruelty. That which Captain Lauder reported of it surpasses any condemnation which could be passed by a commentator. He

[1] White Paper, Cd. 8224 (1916): "Conditions at Wittenberg Camp during the Typhus Epidemic of 1915".

Happy Warriors Again: British wounded released from Germany off for a tour on a mountain railway in Switzerland

[2] Major Priestley and his companions were received by the King on their arrival in England, and were rewarded for their devotion and bravery. Major Priestley received the C.M.G.

said that "many of the prisoners went so far as to look upon the typhus with all its horrors as a godsend; they preferred it to the presence of the German guards".

The brutality in many camps seems to have been purposeful, intended to cow the prisoners and to strike through them at the countries to which they belonged. But when towards the middle of 1916 the number of German prisoners in the hands of France and Great Britain began to mount, the Germans, fearful of reprisals, began to treat prisoners better, and consented to listen to proposals that were made for the amelioration of the lot of those whose wounds had permanently unfitted them for any further participation in the war. Largely owing to the representations of Switzerland, to whom a great debt of gratitude for her humanity is owing, wounded prisoners from both sides were interned in Switzerland, where their comfort and welfare could be assured, and where their near relatives could visit them. The British wounded prisoners of war were received at Château d'Oex and at Mürren, places whose beauty had made them known to many British tourists before the war; and many joyful and pathetic sights accompanied the arrival of the prisoners at these havens of refuge. They were received with the greatest hospitality, kindness, and goodwill by the Swiss people, and gained there some consolation for the trials they had passed through.

At Germany's door lie the deaths of many prisoners and many innocent people. The death of one of them was an act of ferocity which was calculated with precision for a particular end. This was the murder of Captain Fryatt, after a trial which was even more of a mockery than that which sent Miss Edith Cavell to her death. Captain C. A. Fryatt was the master of the Great Eastern Railway Company's steamship *Brussels*, which plied on the Harwich-Rotterdam route.

Captain Charles Fryatt
(Photographed by Miles & Kaye)

On March 2, 1915, while the *Brussels* was on a voyage from Harwich to Rotterdam, Captain Fryatt sighted an undersea boat with two masts, which he recognized as German. The submarine steered straight for the *Brussels*; but Captain Fryatt, sending down every hand he could spare into the engine-room, got nearly sixteen knots out of his ship, and after being chased for a number of miles on a difficult course, escaped from the pursuers. For his skill and determination Captain Fryatt was awarded a gold watch by the Great Eastern Railway Company. Some weeks afterwards, on March 28, the same day on which a German submarine sank the liner *Falaba*,[1] deliberately firing a torpedo at her while passengers and crew were still on board, Captain Fryatt again encountered a German submarine in the North Sea. He sighted it in the afternoon, a submarine of one of the newest classes, some 300 feet long, with a high bow and a large conning-tower. The undersea boat carried no distinguishing marks. Captain Fryatt realized that it was hopeless to run away: the submarine had the heels of him, and could torpedo him almost before he had put on steam. The submarine signalled him to stop. Captain Fryatt determined to make a fight for it, and to take the best chance of saving his ship by threatening the submarine. He therefore starboarded his helm, rang up the engine-room to cram on all speed, sent the crew aft for safety, and steered straight for the submarine's conning-tower. This was his right under international law—to disregard the submarine's summons and to resist her attack to the best of his power. The submarine, when she saw the *Brussels* bent on exercising her right of resistance, immediately submerged. She disappeared about 20 yards ahead. Captain Fryatt did not feel his ship strike the submarine, but when it reappeared it had a decided list, and soon after vanished from view. The British Admiralty showed their sense of his conduct by presenting him with a watch inscribed:—

> "Presented by the Lords Commissioners of the Admiralty to Charles Algernon Fryatt, Master of the s.s. *Brussels*, in recognition of the example set by that vessel when attacked by a German submarine, 28th March, 1915."

The award of the watch by the Admiralty was announced in the House of Commons on April 28, 1915. More than a year later, on June 22, 1916, Captain Fryatt sailed from the Hook of Holland on the *Brussels* for England. The ship had a cargo of foodstuffs and some Belgian refugees. When well on her voyage to Tilbury she was captured by a flotilla of German torpedo-boats and taken as a prize to Zeebrugge. Few incidents of the capture have been made public, for it was some months before any of those on board the *Brussels* were permitted to return to England. One of the stewardesses who at length did so said that Captain Fryatt was pressed to try to get away, but refused to do so because he said the Germans would shell the ship, and he had women and passengers to think of. There are rumours that there was a spy on board, and that the capture was in some measure due to treachery.

On July 1 the United States Ambassador, in reply to an enquiry from the British Foreign Office, assured Sir Edward Grey that the officers and crew of the *Brussels* were safe and well, and that Captain Fryatt "desired that his wife might be informed". Not until July 16 was it learned from

[1] One hundred and four men and women were drowned.

the columns of the Amsterdam *Telegraaf* that Captain Fryatt was to be tried by court martial on the charge of ramming a German submarine. No particulars of this hasty and illegal trial have been made public. It was hurried on in spite of a request for postponement, and Captain Fryatt was at once condemned to death on the ground that

British Official Photograph

Prisoners in British Hands: bringing in a batch of wounded during the Battle of the Somme

"Although he was not a member of a combatant force he made an attempt on the afternoon of March 28th, 1915, to ram the German submarine U 33 near the Maas Lightship".

The sentence, which was immediately carried into execution, was contrary to the prize law of all the great States, and finds no warrant even in the German prize regulations. The German pretence was that Captain Fryatt was a *franc tireur.* "One of the many nefarious *franc tireur* proceedings of the British Merchant Marine against our vessel", ran the German official wireless, "has thus found a belated but merited expiation." Great Britain could exact no expiation for this crime till the war was ended; but then, Mr. Asquith assured his countrymen, no diplomatic relations would be entered upon with Germany till those responsible for this judicial murder were punished. It was no mere ferocity which dictated this German crime. The reason for it appeared some months afterwards when, in October, 1916, Germany began her new "ruthless" campaign against merchant vessels. It was obviously to her advantage in carrying out this campaign that merchant captains should be made to fear that if they offered resistance to German submarines they would share the fate of Captain Fryatt. E. S. G.

# CHAPTER VII

## THE BATTLE OF THE SOMME

(July–November, 1916)

Aims of the Somme Offensive—New Army's Supreme Test—Fate of Verdun—Enemy's Attempts to upset Allies' Plans—Strength of his Defences on the Somme—Preliminaries of the Battle—Leaders of the Opposing Armies—First Phase of the Battle—How Montauban and Mametz were captured—The Check on the British Left—Results of the First Day's Operations—Concentrating on the Main Battle-front—Fall of Fricourt, La Boisselle, and Contalmaison—The Grand Assault of July 14—Messages from the King—Close of the First Phase—Advance up the Main Ridge—The Battle of the Woods—The Epic of Delville Wood and Longueval—Australian Heroism at Pozières—The Struggle for Guillemont, Falfemont Farm, Leuze Wood, and Ginchy—A Real Trial of Strength—Progress of the French Advance—Eighty Battles in Eighty Days—Close of the Second Phase—General Gough's Ordeal of Endurance on the Left—Foot-by-foot Advance on Thiepval—Allies' Combined Attack on September 15—First Appearance of the Tanks—Their Share in the Day's Successes—Capture of Flers, Martinpuich, Courcelette, and High Wood—New Zealanders' Fine Performance—Grand Attack of the Guards—Fall of Morval and Combles—Thiepval and Main Ridge carried—Position gained for overwhelming Success—Germans saved by Bad Weather—Net Results of the Allied Victory.

NOT until winter, with its sodden fields and impassable roads, had at length cried "Halt!" to the Joint Offensive on the Somme was Sir Douglas Haig able to write his dispatch upon the first operations on a large scale which had fallen to his lot, as well as, to quote his own words, "one of the greatest, if not absolutely the greatest, struggle that has ever taken place". That straightforward and weighty document, dated from General Head-quarters in France on December 23, 1916, and published in the newspapers a week later, cleared up a number of vital points concerning the objects and results of the battle. It furnished the first authoritative statement that the object of the Allied offensive, which began on July 1 and continued until towards the close of the year, was threefold:

"1. To relieve the pressure on Verdun.

"2. To assist our Allies in the other theatres of war by stopping any further transfer of German troops from the Western front.

"3. To wear down the strength of the force opposed to us."

Those were the immediate aims of the battle, but of greater moment than any of these was the unwritten purpose of answering the question whether Britain's New Army, the army of continental dimensions — largely composed of amateurs, but of Lord Kitchener's shaping, and endowed with the great traditions of the Old Contemptibles—would be able to hurl back an all-powerful enemy from seemingly impregnable strongholds. It was not a question of courage; that had been proved beyond dispute along every yard of the British front. It was largely a question of strength and skill in the face of the best-equipped and the most highly-trained force the world had ever seen. Ours was an absolutely new army—new men, new officers, generals unaccustomed two years before to warfare on any similar scale, new guns. No longer merely an Expeditionary Force, it had become a mighty host, which transformed Great Britain for the first time into a modern military Power of the leading rank. Though well blooded in the costly victory at Loos, as well as along the slopes of the Vimy Ridge, the deadlier salient of Ypres, and other stricken fields of France and Flanders, it was now to be put to the supreme test as a weapon of offence.

The quality of the men and the leadership of the officers, as we have said, were known to be above and beyond reproach, but other qualities were largely untried. The highest courage, for example, would avail nothing if the artillery failed against the strength of modern defence-works. We could at length boast the best guns at the front, but, after all, we had not the gunners with the years of training of those in the older Continental Armies, especially in the army which had all the knowledge and science of the greatest military empire at its back. Mr. Lloyd George afterwards confessed that this was the chief anxiety of the British Higher Command before the Battle of the Somme removed once and for all the not unnatural doubt whether we could in the course of a few months have turned out gunners fully competent to work their very delicate, subtle, and complex machines in such a way as to hit a target three, four, and five miles off —and a very small target at that. The gunnery of the Somme, if it proved anything, proved not only that the intelligence and brains of the nation had been enlisted in the war, but also that they were devoting to the task their whole energy and determination.

Had the army been larger and more experienced, there is little doubt that the battle would have been begun earlier in the year. Sir Douglas Haig himself tells us that, though the principle of an offensive campaign during the summer of 1916 had been decided on by all the Allies before the date of his previous dispatch (May 19), he desired to postpone his attack—with due regard to the needs of the general situation—as long as possible. Every week made a great difference to his numerical strength and his steadily increasing supplies of munitions. "Moreover," he writes, "a very large proportion of the officers and men under my command were still far from being fully trained, and the longer the attack could be deferred the more efficient they would become." General Joffre was well aware of this, as well as of Sir Douglas Haig's readiness to launch his attack — having received the consent of His Majesty's Government to that effect — whenever the general situation required it with as great a force as he might then be able to make available. Instead of undertaking an offensive with an unready army it was arranged, as mentioned in an earlier chapter, to take over more front from the French. General Sir Henry Rawlinson, Sir Douglas Haig's right-hand man in the Battle of the Somme, subsequently ascribed this decision as a tribute to the judgment of the French that they could meantime hold the Germans at Verdun.

Those who waited impatiently at home as month after month slipped by, and the Germans were hacking their way nearer and ever nearer to that "inviolate citadel", little realized what those months meant to the Allied Commanders. It was a desperate fight for time. By the end of May the immortal defence, begun by the French on February 21, had already gained many precious weeks for our gathering army. Yet the issue at Verdun was still in doubt. So doubtful, indeed, that, with the Austrians also making their serious inroads on the Italian front, it was decided by the Allied Council of War to open the Russian campaign early in June. Broussilov's brilliant strategy at once caused a movement of German troops from the Western to the Eastern front, but it did not relieve the pressure on Verdun. The German Crown Prince, with his advance troops almost on the outskirts of the town, seemed at long last to have almost within his grasp the prize for which he had made such appalling sacrifices. It was perfectly true, as Sir Douglas Haig bore witness, that the desperate struggle for the possession of Verdun had invested that place with a moral and political importance out of all proportion to its military value. "Its fall would undoubtedly have been proclaimed as a great victory for our enemies, and would have shaken the faith of many in our ultimate success." In the hour of its greatest need, and in view of the situation in the various theatres of war, it was accordingly agreed that the combined French and

Field-Marshal Sir Douglas Haig, Commanding the British Army in France
(From a photograph by Russell)

British offensive should not be postponed beyond the end of June.

Two attempts, as we have already seen, were made by the enemy to interfere with Sir Douglas Haig's final preparations—the attack on the Vimy Ridge near Souchez on May 21, and the more formidable onslaughts against the Canadians in the Ypres salient early in June. The earlier attack, as already described,[1] had robbed us of a promising foothold on the crest of the Vimy heights, but this was not regarded by Sir Douglas Haig as of sufficient strategic or tactical importance to warrant any weakening of the preparations for his coming offensive in order to recover the lost ground. It was for this reason, as he explains in his dispatch of December 23, 1916, that he decided to consolidate the new position in rear of our original line. The subsequent attack on the Canadian lines in the Ypres salient he regarded as a more serious matter. "As the southern part of the lost positions commanded our trenches", he wrote, "I judged it necessary to recover it, and by an attack launched on the 13th June, carefully prepared and well executed, this was successfully accomplished by the troops on the spot."[2]

No additional forces had been drawn away by either of these enemy onslaughts from Sir Douglas Haig's unceasing preparations for the major operations of the summer. In his official outline of these tremendous events the Commander-in-Chief gives some idea of the immense preparations necessary for a grand attack in modern warfare, and incidentally shows the nature of the task confronting our new and largely untried army. When we realize the strength and extent of the enemy's defences on the Somme, it is hardly surprising that the German Higher Command regarded them as impregnable. Along the whole of their front, situated on high, undulating ground, with the advantage of position almost everywhere in their favour, they had constructed a double system of main defences, each consisting of several lines of deep trenches, and protected in front by wire entanglements. Many of these entanglements were in two belts forty yards broad, built of iron stakes interlaced with barbed wire, often almost as thick as a man's finger. Every wood and village, every mill and isolated building, had been drawn into the defence scheme, like pieces in a mighty jig-saw puzzle, and converted wherever possible into veritable fortresses. Full advantage had been taken of the deep cellars already existing in the villages, and of the numerous pits and quarries common to a chalk country, to provide cover for machine-guns and trench mortars, the cellars being also supplemented by elaborate dug-outs, sometimes two stories down. Many of these were furnished with some of the luxuries of a permanent residence, and connected up by passages often as much as thirty feet below the ground-level. Sir Douglas Haig explains that these various systems of defences, with their self-contained forts, their protecting mine-fields, and other supporting points, were all so cunningly sited as

[1] Vol. V, pp. 267–8.
[2] Described in Chapter III.

to afford each other mutual assistance, and to admit of the maximum development of enfilade and flanking fire by machine-guns and artillery:

"They formed, in short, not merely a series of successive lines, but one composite system of enormous depth and strength. Behind this second system of trenches, in addition to woods, villages, and other strong points prepared for defence, the enemy had several other lines already completed; and we had learned from aeroplane reconnaissance that he was hard at work improving and strengthening these, and digging fresh ones between them and still farther back."

Truly a tough nut for a new army to crack. So confident were the German commanders of its invincible strength that, though they knew the attack was coming, they decided that the troops already on the spot, secure in defences which they had had nearly two years to construct, would suffice to ward off all possible dangers. Verdun, they argued, need not yet be given up; and Broussilov's alarming thrust in the East called urgently for reinforcements on the Austro-German front. It was not long before the German Higher Command realized its mistake. Only for a short time after the first shattering blow on the

British Official

Under the Shelter of a Sunken Road: British troops with ammunition going up to the front line

Somme did the movements of German troops continue from West to East. Thereafter every available division was needed to prevent defeat on the Somme from developing into irretrievable disaster. The mistake which the German Higher Command had made was not in placing a false

British Official

Summer on the Picardy Battle-field: British 18-pounder gun in action

value on the strength of the Somme defences, but in underrating the new British army, as well as the veterans of France, who, by all the hypotheses of German military science, should have been so exhausted by the ordeal of Verdun as not to have another assault left in them.

Sir Douglas Haig, on his part, left nothing to chance. Many miles of new railways and all available roads were improved to facilitate the accumulation of the vast stores of ammunition and other war material beforehand; the whole of the enemy's lines were mapped by aeroplane reconnaissance; miners attacked them underground, charges being laid at various points beneath their vital positions; and to meet the water difficulty—supplies, save in the river valleys, being hopelessly insufficient for the purpose—numerous wells and borings were sunk, and over 100 pumping plants installed. To ensure an adequate drinking supply as our troops advanced more than 120 miles of water-mains were laid. Much of this work, as well as the digging of additional dug-outs as dressing stations for the wounded, magazines for storing ammunition, food, and the like, had to be done under the most trying weather conditions, and often under fire from the enemy. It threw a heavy strain on the troops, "but was borne by them", records the Commander-in-Chief, "with a cheerfulness beyond all praise".

The high undulating battle-field forms the watershed between the Somme on the one side and the rivers of south-western Belgium on the other. Rising gradually from the Somme in a series of long, wooded hills and deep depressions, the ground selected for the main attack on July 1, 1916, spreads out on a plateau which, starting from a point half a mile north of Thiepval, passes through the Bois des Foureaux (High Wood), thence sweeping round to the south by Guillemont to the end of a spur masked by Falfemont Farm, where the battle-front was taken over by the French, and prolonged as far as the Roman road at Estrées. Though the villages had been shattered by shell-fire and the countryside scarred with the cruel marks of two years' conflict, it was a fairer field than the mud flats of Flanders and the dreary plains of Loos and Hulluch. Among the pleasant hills and valleys and verdant meadow-lands of Picardy, Nature had contrived to mask many of the wounds of war, until the long-drawn-out battle changed the whole complexion of the landscape.

On the southern face of the watershed, and well down its forward slopes, the enemy's first system of defence, starting from the Somme opposite the French lines near Curlu, ran at first northwards for 3000 yards, then westwards for 7000 yards to near Fricourt, where it turned nearly due north again. This formed the great angle in the enemy's lines known as the Fricourt salient. Still running northwards, the German defences crossed the road from Bapaume to Albert, where the golden Virgin still hung suspended from the tall campanile of the battered

British Official

The Battered Cathedral, Albert, with the Virgin suspended from the wrecked campanile

cathedral, as if holding the Holy Child as a peace offering to men; pushing thence across the River Ancre—a tributary of the Somme between five and six miles north of Fricourt—and on through the fearsome stronghold of Beaumont-Hamel and over the summit of the watershed, about Hébuterne and Gommecourt, whence they descended the northern spurs towards the city of Arras.

In the main area, along the 20,000-yards front between the Somme and the Ancre, our forward trenches ran parallel and close to those of the enemy, but below them. The configuration of the ground, however, offered some compensating advantages. We had, as Sir Douglas Haig points out, good direct observation on the enemy's front defences, as well as on the slopes above us between his first and second systems. The second system, on the other hand—sited generally on or near the southern crest of the highest part of the watershed, at an average distance of from 3000 to 5000 yards behind—was hidden in many places from the ground in our possession; and nothing at all, save from the air, was visible of his more distant defences. North of the Ancre, the opposing trenches ran transversely across the main ridge. This placed friend and foe alike on level terms so far as command of ground was concerned, but the opposing lines were more widely separated from one another, and our direct observation was not so good as along the main battle-front to the south. The sequel made it clear that the Germans had been misled into expecting the full force of the blow in this direction, from Fricourt up as far as Arras, and had massed their men and guns accordingly. Sir Douglas Haig explains, however, that the main British attack extended only from the junction with the French at Maricourt to the Ancre in front of St. Pierre Divion. The simultaneous assault north of the Ancre as far as Serre was intended to help this main thrust by holding the enemy's reserves and artillery, the subsidiary attack farther north, on both sides of the Gommecourt salient, being planned for the same purpose.

The whole of the attack on July 1, from Maricourt to Serre, was entrusted to the Fourth Army, under General Sir Henry Rawlinson, with five Army Corps at his disposal, the subsidiary operations at Gommecourt falling to the army commanded by General Sir E. H. H. Allenby. Our Allies were under the brilliant leadership of General Foch, whose troops now included the splendid army under General Fayolle. The Germans on the main battle-front were under the chief command of General von Below, whose brother was at the head of one of the Kaiser's armies on the Eastern front; and among his corps commanders was General von

General von Below, the German Commander-in-Chief in the Somme Battle

FROM A PHOTOGRAPH BY MANDY

*H. R. H. King Ferdinand of Roumania.*

General Sixt v
Army Co

Arnim.
tween Go.
German tr
command (
The gur
June 24, ar
emotional r
large force
into action
little idea o
let loose o
tinued with
the mornin
though all
driving at
less tunnel
who hear
each other
Nothing li
guns of ev

General Sixt von Arnim, commanding the Fourth German Army Corps against the British on the Somme

Arnim. In the northern area, between Gommecourt and Serre, the German troops were under the chief command of General von Marschell.

The guns began the prologue on June 24, and Sir Douglas Haig's unemotional record to the effect that "a large force of artillery was brought into action for the purpose" affords little idea of the crashing roar of guns let loose on that occasion, and continued with increasing intensity until the morning of July 1. "It was as though all the trains in the world were driving at express speed through endless tunnels", wrote Mr. Philip Gibbs, who heard it, "in which they met each other with frightful collisions." Nothing like such a concentration of guns of every calibre had ever before been seen on a British battle-field. A French officer, who had been through the worst bombardments at Verdun, declared that he had witnessed nothing to surpass our terrific fire in the vital sectors of the threatened salient. Only thus, as we had learnt to our cost at Loos, Neuve Chapelle, and elsewhere, could we hope to batter down the enemy's defences in order to prepare the way for a victorious assault.

The British bombardment was not confined to the destined battle-field. It was carried out daily at different points along the rest of our front, the German line in the meantime being effectively probed for information in many sectors by means of infantry raids. No fewer than seventy of these raids were undertaken between Gommecourt and our extreme left north of Ypres during the week preceding the grand attack. "These", wrote Sir Douglas Haig, "kept me well informed as to the enemy's dispositions, besides serving other useful purposes." Among other things, they kept the Germans in a constant state of tension, and, with demonstrations of our Allies at various points along the French front, uncertain as to the exact locality of the real offensive. Gas attacks at more than forty places—making a line of frontage, all told, of over 15 miles—were also included in the British preliminaries during the same period; while on June 25 the Royal Flying Corps partially blinded the enemy for the time being by a general attack on his observation balloons, destroying nine of them. A similarly successful attack was carried out at the same time by the French air service. The Allies' flying men, indeed, had now firmly established their supremacy in the air, and maintained their mastery throughout the battle.

## FIRST PHASE OF THE BATTLE

Sir Douglas Haig divides the offensive itself into three phases, and we cannot do better than follow his example. The first opened with the

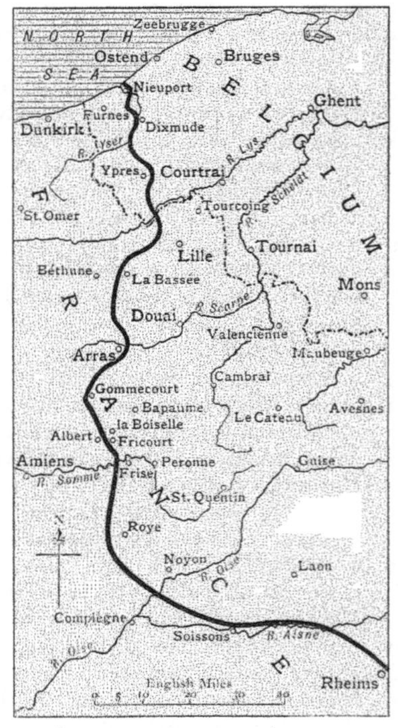


The Allies' Line from the Sea to Rheims, in June, 1916

British Official

Last Moments before the Assault: Lancashire Fusiliers fixing bayonets before charging, on July 1, 1916

joint-attack of July 1, the success of which, though qualified by the setback between Gommecourt, on the extreme left, and Ovillers-la-Boisselle, across the Ancre, must have shaken the enemy's faith in the impregnability of his defences. It began at 7.30 a.m., after a full hour of the most terrific bombardment which the Germans had ever experienced. The guns had been roaring for days and nights together, but this was nothing to the final pandemonium which preceded the attack. Dawn broke with a clear blue sky, which was presently obscured in the distance by a summer mist from the moist earth, and was wholly blotted out for the time being when, immediately before the attack, clouds of smoke were discharged at many points along our front to form a screen for our infantry, who were eagerly awaiting the critical moment in their assembly trenches at all the attacking points. Simultaneously the mines which had been prepared under the enemy's lines were exploded. It was 7.30. The moment for the grand attack had arrived.

In a battle so prolonged and of such magnitude as that which followed, it is only possible, in the space at our disposal, to give a general idea of the whole course of operations. Nor is it permissible at present to particularize the units engaged, save where Sir Douglas Haig himself singled them out for special mention in his daily reports, or where the war correspondents were allowed to associate the fighting representatives of the various parts of the Empire with different phases of the struggle. Certain incidents stand out definitely. On July 1, for instance, the enemy, anticipating a special effort on our part to reduce the Fricourt salient at its apex, had practically levelled our assembly trenches with his concentrated artillery fire, but all his efforts were unavailing against the famous British divisions selected to hold this part of the line. It was a division which had lost most of the officers and men who had filled its ranks in the summer of 1914, but on the morning of July 1, 1916, it proved that it had retained all its steadiness and high traditions. The destruction of the assembly trenches made it necessary for the attacking battalions—English and Scottish regulars together, including the Gordons, Devons, and South Staffordshires—to advance across 400 yards of open ground under a tornado of fire which played havoc with their ranks; but they pushed on without wavering, as if on parade, not only forcing their way into Mametz, but reaching their objective in the valley beyond, first throwing out a defensive flank towards Fricourt on their left. This and the advance of the Lancashire Brigades on their right towards Montauban, with Home County battalions on their left,

British Official

Preliminaries of the Grand Attack: a British mine exploding under the German trenches, on July 1, 1916

were our most successful examples that day of the offensive tactics employed throughout the Battle of the Somme: no attempts to push through at all cost, but methodical attacks sufficiently prepared by the guns, and aiming at no distant objective until each point had been won and consolidated, and the artillery brought up to pave the way for the next advance.

Montauban had been carried in rare style by midday, the Manchester men leading a glorious assault against the Bavarian garrison of 3500 men, and shortly afterwards the Briqueterie—some large brick-yards and buildings about half a mile to the south-east—also fell into our hands. The Briqueterie had threatened to become as troublesome as the terrible brick-stacks at Guinchy, but the sequel showed as conclusively as anything what tremendous strides we had made in our artillery support during the last eighteen months. The troops, sent merely to test its strength, found it so completely destroyed that they captured it, together with the remnants of its garrison, with little opposition. This completed our conquest of the whole of the ridge to the west of Montauban, and linked us with the French left. In a certain trench at Maricourt the Allies had gone over the top together on that historic morning, advancing shoulder to shoulder under the enemy's fire, and literally shed their blood together in the common cause. Continuing in close co-operation—for our right wing kept in touch with the French left throughout—this comradeship and mutual support contributed not a little to the conspicuous success

Drawn by S Begg

First Blood in the Battle of the Somme: the storming of Montauban over the sunken road in front of the village, on July 1, 1916

on this sector of the front. Among our Allies were the Moroccans and the famous Colonial Corps commanded by General Marchand—now happily recovering from his wounds received in the Champagne Offensive, and able in due course to rejoin his troops on the Somme—as well as the immortal Iron Corps of the French army—the army which won its proudest battle honours on the Grand Couronné at Nancy in the first phase of the war, and later at Douaumont, where it helped to save the situation in the most critical days of Verdun.

For the moment, however, we must leave our gallant Allies and follow the more desperate fighting in the centre and left of the British line, where the enemy, having anticipated the full force of the offensive at these points, had prepared his stoutest resistance. Fricourt, on the left of Mametz, was fortified with the elaborate thoroughness of a point which the Germans knew to be of high strategic importance, and for more than a year it had been hurling death and defiance at the British lines, separated from it by lines of trenches full of German snipers. It was one of the deadliest spots on the whole 90 miles of British front, and no attempt was made on July 1 to carry it by direct assault. It was less costly to cut it off; and while the division attacking Mametz was throwing out its defensive flank towards Fricourt the enemy's trenches were entered north of that village, leaving its garrison pressed at nightfall on three sides.

Farther to the north the battle ebbed and flowed all day with varying fortune. The villages of La Boisselle and Ovillers stubbornly resisted our attack; but, driving deeply into the German lines on the flanks of both strongholds, our troops paved the way for their ultimate capture. It was at La Boisselle, towards the middle of January, 1915, that the Kaiser's hopes had been dashed when he decreed that the French were to be driven thence to celebrate the foundation of the modern German Empire by the proclamation of the Emperor William I at Versailles on January 13, 1871. The Kaiser, according to the French official account, had promised a reward of 700 marks to any German soldier who captured a French machine-gun on that occasion; but the only result was the crushing defeat of no fewer than nine German assaults. The ground here, as at Fricourt, had been drenched in French and German blood, and now it was drenched again in German and British; but this time the German troops were on the defensive, and both villages were soon to be wrested from their grasp.

Their hold was even more tenacious on their northern strongholds on both sides of the Somme's tributary stream, the Ancre. It was here that our heaviest losses occurred, and points of vantage won after prodigies of valour, only to be lost again through lack of reinforcements and ammunition. Some day the full story will be told of the terrific struggle as the battle swayed backwards and forwards between Gommecourt and Thiepval, where dug-outs were discovered under dug-outs, and machine-gunners were so cunningly concealed that many of our advancing troops suddenly found themselves under decimating fire from all sides. The German machine-gunners, posted at every nook and corner, and emerging unscathed from their underground lairs after the British bombardment, combined with the impregnability of the enemy's front line of fortified villages, caused the set-back which was destined to place the northern half of the British battle-front practically out of the main offensive until mid-November. The confused accounts of all this fighting on the northern half of our line in the opening day of the battle are best summarized by Sir Douglas Haig as follows:—

> "On the spur running south from Thiepval the work known as the Leipzig Salient was stormed, and severe fighting took place for the possession of the village and its defences. Here and north of the valley of the Ancre as far as Serre, on the left flank of our attack, our initial successes were not sustained. Striking progress was made at many points, and parties of troops penetrated the enemy's positions to the outer defences of Grandcourt, and also to Pendant Copse and Serre; but the enemy's continued resistance at Thiepval and Beaumont Hamel made it impossible to forward reinforcements and ammunition, and, in spite of their gallant efforts, our troops were forced to withdraw during the night to their own lines. The subsidiary attack at Gommecourt also forced its way into the enemy's positions; but there met with such vigorous opposition that, as soon as it was considered that the attack had fulfilled its object, our troops were withdrawn."

Regiments from all parts of Great Britain and Ireland—old regulars and New Army men, as well as many Territorials—shared in this self-sacrificing heroism north of Thiepval, as well as a brave little company of Rhodesians and a battalion of Newfoundlanders. On the extreme left, on each side of the Gommecourt salient, Midland and London Territorials—including some of the crack Metropolitan corps—struck the very centre of the German defence, yet reached their objectives in the face of a terrific fire, advancing with magnificent steadiness across the intervening valley through their covering screen of smoke. Though they broke the German line, however, the Londoners found themselves in a death-trap, cut off from the British positions by a wall of fire from masses of German guns of every calibre, and surrounded by German troops emerging unscathed from their deep dug-outs on all sides, armed with bombs and machine-guns. The Territorials put up a grand fight, sending back 200 prisoners through the barrage of the German guns; and fighting till their ammunition was exhausted. Then, realizing the hopelessness of their position, and the impossibility of receiving fresh supplies, they retired in good order, but with sadly thinned ranks, and with what reluctance may be imagined, robbed as they were by the cruel fortune of war of what otherwise would have proved a fine and fruitful victory.

Another death-trap in the tragic advance north of Thiepval was that into which the Ulster Division fell on the slopes leading from Beaumont Hamel to the Ancre. It was the anniversary of the Battle of the Boyne, and though the Ulstermen — volunteers originally in a very different cause — had been mercilessly shelled in the wood in which they had assembled for the assault, and suffered heavily even before they emerged from it, they advanced across the open towards the German line "with the steadiness of a parade movement", as the General Officer Commanding the Division recorded in his subsequent special order of the day, "under a fire, both from front and flanks, which could only have been faced by troops of the highest quality". In spite of fearful gaps in their ranks none of the battalions wavered for an instant. Line after line of enemy trench was captured amid the ancient battle-cry of "Remember the Boyne!", until, with the impetuosity of those ardent Scotsmen who pushed their victorious way too far beyond Loos in the September offensive of the year before, their leading troops forged a path right into the fifth line of German trenches, only to find themselves "in the air", without supports on either flanks. They had driven a long narrow wedge into the solid body of the enemy's defence, which now had its revenge by gradually closing in on three sides. Far from support on either flank, the intrepid Ulstermen, whose amazing advance had not been achieved without fearful loss, were not strong enough to retain all that they had won in the face of the tornado of bombs and shells now concentrated upon their perilous positions. Many fell in a vain endeavour to hold the advanced lines. The survivors, fighting their way back as they came, at length made a determined and decisive stand in

British Official

The Track of the British Guns: among the ruins of Mametz after the capture of the village on July 1, 1916

the second line of German trenches. Here, as elsewhere, they fought with a valour which made the General Officer Commanding justly proud of them, finally emerging from the ordeal with undying honour—and nearly 600 prisoners. It was in one of many gallant attempts made that day to support the Ulstermen by clearing their advanced flanks, that the Newfoundlanders sacrificed themselves so nobly on the same terrible slopes of Beaumont Hamel. They had proved first-rate fighting men in Gallipoli, and stood the cruel test on July 1, 1917, with the steadiness of veterans, showing themselves, as was subsequently recorded by the General Officer commanding the Division to which they were attached, "worthy of the highest traditions of the British race, and fit representatives of the oldest British colony".

Though the attack in the north had been checked, its costly sacrifices had not been in vain. It had held the enemy's main forces to the sector from which he had from the first expected the greatest danger, thus helping materially towards the successes to the south. An attacking army, as one of the Divisional Commanders in the battle afterwards wrote, is like a football team, "only one kicks the goal, but the credit of success belongs not only to that individual, but to the whole team, whose concerted action led to the desired result". The concentration of the German defence in the north was especially valuable to our French Allies, for whom apparently, the Germans, over-confident that Verdun had left them too exhausted seriously to attack elsewhere, were not so fully prepared. More particularly was this the case on the southern side of the Somme. Reinforcements, however, were soon rushed up. Before the afternoon of the 3rd, the French identified as many as forty German battalions on their attacking front, and the brilliant successes of our Allies on these opening days of the battle were magnificent feats of arms. On the right of the British, above the Somme, the French troops on July 1 established themselves in the approaches to the village of Hardecourt, south-east of the Briqueterie, as well as in the outskirts of Curlu; but their chief progress that day was made to

British Official

Sir Henry Rawlinson, commanding the Fourth Army in the Allied Offensive

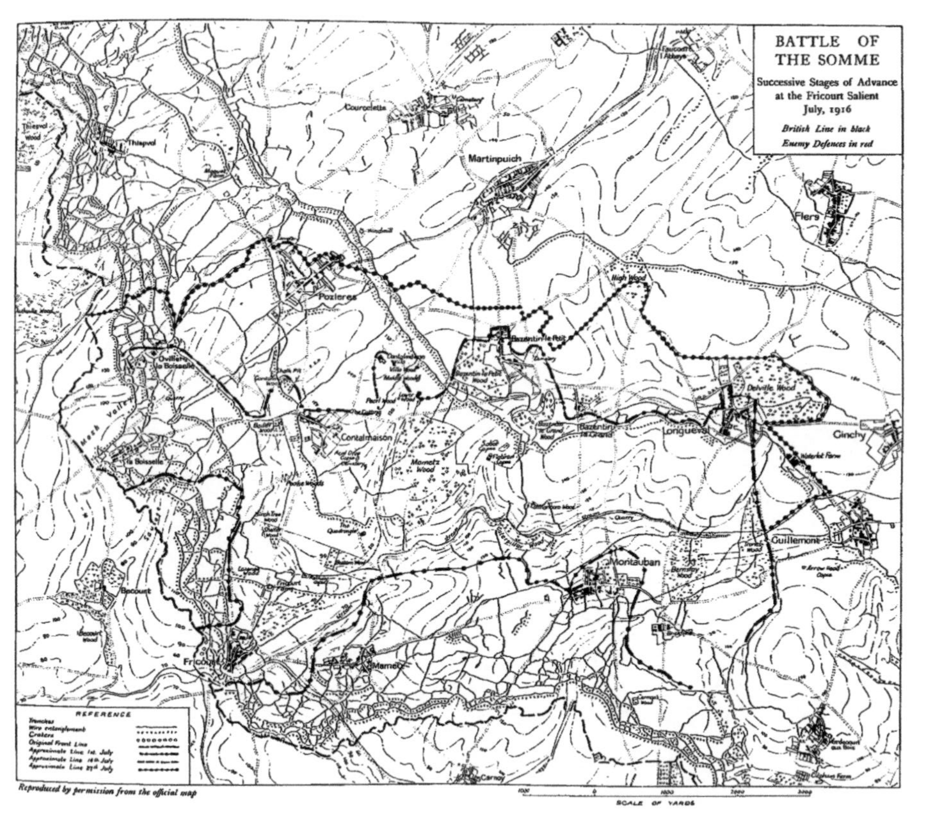

*Reproduced by permission from the official map*

Sir Hubert de la Poer Gough, commanding the Fifth British Army in the Allied Offensive
(From a photograph by Gale & Polden)

the south of the Somme, where the villages of Dompierre, Becquincourt, Bussu, and Fay fell into their hands, together with more than 3500 prisouers. Thanks largely to the remarkable efficiency of their artillery preparation their own losses were relatively small. The prisoners captured by the British on the same day totalled nearly 3000, including two regimental commanders and the whole of one regimental staff.

As a result of the first day's operations, Sir Douglas Haig decided to shorten his offensive front from our junction with the French to a point half-way between La Boisselle and Contalmaison. North of the Ancre, meantime, only such operations were to be undertaken as would hold the enemy to his positions and enable the attack to be resumed there later if desirable. This sector, La Boisselle to Serre, was now handed over to General Sir Hubert Gough,[1] thus leaving Sir Henry Rawlinson free to concentrate his attention on the front where the attack was to be pushed home. It was on these lines that our offensive was continued during the succeeding days, while the German Higher Command rushed up reserves from all directions, quick to realize that Verdun must now be left to its fate, and all hope abandoned for the time being of doing more than hold the Russians on the Eastern front. To save his face the army of the Crown Prince continued its assaults on the outskirts of Verdun, but the attacks had lost half their momentum, and the defenders, exulting in the knowledge that their comrades on the Somme were fully repaying the Germans in their own coin, hurled them back with a fiercer joy than ever. Soon it was judged advisable by those who had loudly boasted to neutrals that they would make their triumphant entry into Verdun on a certain date, to explain that Verdun was of no consequence, and that the objects of their attacks had been achieved without the necessity of entering that city.

Meantime Sir Douglas Haig and General Foch trampled down the German defences on both sides of the Somme with a thoroughness which, if desperately slow, was continuous, carrying them from one German position to another, and adding daily to their prodigious gains in guns,

[1] Sir Hubert Gough's instructions were to maintain a steady pressure on the front from La Boisselle to the Serre Road, and to act as a pivot, on which our line could swing as our attacks on his right made progress towards the north.

British Official

Death-traps in Montauban: German dug-outs, 30 feet deep, which had to be cleared in the British Advance

prisoners, and other spoils of war. It is impossible here to follow day by day the unforgettable record of battle which filled the war news and kept nearly every home in suspense during the next few months. At present we can only sum up the various phases of battle on the lines of Sir Douglas Haig's dispatch. He shows, for instance, how, as a result of the first five days' fighting on the narrowed British front from the Briqueterie to La Boisselle, Sir Henry Rawlinson's troops had swept over the whole of the enemy's first and strongest system of trenches, driving him back over a distance of more than a mile, and carrying four elaborately-fortified villages. In these days of ceaseless fighting Fricourt and La Boisselle had been added to Mametz and Montauban; Bernafay and Caterpillar Woods had been captured on the right; and on the left our troops had pushed on as far as the outskirts of Contalmaison.

Fricourt, pressed on three sides on the opening day of the battle by the men of Yorkshire, Durham, and Northumberland, was carried after a sanguinary struggle on the following afternoon, when the attacking troops seized it by assault, capturing the survivors of the garrison and adding to our already considerable haul of guns. La Boisselle, after similarly fierce fighting and fluctuating fortune until the last remnants of the stubborn defenders had been routed from their caverns, followed the fate of Fricourt on the Monday. On that day a more remarkable surrender took place along the line between Fricourt and Contalmaison. Here the enemy's losses under the continued British attack and bombardment had been particularly heavy, and the 186th Regiment of Prussian Infantry was rushed up to replace the casualties. According to the prisoners' accounts, afterwards transmitted from British Head-quarters, the battalion was moved into trenches affording such indifferent protection to the shattering fire of the British guns, and the daring advance of our infantry, that officers and men alike, after a short show of resistance, could stand it no longer. The survivors, numbering some 20 officers and more than 600 of all ranks, emerged from their defences with signs of surrender, and were marched off in a body by their captors to the barbed-wire enclosures in the rear, there to be shepherded pending their transportation across the Channel.

This was the day on which General von Below, commanding the German troops on the Somme, issued his order forbidding the voluntary evacuation of trenches. Possibly it was inspired by this incident. To the enemy's credit be it added that his troops for the most part stood their ground well, the machine-gunners especially being ready for any post of danger in order to carry out Von Below's injunctions that no more ground must be lost, and that the enemy, if he tried to advance, should have "to carve his way over heaps of corpses". Every day, however, swelled the list of German surrenders, both on the British and the

Drawn by S. Begg

"Kamerad!": a German garrison surrendering to British troops in the opening phase of the Allied offensive, July, 1916

French fronts. At the close of July 5 the number of prisoners passed back from the British lines had already reached the total of 6000 unwounded men of all ranks, besides many guns and other war material. The French total was considerably more. It was at this juncture that the following messages were published as having passed between His Majesty and Sir Douglas Haig:—

MESSAGE FROM THE KING TO GENERAL SIR DOUGLAS HAIG

Please convey to the Army under your command my sincere congratulations on the results achieved in the recent fighting. I am proud of my troops—none could have fought more bravely.

GEORGE R.I.

GENERAL SIR DOUGLAS HAIG'S REPLY TO THE KING'S MESSAGE

Your Majesty's gracious message has been conveyed to the Army, on whose behalf I return most respectful and grateful thanks. All ranks will do their utmost to continue to deserve your Majesty's confidence and praise.

DOUGLAS HAIG.

After five days of such intense and continuous fighting, a lull was inevitable in the general advance. "Apart from the physical exhaustion of the attacking troops," as Sir Douglas Haig explained, "and the considerable distances separating the enemy's successive main systems of defence, special artillery preparation was required before a successful assault could be delivered." The lull, however, was not very apparent at the time, either in the daily news from the front or in such storm-centres of the fighting line as Contalmaison, Mametz Wood, and Trônes Wood, where the defences were particularly strong. Here local operations took place which would have ranked as decisive battles in many previous wars. In each case our new Continental army found itself matched against the flower of the Kaiser's troops—and defeated them. It was this reiterated proof of superiority which gradually told on the enemy's *moral* and shook his faith in his invincibility. Contalmaison, once a sleepy little village of no account, was now thrust into world-importance by its tactical position in the war-game, situated on a ridge just above the big Mametz Wood. It was won and lost repeatedly in the final trial of strength which raged in and about its battered heap of ruins between July 7 and 11, 1916. True to the order of Von Below to yield no more ground but to hold on to the last, the Boche, to give him his due, fought with the greatest courage and determination, as well as cunning—creeping out of deep dug-outs, for example, on the night of its first capture, and making use of the darkness to force our troops back with machine-guns and bombs—and it was only after alternate advances and retirements that this miniature German Verdun, as one correspondent described it, became definitely ours.

Both sides of the Border shared in the glory, as well as the tragic sacrifices, attached to the taking of Contalmaison. Among many memorable episodes in this prolonged battle was the thrilling charge in the first attack, when Royal Scots, Suffolks, Tynesiders, and others swept all before them until they reached the death-trap in Contalmaison itself. Three days later, when the village was again entered and temporarily won, our troops were able to save a handful of Tynesiders who had fallen into the enemy's hands in the first, short-lived triumph. Once again, however, Contalmaison had to be given up under the weight of an overpowering counter-attack; and, as already stated, it was not until July 11, after the capture of Bailiff Wood on the north-western fringe of the stronghold, that the whole of the village was secured and firmly consolidated. It was in the course of this terrific fighting that several battalions of the 3rd Division of the Prussian Guard rushed up to counter-attack, and, hurriedly thrown into the battle-

British Official

Clearing up for the Next Advance: British troops making a road through Contalmaison after its capture from the Germans

field, were cut to pieces. One battalion was practically annihilated by the barrage of our guns, which suddenly caught them on the march; and the others suffered heavily at the hands of our infantry as soon as this barrage lifted. Many of the shattered remnants—700 all told—were taken prisoners. They were incredulous when informed that the gunners and infantry who had dealt them such crushing blows belonged to the "New Army", which so many of them had affected to despise. They thought they were fighting our own Guards.

Trônes Wood, to which the enemy also set great store, was meanwhile the scene of another prolonged and embittered struggle, sharing with Mametz Wood and Contalmaison the doubtful distinction of remaining for some days the hottest part of the battle-front. Trônes Wood, measuring some 1400 yards from north to south, with a southern base of 400 yards, lay on the right of Bernafay Wood, which had been carried by the victorious Lancashire troops on July 4 as a sequel to their capture of Montauban; and on the left of the village of Guillemont, which held out against the combined assaults of the Allies, who joined forces in its forbidding neighbourhood, until the early days of September. Trônes Wood itself, one of the strongest links in the enemy's chain of defence-works, had two lines of railway running through it in direct connection with Combles, via the northern outskirts of Guillemont. Its possession was essential to the safety of both Guillemont and Longueval, and with them the whole centre of the second system of German defences. Hence the exceptional strength of the enemy's positions, especially in the northern and eastern parts of the wood, and the reckless sacrifice by General von Arnim—for Von Arnim was the German commander at this point—of division after division of his best troops to hold it to the death, and afterwards to retake it when, after doggedly fighting their way through it foot by foot from the morning of Saturday, July 8, our indomitable troops had practically the whole of it in their possession. This was on Sunday morning, after no fewer than five determined attempts to drive us from our positions. Then, on Sunday afternoon, came a sixth assault, wave after wave of German infantry storming in succession over hecatombs of dead until once again they succeded in penetrating the southern end of the wood. But it is still the Briton's characteristic, as in Napoleon's day, never to know when he is beaten; and the enemy's costly triumph on this occasion was of short duration. Within the next twenty-four hours we had recaptured nearly the whole of the wood, all but the northernmost end being again in our hands; and it was not long before every tortured foot of it had passed permanently from the enemy's possession.

In the meanwhile a lodgment had been gained on the same Monday afternoon in the larger and even more formidable Mametz Wood, on the slopes leading to Contalmaison, some two miles away to the left. Here the enemy's positions, defended by every artifice known to military science as well as every natural advantage in the shape of cover—the thick tangle of undergrowth hiding machine-gun redoubts, and all manner of frightful obstacles—had hitherto resisted all our efforts. Monday's success was the result of a cleverly-planned surprise assault, and a dashing attack by some ardent Welsh battalions, supported by a progressive barrage of fire—line of high explosive preceding the attack and moving forward as the infantry completed its work. It would have been more decisive but for the lust of battle which seized our advancing troops, who followed the foe even through this curtain of fire, and fell victims, many of them, to our own shells. When the barrage lifted, the survivors were forced back by the

German counter-attack; but they still clung with unbroken spirit to sufficient lodgment in the wood from which to make fresh advance on the morrow. A fight as fierce as that in Trônes Wood raged for three whole days, while friend and foe crouched in shell-holes and shattered trench, or behind fallen tree trunks, to seize the first opportunity of rushing forward with bomb or bayonet to win a fresh foot of ground. Like many another stretch of woodland between these bastions of the German defence it became a place of stark death and terror. Some of its formidable defences were revealed on the closing day of the battle, when the last strongholds of the enemy, together with one heavy howitzer and three field guns were captured, as well as close upon 300 unwounded prisoners.

With Mametz and Trônes Woods practically mastered, we were at last in a position to undertake an assault upon the enemy's second system of defences; for all this isolated clearing of wood and copse, forming as they did the strong points in the continuous system of labyrinthine defences which guarded the whole country between the enemy's first and second lines, was but the preliminary to the next general advance. The systematic nature of the offensive since the beginning of July was recorded by Sir Douglas Haig on the 11th, when he wrote:—

"After ten days and nights of continuous fighting our troops have completed the methodical capture of the whole of the enemy's first system of defence on a front of 4,000 yards. This system of defence consisted of numerous and continuous lines of fire trenches, support trenches, and reserve trenches, extending to various depths of from 2000 yards to 4000 yards, and included five strongly-fortified villages, numerous heavily-wired and entrenched woods, and a large number of immensely strong redoubts.

"The capture of each of these trenches represented an operation of some importance, and the whole of them are now in our hands."

The grand attack on the enemy's second system was fixed for daybreak on July 14—the fête-day of France—when the assault was planned against a front extending from Longueval, facing Trônes Wood, to Bazentin-le-Petit Wood. Contalmaison Villa, on a spur 1000 yards west of Bazentin-le-Petit Wood, had already been captured to secure the left flank of the attack, and the guns had been moved forward for the preliminary bombardment, which began on July 11. For three days our artillery pounded the German second line with the thoroughness with which it had treated the first system in the closing days of June, warning friend and foe alike that a new stage in the battle was about to open. Though the Germans knew only too well what this warning of the guns foretold, they built their hopes on the long stretches of open country which for the most part lay between their elaborate defences and the advanced positions of the new British line. They were not prepared for the daring decision to overcome this difficulty with a night march, which brought the British infantry, in the small hours of July 14, over a distance of from 1000 to 1400 yards, and lined them up just below the crest of the intervening slope, some 300 to

500 yards from the enemy's trenches. It was a bold move, involving heavy risk of failure if discovered; but careful preparations had been made to ensure correct deployment, and strong patrols covered the advance itself.

"The whole movement", records Sir Douglas Haig, "was carried out unobserved and without touch being lost in any case. The decision to attempt a night operation of this magnitude, with an army, the bulk of which has been raised since the beginning of the war, was perhaps the highest tribute that could be paid to the quality of our troops. It would not have been possible but for the most careful preparation and forethought, as well as thorough reconnaissance of the ground, which was in many cases made personally by Divisional, Brigade, and Battalion Commanders and their staffs before framing their detailed orders for the advance."

The results stamped the whole operation as a masterly piece of generalship and organization. The ground to be attacked was first swept from end to end with a concentrated fire in the shape of a final bombardment of the most terrific intensity. Directed as it was against a much narrower front than on the eve of the first great attack, it was again the most tremendous spectacle of the kind ever witnessed. Big and little guns were conjoined in one deafening roar until, as someone present described it, "the earth trembled underfoot and the whole sky was lurid with great spouts and jets of flame". The "zero" hour at which our waiting troops were to deliver the actual assault was 3.25 a.m., when there was just sufficient light to enable our men to distinguish friend from foe at short range. At that moment the troops took the final

Drawn by H. W. Koekkoek

Heroes of Trônes Wood: the Royal West Kents, who held out for forty-eight hours against heavy odds, and were relieved on July 14, 1916

Drawn by R. Caton Woodville

The Pipers at Longueval: how the Highlanders were led into battle on July 14, 1916

plunge from their advanced positions, following the raging inferno of our shells as the barrage swept over the first of the opposing trenches and on to the defences beyond.

One of the first and most dramatic results was the rescue, in the northern corner of Trônes Wood, of some 170 of the Royal West Kents, who, "separated from our own troops in the recent fighting and surrounded by Germans", to quote from Sir Douglas Haig's *communiqué* at the time, in which he made one of his rare exceptions in mentioning the regiment by name, "had gallantly held out for forty-eight hours". Having driven the foe from his last foothold in this ghastly wood and finally consolidated it, the victors sent out strong patrols in the direction of Guillemont and Longueval—or "Long Valley", as Thomas Atkins preferred to call it—where, in the southern half of the latter village, they found the troops who had advanced west of Trônes Wood. Some famous Scottish regiments had played a lion's part in this advance, led on by their pipers; and half of Longueval was in our hands before Glasgow and London had finished breakfast. It had been bloody work among the charred ruins, with their masked machine-guns and their cellars packed with Germans fighting for their lives; but the conquerors, knowing the men they had to deal with, cleared up thoroughly as they went, and, with the reinforcements, had nearly the whole village in their possession by 4 p.m. Two German strongholds to the north of the village, however, still defied all efforts to take them.

In the meanwhile the rapidity of our advance in the centre had not only carried the village and wood of Bazentin-le-Grand but the neighbouring village of Bazentin-le-Petit, as well as the cemetery to the east. Two determined counter-attacks on our new positions were made about midday, but positions was gained without a mighty effort, but all along the line the well-planned blow had fallen with telling effect against the German centre, and brought the British troops, between Longueval and the Bazentins, within measurable distance of High Wood, or the Bois de Foureaux as it is called in

Belgian War Official

Awaiting their Opportunity: Indian cavalry behind the lines in the Somme Offensive

were immediately crushed by our fire. Later in the afternoon, after another fierce counter-attack, the enemy momentarily succeeded in occupying the northern half of Bazentin-le-Petit, but was driven out again by our infantry with heavy loss, leaving the whole village once more in our hands. Bazentin-le-Petit Wood on the left was also cleared, notwithstanding the desperate efforts of the Germans to resist our impetuous advance. None of these the French maps. Once in our possession, with its protecting strongholds swept away, this commanding position on the Bazentin ridge, which overlooked the enemy's lines as far as Bapaume, would seriously threaten his third system of defence.

So severely had the Germans been handled in these attacks and counter-attacks that they began to show signs of disorganization. It was reported early in the afternoon of this memorable 14th of July, while France's Day was being celebrated in Great Britain, and Allied troops were passing in procession through cheering multitudes of Frenchmen and Frenchwomen in Paris, that it was possible to crown the earlier successes with an advance to High Wood. Sir Douglas Haig tells us in his dispatch how General Rawlinson, who had held a force of cavalry in readiness for such an eventuality, decided that the time had at length arrived to employ a part of it at least. It was the first opportunity for mounted action on the British front since 1914, though some of the French cavalry were seen in their legitimate rôle in an isolated part of the Champagne offensive in 1915. Some Indian as well as British cavalry took part in this eagerly awaited operation, burning to prove that the *arme blanche* had not forgotten its art in the dreary business of siege warfare. As the infantry pushed up towards High Wood in this adventurous advance small bodies of cavalry were moved forward gradually, keeping in close touch with the development of the action, and prepared to take full advantage of every chance that presented itself. It was a squadron of Dragoon Guards which earned the proud distinction of special mention in Sir Douglas Haig's daily reports from Head-quarters for having successfully accounted for a detachment of the enemy during the advance, killing sixteen, it was afterwards reported, and capturing thirty-four men. The squadron came up on the flanks of the infantry, who, entering High Wood at about 8 p.m., fought their way through after fierce hand-to-hand fighting, and cleared the whole of the wood save its strongly fortified northern apex. The new advance had forced the enemy back at this point to his third system of defence, more than four miles in rear of his original front trenches at Mametz.

Altogether it had been a day of great achievement and greater promise. The news of its successes added lustre to the celebration of the French National Fête in Paris, and formed a fitting accompaniment to the British army's good wishes on that occasion.

"The British army," telegraphed Sir Douglas Haig that morning to President Poincaré, "fighting side by side with the brave soldiers of France in the bitter struggle now proceeding, expresses on this great anniversary its admiration for the results achieved by the French army, and its unshakable faith in the speedy realization of our common hopes."

To which the President replied:—

"I thank you, my dear General, for the good wishes which you have expressed towards France, and beg you to convey to the gallant British army my great admiration of the fine successes which it has just achieved and which only this morning have been so brilliantly extended. They have produced a profound impression on the hearts of all Frenchmen. Those of your magnificent troops who have to-day marched through the streets of Paris, in company with those of our Allies, received throughout a striking proof of the public sentiment. I am glad to have this opportunity of sending you—to you personally and to your troops—my hearty congratulations."

That day we had captured a further 2000 prisoners, including a regimental commander of the 3rd Guards Division, bringing the total number of prisoners taken by the British since the beginning of the battle to over 10,000. Large quantities of war material had also fallen into our hands, the total number of guns up to July 15 including 8 heavy howitzers, 4 heavy guns, 42 field and light guns and field howitzers, 30 trench-mortars, and 52 machine-guns. These figures are exclusive of many guns destroyed by our artillery bombardment and abandoned by the enemy.

The enemy, however, though dangerously shaken, had now, owing to the great strength and depth of his defences, succeeded in bringing up sufficient reinforcements to check our threatening advance by holding the many powerful fortifications, alike in trenches, villages, and woods, to which he still clung, both on our front and on our flanks. High Wood, lying over the crest of the hill, was held by our advanced troops at heavy cost, as the Germans had the range to an inch, and bombarded our positions over the heads of their own men, who still held the northern edge of the wood. On the night of July 15–16, therefore, the position of the British troops at this point becoming precarious, orders were given for their withdrawal. This movement was effected before daybreak without interruption by the enemy. All the wounded were brought in, and the line straightened out from Longueval to Bazentin-le-Petit village, whence it swung back in undulating irregularities through Contalmaison and Bailiff's Wood towards Ovillers-La Boisselle. This last was the village fortress where, after days and nights of some of the hardest and closest fighting since July 7, when a footing was gained in its outer defences, the struggle had resolved itself into a regular siege, in which many men died for every yard of earthwork gained.

In the centre the battle for the second German system continued throughout the 15th, though on a reduced scale. Against the loss of High Wood, which brought the day's fighting to a close, was to be set the capture of Arrow Head Copse, between the southern edge of Trônes Wood and Guillemont; the strongly-defended position of Waterlot Farm on the Longueval-Guillemont road; and, more important still, the whole of Delville Wood, after one of the most sanguinary fights of the day, followed by a strong counter-attack on the part of the enemy to regain it. It was here that the South Africans won their first laurels on the Western front, carrying the dense defences of the Germans with a dash and determination nobly upholding the high reputation which they had already won in South-West Africa, as well as in the Egyptian desert.

Our airmen, as usual, rendered invaluable assistance, though much hampered at this period by unfavourable weather. In one of their bombing raids this day they derailed an enemy train, overturning a coach, while in aerial combats their bag, officially recorded from British Headquarters, included three Fokkers, three biplanes, and a double-engined aeroplane—all destroyed—while another Fokker was forced to land in a damaged condition. On the other hand, "all our machines', to quote from the official report for the same day, "returned safely to our own lines". No more conclusive evidence was needed to prove how completely our airmen at this period had established their supremacy in the air.

All this while a bitter struggle was raging in Longueval for the possession of the two vital points still held by the enemy in that pulverized village, as well as for the orchards to the north of it; while away to the left, at the northern end of the offensive front, other British troops were creeping up towards Pozières—one of the fortified villages along the Albert-Bapaume road—some from the south, others along the enemy's main second-line trenches north-west of Bazentin-le-Petit Wood. From this last direction they had reached to within 500 yards of the north-west corner of the village, which served, with its formidable defence works, as a sort of outpost of the enemy's main second-line system, which ran behind it.

Farther north, the protracted struggle for Ovillers-La Boisselle reached its climax on July 16–17. In accordance with Sir Douglas Haig's instructions to General Sir Hubert Gough, who commanded along this front, the enemy both in and about the village had been pressed relentlessly, and gradually driven back by incessant bombing attacks and local assaults. Sir Douglas paid a well-earned tribute to a doughty foe at this point when, on July 17, he telegraphed that after continuous hand-to-hand fighting we had captured the remaining strongholds of the enemy, "together with 2 officers and 124 Guardsmen, who formed the remnants of its brave garrison". The whole village, he recorded, was now in our hands; to which we would add an equally merited tribute to the gallant Midland County regiments who captured the place, as well as those other battalions who had isolated the garrison and suffered heroically in helping to seal its fate before they were relieved. Many captured documents bore witness to the undreamt-of hardships and sufferings of the German troops since the Allied offensive began, but none revealed their heavy casualties so eloquently as the following, published at this date by the British Commander-in-Chief:—

"From a company of the 16th Bavarian Infantry Regiment to 3rd Battalion 16th Bavarian Infantry: 'Severe enemy artillery fire of all calibres up to 28 cm. on company sector. Company strength, one officer, twelve men. Beg urgently speedy relief for the company. What remains of the company is so exhausted that in case of an attack by the enemy the few totally exhausted men cannot be counted on.'

"From 2nd Battalion to 3rd Battalion 16th Bavarian Infantry Regiment: 'The battalion has just received orders from Lieutenant-Colonel Kumme that it is placed under orders of the 3rd Battalion 16th Bavarian Regiment as sector reserve. Battalion consists at present time of three officers, two non-commissioned officers, and nineteen men.'"

The operations of July 14 and three following days, which gave us possession of the southern crest of the main plateau between Delville Wood and Bazentin-le-Petit, had rounded off the opening attack of July 1, and completed what Sir Douglas Haig describes as the first phase of the Somme battle.

"We then entered upon a contest", he writes in his dispatch, "lasting for many weeks, during which the enemy, having found his strongest defences unavailing, and now fully alive to his danger, put forth his utmost efforts to keep his hold on the main ridge. This stage of the battle constituted a prolonged and severe struggle for mastery between the contending armies, in which, although progress was slow and difficult, the confidence of our troops in their ability to win was never shaken."

The close of the first phase found us in possession of the enemy's second main system of defence on a front of over three miles, and our new line was definitely established from Maltz Horn Farm—an important point on the spur north of Hardecourt, secured by us on July 9—where we now linked up with the French left, northwards along the eastern edge of Trônes Wood to Longueval, then onwards past Bazentin-le-Grand to the northern corner of Bazentin-le-Petit and Bazentin-le-Petit Wood, and westwards again past the southern face of Pozières to the north of Ovillers. Posts were established at Waterlot Farm and Arrow Head Copse above and below the road between Trônes Wood and Guillemont; and troops were thrown forward both in Deville Wood and towards High Wood, though they had yet to make their positions secure.

High praise is bestowed by Sir Douglas Haig for "the skill, daring, endurance, and determination" displayed in the operations which had yielded the last results. "Great credit", he writes, "is due to Sir Henry Rawlinson for the thoroughness and care with which this difficult undertaking was planned; while the advance and deployment made by night without confusion, and the con-

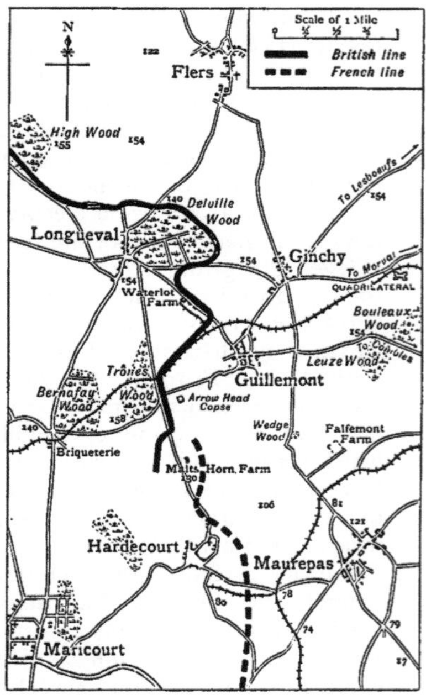


Where the Allies joined Forces: map showing the approximate positions of the British right wing and the French left at their junction at the close of July, 1916

plete success of the subsequent attack, constitute a striking tribute to the discipline and spirit of the troops engaged, as well as to the powers of leadership and organization of their commanders and staffs." This successful completion of the first phase of the battle was marked by a further message of appreciation from His Majesty, between whom and Sir Douglas Haig the following messages now passed:—

FROM THE KING TO GENERAL SIR DOUGLAS HAIG, *July 16*

The continued successful advance of my troops fills me with admiration, and I send my best wishes to all ranks.

The Emperor of Russia has asked me to convey his warm congratulations to the troops upon the great success they have achieved.

GEORGE R.I.

FROM GENERAL SIR DOUGLAS HAIG TO THE KING, *July 17*

The British Armies in France offer most respectful and grateful thanks for this further mark of your Majesty's gracious appreciation of what they have achieved.

They also respectfully beg that their grateful acknowledgments may be conveyed to the Emperor of Russia for his Majesty's congratulations.

DOUGLAS HAIG.

## SECOND PHASE OF THE BATTLE

With evidence visible on every hand that these successes, and those of the French on our right, had considerably shaken the enemy on the battle-front, the Allies were naturally eager to complete his discomfiture with another smashing blow as quickly as possible. Unfortunately, though we had secured a footing on the main ridge, it was only on a front of 6000 yards, and, as Sir Douglas Haig points out, it was first necessary to widen this. For sound strategical reasons it was decided to attempt this on the right rather than on the left flank, where the fortress-villages of Pozières and Thiepval still blocked the way, together with the whole elaborate maze of entrenchments which not only surrounded them, but extended between and on the main ridge behind them. Sir Douglas Haig therefore ordered a continuance of the grim, methodical, step-by-step advance which had been in progress since Sir Hubert Gough took over this portion of the front, knowing that the stubborn defences must eventually be turned by an advance farther east. An advance on the right flank, indeed, was essential, not only to extend our footing on the main ridge, but also to straighten out the dangerous salient which had been created in our lines round Longueval and Delville Wood. The situation at this point, inviting counter-attacks by the enemy on three sides, called for immediate attention. The right flank of the British front swept backwards from Delville Wood towards Maltz Horn Farm, where it came in touch with the French, who continued the Allied front still southwards to the village of Hem, on the Somme, which they had captured on July 5. The French territorial gains had hitherto been greatest on the south of the Somme, where their left wing was continually advancing, clearing up the interior of the angle of the Somme, and thus covering the right of the troops attacking to the north of the river. Here, following the capture of Hem, the French on July 8, while the British were establishing themselves in the southern end of Trônes Wood, had carried the village of Hardecourt, thence pushing up to its junction with the British at Maltz Horn Farm.

When Sir Douglas Haig determined to straighten out the pronounced salient at Delville Wood and Longueval by swinging up his right flank from Maltz Horn Farm with the object of capturing first Guillemont, Falfemont Farm, and Leuze Wood, and then Ginchy and Bouleaux Wood, it was essential that the French on his right should make a simultaneous movement in the closest co-operation with the British troops. This was accordingly arranged, the line of demarcation agreed upon between Sir Douglas Haig and General Foch running due eastwards to the Combles valley, and then north-eastwards up that valley to a point midway between Sailly-Saillisel and Morval—the two villages fixed upon as the objectives respectively of the French left and the British right.

British Official

**Longueval after the British Occupation, July, 1916: a look-out from one of the strongholds captured by the Scottish troops**

The task confronting the Allies was indescribably difficult, entailing, as Sir Douglas Haig remarks, "a real trial of strength between the opposing forces". He also pointed out how seriously they were handicapped at this juncture by the unfavourable weather. There was not only more than the average allowance of rain both in July and August; but even when no rain fell there was an almost constant haze, and low clouds were all too frequent:

"The nature of the ground", he writes, "limited the possibility of direct observation

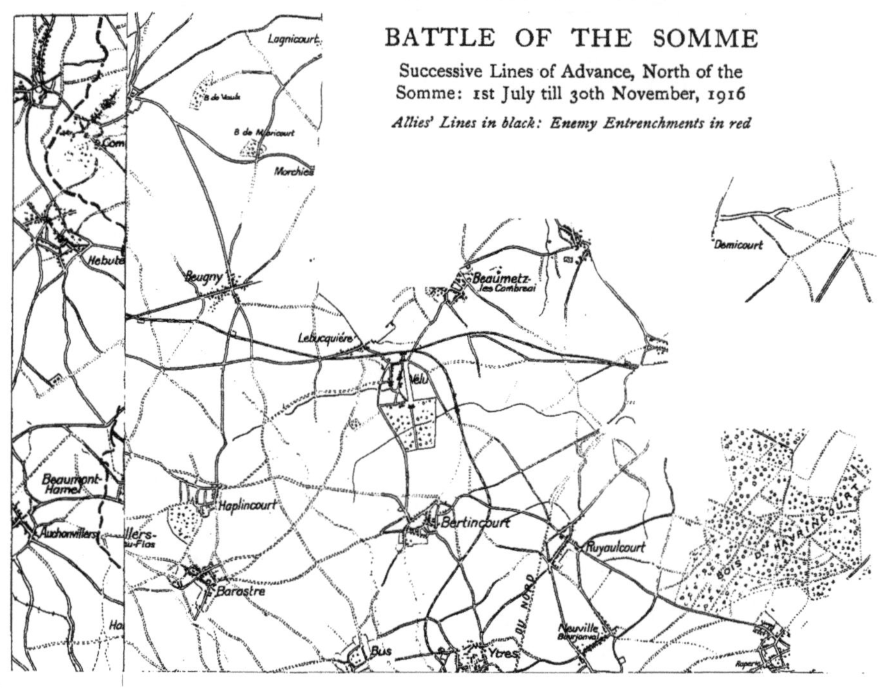


BATTLE OF THE SOMME

Successive Lines of Advance, North of the Somme: 1st July till 30th November, 1916

*Allies' Lines in black: Enemy Entrenchments in red*

by artillery fire, and we were consequently much dependent on observation from the air. As in that element we had obtained almost complete superiority, all that we required was a clear atmosphere; but with this we were not favoured for several weeks."

There was now no longer any possibility of taking by surprise an enemy who had brought up enormous numbers of fresh troops and was prepared for every emergency, as well as burning to avenge the irreplaceable losses inflicted on his ranks. Quick to seize advantage of every weakness, he was as conscious as ourselves of the precarious position of that sharp salient in our line round Longueval and Del-
Wood. Possessing direct obser-
n it all round, from Guillemont
outh-east to High Wood on
east, and knowing every foot
two years' occupation he
a concentric fire of artillery
t only on the wood and
lso on the confined space
e both the French and
nications ran, and great
uns, ammunition, and
f all sorts had neces-
wded together. Obvi-
that if only he could
ient, and so gain direct
the ground behind, the
e whole Allied position
tremely uncomfortable.
ir Douglas Haig, 'there
d grounds for confidence
as not capable of dving
troops who had shown
wrest it from him. the
ve been an anxious one.
s clear that the first re-
ment was that our right
nch troops in extension
of it, should swing up into line with our centre."

Before this could be done, however, communications had to be improved, guns brought forward, tired troops relieved, and fresh dispositions of troops completed; and meantime the Germans, recovering from the shock and confusion of our previous onslaughts, delivered their expected counter-attack against Delville Wood. This was on July 18, when, after an intense bombardment, they forced their way through the northern and north-eastern portion of the wood, and into the northern half of Longueval, which our troops had cleared only that morning. It was subsequently established that the assault, which extended over a front of some 2000 yards, was delivered by at least thirteen battalions, drawn from four divisions, and that their losses were correspondingly great. The brunt of the battle fell on those heroic Scotsmen who, as already mentioned, had carried the battered ruins of Longueval on July 14, and the equally gallant South Africans, who passed through them on the following day to clear out the hornets' nest in Delville Wood. Wood and village here practically merged in one, and in the hurriedly-made reserve line which stemmed the Teutonic flood in the great counter-attack Scotsmen and South Africans fought and fell in places side by side. These battle-worn British troops not only held the line, but flung the Germans back, and though the remainder of the Delville Wood was not wholly recovered until the 27th, and the

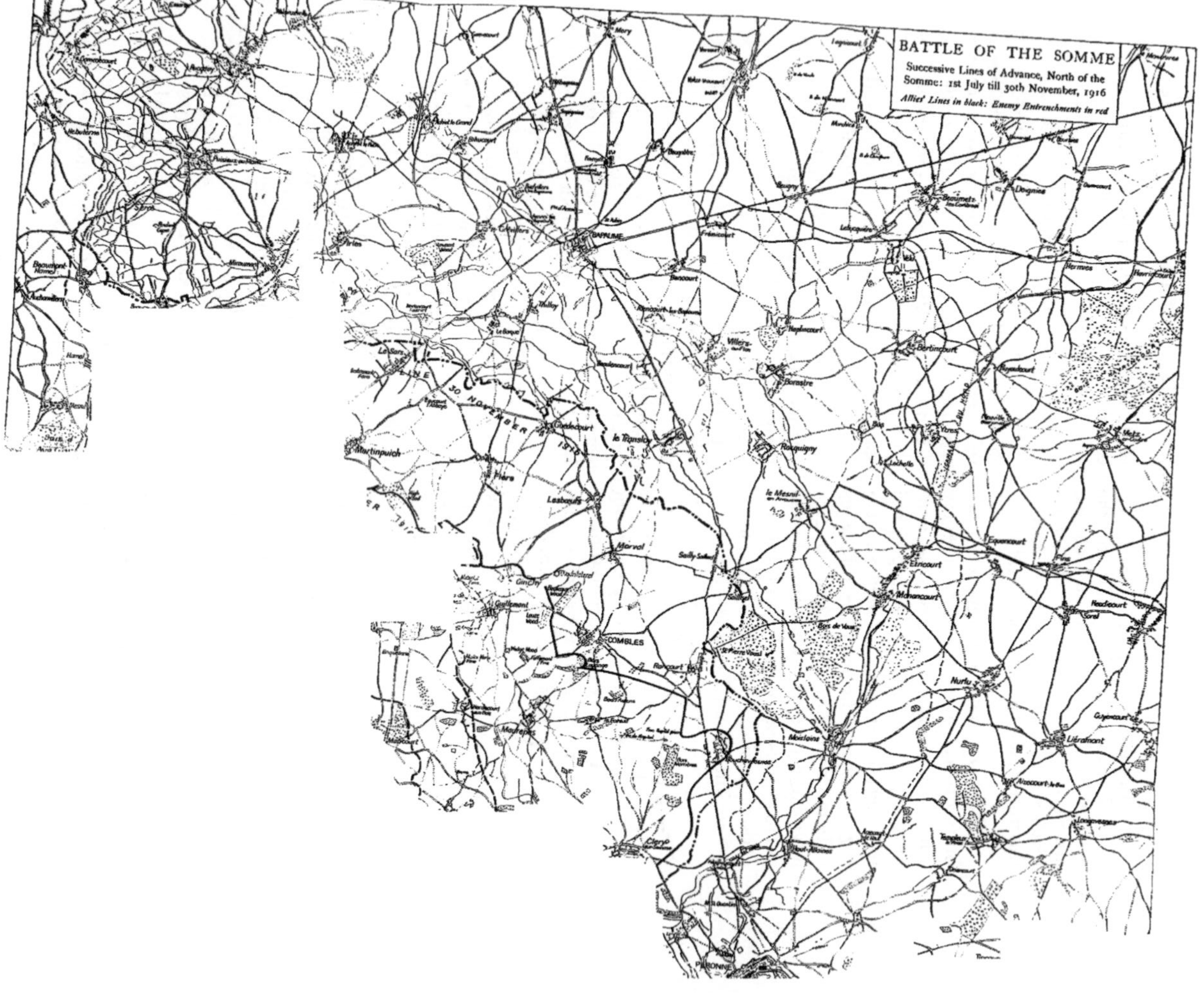

BATTLE OF THE SOMME
Successive Lines of Advance, North of the Somme: 1st July till 30th November, 1916
Allies' Lines in black: Enemy Entrenchments in red
BAPAUME
COMBLES
LINE 30 NOVEMBER 1916
Martinpuich
Flers
Lesboeufs
Morval
Gueudecourt
le Transloy
Rocquigny
Barastre
Bertincourt
Ytres
Equancourt
Etricourt
Manancourt
Nurlu
Moislains
Liéramont
Hermies
Doignies
Guillemont
Sailly-Saillisel
le Mesnil

by artillery fire, and we were consequently much dependent on observation from the air. As in that element we had obtained almost complete superiority, all that we required was a clear atmosphere; but with this we were not favoured for several weeks."

There was now no longer any possibility of taking by surprise an enemy who had brought up enormous numbers of fresh troops and was prepared for every emergency, as well as burning to avenge the irreplaceable losses inflicted on his ranks. Quick to seize advantage of every weakness, he was as conscious as ourselves of the precarious position of that sharp salient in our line round Longueval and Delville Wood. Possessing direct observation on it all round, from Guillemont on the south-east to High Wood on the north-east, and knowing every foot of it from two years' occupation, he could bring a concentric fire of artillery to bear, not only on the wood and village, but also on the confined space behind, where both the French and British communications ran, and great numbers of guns, ammunition, and war material of all sorts had necessarily to be crowded together. Obviously he knew that if only he could drive in this salient, and so gain direct observation on the ground behind, he could make the whole Allied position in that area extremely uncomfortable.

"If", writes Sir Douglas Haig, "there had not been good grounds for confidence that the enemy was not capable of driving from this position troops who had shown themselves able to wrest it from him, the situation would have been an anxious one. In any case it was clear that the first requirement at the moment was that our right flank, and the French troops in extension of it, should swing up into line with our centre."

Before this could be done, however, communications had to be improved, guns brought forward, tired troops relieved, and fresh dispositions of troops completed; and meantime the Germans, recovering from the shock and confusion of our previous onslaughts, delivered their expected counter-attack against Delville Wood. This was on July 18, when, after an intense bombardment, they forced their way through the northern and north-eastern portion of the wood, and into the northern half of Longueval, which our troops had cleared only that morning. It was subsequently established that the assault, which extended over a front of some 2000 yards, was delivered by at least thirteen battalions, drawn from four divisions, and that their losses were correspondingly great. The brunt of the battle fell on those heroic Scotsmen who, as already mentioned, had carried the battered ruins of Longueval on July 14, and the equally gallant South Africans, who passed through them on the following day to clear out the hornets' nest in Delville Wood. Wood and village here practically merged in one, and in the hurriedly-made reserve line which stemmed the Teutonic flood in the great counter-attack Scotsmen and South Africans fought and fell in places side by side. These battle-worn British troops not only held the line, but flung the Germans back, and though the remainder of the Delville Wood was not wholly recovered until the 27th, and the

Drawn by Frank Dadd, R.I.

Heroes of Delville Wood: the glorious defence of the South Africans in July, 1916

northern portion of Longueval and the orchards two days later, their dauntless stand at this vital point was a feat of arms of incalculable value to the Allied cause. An officer of the British Head-quarters Staff, whose son fell with the South Africans in these critical operations, and who visited Delville Wood shortly afterwards to obtain what information he could on the subject, sent home a vivid account—in a letter published in the *Times*—of the splendid gallantry of the South Africans throughout. "Use this letter as you like," he wrote, "in order to let the world know what the South Africans did"; and we cannot do better than tell the story in his own moving words:—

"The dead are lying in Delville Wood, still unburied when I was there (because burial was impossible under the fire going on). Men lie in layers. The South African heroes lie underneath. I wonder whether history will do them justice. Will it tell how, ordered to take and hold the wood at all costs, they took it—and then began one of the most heroic defences known in the history of war? For three days they were subjected to continuous bombardment by guns of all calibres. They held on with very little food or water. Over and over again they were attacked by overwhelming enemy forces. The gallant fellows fell fast under the terrific bombardment and attacks, but not a man wavered.

"Finding them immovable, the Germans at last, on the 18th, concentrated a terrible bombardment for seven hours on what was left of these splendid men, and then about 5 or 6 p.m. launched an attack by three regiments, on the survivors. The front trench was attacked in front and on each flank. My son's trench was attacked from back and front. Our gallant, splendid men, reduced to a mere skeleton of what they were, beat back the Brandenburgers. It was during this awful time that my dear boy fell. They died, our noble South Africans, but they held the wood! Thank God, they held the wood! and thank God they kept up the traditions of our race! And my splendid boy helped. He took no inconsiderable part either.

"I want our South Africans to get the credit they deserve. If you have any friends who can spread the news of what they did, let it be told. I resign my dear son, who was very, very dear to me, into the safe keeping of my Maker, who gave him to me. It is very hard to part with him, but I glory in his glorious end, my splendid chivalrous boy; and if his example inspires others he will not have died in vain."

Our front was strengthened and our hold on the main ridge west of Delville Wood secured on July 20 by an advance in that direction, which gave us a new footing in High Wood, linking up our line with Longueval. Regiments from the Western Counties were among those who measured their strength against the flower of the German army in these encounters, and with a dogged courage which gradually gave them the upper hand worthily maintained the best traditions of the British army.

The great German counter-attack, which began on July 18, marked the beginning of the long, closely-contested struggle, which was not finally decided in our favour until the fall of Guillemont on September 3, and became known as the Battle of the Woods. Mametz, Bailiff, and Trônes Woods, as well as many of the smaller strips of woodland which the Germans had so cunningly included in their defences, had already accustomed our troops to the savage warfare involved in every hand-to-hand fight for their possession. Each wood was a chaos of obstacles, ploughed by shells, strewn with fallen timber, and defended not only by its own dense undergrowth, but also by barbed-wire entanglements among the trees, entrenchments bristling with machine-guns, strong redoubts at all advantageous points, and dug-outs so deep and capacious that one of them was found capable of quartering a whole company of infantry. The fighting which took place in these woods was terrible enough in broad daylight; at night-time it was dreadful beyond words. It was amazing testimony to the valour and superiority of our troops that one after another they cleared these death-traps of an enemy who held them in strength and had spent nearly two years in improving their defences. They could never have done it if, man for man, the Germans had been any match for them.

Progress, nevertheless, as Sir Douglas Haig freely confesses, was slow, and bought only by hard fighting. Three days after the fresh foothold was established in High Wood on July 20, and the line linked up thence to Longueval, the Fourth Army advanced on the whole front from Guillemont to near Pozières; but the enemy, who meantime had been feverishly digging new trenches in advance of his main defences, and held these, as well as every available shell-hole, with forward troops and machine-guns, was everywhere found in immense strength. From end to end of the battle-front the struggle (which began in the early morning after a heavy bombardment) swayed backwards and forwards with a fury which baffles description. Twice the outskirts of Guillemont, round which the Germans had erected the most formidable defences, changed hands, and the day closed with the conflict still undecided. Similarly the enemy was flung in the morning from his remaining strongholds in Longueval, but later in the day regained the northern end of the village. All round the northern areas of Longueval and Delville and High Woods his positions proved for the time impregnable. Although ground was won both here and elsewhere along the line, "the strength of the resistance experienced", to quote from Sir Douglas Haig's dispatch, "showed that the hostile troops had recovered from their previous confusion sufficiently to necessitate long and careful preparation before further successes on any great scale could be secured".

On the left there was compensation for this disappointment in the brilliant success of the simultaneous assault by General Gough's army against Pozières. The honour of attacking the village itself fell to the Australians, with certain British Territorial regiments working up on their left. For days and nights these troops had stood the strain of heavy shelling that never ceased—British shells that screamed overhead and German shells that crashed all round them—and when at length, shortly after midnight of July 22–23, our own torrent of artillery-fire suddenly lifted from the first German lines and turned on the defences behind, they had to stumble in the darkness across more than 500 yards of shell-holes and shattered uplands, through shrapnel, high explosives, and machine-gun fire. Yet nothing daunted these splendid troops. The Territorials, advancing from the south-west, carried the German outer works to the left and pushed up on the farther side of the Albert-Bapaume Road; while the Australians, carrying one advance trench after another, swept onwards through the outlying woods of Pozières into the heart of the village itself. Here the Germans, taking advantage of every ruin, rubbish-heap, and dug-out—for little else remained in this abomination of desolation—and fully equipped at every point with the inevitable machine-gun, offered a resistance which nothing but the bull-dog tenacity of the attackers seemed ever likely to crush. It was the same tenacity which enabled the Australians to hold on to their captured portion of the village through days and nights of bombardment from the German guns on neighbouring heights. This luckless village, reeking with the ceaseless deluge of shells, became the sight of the battle-field for miles round.

British Official

The Scene of an Australian Triumph: Pozières after its capture by the Commonwealth troops

"Now", wrote the official correspondent of the High Commissioner for Australia, who was present at the time, "the enemy would send then crashing in on a line south of the road—eight heavy shells at a time, minute after minute, followed up by burst upon burst of shrapnel. Now he would place a curtain straight across this valley or that, till the sky and landscape were blotted out, except for fleeting glimpses seen as through a lift of fog. Gas shell, musty with chloroform, sweet-scented tear

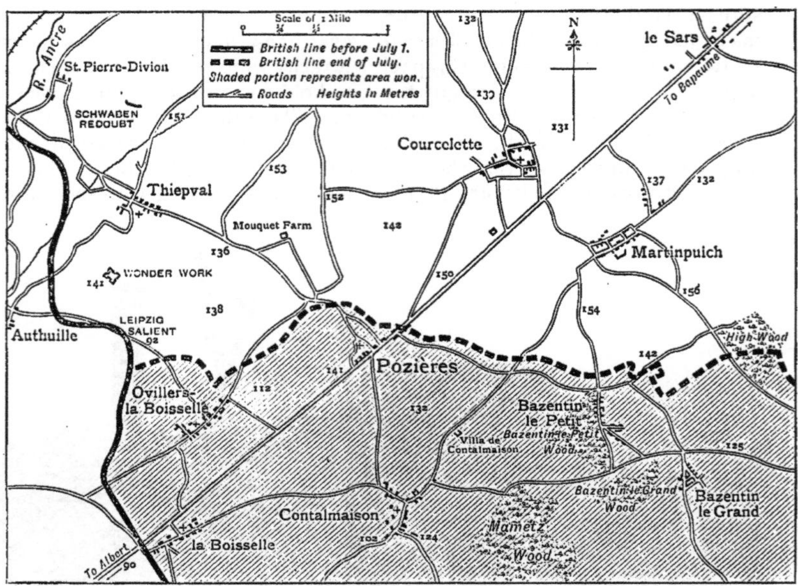


Winning the Ridge in the Centre of the British Battle-field: map showing approximately the position of the British line at the end of July, 1916

shell that made your eyes run with water, high bursting shrapnel, with black smoke and a vicious high-explosive rattle behind its heavy pellets, ugly green bursts the colour of a fat silkworm, huge black clouds from the high-explosive of his five-point-nines. Day and night the men worked through it, fighting this horrid machinery far over the horizon as if they were fighting Germans hand to hand—building up whatever it battered down; buried some of them not once but again and again and again...."

Small wonder that the famous division of British troops on their flank sent them a message to say that they were proud to fight by the side of them. Not until the morning of the 26th was Sir Douglas Haig able to report that the whole of Pozières was at length in our hands. On the evening of the 25th the Australians, who had been steadily fighting their way through the ruins foot by foot, sealed its fate by capturing the main German trench below the cemetery, in the north, where a bunch of prisoners, including two battalion commanders, was captured, together with some machine-guns. The Territorials had meantime been making excellent progress on the left, effecting a junction with the Australians on the 25th at the top of the village. When on the following day the Australians captured the last corner of the place the same Territorials made a further advance, taking two strong trenches, and adding to their bag five officers and a number of other prisoners.

This and much other heroism was rewarded in a notable Honours List published in the following September in the *London Gazette*, when no fewer than twenty new V.C.'s were announced. Five of these fell to the Australian infantry, headed by Second-Lieutenant A. Seaforth Blackburn, who, by sheer dogged determination, captured one of the enemy's strongest points, after personally leading against it four separate parties of bombers, many of whom became casualties. Nothing daunted he first seized 250 yards of the enemy's trench, and then, after crawling forward with a sergeant to reconnoitre, returned, attacked again, and by capturing another 120 yards of trench, succeeded in establishing communication with the battalion on his left. In one assault, when the German bombs were outranging ours, Private John Leak saved the situation by fearlessly leaping from the trench and, after rushing forward under heavy machine-gun fire at close range, throwing three bombs into the enemy's post. It was little short of a miracle that he passed through that storm of fire unscathed. Having done so he jumped into the enemy's position, and clinched matters by bayoneting three unwounded German bombers. Later, however, the enemy returned to the attack in overwhelming numbers, and began driving the small band of Australians back; but Private Leak was always the last to withdraw at each stage, covering

British Official

Back from Pozières: Australian machine-gunners returning from the trenches the retirement by most effective bomb-throwing. "His courage and energy", says the *Gazette* in announcing his award of the Victoria Cross, "had such an effect on the enemy that, on the arrival of reinforcements, the whole trench was recaptured."

The same utter contempt of danger was displayed repeatedly by Privates William Jackson and Martin O'Meara in the gallant work of rescue—Jackson returning to find two wounded comrades after his own arm had been blown off by a shell—and was similarly rewarded; but the supreme example of Australian courage and devotion to duty was reserved for Private Thomas Cooke, who, in adding his name to this list of heroes, sacrificed his life. Private Cooke had been ordered to take his Lewis gun and gun-team to a dangerous part of the line, and continued to do splendid work though one after another of his comrades fell dead or wounded. At length he was the only man left, but he still stuck to his post, continuing to fire on the enemy; and later was found dead beside his gun.

While General Gough's army was clearing up the ground thus thoroughly at Pozières, the Germans strove to avenge this loss on the evening of the 25th with two powerful attacks against our new positions in and around High Wood, and Delville Wood. "Both attacks", writes Sir Douglas Haig tersely, "were completely broken up with heavy losses to the enemy." Two days later, as already mentioned, we turned the tables by recovering the remainder of Delville Wood — or "The Devil's Wood", as it was not inaptly called by our soldiers — supplementing this on the 29th with the recapture of the whole of Longueval, as well as the fortified orchards on the outskirts. The success in the Devil's Wood was again achieved over the proud Brandenburg Grenadiers, "of Douaumont's glorious fame", as the official Berlin report had it when announcing their temporary success at this point; and their defeat was effectively confirmed in the two counter-attacks in which they strove in vain to recover their lost ground. Three officers and 158 men were captured in this crushing defeat of the Brandenburgers, and two or three whole regiments, as officially reported from British Headquarters on July 29, "appear to have been annihilated". The ghastly wood had become little more than a great open grave of unburied dead.

On the following day, July 30—a day of sweltering heat, with a summer haze at times which made artillery observation difficult—a fresh attack was launched, in co-operation with the French on our right wing, against the stubbornly-defended village of Guillemont and Falfemont Farm, one of the enemy's strongholds lying just to the east of Maltz Horn Farm, where, as already mentioned, the Allies joined forces. A day of arduous battle began in the early hours, after the usual bombardment, and found the enemy, who evidently expected us, and was said to have massed from ten to twelve battalions along a front of some 2000 yards, fully prepared to meet us at every possible point of attack. One of our battalions succeeded in fighting its way right into the village, part of it pushing through to the far side; but, unhappily, the supporting battalions on either flank found it impossible to reach their objectives. Machine-gun positions faced them everywhere, the attacking troops also suffering heavily from the German artillery-fire, which could be concentrated on this area at any given spot at the shortest notice. After holding out most gallantly for some hours on the western edge of the village, the survivors of the British regiment in Guillemont were compelled to fall back. The enemy, however, had also suffered severely, and some 200 prisoners were added to our total bag.

In the meantime the French, attacking from Hill 139, by Maltz Horn Farm, as far as the Somme, also took over 200 prisoners, together with the outskirts of the village of Maurepas and the whole system of enemy trenches for a depth varying from about 300 to 800 metres. The following days were spent in improving the Allies' positions, the broiling heat and tiring roads, ankle deep in dust, adding to the hardships of a task which increased in difficulty with every fresh advance in this troublesome sector of the battle-front. Experience having proved how completely the ground to the south of Guillemont was dominated by the German positions in and about that village, it was now hoped to capture these positions first, before pushing farther forward in the direction of Falfemont Farm. A local attack was therefore made on August 7, when our troops again fought their way into Guillemont, only to have to fall back again from the same cause as before —the failure of the supporting attacks against the enemy's trenches on the flanks of the village.

Well aware how Guillemont blocked the path of the Allies at their point of union, the enemy had expended every ounce of his energy in making it, according to all the theories of war, absolutely impregnable, strengthening its defences at every turn, and crowding an extraordinary number of machine-guns in emplacements for enfilade fire. It would probably have remained impregnable if the Allies had not proved themselves superior to all the German theories of defence; and even Sir Douglas Haig was forced to admit that it had now become evident that Guillemont could not be captured as an isolated enterprise. But there were more ways than one of taking it. The method adopted was a series of combined assaults with the French Army on our right, to be delivered in successive stages, embracing not only Guillemont, but also Maurepas, Falfemont Farm, Leuze Wood, and Ginchy. The first Allied attempt to carry out the opening phase of the operation (on August 16) was only partially successful, but we pushed our line slightly forward to the west of Guillemont, while the French made appreciable progress to the south-west, both above and below Maurepas.

The net was drawn still tighter two days later, when we gained more ground both towards Ginchy and Guillemont, and captured over 200 prisoners, while the French, who accounted for about the same number of captives, carried most of the village of Maurepas in the course of a brilliant assault which greatly strengthened the Allies' line. Desperate efforts were now made to repel us in a succession of violent counter-attacks—one of which, as Sir Douglas admits, suc-mark or trace of its former self. Its site was only located by some smashed railway trucks. Progress through these desolate regions, with the Germans clinging to every dug-out and redoubt with grim tenacity, was necessarily slow. On the night of August 23, after a severe bombardment, which

British Official

A Storm Centre of the British Right: all that remained of Guillemont station after its final capture by the Irish troops

ceeded for a time in forcing the French and ourselves back at the point of junction between the Allied armies—but steady progress continued, the British troops establishing themselves in the outskirts of Guillemont village, and occupying Guillemont station. This was now a station in name only, battered by the guns to a mere heap of rubble, and like the village itself, levelled to the surrounding mass of tortured earth, with scarcely a land-

began at 8.45 p.m., they made another infuriated attempt to fling us back from Guillemont station, pressing their infantry assault with such strength and determination that in places it reached our parapets. Here a short, sharp struggle ended in the enemy's complete repulse, with heavy losses. More and more precarious became the enemy's foothold on this high ground about both Guillemont and Ginchy, as the Allies steadily improved their surrounding positions, further important progress being made on the 24th with a fresh British advance on a wide front north and east of Delville Wood. Both villages were now, however, left to the fate awaiting them in the new general assault planned for the early days of September.

While this long, stern struggle for the mastery was in progress at the Guillemont end of the British line, and the French were finally clearing the last Boche out of Maurepas, fierce and obstinate fighting of a local character had been in progress all along the fronts of both the British armies. No general "push" had been attempted during August, but by dint of ceaseless enterprise in bombing, sapping, and bayonet work many gains had been made which, though small in themselves, represented in the aggregate, as Sir Douglas Haig testified, very considerable advances.

"In this way", he writes, "our line was brought to the crest of the ridge above Martinpuich, and Pozières Windmill and the high ground north of the village were secured, and with them observation over the enemy's gun positions in their neighbourhood and round Le Sars."

Therein lies hidden another epic of Anzac and British heroism, the capture of the German main second-line system north of Pozières having been carried on the night of August 4–5, as Sir Douglas announced at the time in his daily reports from General Headquarters, by the Australians and New Army troops from Kent, Surrey, and Sussex. The full story of that gallant fight for the ridge which rolled down at this point to the Promised Land below, has yet to be told, but it is one in which all ranks and all the regiments concerned covered themselves with glory. They carried the whole second-line system on a front of over 2000 yards, captured several hundred prisoners—mostly of the crack 11th Prussian Corps—and held on in the face of repeated endeavours to retrieve the loss. It was a fitting prelude to the solemn services held at various points along the British front on August 6 to commemorate our entry into the third year of the war, and in tune with the inspiring message delivered to all the troops of the Church of England on that occasion by Bishop Gwynne, the Deputy Chaplain-General:—

"English, Welsh, Scotch, Irish, Canadians, Australians, men of New Zealand, Newfoundland, Africa, and India—once more look straight between the eyes the bigness of our task, once more see the greatness of the stake, 'once more unto the breach', dear friends, and we shall keep for our children the Empire of our fathers. We shall free from tyranny and oppression Belgium and Serbia. We shall buy back with our own blood justice and righteousness for Europe, and lasting peace for the world."

A few days later the Australians advanced our lines another 200 yards north-west of Pozières on a front of 800 yards, and the defences were reached of Mouquet Farm, one of Thiepval's key positions, below the crest of the ridge on the German side, which the enemy, with lines of entrenchments, mysterious underground tunnels, and unnumbered machine-gunners, was determined to keep at all costs. So fierce was the fighting that one regiment of the German

British Official

"Advance, Australia!" Commonwealth troops leaving their base camp for the trenches

Guards Reserve Corps, which had been in the Thiepval salient opposite Mouquet Farm—or "Moo-cow Farm" as our men, with their irrepressible sense of humour, preferred to call it—is known to have lost 1400 men in fifteen days. General Von Below had been furious at the loss of Pozières and the surrounding positions on the ridge.

"The Pozières Plateau", he declared in an Army Order found on one of the prisoners, "must be recovered, no matter at what price, for to allow it to remain in the hands of the British would be to give them an important advantage. Counter-attacks will be delivered by successive waves 80 yards apart. The troops who first reach the plateau must hold on until reinforced, no matter at what cost. Any officer or man who fails to resist to the death will be immediately court-martialled."

Many of the Germans obeyed to the bitter end, and their death-roll was heavy enough, but few of them reached the lost crest in these counter-attacks. Every time they advanced our artillery fire descended upon them like a hailstorm, beneath which the doomed lines scattered and fell.

So the month of August, 1916, passed away, with our troops consolidating and gradually increasing the ground won in the month of July and preparing for the new "Push" at the beginning of the following month along the whole of the main battle-front. The month was also memorable for another visit from His Majesty King George, who spent a week with his armies in the field during the comparative lull in the great battle towards the middle of the month. The local struggles at Guillemont and Pozières, however, were still raging fiercely, and the guns were booming all down the line as the King, who landed at Boulogne on August 8, and arrived on the Somme by the shattered regions of Souchez, Neuville St. Vaast, and other "unhealthy" spots in view of the deadly Vimy Ridge, arrived on the greatest battle-field of all. As on the occasions of his previous visits there was no ceremonious display or formal programme. "All the traffic and turmoil of the war", to quote Mr. Philip Gibbs' account at the time from British Headquarters, "has surged about him, day after day, and the endless procession of the Empire's manhood in the fighting ranks—the youth of Britain and of all the Dominions—has passed him on the roads, not in review order, but as men go up to the trenches and do the work of war." Venturing well within range of the enemy's guns the King walked over many of the captured strongholds, following the line of his victorious battalions from their old first-line trenches. He was obviously impressed with the terrific effects of our artillery fire, as well as with the stupendous nature of the task which his troops had to face in carrying the successive fortress lines of the enemy. One day, in the course of his round of visits and informal inspections, there came down the road along the battle-field, quite unexpectedly, a large body of Australians,

British Official

His Majesty's Visit to the Somme Battle-field: the King (behind the first figure in the foreground) passing between two large mine craters near Mametz

just relieved from the thick of the fighting at Pozières, with all the dirt and dust of battle upon them. Mr. Philip Gibbs describes how, in spite of the arduous time they had had, they came back whistling and singing. The King saw the wonderful spirit of these men, and not all that had been told him could have proved so much.

"'Hullo! boys!' shouted an officer. 'Here's the King!' They halted and flung off their broad-brimmed hats and cheered tremendously as he passed among them. It was a fine and stirring scene, better for its unexpectedness."

Fine and stirring also was the scene on another occasion when His Majesty stood in the presence of the Scotsmen and South Africans who would be for ever associated with the critical battles of Longueval and the "Devil's Wood". The King met the general officers commanding these divisions and spoke to some of the officers and men, thanking them for the noble services they had rendered on that occasion. Other war-worn troops, assembled in the old French villages through which His Majesty passed, were also visited and similarly thanked. Besides these and the various departments of our army organization, the King paid a visit to the French Mission; and on Saturday afternoon, August 12, accompanied by the Prince of Wales and Sir Douglas Haig, entertained at luncheon President Poincaré and General Joffre with their suites, including General Foch. The meal, which took place at a French château, was described as of the most

British Official

The King's Visit to Belgium: presenting decorations to heroes of the Royal Naval Air Service

British Official

His Majesty's Visit to the Front, August, 1916: the New Zealanders' welcome

friendly and intimate character, and when, at its close, the President left to see something of the British battle-front, the King and the others walked to the gate to see him off, "the parting there being most cordial". From the Somme His Majesty journeyed to the far end of Joffre's Wall, across the Belgian frontier, to meet King Albert and his consort, conferring upon the Queen of the Belgians the Order of the Royal Red Cross for her devotion to the wounded, and decorating a number of officers and men for gallantry in action. On the Monday of August 14 King George concluded his eventful tour by a visit to the sinister region of the Ypres salient, where the New Zealanders gave him a great reception. Here, too, from an observation post, His Majesty watched a heavy bombardment of the enemy's trenches. Withdrawing at last from this close view of the great drama of war he motored back through the Canadian camp, where the cheers of the Dominion troops furnished one more convincing proof that the whole Empire was heart and soul with him in the great fight for freedom. At the close of his visit His Majesty issued the following General Order to his troops:—

"OFFICERS, N.C.O.'S AND MEN

"It has been a great pleasure and satisfaction to me to be with my Armies during the past week. I have been able to judge for myself of their splendid condition for war and of the spirit of cheerful confidence which animates all ranks, united in loyal co-operation to their Chiefs and to one another.

"Since my last visit to the front there has been almost uninterrupted fighting on parts of our line. The offensive recently begun has since been resolutely maintained by day and by night. I have had opportunities of visiting some of the scenes of the later desperate struggles, and of appreciating, to a slight extent, the demands made upon your courage and physical endurance in order to assail and capture positions prepared during the past two years and stoutly defended to the last.

"I have realized not only the splendid work which has been done in immediate touch with the enemy—in the air, under ground, as well as on the ground—but also the vast organizations behind the fighting line, honourable alike to the genius of the initiators and to the heart and hand of the workers. Everywhere there is proof that all, men and women, are playing their part, and I rejoice to think their noble efforts are being heartily seconded by all classes at home.

"The happy relations maintained by my Armies and those of our French Allies were equally noticeable between my troops and the inhabitants of the districts in which they are quartered, and from whom they have received a cordial welcome ever since their first arrival in France.

"Do not think that I and your fellow-countrymen forget the heavy sacrifices which the Armies have made and the bravery and endurance they have displayed during the past two years of bitter conflict. These sacrifices have not been in vain; the arms of the Allies will never be laid down until our cause has triumphed.

"I return home more than ever proud of you.

"May God guide you to Victory.

"GEORGE R.I."

British Official

Captured German Trenches at Ovillers

Before the renewed general offensive on the Somme was begun on September 3 General Gough's army, on Sir Henry Rawlinson's left flank, had been steadily and remorselessly preparing the doom of Thiepval, the village fortress which had defied all efforts to take it on July 1. The end of August found the right front of General Gough's army bent back from the main ridge near Mouquet Farm—towards which the Australians, as already described, had advanced from Pozières—down a spur descending south-westwards, and then crossed a broad valley to the "Wonderwork", a powerful buttress of the enemy's defences near the southern end of the spur on the higher slope of which stood Thiepval itself. We had bitten off the nose of the strong point known as the Leipzig salient, at the end of this spur, but we had still to carry the village itself, and the defences below and beyond it, defences described by Sir Douglas Haig as being "as nearly impregnable as nature, art, and the unstinted labour of nearly two years could make them". Their immediate possession had not been necessary to the development of the Allied plans after July 1, General Gough's Army being used, indeed, as a pivot to the remainder of the attack, meantime, in accordance with the Commander-in-Chief's instructions, increasing its grip on the Thiepval garrison with a slow but ever-increasing tightness, which gradually transformed the forbidding German stronghold into little more than a death-trap. It was all done, to quote from Sir Douglas Haig's dispatch, "with great skill, and much patience and endurance"; and the daily reports from Head-quarters, published in the newspapers at the time, conveyed little idea of the dogged courage and terrific fury of the local battles in which each fresh advantage was won. For instance, "Between Ovillers and Thiepval we have pushed forward on a front of over half a mile", to quote from the morning report of August 19, was all that Head-quarters could devote to the brilliant assault which carried the British troops over the network of German trenches and dug-outs on the lower face of the Leipzig salient, and brought them appreciably nearer to Thiepval itself. In this action the Royal Warwickshire Regiment, which had fought and suffered with stoic fortitude in the hopeless battle north of the Ancre on July 1, and subsequently distinguished itself in the capture of Ovillers-la-Boisselle, now added to its laurels by carrying a German strong point which had beaten off several previous attacks, and taking, all told, no fewer than 600 prisoners, with a total loss to themselves of 300 officers and men. It was a fine performance, and earned a special message of thanks from their Army Commander. They had to force their way over a ground honeycombed with entrenchments and torn into gaping pits by mines and high explosives, storming miniature fortresses, where deep, underground galleries were crowded with bombers ready to come up and attack from front and rear. From one of these great dug-outs alone the Warwicks took 250 prisoners, nearly all unwounded.

British Official

A View of the Battle-field from one of the Captured German Trenches looking towards Ovillers. (This white chalk trench could be followed for miles.)

The battle-ground between Ovillers and Thiepval remained for several days the central point of conflict, with attacks and counter-attacks preceded by hurricane bombardments which made the whole region, as one who was there described it, "a perfect hell". Some of our Territorials were among the troops who did conspicuously well in this inferno, and gradually decreased the distance between their battered trenches and the high ridge beyond. Between now and the end of August a further succession of local "pushes" extended our gains in the Leipzig salient and near Mouquet Farm, and brought us within 500 yards of Thiepval Church, several strenuous counter-attacks by the enemy being completely repulsed. Other regiments specially distinguished themselves in this stubborn fighting, as will be seen from the following unusually detailed account telegraphed by Sir Douglas Haig on August 26:—

British Official

On their Way to Battle: some of the Worcesters, mentioned by Sir Douglas Haig for their gallantry against the German counter-attacks

"The importance attributed by the enemy to the Thiepval sector of his line is shown by the great efforts he is making to recover his lost ground in the Leipzig salient. He has recently been effecting a great concentration of guns in this area to oppose our progress and to support his attacks. Last night he delivered an attack in considerable force on our new trenches south of Thiepval village. This attack was made by troops of the Prussian Guard, and was preceded by a very heavy bombardment, which commenced at 7 p.m. The attack was launched about 7.30 p.m., and was pressed with determination, but was everywhere repulsed with heavy loss to the enemy, and we have maintained all our positions. The success of our defence is largely due to the steadiness and determined gallantry of Wiltshire and Worcestershire men, who, in spite of being subjected to a very heavy bombardment, steadily maintained their positions and repulsed the determined assault of the enemy."

Simultaneously with this stern, uphill way for the ridge at Thiepval, we were delivering a similar series of stunning blows in the fiercely-contested region of Delville Wood, to the northern outskirts of which the Germans were still obstinately clinging in various strong points, behind barricades, or in shell-holes and strongly-constructed trenches, defended, as always, by bombers and machine-guns. While the West Country troops were winning fresh laurels below Thiepval, the Rifle Brigade added to its great reputation by a dashing attack which gave us a strong grip all round and beyond that pestilential wood. Several hundred prisoners were taken in this gallant affair, some Scottish battalions also playing their part in thus advancing our line until from our new positions we could look down on the village of Flers, just as, from the left of High Wood, we could now look down on Martinpuich, and from the high ground beyond Pozières on Courcelette.

The long, embittered battle for Delville Wood, however, was not yet over. When our heroic Riflemen chased the enemy from his stronghold among the charred tree-stumps, and over the maze of trenches and shattered gun emplacements towards High Wood and Ginchy, they had to re-dig a new line beyond the wood under an appalling hurricane of shells from the German artillery, the enemy having vastly increased the number of his guns in this vital sector since the beginning of the battle. To add to their difficulties the weather broke, flooding the new trenches and reducing the whole ghastly region to little more than a quagmire. Seizing their opportunity the Germans, under cover of all the guns they could muster, launched a series of strong counter-attacks in the hope of winning back their lost ground. Wave after wave of infantry was flung towards our sorely-tried troops, and either hurled back at bayonet point, or wiped out by our machine-gun fire and barrage of high explosive. Still others came with a persistence and undeniable courage which, at a fifth attempt, forced back in two places our thinly-held front line, where the new trenches had been practically flattened out, and the only cover left was that afforded by shell-holes. Thus for a time the enemy secured a fresh foothold along the north-western fringe of the wood. It was a precarious foothold at the best, won at a frightful cost in blood, and maintained but a few days longer, when, as a result of minor operations in the wood itself, and of the fall of Guillemont on September 3, the whole savage contest was finally decided in our favour. Many heroes fell on both sides in that prolonged trial of strength, but none more nobly than Major William Congreve, of the Rifle Brigade, who, having already won in two years of the Great War the Distinguished Service Order, the Military Cross, and the Cross of the Legion of Honour, now crowned his brilliant record by earning the posthumous honour of the Victoria Cross. He was the first officer to win all three

British decorations for gallantry in the field. The official record in the *London Gazette* not only shows how richly he deserved his last award, but also throws some light on the operations themselves:—

"For most conspicuous bravery during a period of fourteen days preceding his death in action. This officer constantly performed acts of gallantry and showed the greatest devotion to duty, and by his personal example inspired all those around him with confidence at critical periods of the operations. During preliminary preparations for the attack he carried out personal reconnaissances of the enemy lines, taking out parties of officers and non-commissioned officers for over 1000 yards in front of our line, in order to acquaint them with the ground. All these preparations were made under fire. Later, by night, Major Congreve conducted a battalion to its position of employment, afterwards returning to it to ascertain the situation after assault. He established himself in an exposed forward position from whence he successfully observed the enemy, and gave orders necessary to drive them from their position. Two days later, when Brigade Head-quarters was heavily shelled and many casualties resulted, he went out and assisted the medical officer to remove the wounded to places of safety, although he was himself suffering severely from gas and other shell effects. He again on a subsequent occasion showed supreme courage in tending wounded under heavy shell fire. He finally returned to the front line to ascertain the situation after an unsuccessful attack, and whilst in the act of writing his report was shot and killed instantly."

Like Brigadier-General Sir J. E. Gough, V.C., who was mortally wounded in the trenches early in 1915, Major Congreve was the son of another Victoria Cross hero, his father being Major-General Walter N. Congreve,[1] whose own distinguished services in the battle of the Somme earned him the honour of a K.C.B. Major Congreve was only twenty-five, and not many weeks before his death in action had married Miss Pamela Maude, daughter of Mr. Cyril Maude, the well-known actor.

## THIRD PHASE OF THE BATTLE

In the two months' operations—to sum up the position at the beginning of September—we had not only estab-

[1] Sir W. N. Congreve won his Victoria Cross at Colenso, in the South African War, when he was wounded. It was in this action, by a remarkable coincidence, that he went out under heavy fire and brought in the body of the hero son of Lord Roberts, V.C., Lieutenant F. H. S. Roberts, who was mortally wounded. Lieutenant Roberts himself earned the posthumous honour of the Victoria Cross that day, thus furnishing the only other precedent, besides that of the fighting Goughs and Congreves, for the award of the V.C. to both father and son.

Major William Congreve, who, after gaining the Military Cross and the Distinguished Service Order, lost his life in winning the Victoria Cross

Major-General Walter N. Congreve, V.C., rewarded with the K.C.B. for his Distinguished Services in the Battle of the Somme

lished a fighting superiority over the enemy, of which, as Sir Douglas Haig pointed out, the possession of the ridge was merely the visible proof, but had also opened the way for the third phase, "in which our advance was pushed down the forward slopes, and further extended on both flanks until, from Morval to Thiepval, the whole plateau and a good deal of ground beyond were in our possession".

Many guns had been added during this period to the list already mentioned of British war booty, and our total number of prisoners had grown to nearly 16,000, the French meantime accounting for about 23,000. Nothing could exceed the cordiality of the close relationship existing throughout the battle between the Allied armies. The progress of the French and British forces was still interdependent, and the most intimate co-operation was always necessary. In most cases of the kind unity of command would have been essential, but Sir Douglas Haig bears witness to the fact that the new bond of union between both nations and armies, and the earnest desire of each to assist the other, proved equally effective and removed all difficulties. The greatest progress of the French troops had continued south of the Somme, but north of the river, where they faced extremely difficult tactical conditions, they had pushed their advance up the long slopes on our right flanks, in the face of the fiercest opposition. Now, while we were preparing to push down the forward slopes beyond the British front, they arranged to continue their line of advance from the Somme to the heights above Combles, but directing their main efforts northwards against the villages of Rancourt and Frégicourt. This would complete the isolation of Combles and open the way for their attack on Sailly-Saillisel.

The main assault on the British battle-front on September 3, 1916—extending from our extreme right to the third enemy trench on the right bank of the Ancre, north of Hamel—was preceded three hours—at 9 a.m.—by an attack on Falfemont Farm, in order to keep touch with the French, who joined us at this point. It proved a red-letter day for our Allies, whose offensive, according to confident German reports, had come definitely to an end. On the whole front of 4 miles between the region north of Maurepas and the river they proved the fallacy of this, after an artillery fire described as more intense than anything hitherto experienced, by sweeping the hostile positions with a dash "against which", to quote from the official French report, "the resistance of the enemy was unable to hold out for a moment". The villages of Le Forest, to the east of Maurepas, and Cléry-sur-Somme fell entirely into their hands, and much of the ground above and beyond those two places.

Hurling back a succession of determined counter-attacks during the night from the direction of Combles—the most important strategic point in the immediate district, now seriously threatened by the new advance—they extended their gains on the following day by a fresh assault on both sides of the river, pushing towards Rancourt on the left bank, and on the right not only capturing both Soyecourt and Chilly, but flinging back the German line on a total depth of some 2½ miles. In these two eventful days the French alone took some 6000 prisoners, 14 guns, and 60 odd machine-guns. There was no further reference in the Berlin reports to the impotence of an exhausted French army.

Though our gains during the same period were less striking they were also of the first importance, and paved the way to greater triumphs. When our troops on the left of the French sprang from their trenches in the preliminary thrust towards Falfemont Farm they reached their objective in the impetus of the first rush, but found the Prussian Guards in such tremendous strength that they were forced to loosen their hold, pushing round instead to the north of it. The only way to master this immensely strong position was to occupy it piece by piece. It was no longer a farm, but a place of scattered ruin packed with every kind of modern defence, and marked only by the gaunt tree stumps surrounding it, like shattered telegraph poles. Bit by bit it was conquered in a series of fresh assaults from the west and north, but it was not until the morning of the 5th that we had the whole of it in our possession.

Elsewhere along the British front the tide of battle had ebbed and flowed with similar violence. Our greatest success on the 3rd was the capture and consolidation of Guillemont by the Irish troops—this time from the division established two years before in response to the appeal of the Irish Nationalist leaders, and composed of battalions of all the famous Irish regiments, the Dublins, Munsters, and so on. The brigade which took part in this assault had only arrived on the previous night from another part of the battle-front, after a long and trying march in a drenching rain. Bivouacking on the bare side of a hill, they had been visited by their devoted priest, who, after a moving address round the camp fires, held an impromptu service, at the close of which the Irish troops knelt to receive the General Absolution administered in times of emergency. It was a deeply impressive scene amid the gloom of that bleak hillside, and sent the troops into action on the following morning with a burning faith in the justice of their cause, and a determination to win the day for which their new battalions had been training so long. Nor did they fail. They advanced on Guillemont with an impetuosity which carried all before it: charged through the German positions with the wild music of their pipes playing them on. Before the afternoon was out the 2000 Prussians who constituted the garrison—with imperative orders to hold the ground at all cost—were killed, wounded, or captured. Not many escaped. Of the prisoners the Irishmen alone accounted for 600. While the savage struggle was proceeding among the dug-outs and wreckage of the village, English riflemen on the right were contributing largely to the Irish triumph by clearing the southern area of the attack and seizing the sunken road running southward from the village—a road which had proved a tower of strength in the enemy's defence, and became a shambles in the earlier assaults on the place.

These notable successes had been achieved in the face of an artillery fire which showed that the Germans were massing more and more guns against the British front. In this day's fight it was computed on good authority that they must have hurled against us upwards of 10,000 gas shells alone, to say nothing of "heavies", high explosives, common shells, and shrapnel. Everywhere our advance was stubbornly contested, but the net result of a day of deadly strife was that we carried the enemy's defences on a front of 3000 yards to an average depth of 800 yards. A premature triumph was achieved at Ginchy, the whole of which

British Official

Heroes of Guillemont: part of the Irish Brigade returning after the capture of that hotly-disputed village

was at first captured by the troops who pushed on thence from Guillemont. In the afternoon the Germans, counter-attacking in overwhelming strength, forced us at this point to give ground, but we still clung to part of the village, despite repeated endeavours during the night to fling us back. "For three days", writes Sir Douglas Haig, "the tide of attack and counter-attack swayed backwards and forwards among the ruined houses of the village till, in the end, for three days more the greater part of it remained in the enemy's possession."

On September 9, however, when the attack was reopened on the whole of the Fourth Army front, our troops again forced their way into Ginchy and wrested it finally from German hands, passing beyond it and carrying the line of enemy trenches to the east. The men responsible for this decisive success were the same Irish troops who had captured Guillemont six days before—the men from Munster, Dublin, Leinster, and Connaught. They had charged into Ginchy again as they charged into Guillemont, through the barrage of shells and the storm of machine-gun fire, clambering over shell-holes, fallen trees, and the great mounds of bricks and rubble which were all that remained of the village itself; cheering like mad, and driving the enemy before them in a fierce assault against which nothing could stand. The Germans, chiefly Bavarians, put up a stout fight, but after one of the hottest hours of the great offensive, the Irish had not only overrun the whole of the village, but had

British Official

"Scotland for Ever!" The Black Watch marching back from the trenches headed by their pipers

thrown out patrols 400 yards north of the place. Some stiff, close-quarter fighting remained to be done before the last remnants of the garrison were rooted out of their cellars and dug-outs, but it was not long before the only Germans left were those who were killed, wounded, or captured. Some 200 were taken from one trench alone in the heart of the village. Altogether it was a great achievement, and the brigadier who greeted their worn, shrunken battalions on their return after being relieved, spoke no more than the truth when he cried: "Well done, my lads! you did gloriously!"

While the earlier battles were raging for the pulverized village of Ginchy we had made appreciable progress to the south, following upon the fine advance of the French on our right. Much ground was gained to the north-east of Falfemont Farm, "where considerable initiative", writes Sir Douglas Haig, "was shown by the local commanders". By the evening of September 5, on the morning of which the bitter struggle for the ruins of the farm itself had ended in our favour, our troops were strongly established in Leuze Wood, midway between Guillemont and Combles. This gave us possession of all the ground between Falfemont Farm and Leuze Wood—or "Lousy" Wood as our men insisted upon calling it—and between that wood and the outskirts of Ginchy. The West Country troops had a large share in the great fighting which gained this supremely important ground. From first to last, according to Mr. Philip Gibbs, in his dispatch from British Head-quarters on the following day, it was a soldiers' battle from the moment that the first orders were given.

> "Its success was due to young officers and N.C.O.'s and men using their own initiative, finding another way round when one had failed, and arranging their own tactics in face of the enemy to suit the situation of the moment. Such a thing has been done very rarely since the first days of trench warfare, except in raids over No Man's Land and bombing fights in such places as Ovillers and Longueval."[1]

In acknowledging the fine work of the Irish troops at Guillemont and Ginchy, Sir Douglas Haig mentioned that some of our rifle battalions, and regiments from Scotland, Warwickshire, Kent, Devonshire, Gloucestershire, Surrey, Cornwall, and Wales, had all done splendidly in the severe fighting since the September advance began. "The spirit and dash of our troops in the face of frequent determined counter-attacks and constant intense artillery fire", he added, "have been magnificent"; and the net result of the week's fighting had been that our line had been advanced on a front of 6000 yards to a depth varying from 300 to 3000 yards. Every day some hundreds of prisoners were brought in, carrying the British total since July 1 to over 17,000. The Commander-in-Chief found much food for encouragement in the progress of the battle at this point. With the rapid advance of the French on his right, bringing their line forward to Louange Wood (just south of Combles)—Le

[1] *The Battles of the Somme.* By Philip Gibbs. (Heinemann, 1917.)

Forest—Cléry-sur-Somme, the weak salient in the Allies' front had disappeared, and the line straightened out in readiness for further developments.

What was of still greater importance, as Sir Douglas pointed out in his subsequent dispatch, was the

British Official
Creeping up to Thiepval: a look-out within 100 yards of the German fortress-village

effect of this long succession of defeats on a disillusioned enemy. We had already proved, not once, but repeatedly, that we could rush his strongest defences, and now we had furnished equally convincing proof of our ability to wear down and break his power of resistance by a steady, relentless pressure. The success of the great advances of July 1 and 14 had fully convinced him of his grave danger, and nothing but the depth of his system of fortifications, which had enabled him to reorganize his defeated troops and hurry up more guns and reinforcements, saved him from crushing disaster. As it was, he was being pushed back, slowly it is true, but none the less continuously. Rarely did he succeed in his repeated counter-attacks in regaining some of his lost ground, and every yard, dearly won, was soon lost again. Although, as Sir Douglas Haig admitted, the enemy had delayed our advance considerably, "the last few days of the struggle justified the belief that in the long run decisive victory would lie with our troops, who had displayed such fine fighting qualities, and such indomitable endurance and resolution".

Turning to his left flank, where our gain in ground had been slight in this early September fighting, though heavy losses in *personnel* had been inflicted on the enemy, the Commander-in-Chief pointed out that the time was approaching when the powerful Thiepval fortresses would have to be captured, but that it had not yet arrived, General Gough's army meantime playing its self-sacrificing part as a pivot to the remainder of the attack. The front of this army still bent back from the main ridge near Mouquet Farm and descended southwards towards the German strong point known as the Wonderwork, the outpost guarding the southern approach to Thiepval from the Leipzig Salient. On this, as on our right flank, the enemy continued to bring up against us the flower of the Kaiser's army. The Australians, pressing ever nearer over the ridge from Pozières, received the best tribute to their valour by having pitted against them at Mouquet Farm on September 3 the 1st Prussian Guards Reserve Regiment —all picked men, and the special pride of the Kaiser's heart. While the main attack on the 3rd on the right flank began at noon, that on the left took place at dawn, after a torrential rain of shells on the enemy's positions. The farm itself, as already mentioned, was now only a mass of desolate rubbish, with the remains of a few shattered trees; but every heap was a stronghold defended by bombers and machine-guns, while deep entrenchments with wire entanglements and subterranean passages guarded the approach from all directions. The trying scramble in the half light across the 200 yards of crumpled and shell-marked No Man's Land was not effected without considerable loss from the enemy's artillery and cross-fire of machine-guns; but the Australians were soon not only at Mouquet Farm itself but beyond it, beating back the Prussian Guards and making many of them prisoners. As the day wore on, however, Mouquet Farm became untenable, and the battle resolved itself into a series of fierce isolated engagements between scattered parties of Prussians and Australians, leaving the Anzacs in possession of a new line flanking the ruins and threatening them from the north-west.

The next step forward in the Thiepval region was the capture on the evening of September 14 of the enemy's trenches south-east of that fortress on a front of about 1000 yards, when the Wonderwork was stormed and the path cleared for the final overthrow of Thiepval towards the end of the month.

The Wunderwerk—to give it its German spelling—was one of the enemy's most villainous systems of dug-outs and entrenchments, and its capture was expected to prove a costly business, but the poor spirit displayed by the garrison was one of an increasing number of instances pointing to the gradual collapse of the Boche's power of resistance.

This stronghold fell on the eve of the great Allied attack on September 15, when our new heavily armoured cars, the "Tanks", made their first appearance on the battle-field, and helped us to gains "more considerable", to quote Sir Douglas Haig's own words, "than any which had attended our arms in the course of a single operation since the commencement of the offensive". Though we had straightened out our line to Ginchy, and the French were advancing victoriously across the Combles Valley, there was still, on the eve of this new advance, much difficult ground to be won in that direction, as well as on our left, before our flanks were as firmly planted on the main ridge as was the centre of our line.

Sir Douglas describes how the crest of the high ground runs northward from Ginchy for 2000 yards, and then eastward for nearly 4000 yards, in a long spur, near the eastern extremity of which stands the village of Morval, commanding a wide field of view and fire in all directions. It is necessary to follow his description at this point in order clearly to understand the problem presented both by the capture of Morval by the British and that of Sailly-Saillisel—situated due east of Morval and standing on the same level—by the French, who were working their way towards this objective up the high ground on the other side assault on Combles would not be necessary, as the place could be rendered untenable by pressing forward along the ridge above it on either side." Our advance on Morval, however, presented many difficulties. That village stood not less than 2000 yards from our right at Leuze Wood, across a broad and deep branch of the main

French Official

Combles, captured by the Allies in the Somme Offensive

of the Combles Valley. Between the two advancing armies lay the Combles Valley, with the townlet of Combles itself—once peacefully sleeping at the bottom, but now strongly fortified and held by the enemy in force, though dominated by the British right at Leuze Wood, and by the French left on the opposite height. The Allies had no intention of taking the place by direct attack. "It had been agreed between the French and myself", explains Sir Douglas Haig, "that an Combles Valley which was completely commanded by the Morval spur, and flanked, as the Commander-in-Chief points out, not only from its head north-east of Ginchy, but also from the high ground east of the Combles Valley, which looks directly into it. In some respects the French advance —with Sailly-Saillisel at that time lying some 3000 yards to the north of our Allies' left—was even more difficult. They had captured the Marrières Wood and the village of Bouchavesnes in another of their lightning advances on the 12th, and extended their line along the Peronne-Bapaume road as far as the southern outskirts of Rancourt. Thence, however, "the line of the French advance", in the words of Sir Douglas Haig, "was narrowed almost to a defile by the extensive and strongly fortified wood of St. Pierre Vaast on the one side, and on the other by the Combles Valley, which, with the branches running out from it, and the slopes from either side, is completely commanded by the heights bounding the valley on the east and west".

The capture of Ginchy, however, had robbed the enemy of his old point of vantage from which he could overlook the Allies' lines to the south and west, a point of the greatest value in watching our movements and registering upon our batteries. The appearance on September 11 of sixteen of his kite balloons—"German sausages", as our men called them—above the battle-front beyond Ginchy was a confession that his only means of full observation was from the air; and it was not long before several of these great gas-bags, in spite of the batteries of new anti-aircraft guns defending them—firing high-reaching flames at all intruders—fell victims to the fearless hawks both of the Royal Flying Corps and the French Air Service. Our own airmen accounted for one on the eve of the new Allied Offensive, and brought down another—reduced in a second to a mass of flame and smoke—on the morning of the advance itself.

Our preliminary bombardment for the new combined assault began at 6.0 a.m. on September 12, and was continued steadily and uninterruptedly until the moment of assault three days later. Sir Douglas Haig describes the general plan of attack as intended to pivot on the high ground south of

British Official

A Kite Balloon ascending on the British Front

the Ancre and north of the Albert-Bapaume road, while the Fourth Army devoted its whole effort to the rearmost of the enemy's original systems of defence between Morval and Le Sars.

"Should our success in that direction warrant it," added the Commander-in-Chief, "I made arrangements to enable me to extend the left of the attack to embrace the villages of Martinpuich and Courcelette.

As soon as our advance on this front had reached the Morval line, the time would have arrived to bring forward my left across the Thiepval Ridge."

Meantime the French on his right arranged to begin the complete encircling of Combles, and open the way for their advance upon their objective at Sailly-Saillisel by pushing northwards towards the villages of Frégicourt and Rancourt.

The abnormal concentrations of troops which the Allied assault at once disclosed behind the enemy's front led at the time to the impression that we had taken the Germans by surprise, and unwittingly disorganized their plans for a great counter-attack to recover the ground lost since July 1. The truth was, apparently, that these heavy reinforcements had been specially brought up to meet our new offensive, it being subsequently discovered, as Sir Douglas Haig mentions in his dispatch, that "the attack did not come as a complete surprise to the enemy". In preparation for this, the German Higher Command had massed over 1000 guns against the 6 miles of British battle-front alone, and made the whole area as uncomfortable as possible throughout the previous day and night. When, however, our own batteries broke out together in their intense bombardment at the moment of attack on September 15, they did so with a stupendous roar which seemed to smother all reply. One correspondent described this accompaniment to the infantry advance as more shattering and overwhelming than ever—as "a fury of flame and whirling smoke, and deafening noise".

Other ominous signs at daybreak on that memorable Friday of September 15 were the Allies' aeroplanes, winging their way alone and in squadrons to co-operate with the artillery and infantry, and bombard the enemy's Head-quarters, stores, and lines of communication in the rear. Our air service played a great part in the ensuing battle, not only bringing down one of the German kite balloons, besides destroying thirteen hostile aeroplanes and driving down nine others, but also supporting our infantry in the advance, descending with superb audacity to a close height from the ground, and sweeping the German trenches with machine-gun fire.

Although the advance was not unexpected, it proved a day of dreadful surprise for the Germans. They had taught the Allies so many fearsome tricks of modern warfare that they regarded almost as an impertinence the mechanical monsters which now came lolloping from the British front; land Dreadnoughts which took shell-holes and trenches in their stride as though to the manner born, spreading death from armour-plated sides, and crushing everything which barred their passage like veritable juggernauts. Yet the fundamental idea of the "Tanks", as the new armoured cars were called, was almost as old as the hills, even without the wooden horse of Troy. Rhodes was besieged some six centuries before Christ by a king of Asia whose son invented what was called the Helepolis—a movable wooden fort nine stories high, plated with iron, and manned by archers. The new machines were not so much armoured cars as forts on wheels, but of extraordinary mobility. Mr. H. G. Wells, who so vividly anticipated the war in the air, foretold them in his short story, *The Land Ironclads*; and many people had a hand in the elaboration of the idea in the form in which it took shape in the Somme offensive.

It was not until some months after the Germans had been introduced to these land cruisers that the War Office permitted any details, or illustrations of them, to be published. In due course, however, official photographs were issued, and discreet details given of their general appearance. The new craft were officially designated His Majesty's Land-ships ("H.M.L.-S."), and each was as proud of its name—Cordon Rouge, Crême de Menthe, Delphine, Daphne, Delsie, and so on—as any of His Majesty's ships at sea. In size they were described as something between a touring motor-car and a tiny bungalow; and to render them as inconspicuous as possible they were painted a mixture of colours to harmonize with their surroundings. They crawled along their bodies like mammoth slugs, slowly, but with sufficient momentum to crash through a wall, let us say, or bring down the fortified ruins of a house, and then climb over the debris. Inside they were crowded with engines, guns, and ammunition, and each was manned by a commanding officer and a crew of driver and gunners. All

Canadian War Records

A "Tank" in Action: one of His Majesty's land-ships astride a large shell-hole on the Somme Front

were picked men, ready to do and dare anything; and, as Sir Douglas Haig bore witness in his dispatch, they "performed many deeds of remarkable valour".

Naturally the new-comers heartened our men advancing across No Man's Land on September 15 as much as they horrified the enemy, who soon found that they were proof against everything save a direct hit from a fair-sized shell. Some of them came to grief; but the excellent results of the day's work amply justified their astonishing existence. The day's successes, indeed, were the reward of infinite pains both in scheming and organization, and in the complete co-ordination of all arms. For days, while the guns were methodically preparing the way for the infantry, a steady forward movement of troops had taken place and a rapid concentration of all the men and machinery necessary for the purpose. The gunnery throughout was described by Mr Philip Gibbs from British Head-quarters as the most remarkable achievement ever done by British artillery.

"Every detail of it was planned beforehand. Every 'heavy' had its special objective, and its own time-table, working exactly with the infantry, concentrating upon the enemy's trenches and strong points, barraging his lines of communication, following the tracks of those motor monsters . . . and co-operating with the air service to reach out to distant targets. The field batteries were marvellously audacious in taking up new positions, and the F.O.O.'s (the forward observing officers) were gallant in getting up to the high ground as soon as our infantry had taken it, and registering their batteries from these new view-points."[1]

Success, though here and there delayed, had awaited the attack from the

[1] *The Battles of the Somme.* Philip Gibbs. (Heinemann, 1917.)

British Official

Reinforcements moving up towards Flers: view across the front German trenches captured on September 15, 1916

Canadian War Records

General Sir Sam Hughes, as Canadian Minister of Militia and Defence, reviewing Canadian troops in England before their Departure for the Front

moment the infantry started from the trenches along the six-mile battle-front from Leuze Wood on the right to Pozières on the left. It was not easily or cheaply won, for the hostile defence, backed by more than 1000 guns of all calibres, was everywhere of a formidable nature. In addition to his treble line of entrenchments linked together by strong subsidiary trenches, the enemy kept a grim hold on numerous advanced posts, with machine-guns in trenches, dug-outs, and shell-holes; while behind all these positions, at a distance of some 7000 yards from our front, he had recently constructed and wired a fourth nine-line of defences in front of the Le Transloy-Bapaume road.

Under cover of our field artillery barrage the unexpected Tanks led the action in fine style, "knocking out hostile machine-guns, inflicting heavy losses by their machine-gun fire, enfilading the German trenches, and causing", in the unwonted language of the official dispatch at the time, "indescribable demoralization in the enemy's ranks". Moving forward to the assault at the same time, our cheering infantry carried the whole of the front German line at the first onset, save at two deadly points, one on the high ground between Ginchy and Leuze Wood, and the other on the long-disputed battle-field at High Wood. Failing to carry these by frontal attack, the troops swept round their flanks, and held on, to clear them up later. By 8.40 a.m. other troops were seen to swarm into the village of Flers, headed by the imper-

British Official

New Zealand in the Great Advance: Dominion troops on the road to the trenches

turbable Tanks. The garrison, probably receiving the surprise of their lives, were not proof against this monstrous invasion. It was difficult to say, according to the *Times* correspondent, how far the comparative lack of resistance in the village, which was not so well provided with defence works and dug-outs as were most German strongholds, was due to these new terrors that stalked there by day.

> "Certain it is that Tanks walked majestically ahead of our advancing line of men, and there are those who say that one of the finest sights of a thrilling day was the spectacle of one huge pachyderm sauntering down the main street of Flers all alone, while from among the ruins rifles and machine-guns played on it like pea-shooters."

The New Zealanders played a brilliant part in the attack on this sector of the front. Advancing at dawn in waves that never faltered, they carried the first position assigned to them unaided by Tanks, though these accompanied them in the later stages of the advance, when they pushed northward to the Flers road through the third German line. Here their final task was to throw their left flank roughly in the direction of Martinpuich, but the check at High Wood had robbed them of their expected support, and finding themselves, as a result, severely enfiladed, there was nothing for it but to swing back their left and hold on. A thrilling chapter could be written of their share in this tremendous battle, and of how they clung for days and nights to their perilous position, with true Anzac courage, in the face of continuous shelling, beating back a succession of determined enemy counterattacks. A summary of their achievements on the 15th was provided by their official war correspondent, Mr.

Malcolm Ross, in the following telegram issued by the High Commissioner, Sir Thomas Mackenzie:—

"*September 16.*

"The New Zealanders, who have the honour of being in the new phase of the Somme advance, fought hard and successfully all yesterday, capturing several lines of German trenches and pushing on right behind Flers village, which they assisted in taking and holding during the night. Leaving their assembly trench in the early morning, they went over the parapet and took the first weakly-held German trench in their stride. Then, pushing on behind a creeping barrage, they went gallantly through the German shrapnel, high explosive, and machine-gun fire, and captured an important trench. This trench taken, the brigade passed over it, and they advanced close behind a further creeping barrage. The leading waves assaulted and took a trench 1000 yards farther on. Here one of the armoured land cruisers did good work. In one place it charged through uncut German wire. All this time the brigade was moving steadily onward, and the leading waves found two lines of trenches and a long communication trench. These trenches they also took. One armoured car charged slowly right into the village in front of the cheering infantry, a scene unparalleled in war. We got beyond this objective, but as there were some gaps in the line [between Flers and Martinpuich] the men had to be brought back a short distance. They dug in on the line."

While the New Zealanders were thus establishing themselves on the new line west of Flers, and Londoners were clearing up Flers itself, the Canadians were similarly distinguishing themselves at Courcelette. A powerful raiding party of Germans had been sent, just before the time fixed for the assault, to probe the Canadian positions for information, and the fierce fight which ensued might have unsettled the plans of less reliable troops. But the Canadians finished off the raiders—not one of whom got back—and were ready for the greater adventure at the exact moment fixed for the general advance. Accompanied by three Tanks, they swept down the broken slopes towards Courcelette, shouting and cheering as they went, through an inferno of shrapnel and high explosives, as well as a storm of rifle and machine-gun fire from a trench lying at right angles with the general

Canadian War Records

Canada in the Trenches: fixing bayonets before an assault at Courcelette direction of the advance. Making at once for this entrenchment, certain sections of the Canadians bombed their way down, and cleared it from end to end, while their comrades overran the rest of the ground as far as their objective round the southern outskirts of the village, where they dug themselves in. When this news reached the Commander-in-Chief, as well as the fact that other victorious troops had pushed to within striking distance of Martinpuich at the same time, Sir Douglas Haig decided to carry out that part of his plan which provided for the capture of both these villages.

Among the brave Dominion men who stormed their way to Courcelette down the shell-swept slopes from the high ridge at Pozières was a body of French-Canadians, many of them of the same type as the very people whose ruined homesteads they were now winning back, foot by foot, from the common enemy. When, late in the afternoon, permission to carry Courcelette itself reached the captured trenches south of the village, these and the other Dominion troops took it with such an impetuous rush that though the garrison of 1500 Germans actually outnumbered the assaulting force, the defence melted away amid loud cries of surrender, after a determined resistance in which, in the words of the Canadian *communiqué*, "the Germans fought with the courage of despair", the bodies of machine-gunners being found chained and padlocked to their guns. Some desperate Bavarians put up a last fight in the quarry, and machine-guns defended the cemetery, but the Canadians fought their way from one strong point to another, and soon had the whole village in their hands. The enemy's submission was then complete. Stories are told of dug-outs packed with Germans being cleared by a few men who could easily have been overwhelmed; and of one Canadian boy in particular who, single-handed, emerged from a large cellar proudly leading a string of thirty-two Bavarians, all with their hands up in token of surrender.

Holding Courcelette proved even sterner work than taking it, as the Canadians found when, having cleared it, they dug in round the northern end. The Germans made no fewer than seven counter-attacks to recover the lost ground, and the Canadians, holding a thin irregular line—chiefly shell-holes—only some 70 yards from the trenches to which the enemy had retired, were more than once hard pressed. But they held on, and when at length they were relieved the whole of their battle-field was found strewn with the bodies of Bavarians sacrificed in these abortive efforts. Tidings of the splendid gallantry and resourcefulness of the Canadians were naturally received in the Dominion with deep appreciation, Sir Robert Borden, on behalf of the Dominion Government, cabling the warmest congratulations to General Sir Julian Byng, commanding the Canadian Army Corps, who replied expressing his pride in all the troops for the skill and courage with which they had fought.

The story of two Victoria Crosses awarded to the Canadian Infantry shows the mettle of the men. One was conferred upon Corporal Leo

Clarke, who, after most of his section of bombers in a newly-captured trench had become casualties, started building a "block", when about twenty of the enemy, with two officers, counter-attacked.

"He boldly advanced against them," states the official record, "emptied his revolver into them and afterwards two enemy rifles which he picked up in the trench. One of the officers then attacked him with the bayonet, wounding him in the leg, but he shot him dead. The enemy then ran away, pursued by Acting Corporal Clarke, who shot four more and captured a fifth. Later he was ordered to the dressing-station, but returned next day to duty."

The other Victoria Cross fell to Private John C. Kerr for similar heroism during a bombing attack, when he was acting as bayonet man.

"Knowing that bombs were running short, he ran along the parados under heavy fire until he was in close contact with the enemy, when he opened fire on them at point-blank range, and inflicted heavy loss. The enemy, thinking they were surrounded, surrendered. Sixty-two prisoners were taken and 250 yards of enemy trench captured. Before carrying out this very plucky act one of Private Kerr's fingers had been blown off by a bomb. Later, with two other men, he escorted back the prisoners under fire, and then returned to report himself for duty before having his wound dressed."

While Courcelette and Martinpuich were being conquered on Sir Douglas Haig's left on September 15, prodigies of heroism were being performed elsewhere by other troops. One of the unforgettable episodes was the daybreak advance of the Guards, when, for the first time in the history of the regiment, three battalions of the Coldstreams — the old "Lilywhites" — charged together in line. Followed

Preparing for Battle on the Somme: respirator drill for the Guards behind the lines British Official

by other regiments of the Guards Division, it was a charge which none privileged to witness it could ever forget. It was heavily handicapped from the fact that the starting line was below the crest of the ridge, and that once over the top the Guards were in unknown land and faced by trenches still defended, as they now discovered for the first time, by uncut wire. Yet the men advanced, as an eye-witness described it, as steadily as though they were walking down the Mall.

"The line", to quote from the *Morning Post's* war correspondent, "rippled over the broken ground, never halting or hesitating, while shells burst above and around them. Gaps were blown in their ranks, only to disappear as the battalions closed in again; machine-guns raked the fields over which they passed, but they could not stay the steady, onward drive of the cheering Coldstream Guards. 'At them, the Lilywhites!' shouted the sergeants: 'Come on, Lilywhites!', and on they went."

Needless to say, all the Guards fought gloriously, killing a great number of Germans, sending back several hundred prisoners, and after overcoming more than one critical situation, advancing some 2000 yards into the enemy's country. Here, with an exposed flank—the troops on their right having been held up by the enemy's impregnable defences—and heavy losses among both officers and men, they decided to dig themselves in, taking such cover as they could in shell-craters and broken ground, and throwing out advanced posts. They faced the deluge of fire which now descended upon them from the enemy's guns with the same invincible courage and discipline, holding the ground they had won until they were relieved, when their thinned and battle-stained battalions marched back as steadily as they had advanced.

Their thrilling achievements are but vaguely hinted at in the official account of the award of the Victoria Cross to Lieut.-Colonel J. Vaughan Campbell, commanding the Coldstream Guards.

"Seeing that the first two waves of his battalion had been decimated by machine-gun and rifle fire he took personal command of the third line, rallied his men with the utmost gallantry, and led them against the enemy machine-guns, capturing the guns and killing the *personnel*. Later in the day, after consultation with other unit commanders, he again rallied the survivors of his battalion, and at a critical moment led them through a very heavy hostile fire barrage against the objective. He was one of the first to enter the enemy trench. His personal gallantry and initiative at a very critical moment turned the fortunes of the day and enabled the division to press on and capture objectives of the highest tactical importance."

Lieut.-Colonel Campbell, a grandson of Earl Cawdor, still retained his position as Master of the Tanat-side Harriers, and it is stated on good authority that he rallied his command on September 15 to the sound of an old hunting-horn. In the same Honours List appeared the award of the Victoria Cross to Lance-Sergeant F. M'Ness, of the Scots Guards, who, when the left flank of his regiment was exposed after the first line of the enemy's trenches was reached, and the enemy began bombing down, at once organized a counter-attack and led it in person.

"He was very severely wounded in the neck and jaw, but went on, passing through

the barrage of hostile bombs, in order to bring up fresh supplies of bombs to his own men. Finally he established a 'block', and continued encouraging his men and throwing bombs till utterly exhausted by loss of blood."

British Official

The Great Advance on September 15, 1916: the main street of Flers after its capture by the British

Captain Sir Iain Colquhoun, Bart., who won the D.S.O., also showed how the Scots Guards could fight when, after leading his company with the greatest dash, and, with a few men, reaching the enemy's second line, he found it full of bombers. "He personally accounted for six of them, and knocked over several others with a stick." We are not surprised to learn, on the same official authority, that Sir Iain "has done other fine work". Captain the Hon. Harold R. L. G. Alexander, of the Irish Guards, who had already earned the Military Cross in the Great War, held the trenches gained in spite of heavy machine-gun fire, and won the Distinguished Service Order. "He was the life and soul of the attack, and throughout the day led forward not only his own men but men of all regiments." Only one other honour—all the famous regiments of the Guards Division earned their share—need be mentioned to illustrate this splendid page in the history of the Somme. It is the D.S.O. awarded to Captain Eugene Napoleon E. M. Vaughan, of the Grenadiers, who, when in command of an isolated trench, was attacked by the enemy in front, flank, and rear. He not only drove off the enemy, records the *London Gazette*, but killed over 100 of them, and took 20 prisoners.

The advance on Sir Douglas Haig's right flank had been checked by the enemy's hold on the high ground north-west of Leuze Wood, particularly at the strongly-fortified redoubt known as the Quadrilateral, on the Ginchy-Morval road. From this dominating work, with its series of surrounding entrenchments, the enemy could enfilade all our troops advancing from east of Ginchy. Its own defences were formidable enough, including, besides its rows of protecting trenches, a deep, neighbouring ravine with wooded sides all honeycombed with dug-outs and machine-gun emplacements; but its approaches were doubly guarded in the south by other strong points in and about the northern end of Bouleaux Wood. Noble sacrifices were made in vain attempts to carry these death-traps by storm on September 15, and it was not until the 18th, after a ferocious hand-to-hand fight with bombs and bayonets, that they were finally conquered. The survivors of the garrison—Bavarians, who, to give them due credit, had offered a stout resistance—then surrendered, seven machine-guns also being captured. The conquest of the neighbouring ravine was a more bloodthirsty affair. Many of the Germans clung to their dug-outs, refusing to surrender, and, when forced out by bombs, fought to the death. As a result of this clearance our lines on our right flank were advanced to a depth of 1000 yards on a mile front.

British Official

After the Great Advance on September 15, 1916: cavalry patrol on the broken road from Flers

The battle for High Wood reached its climax on September 15, after two months of ghastly fighting—for our first foothold, it will be remembered, had been won there as far back as July 14, and it had since defied all our efforts to make a clean sweep through, chiefly on account of the vast mine crater in the eastern extremity of the wood, which the Germans had converted into a fortress of extraordinary strength, with machine-guns sweeping every approach. The final struggle, in which, as in the capture of Flers, many London regiments greatly distinguished themselves, raged with undiminished fury for many hours, but was at length decided finally in our favour, the whole of it being carried with a heroism which, in the Commander-in-Chief's own words, "reflected great credit on the attacking battalions". One of the Tanks, arriving in the nick of time in the critical moments of the first advance, saved the lives of not a few gallant Londoners who, having pushed ahead at all costs, were in danger of being wiped out by German snipers and machine-gunners. Thus, when High Wood had finally fallen into our hands, we had conquered practically all the high ground between the Combles Valley and the River Ancre, and, more than that, were well down the forward slopes, from the commanding positions of which our gunners could inflict continual punishment on the Germans.

Many famous regiments—English, Scottish, Welsh, and Irish—as well as London and Northumbrian Territorials, shared with those already mentioned the glory of this great achievement. At present it is not permissible, even were it possible, to particularize more exactly. Enough for the moment that all ranks, from the newest Derby recruit to the war-worn survivors of the Old Contemptibles, were splendid. The result of their blow on September 15, and following days, when our troops straightened out our dented line between Martinpuich and Flers, and also made further progress in the direction of Lesbœufs, was described by Sir Douglas Haig at the time as "probably the most effective blow which has yet been dealt to the enemy by British troops". It was certainly the most productive in our territorial gains since the Allied offensive began.

"In the course of one day's fighting," he wrote in his full dispatch, "we had broken through two of the enemy's main defensive systems and had advanced on a front of over 6 miles to an average depth of a mile. In the course of this advance we had taken three large villages, each powerfully organized for prolonged resistance. Two of these villages had been carried by assault with short preparation in the course of a few hours' fighting. All this had been accomplished with a small number of casualties in comparison with the troops employed, and in spite of the fact that, as was afterwards discovered, the attack did not come as a complete surprise to the enemy."

The damage to the enemy's *moral* was even greater than his territorial losses and our capture of between 4000 and 5000 prisoners, including 127 officers, and many guns. All told, since July 1 we had now taken more than 22,000 prisoners, with upwards of 100 guns and several hundred machine-guns, trench mortars, and the like. It was officially stated, too, that since July 1 the British forces alone on the Somme front had met and engaged no fewer than 38 German Divisions, and that 29 of these had already been defeated and withdrawn

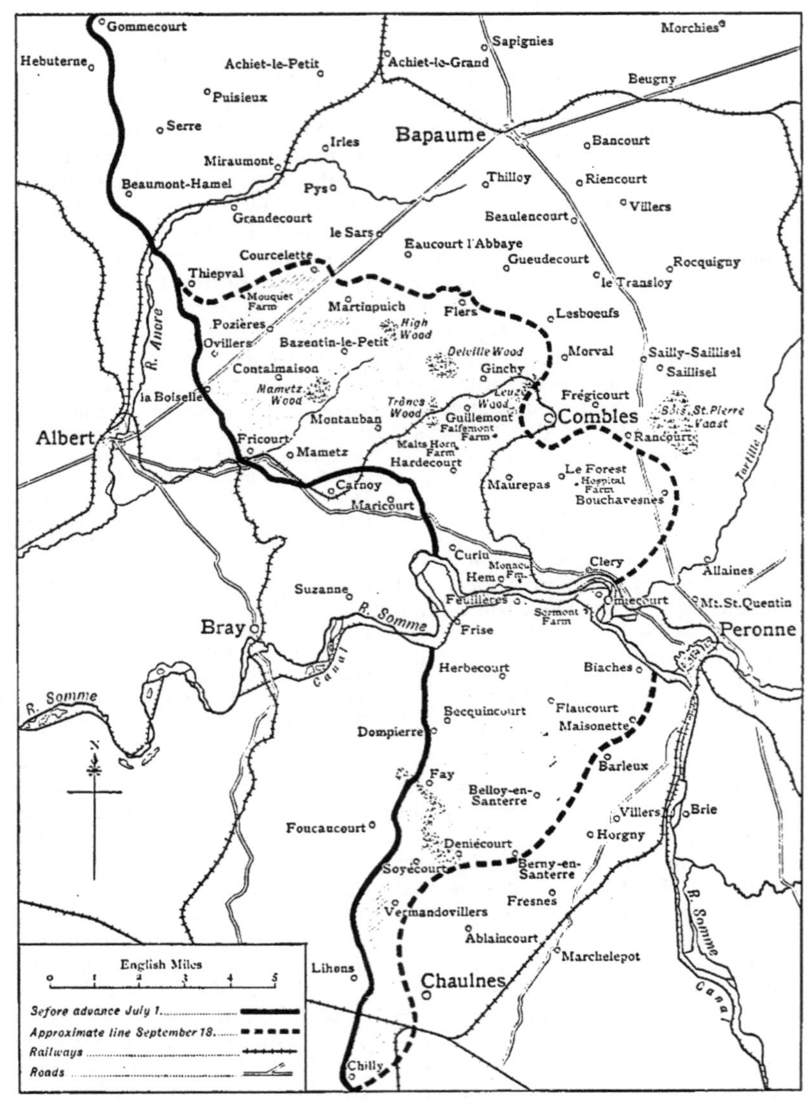


The Allied Battle-field on the Somme: map showing approximately by the shaded area the Franco-British gains from July 1 to September 18, 1916

defeated—truly a proud record for an army which did not exist before the Great War began.

The weather, which had already handicapped the advance in its earlier stages, and was destined to rob the Allies of the crowning triumph which now seemed possible as a result of the enemy's obviously diminishing powers of resistance, seriously hindered Sir Douglas Haig's preparations for a further advance at this time. Days of rainstorms, mist, and mud added to the hardships of the autumn campaign and made rapid progress impossible. Bit by bit, however, we continued to improve our positions, pushing detachments forward in places into the enemy's advanced trenches, and waging a ceaseless, if local, warfare along the whole front.

It was not until September 25, the first anniversary of the Battle of Loos, that the Allies were able to launch their next general attack on the whole front from the Somme to Martinpuich, the main object of which was to complete the encircling movement that was slowly sealing the fate of Combles, and bring the advancing line another definite stage in the direction of Bapaume. Combles was a place of more importance than any that had yet stood in the Allies' path in this war among the woods and villages of Picardy, and the French and British Commanders, as already pointed out, had deliberately refrained from the direct assault for which the Germans were fully prepared. While the British on the left, advancing shortly after midday, following a bombard-

British Official

Where the French and British joined Forces on September 26, 1916: the main street of Combles

ment which had lasted since early the previous morning, closed round on Morval, capturing that village by nightfall, the French, first carrying Rancourt, also captured during the same night the neighbouring village of Frégicourt. By daybreak on the 26th, therefore, the Allied pincers had nearly closed, and a few hours later, with scarce a blow struck in its defence, the conquerors entered the town simultaneously, the British occupying the half to the north of the railway, and the French the half to the south.

When, two years previously, the Germans first captured the place they caused a medal to be struck in honour of what they boasted was a mighty achievement of German arms. Sir Douglas Haig modestly describes its rescue from their hands in this inexpensive fashion as "a not inconsiderable tactical success". Combles, as he points out, though lying in a hollow, was very strongly fortified, "and possessed, in addition to the works which the enemy had constructed, exceptionally large cellars and galleries, at a great depth underground, sufficient to give effectual shelter to troops and material under the heaviest bombardment". According to the orders issued by the German High Command it was to be held at all costs. The garrison, however, deciding that discretion was the better part of valour, had flown, taking most of their guns with them. They had foreseen the doom of their stronghold while the British were advancing towards Morval and the French troops fighting for Rancourt. There was no mistaking the meaning of these moves with an Allied army which had been capturing one German position after another since July 1 with unfailing regularity. So they had seized their last opportunity before the inexorable pincers closed over them, and escaped during the night to Le Transloy—those of them, at least, who survived the curtain of Allied fire which swept this last remaining road of refuge. A half-hearted rear-guard fight by their patrols was soon dealt with by the advancing troops, and many men were captured who, losing their way in the dark, wandered into the Allies' narrowing lines.

"When the morning came," to quote from the *Morning Post's* correspondent at the front, "the men in khaki came down the hill from Morval, streaming through the streets to meet their comrades of the French army advancing from the south. Other British battalions pressed forward from Bouleaux Wood, that sinister strip of ragged trees that blocked our path during many days of fighting. They had taken the wood at last; climbed over the labyrinth of trenches among the stumps and dead branches, and pushed along the sunken road that gives access to Combles from the west. Before dawn they were in possession of the orchard that lies on the edge of the town; stragglers and some machine-gun parties yielded themselves speedily; the way to the market square was free. At sunrise they were in Combles with their comrades from the north. The German rear-guard tried to show its teeth for the last time. It was a poor effort, and the fighting died away before it had become a serious menace."

Great quantities of war material were captured in the cellars, including many thousands of rounds of artillery ammunition and grenades. Combles was only one of many successes in the new advance begun at midday on September 25. Besides Morval and Combles our objectives had included the villages of Lesbœufs and Gueudecourt, with a belt of country about 1000 yards deep curving round the north of Flers to a point midway between that village and Martinpuich. The whole of these objectives were in our hands by nightfall, save the village of Gueudecourt, where a protecting trench to the west, forming a section of the enemy's fourth main system of defence, frustrated all our efforts to take it that day. Early next morning, however, it was very effectively overcome by a combined attack in a form unheard of in any previous war: a combination of Tank, aeroplane, and bombers. The Tank started down the portion of the trench held by the enemy from the north-west, firing its machine-guns and followed by bombers; the aeroplane at the same time, swooping to a low height from the ground, flew down the length of the trench, also firing a machine-gun as it went. There was no means of escape for the garrison from this staggering surprise, as we held the trench at the southern end. Realizing the hopelessness of their position they waved white handkerchiefs in token of surrender. As soon as this was reported by the aeroplane the unprecedented attack ceased, and the infantry accepted the garrison's surrender. "By 8.30 a.m.", records Sir Douglas Haig, "the whole trench had been cleared, great numbers of the enemy had been killed, and 8 officers and 362 other ranks made prisoners." Our total casualties in this amazing affair did not amount to more than five. A remarkable sequel is mentioned by the special correspondents at General Head-quarters, from which it appears that after leaving this captured trench in search of fresh adventures the Tank was forced to stop in order to attend to some slight internal trouble. It was quite alone, and the opportunity to wreak some vengeance on one of Britain's monstrous recruits was apparently too strong for another German garrison still lurking in the neighbourhood. Rushing from their hiding-place the Germans, quickly surrounding it in spite of the bullets which immediately rained upon them from its hidden batteries, clambered up its steel back and jabbed it with their bayonets, pelted it with bombs, and in short, to quote one writer, "made a wild pandemonium about it".

"Then", adds Mr. Philip Gibbs, "our infantry arrived, attracted by the tumult of this scene, and drove the enemy back. But the Tank had done deadly work, and between 200 and 300 killed and wounded Germans lay about its ungainly carcass. For a little while it seemed that the Tank also was out of action, but after a little attention and a good deal of grinding and grunting it heaved itself up and waddled away."[1]

The double capture of Morval and Lesbœufs on the previous day had been a very fine performance. Morval, standing on the heights north of Combles, constituted, with its subterranean quarries, trenches, and wire entanglements, "a formidable fortress", to quote Sir Douglas Haig's own words, and its possession, with that of

[1] *The Battles of the Somme.* By Philip Gibbs. (Heinemann, 1917.)

Lesbœufs, was of considerable military importance. Their comparatively easy capture strengthened the well-founded belief in the growing discouragement of the enemy. Here and there the Germans put up a dogged face-to-face fight to the last, but there was little organized resistance once the confident British infantry, carrying the advance position in a rush, fought their way into the ruins, and swept both villages clean with bombs and bayonets.

This triumph on the British right, completed on the following day by the fall of Gueudecourt, was rounded off on the left by the conquest of Thiepval and the high ridge east of it, including the Zollern Redoubt. Sir Douglas Haig now decided that the moment had arrived when Thiepval itself should be taken in order to bring his left flank into line and establish it on the main ridge above that infernal fastness. While, therefore, the enemy was still reeling under the succession of blows delivered by Sir Henry Rawlinson's troops, the Fifth Army under Sir Hubert Gough, released at last from its patient, self-sacrificing task of acting as a pivot to the remainder of the attack, launched a general assault against the salient which had barred its path through so many weeks of deadly warfare. In systematic preparation for this, New Army troops since the middle of September had been very skilfully and gallantly extending our gains south of Thiepval in the region of the captured Wonderwork, seizing trenches and taking some hundreds of prisoners. All these minor operations helped the decisive assault begun on September 26.

The result was a brilliant success, though the whole ridge was powerfully fortified, with an elaborate system of heavily-wired trenches, and defended with desperation. There was little sign here of the demoralization displayed by the defeated Prussians on

British Official

The Enemy's Underground Barracks on the Somme: entrance to a captured dug-out

the right flank. Thiepval, regarded as the strongest of all the enemy fortresses between the Ancre and the Somme, was defended to the last with a disciplined courage which Britons are always ready enough to recognize and honour. They were nearly all Wurtembergers in the garrison; and the 180th Regiment, which had held the place for nearly two years, strengthening it above and below ground with indefatigable zeal and ingenuity, were so proud of their handiwork that they had begged for the honour of holding it till the end of the war. Sure of its invincibility even before the Allied offensive, the tragic advance of July 1 had but confirmed them in their faith. So deep were their vaults and tunnels, which they had pierced and enlarged in all directions, extending in the east as far as their key position at Mouquet Farm, that when not on duty above ground they could live in perfect safety in an underworld of their own, untroubled by the fiercest bombardment. These subterranean barracks were subsequently found to be wired for electric light and fitted up in every way as a permanent habitation, with a completely equipped hospital and dressing-station thrown in.

When at last its doom was fulfilled, and we came to realize the amazing strength of the place, the possibilities of its underground fortifications, and the fighting spirit of the garrison, their confidence was hardly surprising. It was not until the British line came creeping ever nearer in those preliminary thrusts in September, and the British barrage which had been blasting so many other redoubts to bits was concentrated on their own quarters, that they began to lose their sense of security. But they fought tooth and nail for their buried battle-ground when the British attacking battalions advanced from the direction of the Wonderwork on September 26, preceded by their heavy curtain of protecting fire, and accompanied on the left by more than one of the mysterious Tanks, destined to play no small part in driving the British blow home. Only when our men were well over No Man's Land did the garrison reveal the full strength of their underground defences. Shell-holes were suddenly peopled with German machine-gunners, seemingly emerging from the bowels of the earth. Machine-guns began spitting death everywhere: behind every heap of rubbish; behind the shattered trunks of the apple orchard just before the village was reached; from every hole and corner of the place, until it seemed as though nothing could enter and live. Yet successive waves of our cheering infantry swept a path through the apple orchard and into Thiepval itself with a rush which gave them possession of three parts of the surface of the village within an hour. Then, however, came the long and close fighting in the underground labyrinth, and the enemy's determined struggles for his strong works in the north. A great stand was also made by the defenders among the fortified ruins of the château, which, bristling with machine-guns, defied all efforts to take it until a timely Tank appeared on the scene.

"Up it came, ponderously and deliberately," wrote the *Morning Post* correspondent, "head on at the château, impervious to the bullets that pattered on its armoured sides; charging the mound of brick and earth like a battering-ram, with its batteries in full action. The 'château' crumbled; the gunners ceased fire. Then, as the cheering infantry (they always cheer when they work with a 'Tank') pressed over the trenches around it the Wurtembergers grimly held up their hands, and the battalion commander tendered his submission."

Unfortunately some internal trouble put the Tank out of action shortly after this performance, and the infantry were deprived of its powerful assistance in the fierce struggle which ensued for the remainder of the place. They were New Army men, and unaccustomed for the most part to this murderous form of fortress warfare; but no troops in the world could have done better. They had to fight all day and night in the labyrinth of tunnels and deep dug-outs before Thiepval was finally won, but by 8.30 the next morning the whole of the village was in their hands, together with more than 1000 prisoners, including 26 officers. These were mostly of the 180th Wurtembergers, but units of seven other regiments were included in the remnants of the captured garrison.

On the right of Thiepval the attack had been equally successful, and was chiefly remarkable for the manner in which the last nest of Germans was destroyed at Mouquet Farm. "Moo-Cow" Farm deserves a chapter to itself when the full history of the war comes to be written. It was stormed by the Australians from the Pozières ridge on September 3, as described on p. 171, but, decimated by machine-gun fire from unknown quarters all round them, they had found the ruins untenable and dug themselves in a good 200 yards beyond the ruins to the east. The now famous "farm", with its mysterious powers of defence, thus remained the key position to Thiepval; and twelve days later, while the Tanks were making their sensational debut in the Allies' renewed offensive, the Canadians, not content with taking Courcelette, made an equally bold bid for the Mouquet ruins. Their success was as glorious and as tragic as the Australians'. Carrying the whole position with an irresistible rush they regarded the farm as definitively theirs, "having", to quote from their official *communiqué*, "finally overcome a desperate resistance"; but once more the enemy, counter-attacking with all the known and unknown means at his disposal, won the place back. It had long been obvious that all the ground in the neighbourhood was honeycombed with tunnels, and though many of these were discovered and blocked, others remained with hidden

Canadian War Records

Hazardous Work in the Canadian Trenches: sniping at a loophole in the enemy's defences

British Official

A Bombing Post: photograph taken at the moment of explosion

exits which were a continual menace to our troops. Later in the north a night attack gave us part of the farm, but two evil bits of ruin remained in the enemy's possession to the north, beyond our new front line. When we tried to wrest these from him he retreated to his caverns and connecting tunnels, refusing to budge, and continuing to harass us by sniping from positions which none could identify. One morning an officer talking to a sentry saw two Germans emerge from a heap of ruins behind our line. When they beckoned to him he not unnaturally thought they had strayed in and wished to surrender, as often happened. He was accordingly advancing in their direction when one of them deliberately shot him dead, and before the sentry could rush to his assistance both Germans had vanished as mysteriously as they had come.

That was the position at Mouquet Farm on the morning of the new advance on September 25, when its last secrets were to be given up after an underground battle which brought this savage form of warfare to a climax. While other battalions were advancing on Thiepval three waves of our attacking troops carried the outer defences of Mouquet Farm "and, pushing on", to quote the terse phrase of Sir Douglas Haig's dispatch, "entered Zollern Redoubt and consolidated". Behind them, however, had occurred an incident which might have broken down this assault—as so many other fine attacks had been broken down in this so-called "mystery corner"—but for the prompt intervention of a working party of a Pioneer Battalion acting on its own initiative, under one young officer. Our waves of infantry had scarcely swept over the wreckage of the farm towards the Zollern trench when parties of German machine-gunners emerged from unsuspected tunnels in the ruins and began firing into the backs of the British soldiers ahead. Luckily they were at once seen by the Pioneers at work not far away. "Come on, boys!" shouted the officer; and without a moment's hesitation they flung themselves into the fight at the critical moment, nipping in the bud what might otherwise have proved another local disaster. Thinking they were the advance party of a

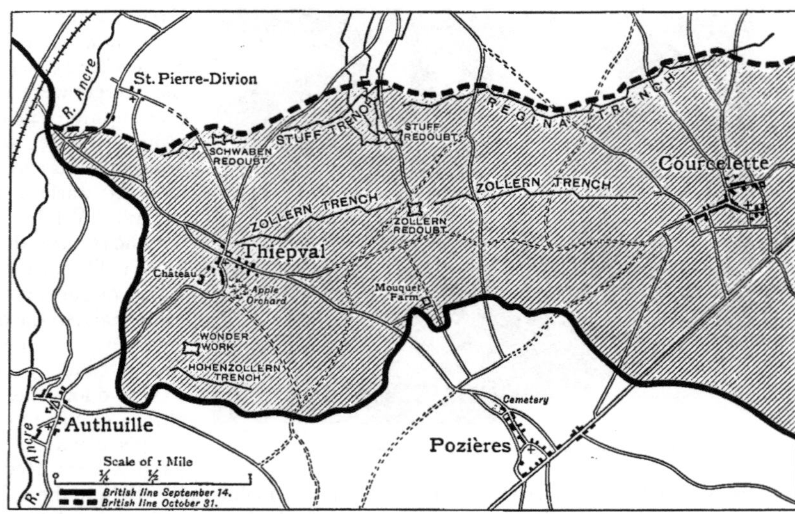


Map showing approximately the area gained on the Thiepval Ridge between September 14 and October 31, 1916

superior force the German machine-gunners surrendered; but there was still the main enemy garrison below, securely posted in deep cellars. Determined to wipe out this nest of hornets once and for all the Pioneers followed up their initial success by a pitched battle underground, which lasted until 6 p.m., when the enemy's last defences were forced. It is recorded that of these gallant Pioneers only thirteen were left at the end of the fight, but all had covered themselves with glory. When at last the survivors emerged in triumph they brought with them fifty-six prisoners, including one officer; and the only Germans now left under Mouquet Farm were never likely to worry us again.

All told some 2300 prisoners had been taken in the course of the successful advance on the Thiepval Ridge on these and subsequent days, bringing the total number of Germans taken in the whole battle area during the operations of the 14th–30th September to nearly 10,000. In the same period we had taken 27 guns, over 200 machine-guns, and some 40 trench mortars. These operations had included the reduction of the strong fortress called the Stuff Redoubt, while on September 27 we mastered most of the even more formidable Schwaben Redoubt, 500 yards north of Thiepval village. This last fortress, occupying the crest of the ridge, and representing the highest ground on the Thiepval spur, with a commanding view over the northern valley of the Ancre, was regarded by the enemy as the pivot of the whole position, and was defended with the utmost tenacity. The capture of the greater part of it was a fine feat of arms, and incidentally led to the taking of nearly 600 prisoners. Our gains were increased on the following day, only a minute portion of the redoubt then remaining in German hands. The importance attached to the position by the enemy was shown by the number of determined counter-attacks delivered during the next few weeks for its recovery, all of which, however, were repulsed, often with heavy losses.

On the right the Fourth Army had also pushed forward in the direction of Eaucourt-l'Abbaye, where, among the ruins of a French monastery, the enemy was making his new effort to stem our advance towards Bapaume; while in the direction of Sars, following an advance of the Canadians north of Courcelette, the Dominion Cavalry got to work for the first time since the Canadians participated in the war, their mounted patrols now being employed to establish the location of the enemy's retreating forces. In consequence of their reports the Canadians were able to advance their lines and occupy a fresh position, nearly 1000 yards farther forward, to the north-east of Courcelette. Since the beginning of their offensive in this field the Canadians, fighting nearly every yard of the way, had now won back for France over three square miles of fortified territory.

Since September 15 the Germans had brought up seven new divisions against the British front and five against the French. "The severe and prolonged struggle", telegraphed Sir Douglas Haig in his *communiqué* of October 3, "has demanded on the part of our troops very great determination and courage"; and all, he

Drawn by S. Begg

Winning the Strongholds of the Thiepval Ridge: the battle for Schwaben Redoubt on September 27, 1916

added, representing every part of the British Empire and British Islands, had behaved with the discipline and resolution of veterans. After battling for three months the situation at the end of September was officially summarized as follows:—

"1.—Since the opening of the battle on July 1 we have taken 26,735 prisoners.

"2.—We have engaged thirty-eight German Divisions, of which twenty-nine have been withdrawn in an exhausted or broken state.

"3.—We hold the half-moon of upland south of the Ancre, occupying every height of importance, and so have direct observation of the ground to the east and north-east.

"4.—The enemy has fallen back upon a fourth line behind the low ridge just west of the Bapaume-Transloy Road."

In a later telegraphic dispatch it was stated that during the same three months the British had captured and recovered from the Somme battle-field, besides large quantities of other war material—

29 heavy guns and heavy howitzers,
92 field guns and field howitzers,
103 trench artillery pieces, and
397 machine-guns.

It was pointed out at the time, and emphasized in the full dispatch at the end of the year, that the value of the prolonged offensive must not be judged in terms of territorial gains. "It must be looked for in the effect upon the enemy's strength in numbers, material, and *moral*"; and in all these respects Sir Douglas Haig was well content. Sufficient evidence was obtained to prove beyond a doubt that the German losses in men and material had been considerably higher than those of the Allies; and not only was the enemy using up his reserves in repeated costly and unsuccessful counter-attacks, but the steady deterioration in the fighting spirit of large numbers of his troops

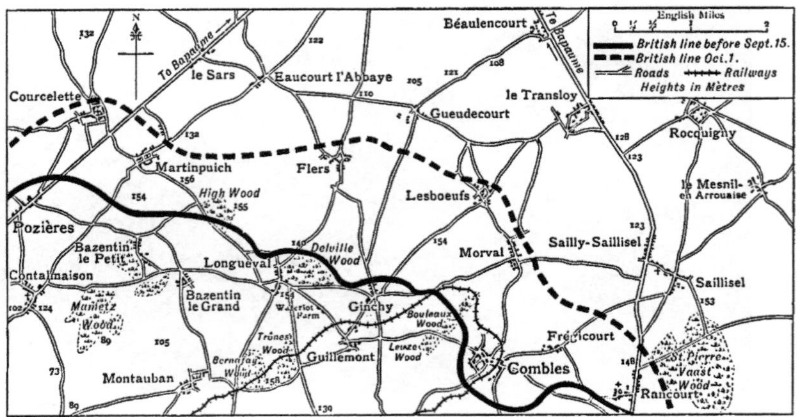


Map showing approximately the Allies' Lines before the attack of September 15 and at the beginning of October, 1916

After the Capture of Lesbœufs: British troops returning, headed by their fifes and drums British Official

was unmistakable. "Many of them, it is true," admitted Sir Douglas Haig, "fought with the greatest determination, even in the latest encounters, but the resistance of still larger numbers became latterly decidedly feebler than it had been in the earlier stages of the battle." That being the case, October found the British Commander-in-Chief not only confident that he could drive the enemy from his last foothold on the whole of the main ridge lying between the Tortille and the Ancre, when it should suit his plans to do so, but also hopeful that he was at length reaching a stage at which a successful attack, in his own words, "might reasonably be expected to yield much greater results than anything we had yet attained".

This hope, in spite of threatening weather, seemed to be drawing nearer and nearer to realization in the local operations which gradually cleared up the situation on both flanks in the early days of October, and brought our front at more than one point within a mile of the German fourth position west of the Bapaume-Transloy Road. Eaucourt l'Abbaye was stormed on the first day of the month, and, after days and nights of fierce bomb fighting among the battered buildings, in which the ruins changed hands more than once, remained finally in our possession by the evening of the 3rd. This brought us in line with the new position won towards the close of September at the strongly defended Destremont Farm, 500 yards south-west of Le Sars, which, after stubbornly resisting a first attempt, had been carried in gallant style by a single company.

A word is here due to the New Zealanders, whose heroic work, overshadowed by the magnitude of the battle as a whole, drew forth at this period a message from Sir Douglas Haig himself. The message was to statesmen from the southern Dominion

who arrived in October in London, and was to the following effect:—

"New Zealand Division has fought with greatest gallantry in Somme battle for twenty-three consecutive days, carrying out with complete success every task set, and always doing more than was asked of them. Division has won universal confidence and admiration. No praise can be too high for such troops."

Guarding against Underground Attack: British listening post on duty in the open

Note the position of the bayonet for the transmission of sound to the ear of the man on the left of the picture.

On October 7, after a postponement rendered necessary by three days continuous rain, a new combined offensive took place, in which the French made a considerable advance towards Sailly-Saillisel—Sir Douglas Haig having handed over Morval to our Allies in order to facilitate this attack—while the Fourth Army advanced in their support along the whole front from Destrement Farm to Lesbœufs. On that day the village of Le Sars, one of the gates barring the passage of our troops to Bapaume, and packed with Bavarian reinforcements, was carried with a dash and determination before which nothing could stand. According to common report among the prisoners—some 300 in all—our men fought like furies. Within an almost incredibly short time the whole defence had collapsed, and our twenty-second village since the offensive began had been won back for France. In the course of this action one division alone, which had previously had many days of hard fighting, took, all told, over 480 prisoners, including 8 officers. On the outskirts of Le Sars, and especially between that place and Eaucourt l'Abbaye, the assaulting troops were confronted with a harder task. It was ground swept by machine-gun fire from many strong points, and extraordinarily difficult by reason of its maze of entrenchments and sunken roads; but here, too, with the help of a Tank, the defence gradually crumbled before our invincible infantry. Good progress was also made to the west as well as to the east of Le Sars, while our line between Gueudecourt and Lesbœufs was advanced from 600 to 1000 yards.

East of Gueudecourt our right wing, marching in line with the French left, carried the enemy's trenches on a breadth of some 2000 yards, gaining a footing on the crest of the long spur which screened the German defences of Le Transloy from the south-west, while the French battalions pressed forward towards Sailly-Saillisel. Our Allies made a big thrust forward, crowning the western slopes of the Sailly-Saillisel Ridge, and bringing their line along the Bapaume Road to within 200 yards of the village itself. But it was essential to capture all the Sailly-Saillisel heights before an assault could be made on the Germans' last completed system of defence before Transloy; and meantime whole precious days were lost on account of the unfavourable weather, which now continued without a break during the remainder of October and the early part of November.

This fatal but unavoidable delay must have been galling beyond words to Sir Douglas Haig and all who had worked and planned so hard with him to bring the operations to a point when they could reasonably hope to deal the enemy a really smashing and decisive blow. Although well aware that the Germans were digging with feverish haste to strengthen the threatened system of defences covering the villages of Le Transloy and Beaulencourt, and the town of Bapaume, they knew that the enemy had as yet no very formidable defences behind that line; and the resistance of the opposing troops had weakened so perceptibly during the recent operations that "there was no reason to suppose", in the Commander-in-Chief's own words, "that the effort required would not be within our power". All that the Allies needed to break right through was a sufficient spell of dry weather. But the rain descended in torrents, and with never a break long enough to make the roads passable again. What this meant is defined clearly enough in Sir Douglas Haig's dispatch —:

> "Poor visibility seriously interfered with the work of our artillery, and constant rain turned the mass of hastily-dug trenches for which we were fighting into channels of deep mud. The country roads, broken by countless shell craters, that cross the deep stretch of ground we had lately won, rapidly became almost impassable, making the supply of food, stores, and ammunition a serious problem. These conditions multiplied the difficulties of attack to such an extent that it was found impossible to exploit the situation with the rapidity necessary to enable us to reap the full benefits of the advantages we had gained."

The enemy, on the other hand, did not fail to make the most of this involuntary respite. He now had time not only to strengthen all the weak points in his armour, but also to reorganize and rally his demoralized troops. His resistance gradually stiffened and became as stubborn as ever. With renewed strength, both in men and guns, he counter-attacked again and again. Trenches changed hands so frequently that it becomes increasingly hard to make either interesting or clear the confused and widely-scattered operations which characterized this disappointing phase of the battle. The conditions of ground, as Sir Douglas Haig points out, made it difficult either to renew exhausted supplies of bombs and ammunition, or to consolidate the ground won. Thus it was always an easier matter to take a battered trench than to hold it in this high, desolate country swept by the enemy's fire. It was a phase involving some of the hardest and sternest fighting of the whole campaign, though for the most part of a local and isolated nature: a thrust forward here for some German strong position; a slight advance there to storm some section of the enemy's defence in order to straighten our new front; constant bombing, sniping, and artillery bombardments; and all the time the execrable weather which prevented anything in the nature of a general advance.

There was none of the glamour of a grand attack about this phase of the battle, but it called for just as high qualities of courage and endurance. The manner in which our troops not only clung to their hard-won ground under the terrific pressure of the enemy's counter-attacks, but also continued slowly but steadily to win their way over the extreme shoulders of the ridge and down the beginning of the slopes beyond, was sufficient testimony both to their grit and gallantry. A minor thrust forward on October 12 forced the Germans back still farther over the right shoulder of the ridge, the French at the same time advancing on our right another and final stage on the hard road to Sailly-Saillisel. The enemy proclaimed this modest advance as "another great attempt to break through", which they had frustrated at frightful cost to the Allies; but, save for an isolated action near the Schwaben Redoubt, the new "push" only extended along the British front from the right of Eaucourt l'Abbaye to beyond Lesbœufs. Thence the French continued the attack, the main object being to clear the enemy from his defences on the Sailly-Saillisel heights and the spur lying between Le Transloy and Lesbœufs, which screened the enemy's last completed system of defences on the road from Peronne to Bapaume. We advanced our front in these operations between Gueudecourt and Lesbœufs, and also north-west of Gueudecourt, besides taking about 150 prisoners and a number of machine-guns.

Most of these later operations had been afternoon affairs, but on October 18, when we still further improved the British line in this region, and the French completed the conquest of Sailly-Saillisel, we took the enemy by surprise in the rain and darkness of the early morning, when the British barrage, short and sharp, suddenly foretold an impending assault. The British advance was in the nature of a triple attack, like a thrust with an ancient trident, one prong pointing beyond Lesbœufs, another to the north-east of Gueudecourt, and the third, in the same direction, from Eaucourt l'Abbaye. It had rained all night, and the bare slopes of the low ridges up which our infantry clambered, over a maze of mine craters and shell-holes — a mere wilderness of pools and puddles intersected with chalky, glutinous mud —became the scene of a breathless struggle in which men fought to the death for every foot of ground. It needed no ordinary courage to attack over such a battle-field in the dark; but here, as elsewhere, our eager infantry displayed their wonted gallantry and devotion. Picked Bavarian, Brunswick, and Hanoverian regiments were pitted against certain distinguished British battalions, and were forced to give ground. We captured altogether, in these three enterprises, some 300 prisoners, and extended our front at various points, especially north of Gueudecourt and towards the Butte de Warlencourt, commanding the Bapaume Road above Le Sars. The Butte, at one time a notable landmark on the battle-field, and a tower of strength in the German defence, standing 50 feet high, had been so pounded by British shells that it was now little but a battered, shapeless mound.

The Impassable Battle-field: scene on the Ancre after the autumn rains of 1916 — Official Photograph

While we were thus pushing our line forward at several points the French, as already mentioned, completed the conquest of Sailly-Saillisel, after several days of house-to-house fighting, in the course of which one group of ruins was lost and retaken no fewer than six times. This costly

Official Photograph

After the Battle: searching German prisoners of war

triumph had at length removed practically the enemy's last vital defence fronting the great Cambrai Plain, and hopes were raised that the road was now clear for an advance which would secure for the Allies complete victory in this field before another winter campaign began. But the moment for decisive action, as Sir Douglas Haig realized only too well, "was rapidly passing away". The weather, too, was as bad as ever. Even in the rare intervals between the downpours of rain the air was "muggy", with only fitful gleams of sunshine. "The ground", writes Sir Douglas Haig, "had now become so bad that nothing less than a prolonged period of drying weather, which at that period of the year was most unlikely to occur, would suit our purpose." These fears proved only too well grounded. The disheartening weather did not take a turn for the better until towards the middle of November, when a great battle on the Ancre, with its capture of Beaumont-Hamel, formed the crowning achievement on the British left, and one of the most remarkable triumphs in all this ensanguined fighting.

The capture of Beaumont-Hamel, however, and the operations which preceded and followed it on the line from Regina Trench to Schwaben Redoubt, on the Thiepval ridge, must be left for a later chapter on the Battles of the Ancre. On the right flank, in conjunction with the French on the Somme, we had to rest content with two minor thrusts, one on October 23, and the other on November 5. In these considerable further progress was achieved to the east of Lesbœufs and Gueudecourt, our footing on the crest of Le Transloy spur being extended and secured, "and the much-contested tangle of trenches at our junction with the French left", to quote from the Commander-in-Chief's dispatch, "at last passed definitely into our possession".

Though robbed by the abnormally heavy autumn rains of the full fruits of our advance, "at a time", he observes, "when we had good grounds for hoping to achieve yet more important successes", Sir Douglas could point with pride to the fact that the three main objects with which he commenced our offensive on July 1 had, by November, already been achieved:

> "Verdun had been relieved; the main German force had been held on the Western Front; and the enemy's strength had been very considerably worn down".

The achievement of any one of these results, claimed the Commander-in-Chief, would alone have been sufficient to justify the Somme Battle, and the attainment of all three of them had not only afforded "ample compensation for the splendid efforts of our troops and the sacrifices made by ourselves and our Allies", but had also brought us "a long step forward towards the final victory of the Allied cause". The fact that in November the enemy mustered more men and guns on this battle-field than at the beginning of July, after four-fifths of the total number of German divisions engaged on the Western front had been thrown one after the other into the Somme furnace—some of them twice, and

British Official

Shepherding the Prisoners on the Somme: German captives in one of the enclosures behind the British firing-line

some three times—was sufficient proof that our combined efforts had not only relieved Verdun but also held large German forces which would otherwise have been employed against our Allies in the east. Discipline and training, combined with the great depth of his defences, and his vast resources in man-power, enabled the enemy to keep his mighty war machine going after each defeat, but every set-back added to its difficulties, and towards the end of the operations, when the weather unfortunately broke, there was no doubt in Sir Douglas's mind that its running powers had been very seriously diminished. Captured documents in growing numbers bore witness at that time to the degenerating *moral* of a badly-shaken enemy, and to the horrors of what German soldiers called "the blood bath of the Somme".

And while the *moral* of the enemy was steadily declining the *moral* of our own troops, always magnificent, was as steadily advancing. The confidence of our men in ultimate victory increased every month. Numbers and all other resources were on their side, and man for man they were never so sure of their superiority over the foe. Day after day, in battle after battle, they had driven the Germans from the strongest entrenchments ever devised by human skill, and knew that they had simply to press on, with all their strength and resources, and decisive victory must be theirs. It was one of the most astounding feats in military history that this absolutely new Army had faced the greatest army the world had ever seen, as Mr. Lloyd George said shortly after succeeding Mr. Asquith as Prime Minister, "and had beaten them, beaten them, beaten them". The truth was fraught with significance for the foe, as well as for ourselves. "Neither victors nor the vanquished will forget this," wrote Sir Douglas Haig, towards the close of his dispatch; "and though bad weather has given the enemy a respite, there will undoubtedly be many thousands in his ranks who will begin the new campaign with little confidence in their ability to resist our assaults or to overcome our defence."

One of the most significant signs of our increasing strength, and a remarkable testimony to the revolution wrought by the Ministry of Munitions, was the fact, disclosed by Mr. Lloyd George at Carnarvon on February 3, 1917, that after four months of incessant bombardment, night and day, along the whole Somme battle-field, there were more British guns and there was more British ammunition than on the opening day of the battle. Sir Douglas did not forget the efficient artillery support throughout the operations in acknowledging the noble services of all arms engaged in the battle. Against such defences as the Germans had prepared—"far more formidable in many respects", he said, "than those of the most famous fortresses in history"—any infantry, with the greatest courage in the world, would have been powerless without thoroughly efficient artillery preparation and support.

"The work of our artillery", he added, "was wholly admirable, though the strain on the *personnel* was enormous. The excellence of the results attained was the more remarkable, in view of the shortness of the training of most of the junior officers and of the N.C.O.'s and men. Despite this, they rose to a very high level of technical and tactical skill, and the combination between artillery and infantry, on which, above everything, victory depends, was an outstanding feature of the battle. Good even in July, it improved with experience, until in the latter assaults it approached perfection."

As already mentioned, the German casualties in killed and wounded were officially estimated to be greater than those of the Allies, while their losses in prisoners, taken by the British alone up to November 18—this date including the capture of Beaumont-Hamel—were given as just over 38,000, including over 800 officers. We captured during the same period 29 heavy guns, 96 field guns and field howitzers, 136 trench mortars, and 514 machine-guns.

Altogether it was a stupendous performance for a new Army, raised and trained for the most part during the war, and all the troops engaged deserved the glowing tribute paid to them by their Commander-in-Chief in his full dispatch:—

"Many of them, especially amongst the drafts sent to replace wastage, counted their service by months, and gained in the Somme battle their first experience of war. The conditions under which we entered the war had made this unavoidable. We were compelled either to use hastily trained and inexperienced officers and men, or else to defer the offensive until we had trained them. In this latter case we should have failed our Allies. That these troops should have accomplished so much under such conditions, and against an army and a nation whose chief concern for so many years has been preparation for war, constitutes a feat of which the history of our nation records no equal. The difficulties and hardships cheerfully overcome, and the endurance, determination, and invincible courage shown in meeting them, can hardly be imagined by those who have not had personal experience of the battle, even though they have themselves seen something of war."

A fine tribute was also paid by Sir Douglas to his two Army Commanders, Generals Sir Henry Rawlinson and Sir Hubert Gough, who for five months controlled the operations of the Fourth and Fifth Armies respectively in "one of the greatest, if not absolutely the greatest, struggle that has ever taken place", and entirely justified their selection for such responsible commands. It was impossible, said their Chief, to speak too highly of the great qualities which both displayed throughout the battle. "Their thorough knowledge of the profession, and their cool and sound judgment, tact, and determination, proved fully equal to every call on them." This handsome acknowledgment will be endorsed by posterity; but Sir Douglas Haig's modesty in belittling his own share in the battle—the control exercised by a Commander-in-Chief where such large forces are concerned being "necessarily restricted", he declares, "to a general guidance"—will never allow the British race to forget its indebtedness to the Chief who bore the supreme burden of responsibility throughout, and inspired everyone with his own admirable skill, courage, and tenacity. He was promoted to Field-Marshal's rank in the King's New Year Honours List; and some months before, on the occasion of His Majesty's visit to the front, was promoted Knight Grand Cross of the Royal Victorian

Order, Sir Henry Rawlinson being promoted to K.C.V.O. on the same occasion. Sir Douglas's two Army Commanders in the battle also figured in the New Year Honours List, Sir Henry Rawlinson being promoted General and Sir Hubert Gough Lieutenant-General "for distinguished service in the field". Many other soldiers who had borne the brunt of the same campaign received their well-earned rewards on this occasion, including Sir L. E. Kiggell, Sir Douglas Haig's invaluable Chief of Staff, who, like Sir Hubert Gough, Major-General H. S. Horne, Major-General G. F. Milne, and the Earl of Cavan, was raised to Lieutenant-General's rank. Among the new K.C.B.'s were Lieutenant-General W. N. Congreve, V.C., whose son, as recorded on p. 164, lost his life in winning a Victoria Cross of his own; Lieutenant-General Claud W. Jacob, Lieutenant-General C. T. M'Murragh Kavanagh, and Lieutenant-General Edward A. Fanshawe. The new K.C.M.G.'s included Lieutenant-General Sir W. Pulteney-Pulteney; Lieutenant-General Sir Thomas D'Oyly Snow; and Lieutenant-General Sir Thomas L. N. Morland; while Colonel Trenchard, the Commander of the Royal Flying Corps, the supremacy of which over the German Air Service throughout the operations was one of the most striking features of the battle, was promoted Major-General.

With a theme so vast it has been impossible in the space at our disposal to give more than the barest outline of our Allies' brilliant share in a long series of victories, which could not have been achieved, as King George acknowledged in his telegram to President Poincaré after the successes of September, "without the splendid support of the gallant French troops on our right fighting for one common objective". Besides their advance side by side with the British north of the Somme they made appreciable progress on their southern front across the river. Their territorial gains during the first three months, shown at a glance in our map on p. 186, were steadily increased during October and November, when their re-entrant in the line between Chaulnes and Berny-en-Santerre was straightened out by successive thrusts which won the German positions within half a mile of Fresnes, and captured the village of Ablaincourt, besides various hamlets and strong points, and some 4000 prisoners. From July 1 to November 1 the magnificent share of our Allies in the total gains in men and material amounted to 41,605 prisoners, including 809 officers; 77 field guns, 101 heavy guns, 104 trench mortars, and 535 machine-guns. More impressive still were the official figures published at the end of the year, which showed that during 1916 the French troops, on the battle-fields both of Verdun and the Somme, captured all told no fewer than 78,500 prisoners. Faced with such facts as these and the relentless pressure of the British blockade, as well as the certain knowledge that the Allies' blows would only begin with redoubled force in the spring, it was hardly surprising that the close of 1916 found the German War Lords ready to intrigue for peace. F. A. M.

# CHAPTER VIII

## THE BALKAN THEATRE, 1916

Attitude of Greece towards the Allies—The Conditions under which Franco-British Forces landed at Salonika—Greek Benevolent Neutrality—The Treacherous Attack on the Allies' Landing Parties at the Piræus on December 1, 1916—Sarrail's Task at Salonika—The Monastir Advance of September, 1916—Description of the Bulgar-Macedonian Front—Serbian Capture of Kaymakchalan Mountain—Bulgarian Retirement to the Cerna—The Kenali Lines in Front of Monastir—Plan for Attacking Monastir by the Cerna Flank—Capture of the Ridges North of the Cerna Loop—Bulgarians Evacuate Monastir—Roumania's Entry into the War—German Preparations—Roumania's Forces and Leaders—The Strategical Outlook—Plans of Campaign—Invasion of Transylvania—Mackensen's Counter-stroke in the Dobrudja—Roumanians Attacked in Transylvania by Falkenhayn—Falkenhayn and the Southern Passes—Fall of Constanza and Cernavoda—Capture of Craiova and Bucharest—Roumanians fall back to the Sereth.

IN the history of the war as it affected the Balkan States during 1916, the political cannot be divorced from the strategic aspect. It was never possible in 1915 for either France or Great Britain, when they took into consideration their military responsibilities on the Western front, to detach a large enough force, properly supplied with artillery and ammunition and transport, to be of any avail in saving Serbia against a joint attack by Germany, Austria, and Bulgaria, especially when that joint attack was directed by German generals and supported by German artillery; and a great disservice was done to public opinion by the pretence that they could. There was never any question in the minds of the responsible military officers of sending a force to Salonika sufficient to stem the invasion of Serbia, because such a force in a military sense did not exist. The men for it might possibly have been spared: but a million men are not an army. The only way in which Serbia could have been saved was that which was indicated by Viscount Grey when he spoke of the effort to induce Greece to fulfil her treaty obligations. Those treaty obligations were, in general terms, that Greece should go to Serbia's assistance if Serbia were attacked by Bulgaria; and Greece evaded them on the pretext that the chief attack on Serbia was made by Germany and Austria, not by Bulgaria.

King Constantine's attitude towards the Entente is best judged by what he did. Having declined to assist Serbia for the implied reason that to have done so would have been to commit a breach of neutrality against Germany, he steadily adhered to this attitude in his treatment of the Entente. France and Great Britain went to Salonika in response to the Greek Government's enquiry whether they were prepared to replace the 150,000 Serbs who, in conformity with the Serbo-Greek treaty, should have been in Macedonia; and this enquiry implied that Greece would fulfil her treaty obligations if the Allies supplied these reinforcements. France and Britain could not therefore be turned out diplomatically, and certainly not by force.[1] But their presence on Greek soil was

[1]This question was discussed by M. Venizelos in the *Kiryx* of April 23, 1916.

King Peter in Exile, 1916: an historic group at Salonika

On the left of the picture is Sir Bryan Mahon, then commanding the British troops in the Balkans. On the right is General Sarrail, Commander-in-Chief at Salonika.

regarded in certain quarters as a stain on Greek neutrality, and consequently there was no pretence of making them welcome. They were tolerated because there was no help for it; and until General Sarrail made it clear that there was no question of the abandonment of Salonika by the Franco-British forces, there was a great deal of the policy of pin-pricks. Railway facilities were refused; a strong Greek force was kept in threatening juxtaposition to the Franco-British lines. When the Serbian army, having been refitted, was being brought from Corfu in April, 1916, King Constantine's Government refused it the right to use the Greek railways—on the ground of a breach of neutrality. This nicety of regard for neutrality had earlier provoked the suggestion that the Franco-British force ought to be interned in Greek territory. That proposal had been made, however, when General Sarrail's retirement on Salonika had been accomplished with difficulty, and when the prospects of the Entente in this part of the conflict were at their gloomiest. As they brightened, Greek insistence on the rigours of neutrality began to diminish; and the fortunes of the Allies in other fields of warfare could almost have been gauged by the state of the Greek neutrality barometer.

During the earlier months of the year General Sarrail's forces dug themselves in, fortified their positions, and accumulated shell. Salonika was not an ideal port, and its surroundings were far from being healthy. There was a good deal of malaria and dysentery among the Entente forces early in 1916 and during the summer months. To these forces were added contingents from Russia and from Italy, and later in the year Italian contingents pushed forward from Avlona (Vallona) on the other side of the peninsula. General Sarrail found himself strong enough to take a firm attitude at Salonika. He turned out the spies that had found a convenient hive there, and deported the Austrian, German, Bulgarian, and Turkish consuls. He insisted on the removal from close propinquity of the Greek forces, and he took steps to secure his position by destroying lengths of the railway leading towards Bulgarian territory parallel to the frontier.

Throughout the tedious and trying operations at Salonika and on the Macedonian front the cordiality of the relations between the Franco-British forces was complete. This was due not a little to the personalities of the Commanders and to the supreme confidence which divisional generals reposed in General Sarrail. No opportunity was lost of enhancing this cordiality, and one of the pleasantest acts of courtesy of the campaign was the bestowal of a K.C.B. on General Bailloud, who commanded a French division in Macedonia, and had rendered signal services to the British Army in the Dardanelles before he came to the Salonika front.

Meanwhile King Constantine, who had declined to govern through M. Venizelos, observing that in regard to international relations he considered himself "alone responsible before God for their direction",[1] replaced the

[1] M. Venizelos's report of his interview with King Constantine on September 5, 1915.

Venizelos Ministry by a succession of others. That of M. Zaimis succeeded those of M. Skoloudis and M. Gounaris and was succeeded by that of Professor Lambros. All these, echoing the King, never ceased to emphasize the assertion of the benevolent feeling which they entertained towards the Allies.

The hypothesis that their neutrality was maintained solely in the interests of the Hellenic peoples, and had nothing to do with King Constantine's predilection for Germany, received, however, a severe blow on September 12, 1916. A Bulgarian force advanced boldly over the Greek frontier far to the east of General Sarrail's right flank, towards Kavalla on the coast. It was asserted by the Greek Government that they had no *locus standi* in resisting this advance into their territory, because they were countenancing a similar breach of neutrality by allowing the Franco-British forces to remain at Salonika. Such an assertion might have had some plausibility, if the concession to the Bulgarians had not been followed up by the hollow submission of Fort Rupel and other defences on the Struma, and by the subsequent surrender of a whole Greek Army Corps, with all its artillery and transport, to the Bulgarian commander.

General Bailloud, created by His Majesty a K.C.B.
(From a photograph by Walery, Paris)

From this day onward the decision of Great Britain and France was taken towards Greece, though it was hampered by diplomatic delays. The only open question was that of ways and means. M. Venizelos, who had long indicated his intentions, but who had made unceasing efforts to obtain the co-operation of King Constantine, cut himself loose, and forming a Provisional Government with headquarters at Salonika, invited the adherence of Greeks as volunteers in a new national army. It was the aim of the Entente diplomacy to attract as many Greeks to this new army as possible, and to weaken the maleficent powers of the army remaining with King Constantine; but, meanwhile, to avoid either precipitating Greece into civil war or exacerbating the feelings of the Greek people. It was a difficult, almost a hopeless task; and its method, which proceeded by the disarming first of the Greek fleet, and afterwards of the Greek army, was attended by continual dangers. The reality of these dangers was demonstrated in the first week of December, when an attempt to land French, British, and Italian forces at the Piræus was met with armed resistance on the part of Greek reservists armed with machine-guns. This act of open treachery abolished the last diplomatic obstacles among the Allies, and it was significantly followed first by an Allied Conference at Rome, and immediately afterwards by an ultimatum, in which Italy unreservedly concurred, to King Constantine's Government.

Throughout 1916 the attitude of Greece was a condition which the Franco-British Higher Commands had to consider before committing the Salonika Expeditionary Forces to any aggressive action against Bulgaria. It was often urged in 1916, and before then, that the road to victory lay through an attack delivered in force from Salonika, whereby the communications between the Central Powers

Map showing the position of Greece in regard to the Balkan Campaign

and their Bulgarian and Turkish allies might be cut. It was never at any time possible. The attack on the Bulgarian lines must be made by three avenues, which did not communicate with one another. The most easterly was the avenue of the Struma; the next was the avenue of the Vardar; the third was the avenue which led to Monastir and the Monastir plain. For the simultaneous thrust through these avenues, half a million of men, with reserves, might have guaranteed success. It would have been very difficult to find the steamers to carry such a force by sea; a single division with its share of line-of-communications impedimenta demands a shipping tonnage of about 200,000 tons. When the troops had been deposited it would have been still more difficult to feed them through a second-class port such as Salonika. Chief of all the difficulties would have been that of finding the transport for them. In Macedonia, which is a country still in the condition of the Turkish Middle Ages, only pack transport or light-cart transport can be used. For the kind of army that has been postulated, some 100,000 of such vehicles would have been required. It was such commonplace but insuperable obstacles as these which condemned the Franco-British forces in Salonika to inactivity during most of the year, and made any advance on a large scale out of the question for the time being. This would only be possible with the gradual development of the Allies' plans elsewhere, together with the clearing up of the situation in Greece herself. It was out of the question in 1916.

Where the Serbian Army was Reconstituted: view of Corfu, with the French warships in the foreground

These were the reasons which kept Sarrail marking time till the autumn. His forces had sufficiently performed their primary duty of keeping the Central Powers in general, and the Bulgarians in particular, from spreading down to the Mediterranean, to be an active danger on the flank of our shipping; and nothing more was immediately incumbent on them. When, however, in August, Roumania at length abandoned her neutrality, and joined her forces to those of Russia and the other Powers of the Entente, General Sarrail launched the long-deferred blow at one sector of the Bulgarian line, choosing that which protected the Monastir plain. This, if broken, would open a gap by which the Serbians would advance on to their own soil.

The mixed force of British, French, Russian, Italian, and Serbian units which General Sarrail commanded were distributed along the Macedonian frontier of Greece between the Struma and Lake Ostrovo. The British force under General Milne formed the extreme right wing, and held the line of the Struma River and the front between that river and the Vardar. The French prolonged this line westwards to the Moglena mountains. The Serbians, on the French left, were stretched as far as Lake Ostrovo, and on their own left had a Franco-Russian strengthening force. The Serbians were given this post of honour at their own request; and had previously been in action in conjunction with the French on the Vardar. On September 13 the Crown Prince of Serbia, having compelled the retirement of the Bulgarians behind the Moglena ridge, attacked them on Malak Nidje ridge, about ten miles west of Lake Ostrovo. The capture of this ridge (and thirty-two guns) by the Serbians opened up the way towards Florina, the first step towards Monastir. On the 13th of September the supporting Franco-Russian force on the Serbian left extended the Serbian gains to the west by occupying the adjacent Malareka ridge: and the whole force advanced on Florina. Florina was occupied on the morning of September 18. Meanwhile General Milne had been "demonstrating" with effect on the Vardar-Struma front. On the 13th he seized the village of Machukovo, and carried a salient called Machine-gun Hill by assault.

From Monastir the flat country is shaped like a jack-boot with a high heel and a toe pointing upwards to the north-east. The Malareka and Malak ridges won by the Franco-Russian-Serbian forces are beneath the sole of the boot, whose toe points towards the Moglena ridge and the Kaymakalan mountain. Florina is the ankle bone. Monastir lies some distance up the leg, with mountains behind the calf, and the curving River Cerna and other mountains fencing in the shin. After the capture of Florina the Serbians went on to the River Brod, which rises at the foot of the Kaymakalan mountain, and lies in a big loop in the plain. The mountain was the flanking key to the Bulgarian defences on the Brod. The Serbians turned it after many fierce assaults on September 28—a notable victory. It left the Bulgarians no option but to fall back to the Cerna, the river that completely looped the buttress of mountain range which formed the eastern protection of the Monastir plain and positions.

During this fortnight the Franco-Russian force had been clearing up the ankle of the boot, north and west of Florina; and by October 6 had reached a line extending from Presba Lake on the extreme west, through Kishovo, at the foot of the western hills protecting the Monastir Plain, to

Reorganizing the Serbian Army: troops in training on Corfu Island

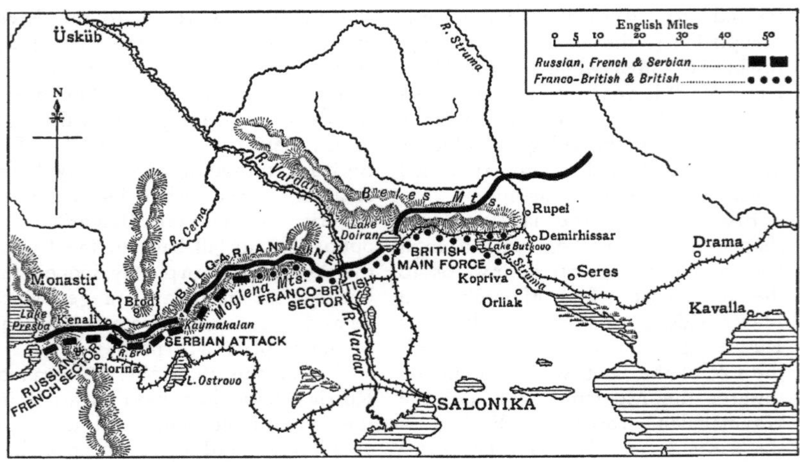


The Allies' Line facing the Bulgarians in the closing Campaign of 1916

Kenali. At Kenali the French linked up with the Serbians, and for some time the combined forces stood in front of the Kenali positions while the French Command reconnoitred the position. During this temporary pause General Milne continued to demonstrate with continuous vigour. He crossed the Struma on September 30 at Orliak, carrying a cluster of villages on October 4 and 5, and advancing during the next few days as far as Kalendra on the road to Seres. In his extended positions he then faced a Bulgarian army holding a strongly-entrenched position on the western slopes of the hills between Demirhissar and Seres.

The Kenali positions which the Bulgarians had fortified in front of Monastir had been prepared with great labour, and the trenches, constructed after the Somme model, had been strengthened by continuous belts of wire entanglements. The situation was one which the peculiarities of siege warfare had rendered not uncommon. The Monastir Plain has just been compared to the leg and foot of a jack-boot. The simile may be amplified in the following way. Monastir stands between two ranges of mountains thus:—**U · U**. Round the right-hand **U** the River Cerna ran in a loop, and the part of the loop nearest to Monastir was fringed with swamps. In old-time warfare the obvious way to approach Monastir would have been by the avenue of plain between the **U U**. But with modern trenches backed up by modern artillery this was the impracticable way, because the whole eight miles of front in the flat plain imposed on its attackers the need of a frontal assault. After repairing the roads, bringing up heavy guns, and accumulating for a fortnight a head of shell, the French Command launched such a frontal attack, after an intensive bombardment. This was on October 14. The attack failed.

It became, therefore, necessary to find some way of taking these lines in flank. They must be turned by either one or other of the **U U**. A scheme was considered of turning them by the left-hand **U**, but was rejected as too perilous. The arm stretched out in that direction would have to extend too far westwards. They must be turned by the right-hand **U**. That was nearer to the Allies' sources and lines of supply; and when the Serbians had made their brilliant capture of the Kaymakalan summit they had taken a great step towards attack in this direction. Before the unsuccessful frontal attack on the Kenali entrenchments had been made, they had come down from the mountain to the loop-like River Cerna, and had fought their way to a rather precarious footing on the other side. This footing was at length consolidated, and was made the basis of the flank attack on the Kenali lines which succeeded. It was a lengthy business, and while all the laborious preparations, the shifting of artillery, the re-accumulation of shell, &c., were going on, General Milne's forces kept up the steady pressure on the Bulgarian forces of the Struma which prevented their removal to reinforce the Kenali-Monastir front.

The difficult rock mass which, encircled by the Cerna, protected Monastir and the Kenali lines from an attack on the east, may be likened to a **W** within a **U**, thus: **W U**. The two points of the **W** are the Tepavtsi ridge and the Chuke ridge. A ravine runs between them, and the ground at the top of the **W**, which is due east of Monastir, rises much higher. If this higher ground could be reached and secured, all the Bulgarian Kenali positions would be exposed to a fire from behind them. If artillery could be got up the ridges, no lines between Kenali and Monastir would be long tenable.

The positions on the Bulgarian side of the Cerna loop, at the foot of the points of the **W**, were Brod and Skochovir. These were the first points seized by the Serbians on November 10. Their next step was to get a footing on the points of the **W**, Tepavtsi and Chuke. They were bound to carry Chuke, the right-hand one, first, though it was the more difficult, because otherwise Tepavtsi would be outflanked. By the evening of November 10 the attack on Chuke had been made, had succeeded, and the Serbians were half-way up it at Polag, and had captured some guns. On Saturday, November 11, half the Chuke ridge and the valley between the points of the **W** was in Serbian hands, and the defences of Monastir began from that moment to crumble. On Sunday, 12th, all Bulgarian counter-attacks failed, and they abandoned the whole of the right-hand half of the **W**, and thus rendered the left-hand half of it vulnerable to the victorious Serbians. Even from the right-hand half which they had won, the Serbian artillery could now throw shells over the left-hand half into the Kenali trenches.

Ready Again for the Fray: Serbian artillery on the way to the front from Salonika

The Serbian infantry, aided by the French, were not long in improving their advantage, and by Tuesday, 14th, the Bulgarians had recognized the peril of their advanced position, and, leaving a rear-guard only to defend them, had begun to retire to their second position on the Bistriza stream, which crosses the plain 2 miles in front of Monastir. The Russians and French were held at bay for most of the day by the rear-guard and a blinding rainstorm, but at night had penetrated the first-line trenches. By next morning they found that the defenders had melted away, and had made their way to the Bistriza, where—according to their published *communiqués*—they would make a renewed stand. They had not the power to do so. The Bistriza lines were not a good position, nor had they been prepared with the skill and industry lavished on the fortified positions of Kenali, on which the enemy had staked everything. Moreover, the Serbian continued advance over the mountain mass made all the Bulgarian positions south of Monastir precarious. The German and Bulgarian commanders were acute enough to realize that they had lost the position and the battle, and made the best of the business by getting their guns away. On the night of the Saturday-Sunday, November 18–19, they marched out of Monastir by the northern road, and began a retreat to the hill positions to the north. The last rear-guard battery left as the advance-guard of the Allies entered the city on Sunday morning. To the brave Serbian troops was given the honour of first marching into the town they had won back, the capital of western Macedonia. It is worth while to remark that throughout the critical period of this struggle, between November 11 and 18, every German *communiqué* distorted the facts so as to give the crumbling resistance of the German and Bulgarian troops the appearance of successful counter-attack, and on the eve of the retirement from Monastir General von Bulow was promoted for retaking a Serbian height which, in fact, remained in Serbian hands.

If the upshot of General Sarrail's advance from Salonika had more than fulfilled the hopes of those who were in a position to judge of the difficulties, the result of the year's campaigning in another and a more conspicuous part of the Balkans, namely, Roumania, was a chilling disappointment. Roumania's entry into the war had been long foretold. It had been rashly proclaimed as certain when the Allies had bought the Roumanian wheat crop of 1914; it had again been assumed as certain when Italy joined the Allies. Even through the period of Russia's disasters in 1915 hopes were entertained that the appeals of her pro-Ally statesman, M. Take Jonescu, would bring her to the Allies' aid. Those who were acquainted with the difficulties which stood in Roumania's way in obtaining either artillery or the ammunition for it were naturally sceptical. When, however, in August, 1916, after Russia had thrust back the Austrian armies south of the Pripet over a 150-mile front, and had burst

Roumania's Military Preparations: cavalry review by King Ferdinand on "National Day", 1916

a way past Czernowitz into the Bukovina and towards the Jablonica and Kirlibaba Passes in the Carpathians, it seemed clear that the time had come for Roumania to declare herself. The only question was—had she enough ammunition? Roumania declared war against Austria-Hungary on August 27. It was assumed, therefore, that she had enough ammunition, and was able to play her part in prolonging the Russian left in the Bukovina along the whole line of the south-eastern Carpathians. That is to be regarded as a military view of the situation. The political view had more than one aspect. Roumania's declaration for the cause of the Entente was regarded by the practical-minded as significant of the Roumanian belief that the balance of the war was inclining to their side. In Germany her act was denounced as one of treacherous self-seeking.

If the last of these views was untrue, the first of them is not the whole truth. It would have been most to Roumania's advantage to keep out of the war. She had nothing to lose as a neutral, and a great deal of material profit to gain. History will probably reveal that it was Germany which insisted on Roumania's abandonment of neutrality, though Germany may have believed that under pressure Roumania would join the Central Powers. If she did not, Germany had a well-thought-out plan of campaign for crushing her, and had also made preparations, both political and military, to put it into execution. The political preparation, which was important, was to secure that Bulgaria should be ready and able (with Turkish assistance) to co-operate in an attack on Roumania. Thus Roumania would be caught, as Serbia had been caught on the previous year, between the pincers of an attack on two sides. It is doubtful whether Roumania expected this; it is certain she was not prepared for it. If she believed, as she seems to have done, that Bulgaria would not attack her, the hope was speedily dispelled, and her plan of campaign broke down as fully as her expectations.

On paper, Roumania's armies were a valuable accession to the Allies. Before the Balkan War Roumania's mobilizable forces were calculated at 400,000, with 100,000 men in reserve, and the calculation proved to be justified by the numbers she was able to put into the field to give effect to her threat to march on Bulgaria. These numbers were augmented afterwards, and when Roumania declared war on August 27, 1916, her forces were estimated at 600,000 fully-trained men, with a reserve of 100,000 untrained. The Roumanian army was organized in 10 army corps, of 20 divisions. It was stated that for fifteen months the men had been in training, and that ample munitionment had been received through Russia by way of Archangel, so that the army was prepared for a two years' war. Unlike the peasants of the other Balkan States, the Roumanian soldier had endured no experience of war; but it was believed that he would make a good fighter and a good marcher, and that the officers were energetic and competent. There is no other means of judging these representations than by subsequent events. In the early stages of the war the marching and fighting quality of the Roumanian soldiery responded to the call made on them. They were placed in many difficult situations by the mistakes of their higher commands, and from some of them they were extricated by their own fighting ability and by the handling of their regimental, battalion, and company commanders. But, like an elastic string stretched beyond its coefficient of resistance, when they did break they broke badly. As an army the Roumanians had to meet one which was made up of comparatively veteran soldiers, and which was better generalled, better gunned, and very much better organized. The result was written on the fields of Cernavoda and Craiova. Before imputing sole blame to the Roumanian Higher Command, it must be said that Roumania's preliminary action in her campaign provoked no remonstrance from her allies, and was applauded by some who afterwards bitterly blamed it. The Roumanian Chief of Staff was General Iliesco, a man of forty-eight, whose military education had been received in France, and he was by training an engineer and artillerist. General Avaresco, the Commander-in-Chief, had been a lieutenant in the Russo-Turkish War of 1877, and was a cavalry leader. General Coanda, Inspector of Artillery, and Colonel Rudeano, whose names were prominent in the early stages of the campaign, were also of French military education. Colonel Rudeano was responsible for munitions and transport. At the beginning of the war the King, Ferdinand of Roumania, following the example of the Tsar, placed himself at the head of his armies. The Queen, who was an English princess, daughter of the Duke of Edinburgh, busied herself with the organization of hospitals for the wounded.

Roumania is shaped like a **J**. The thick stumpy foot of the **J** is bounded on its sole by the Danube and Bulgaria; its heel juts into the Black Sea, and the bottom of the heel is the Dobrudja. Its toe touches Serbia at Turnu Severin, and Austria-Hungary at Orsova and the Iron Gates of the Danube. The instep of the foot is protected by the Carpathians, pierced by the chief inlets of the Jiul Pass, the Vulcan Pass, the Rother Thurm, or Red Tower, Pass, which form one group; the Torzburg Pass, the Predeal Pass, and the Bodza Pass, which form the second; and the Oitoz, Gyimes, Bekaz, and Tolgyes Pass, which form the third group. Bucharest, the capital, is south-west or south of all of these.

South of the Danube, which has no bridges for 300 miles of its length, is Bulgaria, and, as the Danube curves northward, the desolate land of the Dobrudja, which abuts on the Black Sea coast. Constanza, which is Roumania's chief port on the Black Sea, is in the Dobrudja, and is joined to Bucharest by a railway which crosses the marshes and stream of the Danube by the great bridge of Cernavoda. Over Cernavoda and by the Dobrudja was the path by which, if Russia and Roumania together should invade Bulgaria and Turkey, they would go.

Roumania, however, elected to regard any campaign by way of the Dobrudja as a secondary or subsequent effort, and to make the invasion of the Austro-Hungarian province of Transylvania her chief and first endeavour. In doing so she was achieving the political object of joining to herself the population of Roumanian descent which inhabited Transylvania. From a military point of view, if she could make her way through wooded Transylvania to the line of the River Maros, and thence to the River Theiss, she would be lending very valuable aid to Russia by striking a flanking blow at the Austro-Hungarian communications with the Galician Carpathians. In the opinion of some who criticized her after the event—but before the cup of her disasters began to fill—she should have taken time and opportunity by the forelock, and have at once marched on Bulgaria by way of the Dobrudja. What she ought to have done is, however, a futile speculation in the absence of knowledge of what means she may have had for doing it, or what the obstacles may have been in transport or localities of mobilization. It is sufficient to record her actions.

Photo. Mandy

The Queen of Roumania and Princess Ileana

For a time all went well. An assortment of official and semi-official dispatches of the dates of August 31 and September 1 describes the Roumanian "rush into Hungary"; an advance of 20 miles through the Gyimes Pass; and the statement that "the troops of our Imperial ally Russia have begun to pass through the Dobrudja. . . . Units of the Russian fleet have arrived at Constanza"; and, finally, a royal proclamation of Roumania's intention to unite "a great and free Roumania from the Theiss to the Black Sea". The whole of the passes were secured without serious fighting, and on the other side of the frontier Vasarheli, Kronstadt (Brasso), and Petroseny fell into Roumanian hands. Farther south, at the Iron Gate defile, the Roumanians encountered strong opposition, but they occupied Orsova by September 7. By the 16th their more northerly forces were holding the strategical frontier railway on the enemy's side of the border.

Meanwhile Germany was preparing to strike, and struck where the blow appears to have been least expected.

On September 2 a large composite army of Germans, Bulgarians, and Turks, under the command of Field-Marshal Mackensen, crossed the Bulgarian frontier on the Danube side, and, advancing with great rapidity, pushed back the Roumanian detachments strung along the 70-mile river line. With disarming suddenness Mackensen attacked the bridgehead of Turtukai, which the Roumanian 15th Division were holding, smashed their defences to pieces with heavy guns, and overwhelmed the garrison. The 17th Roumanian Division, coming up river from Silistria in aid, was caught unprepared and similarly destroyed. The surrender took place on September 6, and according to the Sofia *communiqué*, which was not contradicted, 25,000 men, 462 officers, and over 100 guns were captured—a very bad beginning for the Roumanian cause. Mackensen pressed his victory home with the swiftest determination. He drove back the Russian force advancing through the Dobrudja, and after two battles forced them to retire on a prepared position, Rasova to Tuzla, covering the railway line which ran from the Cernavoda Danube bridge to the port of Constantza. Here General Avaresco took command, and preparations were made for a trench-warfare resistance. On September 16 Mackensen made a fierce attack intended to shake the Roumanian defences before they could be consolidated, but his attack was premature, and he was beaten off after a five days' battle, and had to fall back to defensive positions of his own. Here he awaited fresh supplies of shell for his bigger guns, and beat off Roumanian attacks designed to compel his retreat.

King Ferdinand of Roumania
(From a photograph by Mandy)

Meanwhile the Roumanian advance into Hungary had spent itself without achieving results, and the advancing troops were subjected to a systematic counter-attack. The first slackening of the tide was notified on September 19, when the Roumanians were forced to fall back on Petroseny at the head of the Vulcan Pass. The tide began to ebb rapidly a week later, when the First Roumanian Army was assailed, as it was preparing to occupy Hermannstadt, by an Austro-German army under General von Falkenhayn. The Roumanians, according to the German official *communiqué*, suffered a disastrous defeat at the mouth of the Rother Thurn Pass. The defeat was greatly exaggerated, and, in fact, the Roumanian force was withdrawn with the comparatively small loss of 3000 men and 13 guns. None the less a defeat was inflicted, and, with one exception, no Roumanian success against the gathering strength of the German armies was to be recorded in the ensuing three months, which were a time of very severe trial for Roumania, and for Russia, who strove to redeem the situation. The defeat of the First Roumanian Army compelled the retreat of the Second Roumanian Army, which was fortunately effected in time through the central (Bodza and Torzburg) and northerly (Oitoz, Gyimes, Bekas) Passes. Falkenhayn pressed hard on them, coming up with their rear-guards and getting a part of his forces through the Torzburg Pass. On October 12 he had a small force on the Roumanian side of the frontier at Rucar, 10 miles from Campolung and the Bucharest railway. By the 18th he had a hold on the three passes Gyimes, Torzburg, and Rother Thurn.

While Falkenhayn was gathering momentum for a fresh spring, Mackensen in the Dobrudja, having received his heavy shell, advanced again and bombarded his way through the Russo-Roumanian line at its centre, taking the key positions of Kobadin and Topraisar on October 19, and compelling the whole line to fall back and uncover the railway. Mackensen took Constantza on the Black Sea on the 22nd, and, what was far more important, Cernavoda, and its commanding bridgehead over the Danube, on the 28th. He had thus shattered any hope that a Russo-Roumanian army could invade Bulgaria through the Dobrudja in force. Whatever the future might have in store, that was one of the vanished dreams of 1916. As soon as the Russian Chief of Staff heard of the disaster he sent General Sakharoff from Galicia to take charge, and Sakharoff, coming on the heels of his reinforcements, at once counter-attacked and succeeded in driving back the forces which Mackensen had brought to. this point. For some weeks the struggle continued, and once, in November, made a strong bid for the recapture of the Cernavoda Bridge. But Mackensen was strong enough just to hold his own here, while higher up the Danube he began to make preparations to cross the river and co-operate with von Falkenhayn in an encircling attack on the great salient which Wallachia forms in the Roumanian J between the Danube and the Carpathians.

Falkenhayn, having compelled the retreat of the Roumanian forces, but failed to invade Roumania by the Tolgyes, Gyimes, and Oitoz Passes, changed his plan and concentrated on the southern passes leading into Wallachia, the Vulcan, Rother Thurn, Torzburg, and Predeal Passes. During this advance a Bavarian division, advancing without supports through the Vulcan Pass, was badly broken up by the Roumanians, leaving 1500 prisoners and two howitzer batteries behind it. This was the solitary Roumanian success to which allusion was made on a previous page. For three weeks the Roumanians put up a very fine fight at these passes; but they were unable to sustain the continuous German attack and the continual hammering by the superior German artillery.

A Zeppelin's Doom in the Balkans: examining the remains of "L 85" in the Vardar Marshes, near Monastir

By the middle of November they were being forced back with continuous rapidity as Falkenhayn advanced on both sides of the Jiu River, and on November 17 and 18 they were beaten at Targa Jiu, and the way was opened for Falkenhayn to Craiova. From that point onwards the continually deploying and increasing forces of Germans. This period came to an

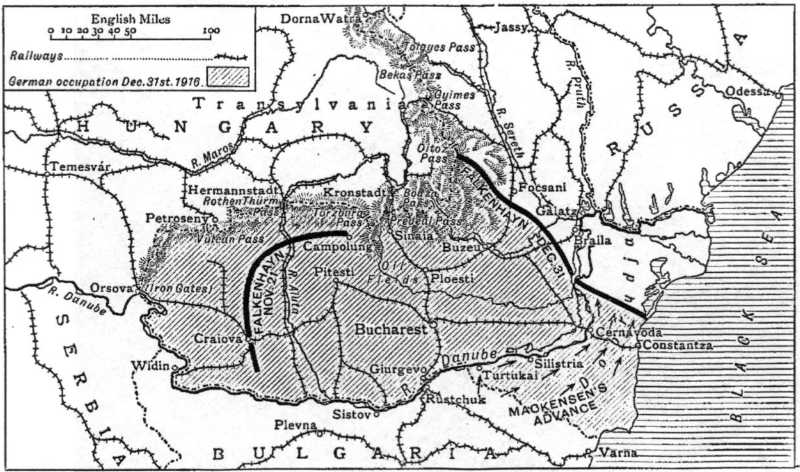


Map illustrating the Roumanian Campaign to the end of 1916

Falkenhayn, aided by the contingents from Mackensen's army which had crossed the Danube, created a salient from which the Roumanian forces could save themselves only by flight. Craiova fell, the Orsova force was cut off, and eventually Bucharest had to be abandoned without a shot fired. The Roumanian army, though so badly hit, preserved its integrity, and fell back towards the line of the Sereth. The oil-fields which they had to abandon were rendered as useless to the invaders as possible by the destruction of wells and machinery. This task was undertaken by a small British mission, and was very thoroughly done.

There was a period on the Salonika front when the ascendancy in the air was not with the Allies, but with the Bulgarians and their supplementary Germans. This period came to an end much about the same time that the Zeppelin, which was said to be a personal gift from the Kaiser to King Ferdinand, came to grief in the marshes of the Vardar, after having been hotly bombarded while over Salonika. The air-ship came from Temesvar in Hungary, and foundered in flames when trying to get back. The metal framework and portions of the gondolas—all that were left—are depicted on the preceding page.

E. S. G.

# CHAPTER IX

## THE BATTLE OF VERDUN: SECOND PHASE

(April–December, 1916)

Reasons for Continuance of German Attack—French Activity in the later part of April—Second Phase of German Activity at the Beginning of May—Hill 304—Attack of May 7—The Attack from Avocourt to Mort Homme and Crow's Wood on May 20 and following days—French Thrust on Douaumont—German Counter-attack on May 23 and 24: Douaumont again changes hands—Renewal of the German Attack at Hill 304, Mort Homme, and Cumières—Thrust to Chattancourt—The French Counter-attacks; and the Renewed German Assault between Hill 304 and Mort Homme—East Bank—The Assault around Fort Vaux—Major Raynal's Defence of Fort Vaux—Capture of the Stronghold on June 6—The Renewed Attack towards Forts Souville and Tavannes on June 6—Assault on the Thiaumont Position, June 23—Loss of Thiaumont Redoubt and Fleury Village—The Last German Attack from Fleury between July 11 and 15—A Month's Attacks and Counter-attacks—Fleury regained, August 18—Two Months' Pause—General Nivelle's Preparation of his Troops and Resources—The Triple Divisional Attack towards Fort Douaumont by the French—Recapture of Fort Douaumont, October 23—Recapture of Fort Vaux, November 3—General Nivelle's New Tactical Methods and their Results—Capture of the Pepper Ridge or Côte du Poivre, December 14–18.

WHEN the German assault, supported with unprecedented fury on either side of the Meuse from April 1 to April 11, 1916, had broken itself alike on the Avocourt-Cumières line and on the Douaumont-Vaux position, it seemed as if concentration of effort could go no further on the enemy's part, and that before Verdun, as before the rest of the front, the operations must relapse into trench-warfare. A semi-official declaration in that sense was made in Paris, where it was held that since the Germans had failed in their first rush, and could no longer secure any such result as that of jamming a disordered French army in a flooded loop of the Meuse, they must discontinue an effort which would become progressively more costly as the French defence stiffened and improved. But if, according to such a way of looking at the situation, the German effort had been a repulse, the German Headquarter staff refused to accept it as such, and falsified expectations by continuing their attempts to convert it into an advantage.

There was nothing stupid about it while they had the men to do it with, the guns with which to support them, and the transport with which to supply them. Costly as the attack was to them in men, many as were the new divisions which had to be imported into the fray, it was at Verdun alone that men could be used to the best advantage, because there the organization for using them had been worked up to the highest pitch. Besides, the desperate struggle, as Sir Douglas Haig said, had invested Verdun with a moral and political importance out of all proportion to its military value, and its fall would undoubtedly have been proclaimed as a great victory for our enemies. Accordingly they continued to hammer the French lines.

During that part of April which

followed the repulse of the double attack of the Crown Prince[1] there was little to prepare expectation for a continuation of the German pressure; there was, on the other hand, much to justify General Pétain's "*On les aura*", and his memorable Order of the Day, thanking the 2nd Army for its past services, and promising it the same success in the future as on "that glorious day" when the German assaults were shattered, one after the other, by the fire of the French guns. On April 19 the German positions east of Douaumont were tested by a smart French counter-attack; and a local success north of Vaux encouraged General Pétain to explore the German advanced positions on the opposite side of the Meuse with a number of sharp and swift thrusts, which always found an opening in lines not yet consolidated. By the end of April the Germans had been pushed back from the base of the Mort Homme, and the safety of that position seemed so far assured as to justify the view that the Germans had arrived at the point of recognizing their failure.

With the beginning of May these theories were blown to fragments by the reawakening roar of the German howitzers, the prelude to a renewal on a greater scale of the fighting which had already lasted between two and three months. More guns had been brought up, old divisions had been reorganized, new divisions thrown in. There was now no idea of surprise: the German purpose was to smash in the French front by weight and determination. It might cost half a million German soldiers and run the stores of ammunition low; but the French must pay the price too; and it might be a price which they could afford the less. The German Intelligence Department knew probably quite well that they had some time to spare before this murderous game of hammer and tongs could be interrupted by an effective intervention on the British-held sectors of their line. The first blow was struck at the left bank of the Meuse again. Instead of attempting to storm the Mort Homme directly the German Staff aimed at securing Hill 304, which lies west of the Mort Homme and the Meuse. If this hill could be freed of Frenchmen and German batteries established on it, the Mort Homme position could be caught by a flanking fire, and the whole ridge of the Côte de l'Oie, on the west side of the river, would fall into German hands. Doubtless the Germans knew the enterprise would be costly. They were prepared with the price.

The plan of attack was extremely simple. The Germans themselves compared it to the strokes of a woodcutter, who hacks alternately at each side of the trunk of a tree, and at each blow drives the axe farther in, till the tree totters. Thus on the left side of the trunk—the western side of the Meuse—each blow strove to bite through the Mort Homme position. On the eastern bank the assaults were symmetrically reversed. The blows of the axe sometimes fell between Douaumont and the river, but more often on its eastern side, towards Fort Vaux.

[1] Vol. V, Chapter XIV.

After three days' preparation three simultaneous attacks were made on the flanks of the main position at midday on May 7. One was directed against Hill 287, which is a north-westerly spur of Hill 304; another against the Avocourt Wood positions (west), and a third against the defences of the ravine between Hill 304 and the Mort Homme. A bitter fight went on all day and all night. At great expenditure the Germans made some headway towards the eastern ravine; and they claimed that they had captured the whole system of trenches on the northern slopes of Hill 304. The French certainly no longer attempted to hold that system, because, owing to the steepness of the slopes, their artillery firing over the hill from its southern side could not command them. They held the crest, and tactically the Germans had made very little headway, while the crest could be swept by French fire. The convincing testimony to a German failure is that they made no attempt at once to push their advantage, as they always did when it was a real one. The action was broken off

Before Verdun: French anti-aircraft post, with observation balloon in the background preparing for an ascent

The main part of their failure was on the French left, the Avocourt Wood, which the French, realizing its importance, had bought at a stiff price some time before. The next German attempt was therefore made here, with a view to easing the prospects of another flank attack on Hill 304. They made two heavy cuts at it on the evenings of May 17 and 18, but the axe did not bite deep enough, and lost a good deal of its edge. But all the while new divisions were pouring in, and the Avocourt attack spread eastwards, and continued to spread till the whole of the battle front from the wood to the river was involved. While the attack was kept up on the Avocourt and Hill 304 defences, the chief weight of the blows fell again on the Mort Homme. Part of the main assault aimed at the ravine between Hill 304 and the Mort Homme, through which the Esnes brook ran; the other part synchronizing with it strove to cut in behind the Mort Homme on the river side. The troops of a German division newly brought up were told off to push through the latter attack from the north-east, to carry Crow's Wood and Les Caurettes, and to join up with the thrust from the north-west.

Sixty German batteries played this double assault in. The new divisions on the Crow's Wood side had little success, though the French trenches had melted under the German bombardment. The Germans occupied the first line with some loss; to the second line they fought their way with a determination undeterred by the machine-gun fire and melinite which barred their way; but they could not hold the second line, and supports were unavailing. The contemporaneous attack made on the west of the Mort Homme got farther. It was an attack made with a resolution which was the high-water mark reached by the best German fighting material. The slight V-shaped wedge which the Germans had already made between Hill 304 and the Mort Homme they widened and deepened to a big U-shaped depression, which on its right-hand side was planted in French trenches south and south-west of the hill the enemy sought. The Germans paid a heavy bill for this advantage, which looks so small on a map, but which had nevertheless solid tactical value, for the Mort Homme was no longer a possession solely French.

For some days the battle on the west side of the Meuse paused—if such a struggle can ever be said to pause for a moment—while the Germans gathered themselves together for another effort, and the French de-

French Troops exploring a Crater made by one of their Mines in the German Line

French Official Photograph

General Nivelle, who succeeded General Pétain at Verdun

liberately extended the area of conflict by a great counter-attack on the other side of the river at Douaumont. This counter-attack was an episode in the history of Verdun, but it was also one of the most daring tactical strokes of the French Higher Command.

Douaumont, since the day in February when it was described, in the same German *communiqué* that prematurely reported its capture, as the north-eastern pillar of the defences of Verdun, had been a critical point of conflict. The capture by the Kaiser's Brandenburgers had proved of exaggerated value, since it no longer implied command of the ridge on which it stood, but it had the great usefulness of furnishing an observation post, and of enabling any force which could establish itself there to sweep the approaches to Vaux, the next fort to the south-east of it. On May 22 the French made their first dash to shake it. The Crown Prince was at this moment pre-occupied with the assault on the other bank of the river, where the new attack on the Mort Homme and the neighbouring ridges was eating up men. General Nivelle, who had succeeded General Pétain[1] (given command of the central group of armies) at the beginning of May, entrusted the operation to General Mangin and to the Fifth Division. The Fifth Division had been in the Vaux-Douaumont sector when the German assault on Verdun rose to what was then believed to be its culminating pitch of violence, and had then been withdrawn to refit their sorely tried and depleted ranks. When they went on leave and to billets for this purpose General Mangin told them to prepare for further battles. "You march under the wings of Victory," said he. Five weeks later they came back to justify his confidence.

The French prepared the attack by two days' bombardment of the battered fort; and they heralded the assault with a device of deadly usefulness. It was a new bomb for the destruction of "sausage", or observation, balloons, and it was so successful that a few minutes after the aeroplanes had been launched to pepper the German observers with them, six of the German sausage balloons had exploded, and

[1] General Nivelle at the beginning of the war was in command of the Fifth Infantry Regiment. In October, 1914, he commanded a brigade. In February, 1915, he commanded the Sixth Division, and then took over the Third Army Corps.

the German artillery was thus temporarily and partially blindfolded. But the significance of the act, joined to the bombardment, was not lost on the enemy, who began to pour a flood of precautionary shrapnel on the lines where the French were in waiting. The Fifth Division waited patiently till nearly midday. They had been divided into three sections for their task; the middle section were to strike directly for the ruins of the fort, the others for the trenches which flanked and protected it to right and to left. They went forward together at the appointed minute, and they moved with great swiftness from shell-hole to shell-hole. In eleven minutes the 129th Regiment in the centre had reached Douaumont Fort across three lines of trenches, and had lit a Bengal flare to signal their arrival. On the left the 36th Regiment had carried out its part of the task, and held the road which led from Douaumont to Fleury. The sappers began now to come in behind the infantry, and got into the fort to block its exits, while the infantry in possession covered the 36th Infantry in its task of destroying the flanking positions. All was going well on this side of Douaumont. On the eastern side matters did not prosper so fast or so fully. The 74th Regiment had been held up by a galling fire from the German communication trenches, and though German prisoners were being sent back from the fort to the French lines, in the north-east corner the enemy still held out—and the German counter-attack, as the French Command well knew, was bound to come. So, restraining their men from pushing on, the French in possession strengthened their hold as much as they could, and all that night fought hand-to-hand combats with Germans grimly holding the passages of the uncaptured corner.

The Germans massed for their counter-attack in Haudremont Wood, and on the morning of the 23rd poured in their turn all the artillery fire at their command on the fort and the French-held trenches. They sent their infantry forward on top of the bombardment, but repeated assaults failed. All day long the 129th Regiment held on; while fresh German troops were brought up. They were too few to hold it; their work had been done—its hardest part began with the dawn of the 23rd—and at last orders had to be given to withdraw them. Two Bavarian Divisions were sent up by the Germans at the close of the day, and by the 24th the ruins of Douaumont had again changed hands—for the last time but one.

The counter-thrust had served its turn, but it had not diverted the Germans from the pursuit of their other attack on the western bank. On May 23 they began an attack on the complementary positions of Hill 304 and the Mort Homme, such as transcended the previous one as an attack in force transcends a reconnaissance, and the violence of which may be estimated by its duration through six days. But if the German effort this week in May rose to greater heights than ever before, it met with a resistance that was less penetrable and more scientific than before. The French had learned the lessons of

Verdun, and were at this time evolving that co-operation between the artillery barrage and the infantry's rifles which, powerful though they proved it in defence, was to become a more deadly weapon when employed offensively on the Somme. The 75's, beautiful weapons though they were, could not stop the waves of German soldiers whose lives their leaders were willing to expend with such prodigality; but the melinite shells of the French heavies, when massed as Pétain and Nivelle massed them, could do so. This barrage stayed the German rushes in bloody confusion east of the Mort Homme on the first day; but between Hill 304 and the Mort Homme the residual onrush of the German waves got through the curtain of fire, and on to the first French trench lines. *Flammenwerfer* were brought up, and the Germans burnt their way in by liquid flame. A French counter-attack threw them out at nightfall: renewed German attacks continued through the night.

While the French were fully occupied with holding on to the Mort Homme and Hill 304 gap with tooth and claw, two fresh German Divisions were flung at the point east of the Mort Homme where the village of Cumières blocked the way. There was little *finesse* about the German method; a few hours' bombardment were followed by waves of infantry; when they returned broken the bombardment was resumed till it was judged time to send in new waves. By this elementary but resistless expenditure of shells and men the Germans, on May 24, got through, and reaped the interest on their outlay. For when the line at Cumières was broken the Germans had nothing there to stop them, and they poured on through the disarrayed French defenders till they got right down to Chattancourt.

The cup seemed to be at the German lips; but once again the French counter-attack, as automatic as the recoil of a gun, dashed it away. The French infantry in reserve bore down on the Germans with a ferocity that would not be denied, and fought them back to Cumières, where they held them through the night of the 24th. The Germans could not again get up the momentum to carry the outskirts, and the French exchanged rushing for bombing, winning here a barn and there a cellar or part of a ruined street. After three days of this two assaulting columns were brought up by the French, and fought their way onward on either side of the village, taking the mill, and bringing back the line to near the point where it had bent and broken.

The Germans counter-attacked, but their counter-attack was not a recoil. It was a blow struck with all the force at the German command, and though aimed at a wider front than the village, and with a greater object, it comprised the Cumières-Mort Homme sector, and made it the chief one. The first attack began on the evening of May 28. It did not get through the curtain fire, nor did the second attack. The task then passed to the German heavy artillery for twelve hours, as a preparation for next day; and next day five new divisions went forward on the

One of the Storm Centres round Verdun: French troops in reserve in the Caillette Wood

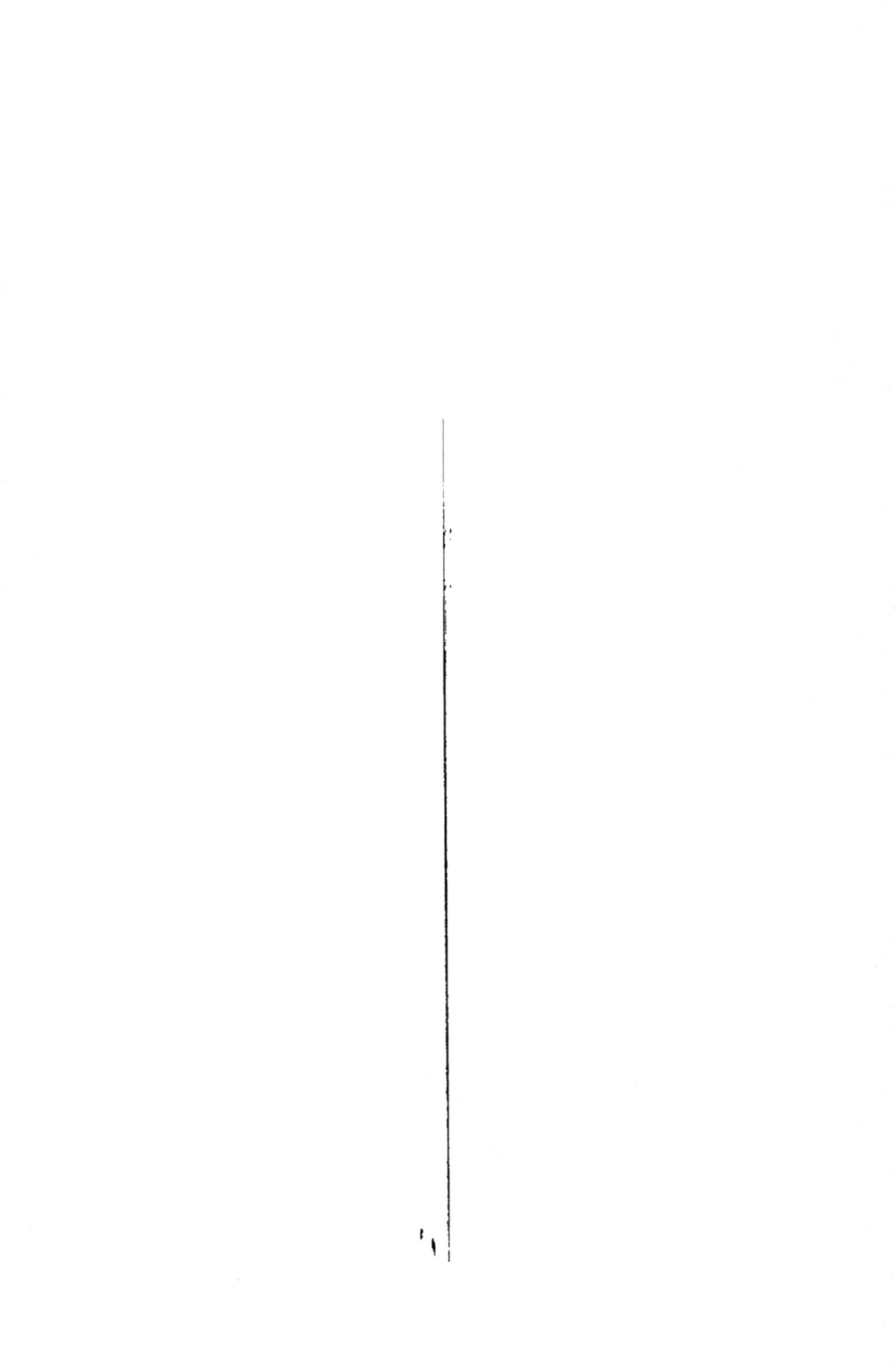

FROM A PHOTOGRAPH BY ELLIOTT & FRY

*Lieut. General The Hon J. C. Smuts.*

heels of the destruction wrought by the artillery fire. But great as that destruction had been it was not enough. The first-line trenches at the French centre no longer existed, for it was there that the German fire had been heaviest. Here the Germans had their greatest measure of success. But summed up this did not amount to a great deal. The French had to abandon the summit of the Mort Homme, as the wedge between it and Hill 304 was deepened, and they established themselves on the western and southern slopes. The crest of the Mort Homme remained untenable by either side. At Cumières the Germans could not materially improve their position. Consequently at the end of the week's battle the Germans had won advantages which were insignificant from a territorial point of view, and which could only be regarded as important taetically if they could be pushed home. They could not be pushed home; and at the end of May the French line, running from Avocourt Wood over Hill 304, along the south of Mort Homme to the Bois de les Caurettes and the remains of Cumières, was as capable of offering resistance to further attacks as heretofore.

On the other bank the Germans began a more piecemeal reduction, which, though less magnificent in aim, was more valuable in moral effect. Failing to place their occupation of the ridge on the west of the Meuse beyond dispute, they determined to hack at the flank of the Douaumont plateau from the east, advancing up the wooded coombes by which the plateau declines to the eastern plain. The first step was to capture Fort Vaux. Fort Vaux is situated on the edge of the ravine which lies between Vaux hill and the triple southerly bastions of the Douaumont plateau, and had to be carried before any further operations east of the Meuse were undertaken. The Germans had other reasons than these tactical ones for bringing to bear on its capture all the resources they could command. If anything was to be done at Verdun it must be done quickly, in order to anticipate or to precipitate the Franco-British push which was in preparation at some other part of the line. On June 1, therefore, the attack was launched, preceded by a bombardment of "extreme intensity". The assault was calculated to encircle the fort by attacks from the north-east and the north-west, as at the Mort Homme. The first of these attacks, advancing under cover of the heavy artillery, spread out from Haudremont Wood and over the Douaumont plateau down to the innermost of the triple-wooded spurs. This was the Bois de la Caillette or Caillette Wood. The Germans seized it, and on the next day (June 2), descending from it into the ravine, began the direct attack on Fort Vaux. At the same time they set in motion their attack from the north-east, and captured the village of Damloup, which is in the ravine on the other or southern side of Fort Vaux. The northern attacking party tried to rush the fort. They were blown back by the guns; but more and more men were brought up to the task, and late at night a brave party of them got into the fort ditch. Here these desperate men remained for four days, unable to enter the fort.

Their courage and their plight found many parallels in the defence of elements of isolated French trenches, where men held on under a pitiless bombardment day after day without water, and with the most shadowy prospect of relief. This individual heroism went on east and west of Vaux, and meanwhile the attack on the fort developed, and developed in a new way. The Germans had learned from their failure in March that it was extravagantly hopeless to try to encircle the fort with infantry; they therefore fed their flank attacks with fresh troops, and maintained so heavy an artillery barrage on the southern slopes of the fort that no troops could get up to succour it. The whole of the southern approaches were closed by this wall of bursting steel; the fort itself was beaten into a ruin. Yet in it a tiny garrison under Major Raynal continued to resist. They could not get out except at the risk of being blown to pieces at every step they took in the open; they could communicate with their own lines only by signal, and imperfectly. The heroism of Fort Vaux's defence became the symbol of all that Frenchmen did and endured there. As on the "little *Revenge*" in Sir Richard Grenville's day, the cry was to fight on, though men were dying of thirst and wounds, and every hour renewed danger and anguish and death. The Germans advanced on the higher levels of the walls, but the Frenchmen organized the debris of the fort. At every window, behind every heap of bricks, machine-guns were placed, or the picked shots took refuge and shot down every enemy who set foot in the courtyard. The Germans, with renewed ingenuity, tried to blast the defenders out with grenades, letting basketfuls of them down by ropes to the level of the windows and swinging them in with a time fuse to burst inside.

The fight went on. The limit to human endurance was not reached till June 6, when Major Raynal got out his last message: "We are near the end. Officers and soldiers have done their whole duty. Vive la France!" A few soldiers, among them wounded, escaped through a grating and crawled towards the French lines; others who had sought to escape with them were killed on the way. Fort Vaux fell on the same day in a renewal of the bombardment. Its defence was one of the greatest testimonies to that spirit of cold unflinching endurance which before the war we associated so little with France, but of which they showed us at Verdun an example the peer of any in our own history. Major Raynal, though a prisoner, was promoted to the rank of Commander in the Legion of Honour; the Germans gave him back his sword—one act, at any rate, to be reckoned to the credit of the Crown Prince.

The fall of Vaux came too late for the Germans. In the exaltation of Raynal's defence the moral effect of its loss on the French was negligible. Its value to the Germans, judged by the standard of its indispensability if any further attack was to be made on the eastern Verdun lines, was considerable; on the other hand, it had not fallen soon enough to assume the character of a dangerous gap in the defences. These defences were now drawn anew on a line from Hill 321 (which is a mile north of the Froide Terre Ridge) through Thiaumont Redoubt, Fleury Village, and the woods of Chapitre and Fumin. It then curled round through the woods of Chenois and La Laufée which look past Damloup eastwards to the plain below. These must be turned or conquered to approach Forts Souville or Tavannes, part of the inner lines of defences. From Verdun on this side the Germans were now less than four miles away. There was a long pause after the fall of Fort Vaux before the Germans gathered themselves together for this new effort. Then, conscious that time was growing short and the need of a superlative effort was vital, they began an attack which retained unchanged all the old weight and violence. On June 12 they had tested the nature of the new French defences by an attack on the lines from Thiaumont Farm to Hill 321. A road runs south-west from Douaumont Fort through Thiaumont Farm to the Côte de Froide Terre. A main German attack was bound to come along the line of this road. Fighting took place to east and west of it. The Germans made some advance on the

Within the Inner Lines of Verdun's Defences: French guns in Fort Souville

slopes of Hill 321. Thiaumont Redoubt was unscathed. They tried again on the 15th, having found that the Thiaumont Redoubt was the key of the position. Then on the 18th and 19th their major attack developed.

It bore down in the three prescribed directions: (1) upon Ridge 321; (2) Thiaumont Redoubt; (3) Fleury village. The Thiaumont position bore the brunt of it, and over a front of just over a mile it was assailed by three divisions. But this was not till June 23rd, when the attack had fully developed, and the whole line had been hotly engaged for four days. The great attack began at eight in the morning; seven hours afterwards a slight break was made in the line, just east of Thiaumont, and into the gap the Germans flung men with promptitude and burst right through. They had got Thiaumont; but they had not then got Fleury. They reached the village, and were thrown out. It was not till the 25th that they had driven a wedge in the French positions and, widening it as before, gained the village. The gap was now wide indeed: but before they could exploit their success at Fleury the French had counter-attacked, had reached and held the outskirts, and were reorganizing their line. On June 23 General Nivelle in an Army Order had told his soldiers that this was the supreme German assault before the enemy in their turn would be assailed, and "Ils ne passeront pas, Camarades!" They did not pass: the Army of Verdun kept its honour intact.

'Ware Gas! bell from a ruined church used by the French to warn their troops of the approach of a gas attack

The hour was fast approaching when the beginning of the combined operations by the British and French armies on the Ancre and the Somme was to compel the Germans to put a period to their endeavour to wear the French down at Verdun. The Somme battle began on July 1, and drew an ever-increasing number of German divisions into its furnace. Though the Germans loudly asserted that the French were mistaken if they thought the pressure on Verdun would be relaxed, guns and men were steadily if stealthily withdrawn, and ultimately it was pressure from the French side which broke through the German defences, and compelled the relinquishment of gains which the Germans had so hardly won. Their last attempt to demonstrate their indifference to the attack on the Somme was made between July 11 and 15, when they attacked on an extending front from Fleury to Damloup. Their chief aim was to burst out from Fleury and, striking along the south-easterly road, break up the French organization between the Thiaumont works and the defences of Fort Souville. This raid in force progressed some distance before it was stopped; but stopped it was, and by the 15th General Nivelle was in a position to strike back. He entrusted the counter-thrust to General Mangin, who was what the British would have called a "thruster" of the General Foch school. Mangin attacked Fleury furiously, and the Germans, instead of being able to develop their success with a new assault on Fort Souville, found themselves battling to hold on to their positions. They resisted with an almost indignant determination, and Fleury and the Thiaumont work changed hands several times in the succeeding weeks. The French won Fleury on August 3: the Germans regained a footing there, and clung on till August 10. Thiaumont work changed hands time after time; the ruins of Fleury were not irrevocably French till August 18. A little more than a fortnight afterwards the German attack flickered up once more for the last time. Instead of taking the south-east road from Fleury to Fort Souville, they came along the road that runs south-west from Fort Vaux to join it. This attack of September 3 shared the fate of its predecessors, a slight advance immediately extinguished by a counter-attack, and for six weeks thereafter the Verdun front relapsed into sniping and regularized exchanges of artillery-fire.

Winged Shells on the French Front: setting an aero-torpedo before launching

A cylinder attached to the shell fits into the tubing which forms the barrel of the gun and receives the propulsion from the discharge.

But now the progress of the Somme battle was such as to enable the French Higher Command to give General Nivelle a freer hand. The steady dwindling of the German forces, now reduced to fifteen divisions along the irregular flat curve from Avocourt Wood to Eix, seemed to promise that the free hand might gather good fruit: and General Nivelle, a tactician who neglected nothing, as well as a strategist who had the vision to perceive the mind of the enemy, had been long preparing his effort. He knew his Generals of Division, he estimated the ability and *moral* of his troops, and those whom he chose he sent behind the lines to a training-ground, where the training was so thorough that there was a reproduction in plan of the country over which they would have to fight, and of the fortifications which they would have to take. It was said of the battalion to which ultimately was assigned the task of taking Douaumont Fort, that every man in it, trained to storm a replica of the fort, knew beforehand exactly what to do and where to go. General Mangin was in command of the triple attack, and the divisional generals were General Lardemelle (on the right in the wood south of Fort Vaux), General Passaga (centre and in a line drawn south through Fort Douaumont), and General Guyot de Salins (left and opposite the Thiaumont works). General Nivelle's plan, stated in the briefest possible terms, was to storm the Douaumont Plateau, which is shaped like a flattish tomato. The sectors of the tomato represent the wooded spurs, the clefts between them the ravines. The French had to get up the ravines and push the Germans off the flat top. Douaumont Fort may be taken to represent the apex.

General Nivelle had stealthily assembled big guns, 150 millimetres and 250 millimetres, as well as some of 400 millimetres, which were to be the surprise, and the attack had been worked out beforehand to the last second. On October 23 the force was deployed on a 5-mile front almost from the river to the Bois Chenois; and a feint attack drew a response in a fierce artillery barrage from numerous German batteries. (It has since been stated that the Germans were not wholly unaware of the French advance; it was the actual hour of attack only which took them by surprise.) The hour was 11.40 a.m. on the 24th, but the day broke so misty that those who watched from Souville trembled lest the attack should be delayed, or having been entered upon

Won Back for France: happy Poilus in the recaptured fort of Douaumont

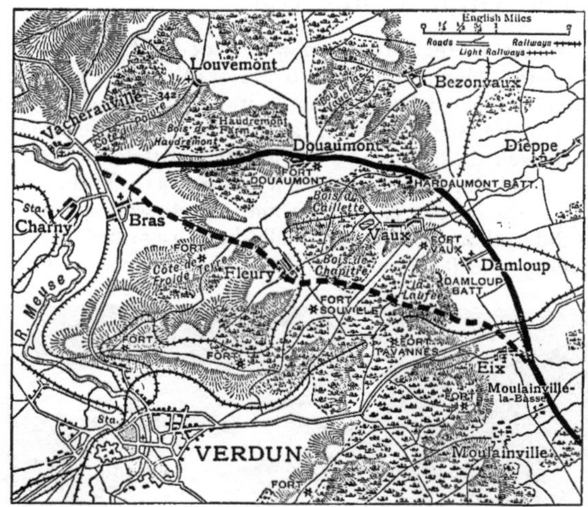


Turning the Tide at Verdun: map showing approximately the French line after the recapture of Forts Douaumont and Vaux

should go astray in the fog. But it had been so minutely arranged, its smallest units conversant with the smallest details of their time table and compass-directions, that the fog aided it instead of throwing it into confusion. Its artillery barrage was perfect, the aeroplanes which went forward with it did not fail it; the infantry went forward through the shell-holes and over the trenches as if there were no living obstacles to be surmounted, no bursting shells or machine-gun fire to survive.

Nobody could witness this sight, for the fog hid it; but had it been visible it would have been strange indeed, for in the force that went onward with a single aim the units were curiously diverse, Zouaves, Moroccans, Algerians, with a stiffening of bluejackets—the Colonial Division under Guyot de Salins—taking in their stride the Thiaumont work so often lost and won; Passaga, with his units picked from nearly every corps in France, driving the Germans in front of their bayonets through the disputed Bois de la Caillette; Lardemelle's Savoyards, and his detachment of black Senegalese from the Gold Coast, walking through the Damloup Redoubt. It was not all so simple as that sounds; there was bitter fighting here and there; but it is undeniable that the Germans were surprised, and were rushed before they could find their feet. Their artillery barrage went astray; it was only when the French found themselves among network defences in the ravines (or in the Haudremont quarries) that the Germans rallied to their machine-guns and fought them as they always did with courageous doggedness.

The attack was devised by General Nivelle as an advance with a pause, followed by another advance; the limits of both these steps being rigidly defined. General Guyot de Salin's men on the left went over and past the German defences of the Thiaumont work, and pursued their way with extraordinary swiftness till they came to the Haudremont quarries, where they encountered suspected but unascertained defences. They bombed the defenders out, but had to stay there. In the centre Passaga's division, which had a very difficult and complicated task, began it well by taking the Bois de la Caillette and getting well on to the ridge beyond. On the clay slopes the going was as hard as the risks were great: but the men did it, though they lost a brigadier-general, who fell at the head of their left advance. They paused according to plan, and when the fog broke Douaumont Fort, the dark tower of their pilgrimage, was before their eyes. The second part of the plan was that in conjunction with de Salins' men on the left they should close in on either side of it, while the specially prepared men should march on it. On this principle the Thiaumont work had been carried; on this principle the fort of Douaumont was won back for France. The fort fell to Major Nicolay's battalion almost as if it had indeed been the spectral castle to which Childe Roland came. When the battalion faced it there was a pause; and little sound came from the ruined walls on which French shells had magnified the devastation that the German artillery had begun. A low-flying aeroplane led the way as the men climbed the ramparts; and then the rattle of German machine-guns from the casemates gave signs that the fort had defenders. They were soon silenced. All the Germans who were not shot surrendered.

**Another recaptured Stronghold before Verdun: French troops again in possession of the Haudremont Quarries**

Douaumont was thus recovered; but the Germans could not let it go without a counter-attack, and four of these followed on the next day, but they made no impression. On the right of Douaumont the fort of Vaux was now left largely unsupported, "in the air" as the soldiers say. General Lardemelle's division, on the right both of Douaumont and Vaux, had made slower progress than the others, because it was here that the Germans had expected the blow to fall, and opposed the French attack strongly in well-prepared defences. But Lardemelle had taken Damloup, and so had begun to put in one leg of the pincers which were to make the fort untenable. In front of the fort, on the 24th and 25th, the Germans fought fiercely in every blockhouse, in every trench, and in every machine-lined shell-crater. It was not till the French brought up another division (General Andlauer), on October 28, that these new men, taking Fumin Wood (west of the fort) with a rush, put in the pincers on the other side. On the morning of November 2 the Germans left in the fort blew up all they could and left it. The French, suspicious of a trick, carefully reconnoitred it before occupying the shell the following day. Next day and on the two days following they took what was left of Vaux and Damloup villages, and so occupied once again all the ridge with its ravines and woods, for which the Germans had struggled so hard and sacrificed so much. They captured in the course of these operations 6000 prisoners and many guns; they had defeated seven German divisions by the employment of four.

There remained one more encounter to seal the French triumph at Verdun and to give assurance that no object which the Germans had declared to be their aim had been or would be attained. The French had learnt many lessons from the German attacks and from their own. Under General Nivelle the new tactics had developed with the extremity of French logic. No longer were advances to be made in long lines which might lose touch or move forward unevenly; the attack must move forward like the spokes of a fan; every object to be reached must be carefully defined, never overpassed, always consolidated when reached; so far as was humanly possible (and the French made it almost inhumanly possible) the artillery curtain must move forward with the infantry like the pillar of fire which led the Israelites, and should be as sentient. These principles were applied to their perfection in that advance from the Douaumont Ridge to the Pepper Ridge, or Côte du Poivre, which having been prepared beforehand by General Nivelle, saluted his appointment to the chief command of the armies of the West.

The preparation occupied a month after the capture of the two forts; and it was designed to push the Germans back off the excellent line, which they had strongly fortified, from Vacherauville, over the Côte du Poivre, round Haudremont Wood and the small wood adjoining, round below Douaumont and its ridge, to the outskirts of Vaux village. This line the Germans held with five divisions, with other divisions in their call; but several of these divisions had been shaken, and one was by no means first class. For the attack on them General Nivelle employed, under General Mangin as before, the two hard-bitten divisions of Generals de Passaga and de Salins, together with

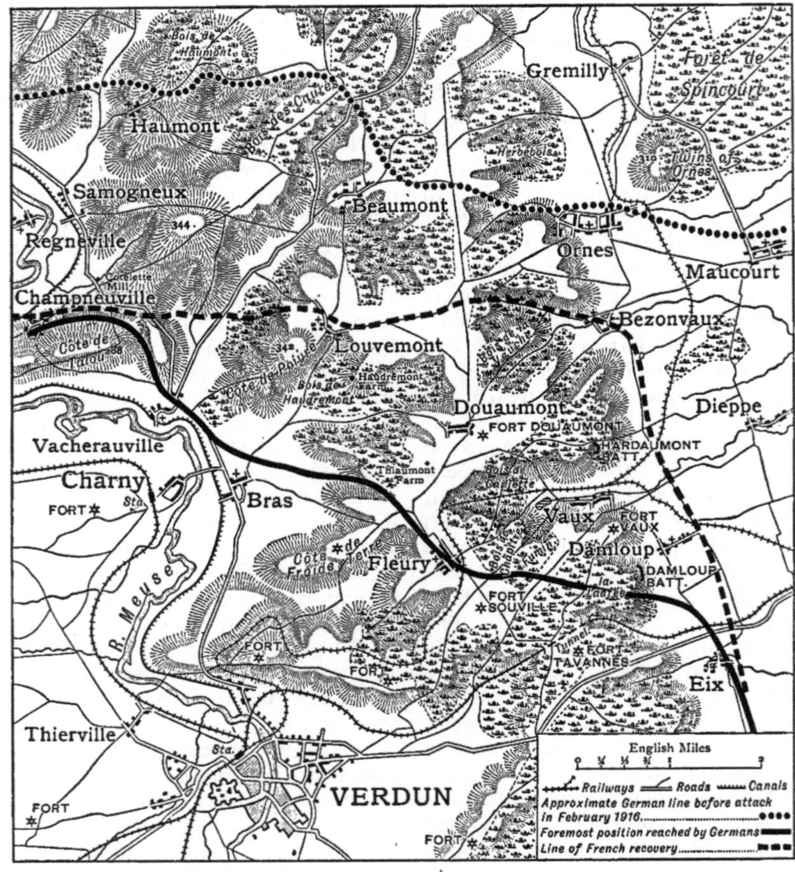


The Mort Homme Area and the Defences on the West Side of the Meuse

The Battles of Verdun, 1916: map—continued on the opposite page—showing approximately the limits of the German advance and the region recaptured by the French by the end of the year.

a veteran division under General du Plessis, and a young one under General Muteau. The young division was set in motion on the extreme left with only half a mile to go and Vacherauville village to envelop. The young troops did all that was required of them. The veteran troops of Guyot de Salins, following close on the wonderful barrage of their artillery, were on the

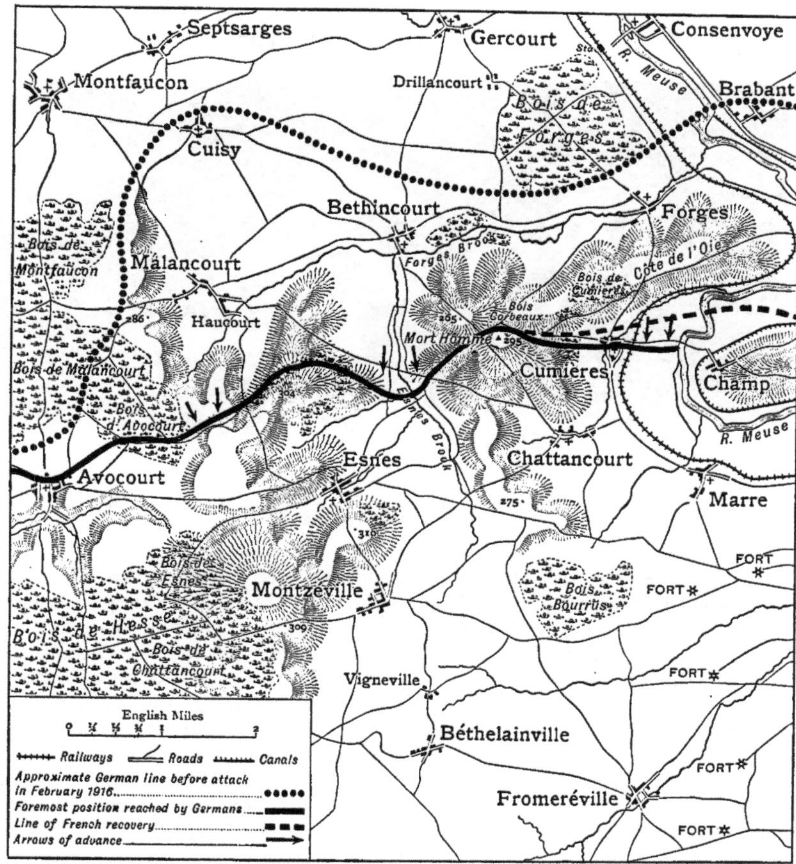


Verdun and its Defences on the East Side of the Meuse

The Battles of Verdun, 1916: map—continued from the opposite page—showing approximately the limits of the German advance and the region recaptured by the French by the end of the Year.

Côte du Poivre thirty-five minutes after the attack had been started, and the Louvemont Ridge was made safe after desperate fighting. De Passaga and du Plessis had the harder task of capturing the Bezonvaux work and the Caurières Wood. They were held up by a salient still wedged in their line at Chambrettes Farm. But on December 15 and the night of the 15th

A Salute from the Vanquished: German prisoners of war passing General Joffre on their way to a French camp of detention

and 16th the line was straightened, Bezonvaux village was captured, Chambrettes Farm retaken, and the French line for all tactical purposes was by the 18th of December as strong on the east side of the Meuse as when the first German onslaught, backed by the 2000 German guns, broke the line on the 21st of February ten months before. The material gains of this last recovery were 11,387 prisoners (including 284 officers), 115 guns, 107 machine-guns.

Four villages, five forts, many redoubts and trenches were occupied, and the better part of six enemy divisions was destroyed. The French losses were extremely small; on the first day of the assault they were under 2000, figures which were augmented only under the counter-assaults sustained. The event came at a happy moment, forming the best possible answer of the French army to Germany's hypocritical overtures for peace, the hollow nature of which was as scornfully detected by our Allies as by ourselves. Nivelle's men had answered with the cannon and the bayonet. "You have been the true ambassadors of the Republic", Nivelle told the army. "You have done well by your country!"

E. S. G.

# CHAPTER X

## WITH GENERAL SMUTS IN GERMAN EAST AFRICA

Germany's Last and Greatest Colony—Inadequate Strength of British Forces—Imperial Government's Appeal to South Africa—How South Africa responded—General Smuts assumes Command—Valuable Preliminary Work by General Tighe—German Strength and Occupation of British Borderland—Gallant Deeds on Rhodesian Front—Opening of General Smuts's Campaign—Conquest of Kilimanjaro—Battle of Latema-Reata Nek—South Africans' Brilliant Victory—Enemy's Stand on the Ruwu River—Flight into the Interior—British Frontier Clear of German Troops—Lord Kitchener's Congratulations—Unparalleled Hardships of the Campaign—Big Game and other Dangers—Portugal's Entry into the War—General Smuts's New Plan—Van Deventer's March to Kondoa Irangi—Typical Boer Tactics—Colonel von Lettow-Vorbeck's Desperate Attack against Van Deventer—His Last Bid for Victory—Guerrilla Warfare as a Forlorn Hope—General Smuts's Main Advance—Fight for the Ngura Mountains—Enemy's Retreat to Central Railway. Advance of other converging Columns from Victoria Nyanza and the Belgian and Rhodesian Fronts—General Northey's Rapid Progress—General Smuts's Cordon Tightening—Congratulations from the King—Visit from General Botha—Enemy's Refusal to Fight—His Escape from Kilossa and Morogoro—The Attack on Kissaki—Germans' Last Refuge—Royal Navy's Share in the War—Fate of Enemy's Western Force—End of Campaign in Sight—General Smuts released for Imperial Conference—His Successor—General Smuts's Tribute to his Leaders and Men.

IT is time to turn from the cockpits of Europe to see how matters stood with Germany's sole remaining colony while the fate of civilization was hanging in the balance. The critical situation in East Africa at the outbreak of war, and the early phases of the campaign on the German borderland, have already been dealt with.[1] As a result of these operations, though deeds were performed which were no less heroic than those in the main theatres of war, it was obvious that the British and Indian forces available were hopelessly insufficient for the task of conquering the last and greatest of the enemy's colonies. With an area twice as large as that of the Fatherland itself, it was not surprising that the campaign had been long and arduous. The hostile border-line included the British possessions of Nyasaland, British East Africa, and Uganda, with a front, all told, of nearly 1000 miles. When it is remembered that none of these British colonies had been prepared for aggression from the outside, while German East Africa, like all the enemy's oversea possessions, had had a military organization from the first, the only wonder was that we were able to hold our own until the arrival of reinforcements. The position in Nyasaland in particular was at first a source of grave anxiety. Of all our possessions, as Mr. Bonar Law told the House of Commons when at length the danger was removed, this was the most precarious when war broke out. Our force available in Nyasaland was small, and could not be increased for a long time. The Colonial Office was in serious apprehension of something disastrous happening there.

Happily these fears proved ground-

[1] Vol. I, Chapter XI; Vol. II, Chapter VIII; Vol. III, Chapter V.

less. The prompt measures taken to destroy the German "fleet" on Lake Nyasa, and the enterprise of our plucky garrison at Karonga—some account of which has already been given — nipped his designs in the bud. Thus robbed of the initiative, he abandoned any idea he may have had of hammering with all his might at the weakest spot, and chose instead to devote most of his attention to the British East African frontier. Failing in his attempt to take Mombasa and Nairobi, the chief object of the German commander, Colonel von Lettow-Vorbeck, became the destruction of our main artery of supply, the Uganda Railway. In this, as already recorded, he had achieved little success. It was easier, however, to drive him back over his frontier than to keep him there or bring him to his knees in the trackless plains and forests which, with mountains and mangrove swamps, rivers and lakes, make up the physical features of German East Africa. He was well-armed, determined, and skilful, and the unfortunate affairs of Tanga and Jassin proved all too clearly that our available British and Indian troops were far too few for the formidable task ahead.

It was at this point that our last chapter on the East African campaign broke off. A long period of stalemate ensued, varied by aggressive activity on the part of German raiders, the British troops for the most part marking time until arrangements could be made for a renewed offensive on an adequate scale. Meantime the Imperial Government had appealed to South Africa to do what was necessary to finish the affair. The appeal was not made in vain. The Union Government at once rose to the occasion, and General Smuts organized a special recruiting campaign, appealing to the manhood of South Africa to recognize the gravity of the position of the Empire and to render personal service wherever possible.

"The Allies", he declared, in a speech which preceded this new call to arms towards the end of 1915, "have now their hands full, and the British Government was doing more than was humanly possible. It was therefore reasonably justified, now that internal hostilities had ceased, in saying to South Africa: 'You must do your duty'."

South Africa, in spite of the bitter hostility of the irreconcilable Nationalists, had already proved her loyalty up to the hilt. Apart from the conquest of German South-West Africa, she had raised other contingents for employment overseas—where they were to distinguish themselves against the Senussi in the Egyptian campaign, and cover themselves with glory on the Western front—as well as in Nyasaland and Northern Rhodesia; and now, in response to the new appeal, so many recruits were forthcoming that a fresh brigade was formed before the end of the year (1915). General Smuts told its members that he was very glad that this special task had been allotted to South Africa and Rhodesia, as they were well versed in the sort of warfare necessary to fight the hordes of barbarians scientifically trained by German officers. Many of the troops had but lately been through the South-West African campaign, and it was not long before the whole brigade was ready to sail for its new theatre of war. The total number originally contemplated for the task was 10,000 men, but before the end of the following March, General Botha announced in the House of Assembly that 20,000 men had already gone, or were going, to German East Africa.

When the Union contingents were being formed, His Majesty's Government offered the command in East Africa to General Smuts, whose record as a guerrilla leader against the British in the South African War, and, later, as General Botha's right-hand man in the conquest of German South-West Africa, stamped him as a soldier endowed with rare gifts both of leadership and organization. For various reasons he was unable at that time to accept the offer, and the choice fell instead upon General Sir Horace Smith-Dorrien, who had served in Egypt, the Soudan, South Africa, and on the Indian Frontier before playing his historic part in the retreat from Mons. Ill-health, however, compelled Sir Horace to relinquish his new command shortly after landing in Africa, and it was again offered to General Smuts, who, in the circumstances, accepted it. This was on February 9, 1916, when the soldier-statesman, who fifteen years before was one of our stoutest opponents, received his first commission in the British army, being given the rank of temporary Lieutenant-General.

At this time the enemy forces in German East Africa were estimated at some 16,000 men, of whom 2000 were white, all well equipped, and possessing sixty guns and eighty machine-guns. The artillery included ten 4.1 guns which the Germans had succeeded in saving from their cruiser *Königsberg*, which had taken refuge up the Rufiji River, eventually to be blown up there by our monitors.[1] The majority of the *Königsberg's* crew had also joined the land forces under Colonel von Lettow-Vorbeck, whose troops appear to have been re-armed in the autumn of 1915 from a blockade-runner which landed a whole cargo of munitions of war. Colonel von Lettow-Vorbeck, it must be conceded, put up a stout fight throughout, and kept his native forces together with rare skill; but his resistance would have collapsed long before the end but for the adventitious aid of those who, on several occasions, succeeded in smuggling fresh stores through to him. One such cargo, landed on the eve of General Smuts's offensive in March, 1916, was known to have included a battery of the latest pattern 10.5-centimetre field-howitzers, with an abundance of shells, besides machine-guns and the necessary ammunition. These proved a heavy handicap to the subsequent British advance. Besides the trained Askaris, drilled for years past with Teutonic thoroughness, and now armed with modern Mausers, there were many raw auxiliaries, and excellent material to draw upon among the Angoni, Wahebe, and other warlike tribes included in Germany's native population of 7,500,000. The whole force was organized in companies varying from 150 to 200 strong, with 10 per cent of whites,

[1] Vol. II, pp. 93-4.

Drawn by Philip Dadd

Railway Warfare in East Africa: British troops preparing to resist an enemy attack on an armoured train along the Uganda line

Africa. After the Jassin affair, which gave them back the coastal borderland, they retained for over a year a considerable tract of British territory. At Taveta, which they had seized at the beginning of the war, and strongly fortified as a defence against a possible invasion of German East Africa—thus guarding the only road along which any overland expedition in force could be attempted basa they maintained a garrison of 500 to 600 rifles, with the object of delaying the British concentration by blowing up the Uganda and the Voi-Maktau railways. "Their numerous attempts to accomplish this end", recorded General Smuts, "were uniformly futile."

Nevertheless, the fact remained that these and other German forces were in possession of British territory, and it

BELGIAN CONGO
UGANDA
BRITISH EAST AFRICA
GERMAN EAST AFRICA
RHODESIA
NYASALAND PROTECTORATE
MOZAMBIQUE
(Portuguese East Africa)
L. Albert
L. Choga
Kakindu
Jinja
Entebbe
Pt. Victoria
Kisumu
Port Florence
L. Edward
Victoria Nyanza
Karungu
Sherati
Bukoba
R. Kagera
Kigali
L. Kivu
Ukerewe I.
Nasa
Mwanza
Naivasha
Nairobi
R. Tana
Kibwezi
Longido
Kilimanjaro
Moshi
Tsavo
Sabaki R.
Voi
Maungu
Taveta
Mombasa
Vanga
Jassin
Vuga
Wilhelmstal
Korogwe
Handeni
Tanga
Pemba I.
Pangani
Sandani
Zanzibar (British)
Bagamoyo
Dar-es-Salaam
Morogoro
Kilossa
Mpapua
Dodoma
Kilimatinde
Usambura
L. Niarasa
UFIOME
Kigoma
Ujiji
Tabora
to Dar-es-Salaam 743 miles
Mkwisa's
Kondoa Irangi
Albertville
Kibwezi
Mpimbue
Ruaha R.
New Iringa
Rufiji R.
Mafia I.
Moliro
Bismarckburg
L. Rukwa
Mahenge
Kilwa
L. Mweru
Kalungwisi (Ft. Rhodesia)
Kituta
Abercorn
Mt. Saisi
Fife
New Langenburg
Lupembe
Old Langenburg
Kazembe
Karonga
R. Chambezi
Muira
Lindi
Mikindani
Kionga
Livingstonia
Sphinxhaven
Mbamba
R. Rovuma
C. Delgado
Bandawe
Likoma
Lake Nyasa
Chiuagulo
Ibo
Pemba Bay
General Smuts's Main Force
General Van Deventer's Division
Combined British & Belgian operations under Generals Crewe and Tombeur
General Northey's advance
Kilwa Column's advance
Portuguese advance under General Gil
Coastal operations in co-operation with the Royal Navy
German Western Force retreating towards Mahenge (defeated and scattered by Northey and Van Deventer)
Mahenge Plateau, the only healthy part left to the Germans
Remnants of Main German Force, sheltering on the Rufiji River

was the none-too-easy task of Major-General Tighe, who had preceded General Smuts to prepare the way for the coming offensive, to sweep them back as far as possible across their own frontier. For this purpose his available forces in East Africa were strengthened by such useful troops as a regiment of volunteers from Southern Rhodesia and the Legion of Frontiersmen, forming a battalion of the Royal Fusiliers, whose ranks included the famous African explorer, F. C. Selous. That mighty hunter and prince of scouts, though sixty-four years of age, had volunteered for the war, and, serving with the rank of captain, was destined to lay down his life for his country after winning the D.S.O. and earning the admiration of the whole British force for his scout-craft and intrepid bravery.

In the coastal region at the beginning of 1916 the Germans were again in occupation of the British borderland, from which they had been expelled by the Vanga Field Force a year before. They maintained a considerable garrison on the Umba River, actively patrolling thence to the vicinity of the Uganda Railway, Mwete Mdogo, and Gazi—about midway along the coastal road between Vanga and Mombasa. These enterprising outposts did their best to harass General Tighe in his preliminary operations; but, though he had to be constantly on the watch for the next move of his active and resourceful enemy, he kept steadily before him, as General Smuts bore witness, "the necessity of doing all in his power to prepare the way for the eventual offensive movement". With 600 miles of land frontier to watch he had widely to disseminate his small force, and was unable to keep any large reserve in hand to meet a sudden call; but he organized such of his infantry as could be spared for active operations into the 1st and 2nd East

Captain F. C. Selous, D.S.O., the famous hunter-naturalist, killed in the East African Campaign (From a photograph by Maull & Fox)

African Brigades, one acting on the Taveta line and the other on the Longido line—the scene of the attack under Major-General Stewart in the first British offensive towards the close of 1914. General Tighe also proceeded to organize the whole of his force into two divisions and line-of-communication troops.

It was during a skirmish in these preliminary operations at the beginning of 1916 that Captain Wavell, of "Wavell's Arabs", was killed. His force of Arabs—mentioned in an earlier chapter[1]—which he had recruited on the coast at the beginning of the war, had rendered yeoman service, and he himself had been severely wounded in the first phase of the campaign. Recovered from this wound and promoted major, he had distinguished himself again and again. A man of rare attainments—full of profound Oriental learning and one of the few Westerners who had visited Mecca—his death was a serious loss to scholarship as well as to General Tighe's force on the East African coast.

On January 15, 1916, Major-General Stewart, commanding the 1st Division, was ordered to reoccupy Longido, the British garrison of which, after holding it for some months as described in our last chapter on the East African campaign, had been withdrawn. Longido was not only a position of exceptional natural strength, as the British and Indian troops had discovered in the first advance, but also of great strategic importance as guarding the road to Kilimanjaro from the north.

While Major-General Stewart was regaining possession of this place, and developing the lines of communication between it and Kajiado, to the north, on the Magadi Railway, Brigadier-General Malleson, with the 2nd Division, began to drive the Germans back from British territory on the other side of Kilimanjaro, advancing on January 22 from Makatau to Mbuyuni. Only slight opposition was offered, and two days later Serengeti camp was occupied. Finding himself thus outflanked, the enemy was now forced to evacuate Kasigau. This accomplished, General Tighe made arrangements for the concentration of a large force at and near Mbuyuni, carrying the railway from Makatau to Njoro, about midway between Mbuyuni and the enemy's entrenched camp at Taveta. General Smuts wrote in warm and generous terms of this and other necessary spade-work before he appeared on the scene in the East African theatre of war.

> "I cannot speak too highly of all the preliminary work done by General Tighe in the direction of organization and preparation for offensive measures. This left me free on arrival to devote my whole energies to active operations, and I take this opportunity of placing on record my appreciation of the fact that the success of those operations is in a large measure due to General Tighe's foresight and energy in paving the way for the expected reinforcements."

For these services General Tighe subsequently received the K.C.M.G. The 2nd South African Infantry Brigade, arriving early in February—a few weeks before the new Commander-in-Chief—soon had its first taste of the hard fighting in store. On the 12th of that month three of its battalions, with three battalions of the 1st East African Brigade, supported by eighteen guns and howitzers, made a reconnaissance in force of Salaita, beyond railhead at Njoro Drift, under Brigadier-General Malleson. Salaita, a position described as of considerable natural strength, had been carefully entrenched, and was found

[1] Vol. II, pp. 91-2.

to be held in force by the enemy, who counter-attacked vigorously.

"General Malleson was compelled to withdraw to Sarengeti, but much useful information had been gained, and the South African Infantry had learned some invaluable lessons in bush fighting, and also had an opportunity to estimate the fighting qualities of their enemy."

Major J. J. O'Sullevan, awarded the D.S.O. for the gallant defence of Saisi
(From a photograph by Elliott & Fry)

That was the last incident of note before the arrival of General Smuts on February 19, 1916, though many heroic little episodes in other parts of the scattered border-line will have to be woven into the narrative when the full story is written of the East African campaign. There was the gallant defence of Saisi, for example, on the Rhodesian front, some 30 miles from Abercorn, by the British and Belgian force under Major J. J. O'Sullevan, of the Northern Rhodesian Police, who received the D.S.O. for his magnificent leadership. Major O'Sullevan had been ordered to the Tanganyika front with his mobile column of British and Belgian troops before the end of 1914, and eventually reached Saisi after a memorable march, the last stage of which, a distance of 430 miles, through most difficult country and in heavy rains, was covered in twenty days—an average of rather more than 21 miles a day. While the war was languishing on the main front the Germans were becoming increasingly troublesome on the Rhodesian border, and Saisi, now strongly fortified by Major O'Sullevan, and held by troops who were always ready to raid any German camp in the neighbourhood, became a perpetual thorn in the enemy's side. Having tried in vain to carry the fort by storm in June, 1915, the Germans laid siege to the place, surrounding it on July 24 with a force of 2000 rifles, supported by several 12-pounders and ten machine-guns. Against this force the defence could only muster 450 Belgian and British native soldiers, with 20 British and Belgian officers, one 7-pounder, one 4-pounder, and two Maxims.

"Fighting", said Major O'Sullevan, in the course of a lecture on his experiences delivered in London some eighteen months later before the African Society, "continued day and night for four days, and all our mules and oxen, besides the sheep and goats upon which we depended for food, were killed by shrapnel. On the fifth day the German officer in command sent in a *parlementaire* with a note asking me to surrender. He stated that he had captured a large convoy of supplies, and had also beaten back our relief forces; that he knew we had no water; and so on. I replied that under no conditions whatever would we surrender."

That night, in the light of a fairly bright moon, the Germans made another attempt to carry the fort by storm; but they only added to their already heavy list of casualties, and after eating up all their supplies were forced on August 3 to abandon the siege in despair. Major O'Sullevan's losses all told during the period did not amount to more than 80, while the enemy lost 60 dead in Germans alone, their casualties in Askaris being proportionately greater. The defenders were "too done up"—in their leader's own words—to give chase to the retreating foe; and a few days later were relieved by a battalion of Belgian troops.

This was one of many brilliant little actions which kept the enemy at bay on the south-western front until the Allies were strong enough to carry the war well into the heart of German territory. Repeated attacks in the direction of Abercorn and Fife were launched from the hostile bases at Bismarcksburg and Neu Langenburg. Once, in June, 1915, the enemy came within measurable distance of rushing our camp at Fife, but after a stiff little fight was beaten back by Major Boyd Cunninghame. Eventually the British troops in Rhodesia and Nyasaland were united under the command of Brigadier-General E. Northey, and the Belgians on the Tanganyika front under Major-General Tombeur. Both forces were then organized to form converging columns in the larger scheme of operations about to be inaugurated under the supreme command of General Smuts.

When the new Commander-in-Chief landed, he was met at Mombasa by General Tighe, who fully explained the situation and the steps he had taken to pave the way for an advance in the Kilimanjaro-Meru area, "probably the richest and most desirable district of German East Africa". With characteristic vigour General Smuts decided immediately to visit the two proposed lines of advance by Mbuyuni and Longido, and, as a result of this personal reconnaissance in company with General Tighe, cabled to Lord Kitchener on February 23 that he was prepared to carry out the occupation of this area before the rainy season, which might be expected towards the end of March. The sanction of the War Minister was received two days later, and by March 4, when the 3rd South African Brigade had arrived in the country, all the necessary concentrations had been made for the advance.

With the enemy's main force, known to be assembled between Salaita and the Kitovo Hills, on the eastern side of the Kilimanjaro, and the road across the border barred by strong defences at Taveta, General Tighe had devised a plan to occupy the whole of the Kilimanjaro area by a converging advance from the German frontier stronghold of Longido, 50 miles to the north-west, and Mbuyuni, in the south-east, with Kahe as the objective in each case. While adhering to this main plan, General Smuts made certain alterations, which he con-

Marching in the Unknown: Rhodesians on their way to the front in East Africa advancing in single file by Kaffir paths untrodden by any white man before

sidered necessary "in order to avoid frontal attacks against entrenched positions of the enemy in dense bush, and to secure the rapidity of advance which appeared to me essential to the success of the operation in the short time at our disposal before the commencement of the rains".

It was no mean task with which the soldier-statesman, making Nairobi the base of his operations, found himself confronted. The enemy, fully prepared for the coming offensive from the British camps at Serengeti and Mbuyuni, lay entrenched in front of these in a most formidable position behind the River Lumi, on the Taveta road. Seven miles of dense bush defended him in front, while he was protected on the right by the Pare Mountains and the swamps of the Ruwu and Lake Jipe, and on the left by the dangerous, broken foot-hills of Kilimanjaro. His own strength in this area was estimated at 6000 rifles, with 16 guns of various calibre and 37 machine-guns.

Unfortunately an essential feature of the attack—the advance of the 1st Division, under Major-General J. M. Stewart, from Longido, on March 5—was seriously delayed, as will presently be explained, and failed to attain its purpose in the chief converging movement, which was to sweep round the enemy's rear and cut his line of communication by the Usambara Railway. The 1st Division was given two days' clear start from Longido before the main advance against Taveta should begin. Its task was to cross the waterless bush which lay between Longido and the Engare Nanjuki River, and then advance between Meru and Kilimanjaro to Bombaja-Ngombe, as shown in the accompanying map. Thence it was to be directed on Kahe, cutting the enemy's communications in the rear while General Smuts was hammering him in front.

Two days after the 1st Division set out on its long march across the bare plains from Longido, General Smuts developed his main advance, the essence of which was a brilliant turning movement by the 1st South African Mounted and 3rd South African Infantry Brigades under the command of General Van Deventer, one of Botha's right-hand men in the South-West African campaign. This movement involved an arduous night march across the Saragenti plains as far as the high ground round Lake Chala, and an advance on Taveta from that direction, thus taking the enemy by surprise, and avoiding the heavy casualties which must have accompanied any frontal attack through the thick bush between Taveta and Salaita. Meantime, another South African column was guarding the Lumi crossing, while the 2nd Division, under General Tighe, bombarded Salaita on the 8th, and prepared for an attack on the following day. General Van Deventer's surprise attack from Chala, however, combined with the bombardment, had persuaded the Germans to yield both Salaita and Taveta without a struggle, both places falling into General Smuts's hands on the 10th. The enemy withdrew from Taveta only after a stubborn rearguard action, hotly pursued by mounted troops and field-artillery towards the Latema-Reata nek. It became clear that the retreat was being pursued along the Taveta-Moshi road towards the west, as well as along the road between the precipitous bush-clad hills of Reata and Latema. Whether this nek was sheltering merely a covering force or the main body preparing for a counter-attack was unknown, but in either case it was necessary to clear it before General Smuts could advance beyond Taveta. On the morning of March 11, therefore, General Malleson was ordered to clear up the situation, and, if possible, seize the nek with the forces then available at Taveta, comprising three weak battalions of the 1st East African Brigade, eight 12-pounder guns, and a howitzer battery. These advanced to the attack at 11.45 a.m., mounted

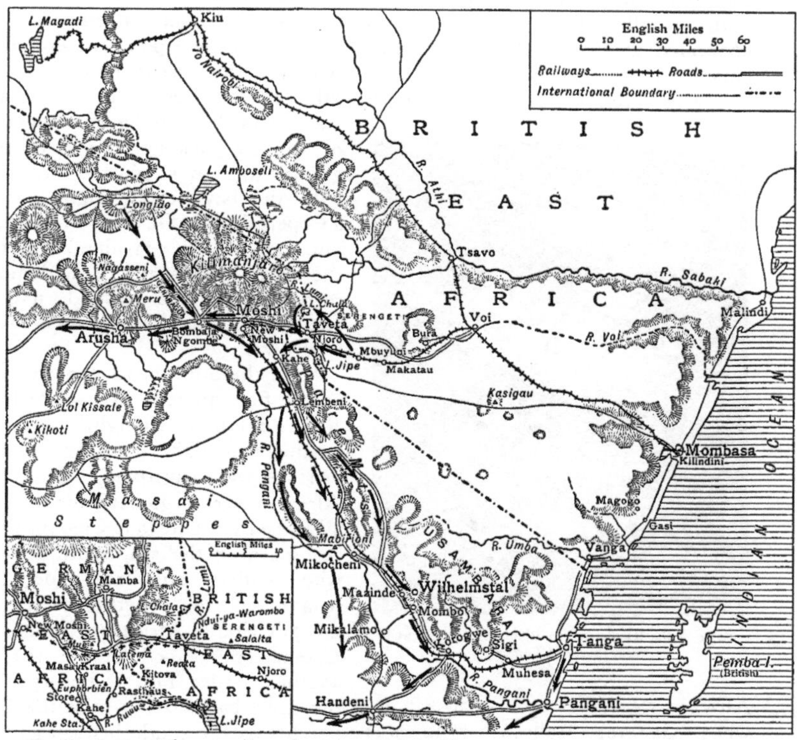


The War in East Africa: map illustrating the conquest of Kilimanjaro and the first phase of General Smuts's campaign in 1916

troops watching both flanks. Approaching the bush-clad slopes of the spur of Latema, which commands the nek from the north, our infantry came under a galling fire from the enemy's concealed artillery and rifle and machine-gun fire, and could make little headway. Reinforcements of South

Some of the King's African Rifles, who fought well throughout the Campaign

Africans were sent up, and at 4 p.m., when General Malleson, who was seriously indisposed, asked to be relieved of his command, General Tighe was directed by General Smuts to take over the personal control of the operations. Bitter but indecisive fighting continued through the rest of the day, portions of the position being taken and retaken several times. The Rhodesians and King's African Rifles especially distinguished themselves by a gallant but unavailing assault on the Latema ridge, the King's African Rifles losing their gallant leader, Lieutenant-Colonel B. R. Graham, and several other officers.

Shortly after 8 p.m., General Tighe, whose reinforcements had included the 5th and 7th South African Infantry Battalions, decided that the only chance of quickly dislodging the obstinate enemy was to send these troops in with the bayonet by night. It was an operation, as General Smuts points out, fraught with considerable risk, for there was no opportunity of adequately reconnoitring the ground, and the strength of the enemy was entirely unknown.

"On the other hand, the moon was in the first quarter, and so facilitated movement up to midnight"; and it was in this dim light that the desperate venture was attempted. The South Africans were organized for the night advance by Lieutenant-Colonel Byron, commanding the 5th South Africans, who, sending one force under Lieutenant Colonel Freeth, commanding the 7th South Africans, to storm the Latema spurs north of the nek, and another, under Major Thompson, of the same battalion, to seize the Reata heights on the south, himself gallantly led a third force to secure the nek. All advanced at the appointed time with great dash through the bush, but this proved much thicker than had been anticipated, and afforded the Germans and their Askaris every opportunity of offering stubborn resistance. Driving the enemy before them, however, both flanking-parties carried out their appointed task with unfaltering determination. It needs no great stretch of imagination to read a tale of magnificent courage between the lines of General Smuts's brief reference to the exploits of the South Africans on this occasion:

"Colonel Freeth fought his way up the steep spurs of Latema till he found that the party with him had dwindled to eighteen men. He was joined by a few of the Rhodesians and King's African Rifles, who had clung on to the crest of the ridge after the assault in the evening, and the small party held on till daylight. Major Thompson wheeled towards Reata with 170 men and dug himself in in an advantageous position. About midnight Colonel Byron reached the nek within thirty yards of the enemy's main position. The opposition here was very stubborn. At one point Major Mainprise, R.E., Brigade Major, and twenty-two men were killed by the concentrated fire of three machine-guns, and Colonel Byron, who was himself slightly wounded, reached the nek with only twenty men. The enemy was still in a position which commanded the ground he had won, and, finding it impossible either to advance or to hold his ground, he was reluctantly compelled to withdraw."

A German Photograph captured at Moshi: view taken before the war within sight of Kilimanjaro—then one of the Kaiser's proudest possessions—with German officers in the foreground

Unaware of the isolated but vital successes of the gallant bands on the northern and southern crests, and faced with the news that Colonel Byron had been forced to order his own party to retire, General Tighe re-formed his troops and dug in astride the road to await daylight. Attempts were made in vain to gain touch with Colonel Freeth and Major Thompson. It seemed that the attempt to force the nek had failed, and General Smuts, judging by the reports received, decided not to press this direct attack further, relying instead on the turning movement of the mounted troops ordered for the following morning. General Tighe was accordingly directed to withdraw his whole force before daybreak to a line farther back from the nek, and the withdrawal was actually in progress when the patrols dispatched to the flank detachments on Reata and Latema returned with the welcome news that they had not only found Colonel Freeth and Major Thompson in possession of both hills, but also that the enemy, finding himself thus commanded from each side, was in full retreat towards Kahe, abandoning guns and much ammunition, and leaving many dead on the ground. General Smuts at once sent the 8th South African Infantry to make good the ridge, and some artillery to complete the discomfiture of the retiring enemy. Effective pursuit, however, was out of the question through the dense tropical forest which stretched all the way to Kahe. Our casualties had amounted to about 270, "which cannot be considered excessive", writes General Smuts, "in view of the important results gained".

While this fight for the nek was in progress, the 4th South African Horse and 12th South African Infantry engaged the enemy along the Taveta-Mosha road, when the Germans were found in considerable strength. Here, too, the foe was driven back with heavy loss, pursued on the 12th by General Van Deventer, and destroying as he fled all the bridges on the road. This proved a heavy obstacle to the pursuit, great difficulty being experienced in rationing the troops.[1] On the 13th, however, Van Deventer occupied Moshi unopposed, and the first phase of the battle for Kilimanjaro came to a close.

It was unfortunate that the 1st Division, under Major-General Stewart, was unable to throw its weight into the final and decisive phase of this engagement. As already mentioned, it had been given two clear days' start on its long march from Longido to Bombaja-Ngombe, where it was expected to arrive in time to bar the retreat of the enemy westward and cut the enemy's line of communication by the Usambara Railway. All went well, apparently, for the first three days, the waterless bush from Longido to the Engare Nanjuki River being crossed in safety, and Geraragua being reached with but slight opposition on March 8. Thenceforward, however, progress was seriously delayed by transport difficulties. Having halted on the 9th to reconnoitre and let his supplies catch up, General Stewart was informed that the direct road from Geraragua to Bombaja-Ngombe was impassable for wheels, all bridges having been destroyed by the enemy.

"As a result of this, and of the exhausted state of his ox transport," records General Smuts, in the following brief summary of the ensuing movements of the 1st Division, "General Stewart considered it necessary to halt on the morning of the 10th and reconnoitre for a road farther to the west. A difficult but passable track was found, and the march was resumed at mid-day. The mounted troops left Geraragua at sixteen hours on the 10th, on which date they

[1] All the way from Taveta to Arusha, 45 miles beyond Moshi, the road has many rivers to cross. There are no fewer than eighteen considerable and minor streams (head-waters of the Pangani River) between Taveta and Moshi alone.

encountered some opposition, sustaining thirteen casualties. The division and the mounted troops eventually joined hands on the Sanja River on the night of the 12th–13th, and on the 13th advanced to Bombaja-Ngombe. On the 14th, when the main force of the enemy had already retired to the Ruwu and Kahe positions, the 1st Division joined hands with General Van Deventer in New Moshi, through which place the six companies of the enemy who had been opposing General Stewart had already passed on the night of the 12th March."

The enemy's next stand was made in the thick forest belt which lies along the Ruwu River, and in view of railway extension and future advance it was essential to drive him south before the rains began. None knew the vital importance of the position better than the Germans, as was presently revealed by the strength of their fortifications and their formidable armament, which included two 4.1 guns from the *Königsberg*—one on a railway truck and the other in a concealed position south of the river—with a range of 14,000 yards. Before attacking this position General Smuts spent the period of March 13–17 in reorganizing his troops and transports, and repairing roads and bridges for motor traffic over the numerous swollen streams. On the 18th the main force renewed its advance through German territory towards Kahe, occupying the line Euphorbien Hill-Unterer Himo without difficulty, but in close contact with the enemy, who for the next few days maintained a defence of the most obstinate character. Desperate fighting took place at Store, four miles south of Masai Kraal, on the 20th, where the 2nd East African Brigade and the mounted troops of the 1st Division, under Brigadier-General S. H. Sheppard, D.S.O., had encamped. That night the camp was heavily attacked by the enemy from 9.30 p.m. to midnight with a force estimated by prisoners at 500 men, with another 500 in reserve, but the assault proved a costly failure.

While the enemy was thus vainly striving to turn the tables on the invaders, General Van Deventer, by order of General Smuts, was in the act of making one of his brilliant night marches, which, as in the capture of Taveta at the beginning of the campaign, was destined to outflank the foe and force him to beat another hasty retreat. Van Deventer's mounted column, comprising the 1st South African Mounted Brigade, the 4th South African Horse, and two field batteries, left Moshi at 2 p.m. on the 20th, with instructions to cross the Pangani River and get in rear of the German position at Kahe station. Marching all the rest of that day and night, they approached the Pangani from the west at a point south-west of Kahe Hill at daybreak on the 21st, and with some difficulty crossed the river in sufficient strength to seize Kahe railway station, as well as Kahe Hill and Baumann Hill to the south. With this threat to their line of retreat the Germans knew that their position on the entire Ruwu line was doomed, but held on throughout the day with the object of retiring under cover of darkness, taking full advantage in the meantime of their skilfully-designed defences in the thick thorn bush to keep both attacking forces at bay. A mounted South African detachment, sent from Kahe Hill to cut off their retreat by the wagon road south of the Ruwu, found them in such force that it had no alternative but to return. Van Deventer therefore decided to wait for the following day to develop his turning movement, after the whole of his brigade had crossed the Pangani.

As soon as General Smuts, in the meanwhile, had heard that Van Deventer was nearing Kahe, he ordered the attack on the enemy's front to be resumed by General Sheppard, who accordingly advanced at 11.30 a.m. on the 21st, with the 2nd East African Brigade on his left and the 2nd South African Brigade on his right, the Masai Kraal-Kahe road being the dividing line. The 3rd South African Brigade advanced at the same time from Euphorbien Hill to co-operate in General Sheppard's plan of enveloping the enemy's eastern flank. Unfortunately the progress of the troops from Euphorbien Hill was so impeded by the dense bush that they were unable to arrive in time, and without their aid, as General Smuts points out, the task proved beyond the powers of the force at General Sheppard's disposal. Though the enemy was driven back within an hour to his main position at the edge of a clearing in the bush, flanked on one side by the Soko Nassai River and on the other by the River Defu, these obstacles, stoutly defended, proved at the time insuperable. General Shepherd's infantry strove gallantly but in

Before the Advance of General Smuts: German Askari (native troops) and baggage-carriers ready to entrain at New Moshi, the northern terminus of the Tanga railway
(From a photograph captured on the occupation of the town by General Smuts's troops)

vain to cross the clearing, which varied in width from 600 to 1200 yards. Commanded as it was both from front and flank by rifle and machine-gun fire, the place was nothing but a death-trap. Two double companies of Baluebis crossed the Soko Nassai and made a brave attempt to turn the enemy's right, but they, too, were held up. Though our guns were well handled—one mountain battery being in action in the actual firing-line—it was practically impossible to get definite targets in the impenetrable bush. "The whole force, in fact," records General Smuts, "was ably handled by General Sheppard, and the men fought like heroes, but they were unable to turn the enemy from his strong position."

The situation now bore a striking resemblance to the position on the night of March 11–12 in front of the Latema-Reata nek, when the tragic fate of Colonel Byron's attack in the centre, and the unknown success of the flanking parties, decided General Tighe to dig in astride the road to await daylight. While battling thus against impossible odds, General Sheppard was equally ignorant of the fact that Van Deventer was already at Kahe station. It proved impossible to establish contact between the two forces through the thick intervening bush. General Sheppard accordingly gave orders to dig in on the ground won, with the object of renewing the attack on the following day. Dawn on the 22nd broke, however, to find the enemy in full retreat. He had only waited for the cover of night to slip across the Ruwu River. Then, avoiding Kahe, where Van Deventer was awaiting his opportunity to take him in the rear, he had retired along the main road to Lembeni, after blowing up his stationary 4.1 naval gun.

Though he had thus succeeded in extracting his main force from a precarious situation, he was known to have suffered heavy casualties, and had obviously been nonplussed by the ingenious development of General Smuts's strategy. The enemy, in the words of the official *communiqué* from British head-quarters, "was outmanœuvred and outclassed by our troops". Our own casualties at the Soko Nassai action amounted, all told, to 288. "Though we mourn the loss of many brave comrades," as General Smuts said in one of his inspiring messages to his force at the time, "the results have thoroughly justified our sacrifices." The immediate effects had been to clear the enemy finally out of British territory, and to complete the conquest of the Kilimanjaro and Meru areas, the healthiest and most valuable settled part of German East Africa.

Arusha, on the southern slopes of Mount Meru, had in the meanwhile been occupied by our mounted scouts, who dislodged the enemy garrison and drove it off to the south. Having achieved the main objects which he had set himself to accomplish before the rainy season began, General Smuts now established his head-quarters at Moshi, and disposed his forces without delay with a view to their comfort and health during the approaching rains, the while he devoted himself with characteristic energy to planning and organizing his next move. The Commander-in-Chief was the recipient of many congratulations on this successful inauguration of his new campaign, among the most gratifying of which was the following telegram from his former opponent and now staunch friend, Lord Kitchener:—

"The Secretary of State for War wishes to congratulate you and all ranks under your command on your brilliant success, and on the dash and energy with which your operations have been conducted in a country with the difficulties of which he is acquainted from personal experience."[1]

General Smuts closed his first dispatch as Commander-in-Chief of the East African Force with a high tribute to the zeal and single-minded devotion of all the troops under his command—a most heterogeneous army, as he subsequently described it, speaking a babel of languages. Shortage of transport had necessitated the force moving on light scale throughout his rapid drive. At times rations unavoidably ran short, and the long marches in the sweltering sun, with occasional drenching rains, were calculated to try the most hardened campaigner. "Yet all these hardships", added General Smuts, "were endured with unfailing cheerfulness, and a chance of dealing a blow at the enemy seemed to be the only recompense required." Though rations at times unavoidably ran short, high praise was bestowed on the work of the supply and transport services in the face of almost inconceivable difficulties. Such roads as did exist were merely clearings through the bush and swamp, and these rapidly became well-nigh impassable for heavy lorries.

"The rapidity of the advance, and the distance to which it was carried, must almost inevitably have caused a breakdown in the transport had it not been for the unremitting exertions of the railway engineers, who carried forward the railway from the Njoro drift, east of Salaita, to Taveta and the Latema nek at an average rate of a mile a day, including surveying, heavy bush-cutting, and the bridging of the Lumi River. This fine performance is largely due to the ripe experience and organizing power of Colonel Sir W. Johns, Kt., C.I.E."

Letters home confirmed these details of the endless difficulties confronting the troops at every turn of this arduous campaign. General Smuts himself confessed, on arriving in London for the Imperial Conference in the following year, that his task had proved considerably harder than he had anticipated. The Germans, it is true, fought their fight against odds with consummate skill, but the campaign was destined to resolve itself, not so much into a contest of arms, as into a costly struggle against immense distances and adverse conditions—execrable roads, lack of food, tropical disease, and bad conditions generally. Wild beasts, too, had always to be reckoned with, especially after an engagement, when it was essential to gather up the wounded as rapidly as possible, and not to leave out for a single night the bodies of those who were killed.

"On one occasion, when out at midnight bringing in some bodies", wrote one of the British chaplains, "two

[1] Lord Kitchener himself possessed an estate of some 5000 acres of agricultural and grazing land in British East Africa, and was thoroughly familiar with the country on the German frontier line. His own estate was on the Uganda line, about 40 miles on the eastern side of the Victoria Nyanza.

lions roared at me from either side of the road in the tall elephant grass." Another officer described the Kilimanjaro country as simply swarming with lions and game of every description; and many tales were told of dramatic meetings in the bush at uncomfortably close quarters. Once, we are told, the lions managed to besiege General Smuts himself in his motor cars, "with developments", according to a *Times* correspondent, reminiscent of Colonel Patterson's encounters with the man-eaters of Tsavo". Giraffes added to the difficulties of the campaign by scratching their necks on the telegraph wire, thereby pulling it down and interrupting communications. The whole region in which the troops were now operating, indeed, was described as one vast natural preserve of big game. "The deeper we get in", wrote Reuter's correspondent, in one of his dispatches, "the more amazing and disconcerting are the animals. We have to confront every animal extant, except the jabberwock and the bandersnatch."

Our Oldest Ally joins in the War: Portuguese cavalry on the march

Beasts of prey, however, formed but an insignificant factor in the task now confronting General Smuts of occupying so vast an enemy territory and compelling the enemy himself to surrender within a reasonable time. It was clear as daylight that the only way to attain these ends was by means of a simultaneous advance by different routes, threatening the enemy from all directions. He was now hemmed in on every side, the Fatherland having closed his only loophole of escape into neutral country by declaring war on Portugal on March 9, 1916. This was at the very beginning of General Smuts's campaign, the chief ostensible reasons being that Britain's oldest ally had requisitioned German merchant-ships which had been lying in her harbours since the outbreak of war, and that British war-vessels had been allowed to remain too long in Portuguese waters. The real reason for declaring war, however, as pointed out by Mr. Hannay in Volume V (p. 224), was that while Germany considered that she had nothing to lose by adding Portugal to her enemies, she would be more free to invade Mozambique if the course of the struggle in East Africa necessitated that step.

Portuguese troops on the frontier, taking up the challenge, at once proceeded to exact redress for a long-outstanding grievance against their aggressive neighbours, who, in 1894, had robbed them, with total disregard for international obligations, of the little coastal town of Kionga, near the mouth of the Rovuma River. This unwarranted seizure in 1894 had been a severe blow to the Portuguese monarchy, but Germany had never attempted to excuse her high-handed action. It was not forgotten when the declaration of war came in 1916. Within a month Portuguese troops had re-occupied the place, and substituted their own flag for that of the Kaiser. Subsequently a Portuguese force, under General Gil, crossed the Rovuma River, and in accordance with the Allies' plans occupied certain strategic points to the north of it.

While the Portuguese were thus threatening the Germans from the south, the Belgians were advancing in the west, all other loopholes of escape being closely guarded by the British. General Smuts's problem was to co-ordinate all those movements, and round up the enemy as speedily as possible. By the end of March, 1916, he had reorganized his own expeditionary force into three divisions—the first comprising the East African, Indian, and other British forces under Major-General A. R. Hoskins, C.M.G., D.S.O., and the second and third consisting of the South African contingents, under Major-General Van Deventer and Major-General Coen Brits respectively. Various alternative schemes had to be weighed in considering the strategy to be followed in the coming campaign, including the obvious plan of advancing inland from the coast along the existing railway lines, as had been done with such signal success by General Botha in the German South-West African campaign. Various considerations, however, ruled out this and other schemes in favour of an advance into the interior from the existing base camps, the most powerful arguments in favour of which were to the effect that the violence of the impending rainy season would be chiefly confined to the Kilimanjaro-Arusha area; that farther west and south the rainy season was less severe and would not seriously interfere with military operations. An advance into the interior, therefore, would not bring the campaign to a complete standstill during the wet months of April and May. Moreover, the enemy, as General Smuts pointed out, had made the mistake of retiring south along the Tanga railway with practically his entire fighting force, leaving the door to the interior standing wide open and unguarded.

The opportunity to enter thus easily into the very heart of German East Africa was too good to be missed.

While, therefore, retaining two of his newly-formed divisions in rain quarters facing the German concentration south of the Ruwu, General Smuts dispatched the 2nd Division, under Van Deventer—comprising the 1st South African Mounted Brigade under Brigadier-General Manie Botha, and the 3rd South African Infantry Brigade under Brigadier-General C. A. L. Berrangé, C.M.G.—to enter this open doorway and march forthwith to Kondoa Irangi, the centre of a rich agricultural district, and about 100 miles from the Central Railway, which cuts German East Africa in two, running right across the colony from the coast at Dar-es-Salaam to Lake Tanganyika. The division entrusted with this adventurous advance was typically South African, and, like all its leaders, largely composed of men who had helped to conquer "German South-West". Van Deventer himself had greatly distinguished himself in that campaign by his long sweeping treks which, time after time, had outflanked the enemy, and helped in no small measure to bring that little war to its speedy end.

Concentrating his force for this new purpose at Arusha, Van Deventer began with a brilliant little success some 35 miles south-west of his headquarters. Here, on Lol Kissale, his scouts on April 1 had discovered a mountain stronghold held by a German force with machine-guns. As this fortress commanded the only water-springs to be found in the neighbourhood, General Smuts ordered the position to be captured. The task was entrusted to three regiments of Van Deventer's mounted men, who, by a swift night march, completely surrounded the mountain, and drew a cordon round it through which there was no escape. The enemy clung to his rocky stronghold with undeniable determination, fighting for it throughout the 4th and 5th, but at daybreak on the following morning the whole garrison, to the number of over 400 Askaris, led by 17 Germans, together with porters and two machine-guns, surrendered—a large quantity of stores and ammunition also falling into our hands. From documents, captured at the same time, General Smuts learned that the enemy contemplated reinforcing his garrisons at Kondoa Irangi and other points along the route of the threatened British advance from Arusha. This would have to be done from his main force on the Tanga railway, and, as several weeks must elapse before the reinforcements could arrive, Van Deventer was ordered to forestall them by pressing forward at once.

It was a strenuous race against time, but with continuous marching and fighting the South Africans won, dispersing the enemy's patrols *en route*, flinging the garrisons in succession out of Ufiome and Umbulu with considerable losses, and finally occupying Kondoa Irangi on May 19, 1916. Typical Boer tactics were employed in this last conspicuous success—founded on the "Zulu Horns" attack which their forefathers had learned to excellent purpose in their early wars with the native warriors in South Africa—the centre being firmly held while the flanks were cautiously but relentlessly enveloped with the help of deadly rifle and field-gun fire. Not a burgher, according to Reuter's correspondent, exposed himself as the net was drawn closer and closer round the strongly held village, until at length the enemy, seizing his last opportunity to escape before the net closed right round him, precipitately fled. The pursuit was at once taken up as fast as the condi-

Colonel von Lettow-Vorbeck, the German Commander-in-Chief in East Africa

tion of the war-worn horses and troops permitted. One happy result was the capture from the enemy and liberation of a considerable number of Boer families whom the Germans had seized from farms in the Kilimanjaro-Meru area, and were marching off for internment as political prisoners.

General Smuts was fully satisfied for the time being with what he had done.

"Van Deventer," he wrote, "with his usual dash and resourcefulness, had secured important results at trifling cost. Within a month of the battle of Kahe we had taken possession of the high, healthy, and fertile plateau which connects Arusha with the Central Railway, and had occupied the dominant strategic points for any further advance."

Hundreds of Van Deventer's animals, however, had died from horse sickness during the month's arduous march of 200 miles from Moshi, and his troops were exhausted. On General Smuts's orders, therefore, the 2nd Division now concentrated at Kondoa Irangi, leaving detachments in possession of Ufiome and Umbulu, and sending patrols towards the Central Railway, Singida, Mikalama, and Handeni, through which the Commander-in-Chief himself intended to move with the main force as soon as the weather abated. By this time the rains had set in with the greatest violence in the whole region between Taveta and Kondoa Irangi. All the rivers came down in flood, sweeping away, as General Smuts feelingly remarked, "almost all our laboriously-built bridges", transforming the roads into impassable tracks of swamp and sludge, and making all transport a physical impossibility. Sometimes as much as 4 inches of rain fell in one day. It would have fared ill, indeed, with the main force in its "rain quarters" but for the fact that by this time the railway had reached Taveta, where sufficient supplies could be dumped for the resting troops.

"The extension of the line," adds the Commander-in-Chief, "was energetically continued to join the Kahe-Moshi railway, although for long distances the track was practically under water, and the attention of thousands of labourers was constantly required to prevent its disappearance in the mud. Van Deventer's division in the interior was cut off, and managed to live for weeks on such supplies as could be collected locally, or could be carried by porters from Lol Kissale for a distance of 120 miles. The strain and privation were, however, bound to be reflected in the general state of health of the troops."

Difficulties of the Advance in German East Africa: British troops wading through the floods

It was in this sorry plight that the South Africans, thus temporarily isolated, were called upon to face and defeat the last serious attempt of the Germans in East Africa to renew the offensive on any considerable scale. Colonel von Lettow-Vorbeck, the German Commander-in-Chief, quick to realize the danger threatened to his whole scheme of defence by this sudden thrust into the heart of the colony, had taken advantage of the rainy season to slip away from the Usambara to the Central Railway with a great part of his force, which he concentrated at Dodoma in order to annihilate Van Deventer's force, or at least drive it back. He was well aware of the extent to which the 2nd Division had been ravaged by sickness and the hardships of the march, and felt confident that his 4000 rifles would prove more than a match for the bare 3000 which the South African commander now had at his disposal in his precarious position at Kondoa Irangi.

In face of this new movement Van Deventer gradually withdrew his advanced posts, but keeping touch with the enemy and finally disposing his force in defensive positions on a perimeter of about 5 miles frontage round Kondoa. The decisive battle began on the evening of May 9, and, from the moment when the enemy drove in our outlying piquets south-east of the village, lasted for nearly eight hours. It was under the personal command of Colonel von Lettow-Vorbeck himself, who had evidently staked all his hopes of victory on this decisive blow. Preceded by a heavy bombardment, for which purpose another of the *Königsberg's* guns was brought into action, the enemy pressed the attack with the fiercest determination, charging repeatedly right up to our positions. Every attempt, however, was shattered by the impregnable defence of the South African Infantry, who bore the brunt of the fighting. At 3.15 a.m. the attack finally ceased, the enemy withdrawing after losing two of his battalion commanders and suffering many other casualties. Thenceforward the Germans, while remaining in position round Kondoa for the rest of May and the greater part of June, 1916, were forced to content themselves with desultory fighting in the thick thorn bush, and occasional long-range bombardment. For the time being General Van Deventer's weakness in horseflesh, and the difficulties of supply along a line of communication consisting of 200 miles of quagmire, prevented him from retaliating with a counter-attack in force, the situation thus resolving itself into affairs of outposts and other minor operations until reinforcements arrived and the interrupted march to the Central Railway was resumed.

The failure at Kondoa having wrecked the enemy's last hope of standing against any considerable force of the invaders, the campaign gradually settled down into a wearisome variety of guerrilla warfare, which, continued long enough, could only have one end. The German Commander-in-Chief's scheme, no doubt, was to hold out until the European War came to an end, when the fate of East Africa would be settled with the rest of the German Empire.

While Colonel von Lettow-Vorbeck was hammering in vain at Van Deventer's camp, the rains began to abate, and by the middle of May the ground was hard enough for General Smuts to push his own advance forward from the Pare and Usambara highlands with the 1st and 3rd Divisions. His general aim was to sweep south towards the Central Railway in a movement parallel to that of Van Deventer, the new concentration of the enemy forces in front of that commander's position at Kondoa simplifying the advance considerably. Even so, however, it was impossible to make rapid progress in a region consisting of huge masses of mountains and verdant valleys. The southern slopes of the Pares and Usambaras are precipitous, with the Tanga railway running immediately below, beyond which dense bush extends from 15 to 20 miles to the Pangani—an impassable river. Expecting General Smuts to advance along the railway, the enemy had prepared strong defences at all convenient points for 100 miles, but was outwitted by the superior strategy of the astute South African Commander-in-Chief, who, while ordering one small column to follow the railway line, and another through the mountains on the north, advanced with his main force along the left bank of the Pangani. In this way, with the British flanks well forward, the enemy soon realized that his carefully-prepared positions in the centre were being outflanked, and discreetly withdrew.

Lieutenant-Colonel Fitzgerald's battalion of King's African Rifles in the north, and General Hannyngton's 2nd East African Brigade on the railway, joined forces on May 22, with instructions to clear the enemy out of Usambara, the advance of the main column—consisting of the 1st East African Brigade under Brigadier-General Sheppard, and the 2nd South African Infantry Brigade under Brigadier-General P. S. Beves,[1] accompanied by the Commander-in-Chief and Major-General Hoskins—continuing steadily along the Pangani. On May 29 a half-hearted stand was made by the enemy near Mikocheni, where the Pangani rejoins the railway close to the mountains, but he was again outmanœuvred by General Smuts, who, while attacking in front with the Rhodesians, made one of his successful turning movements on his left with General Sheppard's brigade. During the night the enemy beat a precipitate retreat, leaving in construction part of a new bridge, which proved extremely useful in the next stage of the advance. General Smuts's progress up to this point had exceeded his best anticipations, covering in ten days a distance of more than 130 miles over trackless country.

It was now clear that the Germans intended to retire to Handeni and the Central Railway. While therefore waiting for his bridges to be completed over the Pangani, and for the railway to catch up with the advance, General Smuts paid a flying visit to Kondoa Irangi by way of Moshi in order to visit Van Deventer and the 2nd Division, and personally arrange plans for the future co-operation between his two widely-scattered forces. Returning to the main body on June 7, to find the Pangani securely bridged, he continued his arduous march, leaving Brigadier-General Hannyngton to occupy Wilhelmstal (June 12) and Korogwe, on the Tanga railway (June 15), whence he was directed to rejoin the 1st Division. Mombo, a health resort at the junction of the narrow-gauge railway with the Tanga line below Wilhelmstal, was found by General Hannyngton full of women and children. The Germans knew that they could be safely left in our care.

For 200 miles General Smuts's troops had to march along routes prepared by themselves, often by cutting their way through almost impenetrable bush; ravaged by fever; handicapped by ever-increasing difficulties of supply; and constantly engaging the enemy in his strongly-prepared rear-guard positions. The retreating forces were

[1] The 2nd South African Mounted Brigade, under Brigadier-General B. Enslin, which, with Brigadier-General Beves's brigade, constituted the 3rd Division under Major-General Coen Brits, did not reach East Africa until this month, and was not ready to take the field until the latter half of June.

beaten time after time, but always managed to elude the net in which General Smuts strove to envelop them. His task was incomparably harder than that of his own pursuers in the great British drives across the veldt in the South African War. Here it was always possible for the Germans and their cunning Askaris to escape complete capture in the trackless depths of the dense bush. Even the aeroplanes were of little use in this form of warfare, for it was almost as hard to find Askaris in the bush as submarines in the Atlantic.[1]

Pushing steadily on in spite of all these difficulties and privations, General Sheppard, with the 1st East African Brigade, captured Handeni and Nderema on June 19, after a double defeat of the enemy's retreating forces. While in pursuit that day Colonel Byron's battalion, the 5th South African Infantry, which had played so gallant a part in the capture of the Latema-Reata Nek, again distinguished itself in a desperate fight with the enemy, whom they found in a concealed position in the heart of the bush. The South Africans lost heavily, "but held on stanchly until night," writes their Commander-in-Chief, "when the enemy retreated".

"Tanks" in East Africa: armoured motor-cars belonging to Sir John Willoughby's command in General Smuts's advance

Now in hot pursuit, General Smuts divided his force in the hope of outflanking the Germans' next position on the Lukigura River, and thus compelling him to make a fight for it. General Hoskins was sent with a flying column, which, after a night march on June 23–4, crossed the river and got astride the road behind the enemy's position, while the remainder of the 1st Division, under General Sheppard, advanced for a direct attack. Both columns engaged the enemy at midday on June 24, assaulting on three sides, and heavily defeated him. The Royal Fusiliers and a composite battalion of Kashmir Imperial Service Infantry specially distinguished themselves in this action, capturing machine-guns and a pom-pom. Sir John Willoughby's armoured car also played a dashing part in the course of the attack

[1] The air service, however, as General Smuts testifies in his dispatches, did most creditable work in this campaign. "In addition to their reconnaissance work", he writes, "there is evidence to the effect that both material and moral damage has been done to the enemy by their constant bombing raids."

engaging one of the pom-poms at close quarters. The car was presently put out of action by a shot in the radiator, and had to withdraw for repairs, but was soon patched up and back in the fighting-line again. Altogether the Germans lost heavily, and only the dense bush enabled them to escape complete capture.

Having reached the eastern slopes of the Nguru Mountains, where the enemy was massing in great strength, and recognizing the urgent need of his own force for rest and reorganization, General Smuts now called a halt. His sorely-tried transport had reached the utmost limit of its capacity. His troops, who had marched considerably over 200 miles in some of the most difficult country in the world, had been reduced to half-rations, and for the last 80 miles since leaving the Pangani there had been frequent shortage of water both for men and animals. Malaria, too, had so seriously reduced his ranks that several units were reduced to 30 per cent of their original strength. General Smuts accordingly formed a large standing camp on the Msiha River, 8 miles beyond the Lukigura, where the troops could rest and refit before beginning the next phase of the campaign.

One reason for this enforced interval was the necessity to await the further progress of General Van Deventer and the 2nd Division before resuming the combined advance against the enemy's main forces on the Central Railway. Van Deventer, who meantime had been holding his own at Kondoa Irangi against the repeated attempts of the Germans to dislodge him, and replenishing his supplies, returned to the offensive on June 24—the day on which General Smuts defeated the enemy on the Lukigura River. The time was ripe, for the Germans, finding themselves caught between two fires, were in the process of transferring their forces to meet this critical development of the situation.

The new advance from Kondoa Irangi began auspiciously with a bayonet attack which swept the enemy from all his surrounding positions, and continued so successfully that by the end of July Van Deventer, who had divided his force into a number of independent columns, was in firm possession of 100 miles of the Central Railway, extending from Kilimatinde to Dodoma. Practically every bridge and culvert across the numerous streams was found blown up, but the rapidity of the advance prevented any further destruction of the track. Brigadier-General Manie Botha, who had rendered great service at the head of the 1st Mounted Brigade, was compelled to return to South Africa on private business during the course of these operations, and his place was taken by Brigadier-General A. H. M. Nussey, D.S.O., who had been acting as Van Deventer's Chief of Staff.

While these sweeping movements were in progress other operations had taken place to prevent the enemy's escape. General Smuts was relying on the Belgians, under Major-General Tombeur, to keep the Germans in play on the Tanganyika front; the British "Lake Detachment" in the region of Victoria Nyanza and the

Uganda frontier; the Northern Rhodesian and Nyasaland forces under Brigadier-General E. Northey in the south-west; and the Portuguese Expeditionary Force, under General Gil, in the south; while the British navy at the same time blockaded the whole coast, and assisted in the capture of the coastal towns. Thus the enemy was surrounded by a ring of converging columns, and it was only a question of time before there would no longer be a place of refuge left to him.

On the Belgian-Congo border General Smuts's chief concern was to facilitate the advance of Major-General Tombeur, part of whose force was destined for Kigali, the capital of the rich German province of Ruanda. In order to avoid a Belgian advance over the barren region of active volcanoes, in face of strong German opposition, the base of this force was shifted from General Tombeur's head-quarters at Kibati, north of Lake Kivu, to Bukakata, on Victoria Nyanza, 150 miles farther east. We undertook the Belgian transport and supply arrangements from this base, and to overcome the difficulties involved thereby General Smuts sent Brigadier-General the Hon. Sir Charles Crewe, of his staff—member for East London in the Union Parliament, and a soldier who had seen much active service in South Africa—to keep in touch with General Tombeur. All difficulties were eventually overcome in April, and the Belgian advance began at once. The column under Colonel Molitor made such rapid progress that Kigali was occupied on May 6, with the result that the German positions farther west on the Belgian border became untenable.

Brigadier-General Sir C. P. Crewe, C.B., K.C.M.G., commanding the Lake Column
(From a photograph by Elliott & Fry)

While Colonel Molitor pushed on thence towards the southern end of Victoria Nyanza, General Tombeur dispatched other Belgian columns from the north and south of Lake Kivu, while the British "Lake Detachment", under Lieutenant-Colonel D. R. Adye, in conjunction with the energetic naval flotilla on the lake, under Commander Thornley, R.N., made a surprise and completely successful attack on Ukerewe—the largest island in Victoria Nyanza, and a favourable base for an operation against the German port of Mwanza. In the middle of June the scattered British posts in this lake region were concentrated into a mobile fighting force, under Sir Charles Crewe, who, by the skilful disposition of his columns, one under Lieutenant-Colonel C. R. Burgess and the other under Lieutenant - Colonel H. B. Towse, drove the enemy out of this fortified town of Mwanza. Hotly pursued by the Lake Column, the Germans, in their headlong flight, abandoned one of their 4.1 naval guns, together with a number of steamers and lighters, a Colt gun, and much baggage and specie. "The rapidity with which the enemy abandoned his valuable Lake Provinces and Mwanza", wrote General Smuts, "was a clear indication that the eventual retreat would not be towards Tabora, but farther east towards Dar-es-Salaam, or south towards Mahenge."

South-west of the Central Railway the German retreat was at the same time threatened by General Northey, commanding the Northern Rhodesian and Nyasaland Field Forces, who had crossed the frontier on May 25 and advanced to a distance of 20 miles into German territory on the whole front between Lakes Nyasa and Tanganyika. It was not long before these British troops mastered an appreciable part of the south-western area of German East Africa. The successful operations which led up to the capture, on May 31, of Neu Langenburg—a military post on the German road between the lakes—caused the British Secretary of State for the Colonies to send General Northey and his force a warm telegram of congratulation. Thereafter the same British columns pushed rapidly northwards towards the Central Railway, one force, on June 8, under Colonel Murray, occupying Bismarckburg — the only German port of consequence at the southern end of Lake Tanganyika, on June 8, and one source of the enemy raids into Rhodesia in the early days of the war—while another column, under Colonel Rodgers, pushed inland towards the important town of Iringa, on the road from Neu Langenburg to the Central Railway. Iringa would have been reached sooner but for General Smuts's advice to General Northey to slow down until the line of the enemy's retreat from the Central Railway became more certain. General Northey's operations, records the Commander-in-Chief, "have been conducted with remarkable ability and vigour"; and the importance of his rôle at that time promised to become more and more accentuated as the campaign proceeded. In the course of their retreat towards Iringa the enemy abandoned a 4.1 - inch how-

Brigadier-General E. Northey, commanding the Advance from the Rhodesian Front
(From a photograph by Elliott & Fry)

itzer and a number of machine-guns. Several Germans were also captured, including Dr. Stier, late Governor of Neu Langenburg District, who subsequently died of wounds received in action.

The sequence of events now calls us back to the operations of General Smuts himself, who, with his main force still encamped on the Msiha River, among the Nguru Hills, was preparing for the combined movement with Van Deventer's troops against the enemy's main position on the Central Railway. In the meantime General Van Deventer, with the same object in view, was concentrating his scattered forces along the railway at Njangalo, on the main road from Kilimatinde to Mpapua. The enemy, at the same time, had skilfully disposed about twenty companies, or 3000 rifles, athwart the main road to the Central Railway along which General Smuts must pass under the Nguru and Kanga Mountains. Elsewhere the general situation in German East Africa in the first week of August, 1916, was summarized by the Commander-in-Chief as follows:—

"In the Lake area the British and Belgian forces were well south of Lake Victoria and preparing for a combined move towards Tabora. Farther west a Belgian force had crossed Lake Tanganyika and occupied Ujiji[1] and Kigoma, the terminus of the Central Railway. In the south-west General Northey's force had occupied Malangali after a brilliant little action, and was prepared to move towards Iringa, 70 miles farther north-east. All coast towns as far south as Sadani had been occupied, and a small column was working its way southward to the Wami River and clearing the country between the Nguru Mountains and the coast."

It was at this juncture that the King sent the following encouraging tribute to General Smuts and his army, dated August 2:—

"I have followed with admiration the continuous progress of the forces under your command, despite the natural difficulties of the country and the efforts of a determined enemy. Please convey to all ranks my appreciation of the skill and courage with which the operations have been conducted.

"GEORGE R.I."

General Smuts addressed in reply the following message to the Private Secretary of the King:—

"On behalf of myself and the troops under my command please convey to His Majesty our deep appreciation of gracious message, which will encourage all ranks to further efforts".

Another notable incident at this period was the brief visit paid to the East African front, at General Smuts's request, by General Botha, whose arrival and comprehensive tour, even of the most advanced British positions, was greatly appreciated by the troops.

The task confronting General Smuts, now that the time had arrived for his 1st and 3rd Divisions to resume the advance to the Central Railway, was

[1] Ujiji, known also as Kaveli, is historic as the place where H. M. Stanley found David Livingstone at the end of his long search in 1871. Some thirteen years before, Ujiji—long a great slave and ivory mart, and the terminus of the caravan route from Dar-es-Salaam before the railhead port of Kigoma, 4 miles to the north, took its place—was visited by Burton and Speke, who were the first Europeans to set eyes on Lake Tanganyika. The town was brought within the German sphere of influence in 1890.

What Forest Fighting in East Africa means: a typical path in the interior

indescribably difficult. His hope was that, even if he failed to corner the Germans in the mountains, they might still be brought to bay at Kilossa, on the railway. At any rate his information gave him some justification for that hope. His main road, however, passing close under the Nguru and Kango Mountains, was so strongly held by the enemy entrenched along the numerous foot-hills which it crossed—with much heavy and light artillery in cunningly concealed position—that to attempt its passage was to court disaster. "If we forced our way down the road against these formidable obstacles, or moved by our left flank through the bush and tall elephant grass, part of the enemy's force in the mountains on our right would get behind us and endanger our communications." The only way, therefore, was to push through the Nguru Mountains themselves, clearing them as the advance proceeded southwards by wide turning movements, thus threatening or cutting off the enemy's retreat if he delayed his retirement unduly.

General Smuts made his dispositions accordingly, the brigades of Generals Sheppard, Hannyngton, Brits, and others taking part in the turning movements. The advance through the Nguru Mountains began on August 5, when General Enslin moved with the 2nd Mounted Brigade from Lukigura. One of his mounted regiments lost its way in the mountains, and finally emerged at Matamondo, but with the balance of his force he pushed through to Mhonda, which he occupied on the 8th, sending back word that the route through the mountains, contrary to the information upon which General Smuts had previously relied, was entirely impracticable for wheeled traffic of any description. This might have been disastrous if Enslin had not made good his hold on Mbonda, thereby forcing the enemy, who was strongly opposing Hannyngton at Matamondo from the 9th to the 11th, hurriedly to abandon his defence in the mountains and retire as fast as he could. All war transport, however, had to be sent back to Lukigura to follow by the main road. "If", as General Smuts pointed out, "the terrain had permitted of the original scheme being carried out, and the whole 3rd Division had proceeded to Mhonda, the retreat of the enemy from these mountains would probably have been impossible."

Seeing that their last hope had gone of holding the Nguru Hills, the Germans retired with the bulk of their force towards the Central Railway in the direction of Morogoro and Kilossa, leaving rear-guards to hamper the British advance. They did this with their usual thoroughness, destroying every bridge over the numerous rivers which the advancing troops had to pass. Undeterred by these difficulties, General Smuts harried the retreating troops by flying columns, while the brigades of Generals Enslin and Sheppard, thanks to a turning movement of mounted men after stiff fighting for two days, captured the Wami crossing at Dakawa on August 18. Our losses in this affair amounted to 120. "The enemy", reported the Commander-in-Chief, "had been very severely handled."

While General Smuts, with the 1st and 3rd Divisions, were thus engaged, and the Cape Corps was following the German rear-guards towards Kilossa, General Van Deventer was making rapid progress with the 2nd Division along the Central Railway, though faced at every stage not only by a stubborn enemy, with a succession of prepared positions to which to retreat in the last extremity, and supported by machine, field, and heavy guns, but also by inadequate food supplies and physical difficulties which would have broken the hearts of less resourceful leaders and less courageous troops. The first stage from Njangalo, where, as already mentioned, the scattered troops of the 2nd Division had been concentrated, began on August 9, while General Smuts's fight for the Nguru Hills was at its height. Two days' march over a waterless area brought them in touch with the enemy at Tschunjo Pass, and they went into action without stopping to rest.

The action continued all night, and morning broke to find the enemy gone. He was immediately pursued towards Mpapua, where he was again engaged and defeated.[1] So the running fight

[1] His tactics were always the same, one or more ambushes being laid for our advanced-guard, followed by retreat to well-prepared positions, repeating the process as often as necessary, and meantime subjecting the less-advanced of Van Deventer's troops to vigorous shelling from his long-range naval guns.

went on, becoming every day more arduous. The pursuit from Mpapua to Kilossa led them through one continual fly-belt, where practically all the animals were infested, and where the underfeeding and overworking of the troops — inevitable, as General Van Deventer himself explained, owing to bad roads, shortage of transport, and the rapidity of the advance—were reflected all too sadly in their weakened ranks. It was almost the last straw when, after capturing Kilossa with his exhausted troops on August 22, a telegram came from the Commander-in-Chief asking for a further advance, four days later, on Kidodi and Kidatu. This was to drive out the enemy, who was now ascertained to be holding Uleia, 20 miles south, in force, having been reinforced by the troops of the German Southern Command, retreating before General Northey's advance; but "it imposed a task", writes General Van Deventer, "which I had not intended to ask from my troops before they had had some rest". However, the request was faithfully carried out, with the loyal co-operation and splendid spirit which alone had enabled the South African leaders to command success.

Conducted throughout over high mountain ridges against an enemy strongly entrenched in positions long since completed for their defence, the operations called for an extraordinary amount of mountain-climbing and constant fighting. The spirit and endurance of Van Deventer's men throughout, especially during their long marches through dry and waterless stretches of tropical country on scanty rations, formed an achievement which their leader justly claimed as "worthy of South African troops"—a tribute fraught with a new and inspiring significance by the glorious stand of the South Africans in Delville Wood, thousands of miles away on the Western front. Fortunately their losses in action were not heavy, thanks to the employment by Van Deventer of his favourite tactics.

"The slight casualties sustained in the various engagements over an enormous tract of country, bristling with dongas and difficulties at every point, were mainly due to the advance being carried out by avoiding as far as possible frontal attacks. Dispositions were made with a view to carry out flanking movements while holding the enemy to the position occupied by him, but this the enemy carefully avoided, and under cover of darkness the engagement was usually broken off and a retreat effected."

On the day following Van Deventer's first entry into Kilossa (August 22, 1916), General Smuts had resumed his advance on the Wami River towards the Central Railway. Disappointed in his hope that the Germans might be cornered at Kilossa, his chief object now was to bring their main forces to bay, if possible, at Morogoro—some 50 miles nearer the coast on the Central Railway—to which the bulk of their troops were known to have retired. Morogoro had been the seat of the German Provisional Government since its hurried removal from Dar-es-Salaam. The centre of a thriving plantation district, it was a prosperous town of considerable dimensions, with splendid avenues and many European residences. High hopes were entertained that Colonel von Lettow-Vorbeck would here be forced to fight to a finish for the last remnant of Germany's colonial empire. Converging columns were sent round the flanks of the mountains in order to bottle up the enemy, while General Smuts himself marched on the 23rd with his main force first backward for 9 miles down the right bank of the Wami and thence due east for 25 miles across the waterless belt to the Ngerengere River, some 18 miles north-east of Morogoro. The difficult nature of the country, the bush, the heat, and the absence of water made this march, which lasted until the night of August 24, one of the most trying of the whole campaign. August 25 was spent in reconnoitring, and in affording rest to exhausted man and beast. Though worn out with their labours the troops were buoyed with the hope that at long last they had the enemy in their toils. Threatened on all sides, there seemed no possibility of his escape.

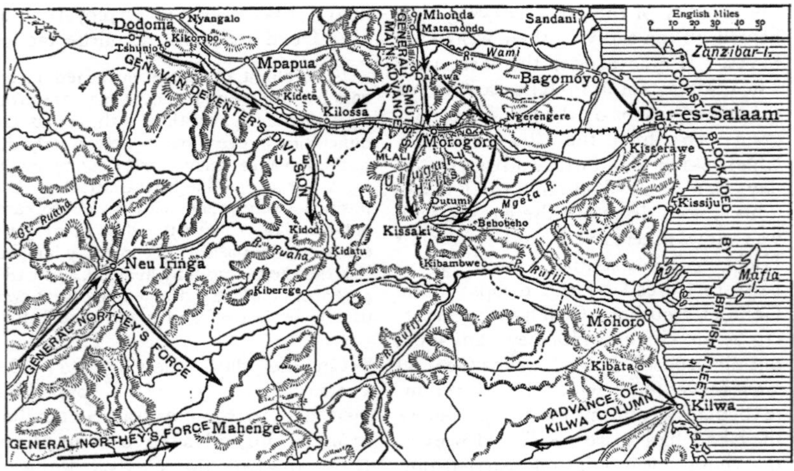


The Campaign in East Africa: map illustrating General Smuts's operations in the heart of the German colony

Alas! they were all unaware that another track lay open from Morogoro through the mountains to Kissaki, thus rendering useless the capture of the flanks of the mountains, and all the carefully-laid plans to cut off the retreat of the main enemy force farther south. Though obviously taken somewhat by surprise by General Smuts's sudden appearance in the north-east, the enemy was not to be lured into action. Both Ngerengere and Morogoro were occupied on August 26, only to find him vanished, leaving abundant proofs of the disorganized flight and demoralized condition of his troops.

Morogoro fell with scarcely a shot fired in its defence.

"The Indian troops", to quote from the account by Reuter's correspondent, "pushed the frontal attack and the eastern enveloping movement on short rations with sturdy endurance and devotion, but the elusive enemy, taking severe punishment, made good his retreat, leaving a heavy toll of dead behind. The Rhodesian Regiment added to its fine record in East Africa by being the first, in company with the Baluchis, to occupy Morogoro."

The march of General Brits's division, with the South African Horse, over the Nguri Mountains, in the vain attempt to cut off the enemy retreating to Morogoro from Rusungu, was described by the same correspondent as a remarkable instance of the adaptability and endurance of the South African troops. The mountains were impossible for wheeled traffic, and the men were forced to eke out their rations with captured cattle and mealies, bananas, pawpaws, and other of the numerous wild fruits for which these mountains are famous.

"Climbing by rugged mountain paths, they struck the enemy heavily on the flank, inflicting severe loss. There were no complaints of the hardships suffered. They were only disappointed at the failure to capture the German heavy artillery, which the enemy hastily extricated at the first sign of the advance of our troops."

The main German force, with the commander-in-chief, Von Lettow-Vorbeck, and Governor Schnee, had slipped along the unsuspected track due south through the mountains. Another force had escaped by the Kiroka route to the east, while a third fled westward towards Mlali, possibly in the hope of saving the situation created there by the advance of General Enslin's 2nd South African Mounted Brigade. These troops, reaching Mlali on August 24, had captured a German ammunition depot, in which were found about 1000 shells for the enemy's naval and other guns. One of Enslin's regiments galloped up the valley just as the German force came marching down the Morogoro road, and put up a gallant fight in the hope of beating them single-handed. Eventually, however, the regiment found its position in the valley untenable, as the enemy was gradually working round in the hills, and bringing converging fire to bear on them. The regiment withdrew a short distance, but doggedly held on to the road, while the enemy, finding it impossible, after fighting for twenty-four hours, to dislodge our men, destroyed two of his naval guns, and retired towards Mgeta Mission Station, some 10 miles farther into the mountains. Leaving their horses behind them, Enslin's victorious South Africans followed in hot pursuit, and, moving in a more southerly direction, hoped to cut off the enemy's retreat. General Smuts himself presently arrived on the scene, and threw a wider net round the fugitives, General Nussey's brigade joining in the chase along the course of the Mgeta River, while General Enslin's brigade was reinforced with General Beves's two infantry regi-

With one of the British Service Corps in German East Africa: a motor tractor and its armed guard

ments, and accompanied by General Brits. Though the elusive enemy again slipped through our fingers, he had undoubtedly been dealt a heavy blow.

"It was clear to me from the vast quantities of heavy-gun ammunition captured at this and various other points in the Uluguru", writes General Smuts, "that the enemy had intended a long and elaborate defence of these mountains, and that it was the unexpected arrival of General Enslin at Mlali and the audacious and successful pursuit into the mountains, combined with the operations of General Hoskins's division on the other side of the mountains, that had forced the enemy to abandon his plans and retreat towards Kissaki. Nussey, followed only by porter transport, slowly worked his way southward through the mountains, finding much ammunition abandoned everywhere. General Brits, on arriving at Mssongossi River, found that it was impossible to take his guns or wagons any farther, and from there they had to return to Morogoro and rejoin him later at Kissaki by the eastern route."

His road to Kissaki lay over historic ground, following the elephant track, as General Smuts tell us, which had been the route of Burton and Speke's pioneer journey into the interior close upon sixty years previously—long before Germany dreamt of holding any part of Africa. Meeting no serious opposition, General Brits reached the neighbourhood of Kissaki on September 5, and two days later, though General Nussey had not yet arrived, and communication with him was impossible, he decided to attack. Nothing illustrates more clearly the extraordinary difficulties of the terrain in all these repeated engagements than the story of the fight which followed. While General Beves was ordered to follow the footpath southward along the Mgeta into Kissaki, General Enslin, with the mounted men, marched round by the right in order to attack from the west and south-west. Instead of reaching their objectives, both forces suddenly found themselves counter-attacked by an enemy who knew how to make use of every inch of the ground. The mounted men were hopelessly outnumbered by the bulk of the hostile force, but unable, owing to the density of the bush, to receive any help from General Beves. With his superiority of strength and position, indeed, the Germans, in the words of General Smuts, "found it possible first to threaten Enslin's left flank by moving between him and Beves, and when Enslin weakened his right flank to reinforce his left, the pressure of the enemy again became too strong on his right". Having already lost twenty-eight men in killed, wounded, and captured, General Enslin decided at night to retire, General Beves being also ordered to withdraw, the whole force thereupon entrenching at Little Nhigu, 6 miles to the north of Kissaki, to await the arrival of General Nussey's brigade.

Entirely ignorant of these events, or even of General Brits's whereabouts, General Nussey arrived before Kissaki on the following morning. Another action developed, in which General Nussey gallantly held his ground against much stronger forces until the evening, when messengers reached

Campaigning in German East Africa: South Africans bringing a gun into action

him from General Brits ordering his withdrawal to Little Nhigu. His losses amounted to some twenty-three killed and about the same number wounded. The most exasperating feature of the whole affair was that though the action could be plainly heard from General Brits's camp, it proved impossible, owing to the ruggedness of the terrain and the thickness of the bush, to render him any assistance. "If", writes General Smuts, "communication between Brits and Nussey could have been maintained there is no doubt that a joint attack would have led to the capture of Kissaki, whereas the two isolated efforts led to a double retirement and a regrettable recovery of enemy *moral*." A week later, however, the foe, finding his retreat to the Rufiji threatened, abandoned Kissaki, leaving in our hands his hospital full of sick and about seventy-two Germans. Now driven from his last stronghold in the Uluguru Mountains, he took up a new defensive line along the Mgeta River, and farther to the west astride the road from Kissaki to the Rufiji, along whose course, it will be remembered, the fugitive German cruiser *Königsberg* had long since met her fate. Here, for a time, he was left undisturbed, our men being too exhausted, after weeks of ceaseless fighting and marching, to press the attack at once. "A thorough rest", records their Commander-in-Chief, "was imperatively necessary, not only on military, but also on medical grounds." Operations on this front remained practically at a standstill until the resumption of the general offensive

With General Northey's Force: landing German prisoners near the Rhodesian front

at the end of the year, the conditions being described by the Commander-in-Chief in his final dispatch as "closely resembling those of trench warfare".

This breathing-space enables us to link up the subsidiary operations scattered over the rest of the interior as well as along the coast, but all neatly joined together in General Smuts's scheme of co-ordination. The British fleet, without whose supremacy at sea the conquest of German East Africa would have been impossible, not only maintained its rigorous blockade but swept the coast line until one after the other of its ports had fallen into our hands. Sadani was taken on August 1, 1916, and a fortnight later Bagamoyo shared the same fate. Here a column of about 1800 rifles was assembled by Brigadier-General W. F. S. Edwards, D.S.O., Inspector-General of Communications, and placed under Colonel Price to march down the coast, in co-operation with the naval forces, towards Dar-es-Salaam, the principal port and the official capital of the colony until the guns of the British navy caused the removal of the seat of Government to Morogoro, 140 miles inland. Dar-es-Salaam—"the harbour of peace"—had already been raided by our war-ships: once, at the beginning of the war, when the wireless station was destroyed and several vessels in the harbour sunk; and again in the first half of the following December, when the town was bombarded and further vessels were damaged in reprisal for deliberate abuse of the white and Red Cross flags, and the sinking of the *Pegasus* at Zanzibar by the *Königsberg*, which had made Dar-es-Salaam her headquarters.

No attempt was made to defend it on the present occasion; the enemy, anxious to avoid siege operations against a town which it had laid out in a very costly and substantial manner, and hoped one day to recover, fell back everywhere before our combined attack. Before leaving he took care to destroy the railway station and harbour works as effectively as usual, but it was found possible to salve the floating dock and one of the vessels lying sunk in the harbour. Continuing the conquest of the coast, General Smuts now made arrangements with Rear-Admiral E. F. B. Charlton, C.B., for convoying forces and co-operating in the seizure of all the important points on the coast south of the capital. This was done before the end of September, 1916, while the main operations under General Smuts were suspended. "This occupation of the southern coast", wrote the Commander-in-Chief, "not only helped to pen the enemy up in the interior, but was intended to prevent any assistance from reaching the enemy from oversea"—attempts still being made, apparently, to run the blockade. In his dispatch General Smuts expresses his deep indebtedness to Rear-Admiral Charlton and all ranks of the Royal Navy "for the very able and thorough manner in which they have furthered my plans, not only by occupying points on the coast, sometimes even without military assistance, but by enabling a change of base to be carried out, first to Tanga and then to Dar-es-Salaam".

The new base rendered imperative

the speedy restoration of the Central Railway for supply purposes. Though the track for the most part had been left undamaged, the bridges had been most carefully destroyed. There were sixty wrecked bridges—some of very considerable dimensions—between Kilossa and the capital alone, and to restore these to bear the strain of heavy locomotives meant the sacrifice of many precious months. The difficulty was overcome by the ingenuity of the South African Pioneers, who repaired the bridges with local material to carry a weight of about six tons, and narrowed the gauge of the heavy motor lorries so that they could run on railway trolley wheels over the restored line. In this way General Van Deventer had already supplied his division over the railway track for the 120 miles advance from Dodoma to Kilossa. Otherwise his advance to the Great Ruaha River at this stage, as General Smuts points out, would have been a physical impossibility. When Morogoro was occupied that section of the line was similarly treated, and by the end of October, 1916, the railway was thus opened for motor traffic right from the sea base at Dar-es-Salaam to Tabora.

This brings us to the combined operations against the enemy's western force concentrated at Tabora—some 200 miles from Lake Tanganyika, on the Central Railway, and one of the principal interior towns of the colony—by the Belgian columns under General Tombeur, and the British force under General Sir C. P. Crewe. Transport difficulties had hindered the operations on both sides, but one Belgian column, under Colonel Olsen, had been able to make steady progress from Ujiji, and, with the co-operation of Colonel Molitor's Belgian column, succeeded in occupying Taboro on September 19, 1916. A week later General Crewe's advanced troops reached the railway east of Tabora, the enemy

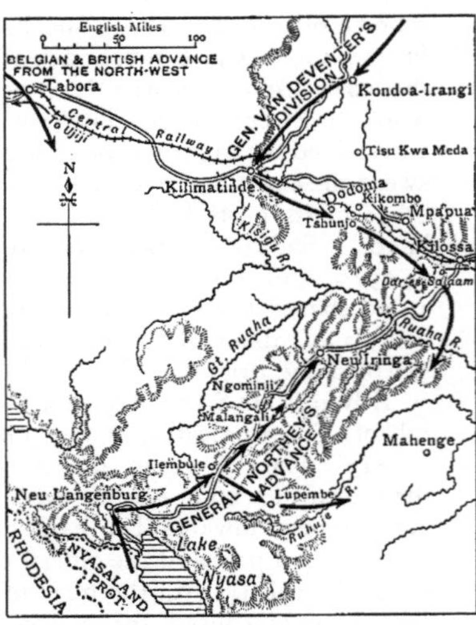


Map illustrating the Retreat of the German Western Force from Tabora, and its Attack on General Northey's Lines of Communication barring the roads to Mahenge

retiring in two columns, one under Major-General Wahle, and the other under Wintgens, their aim being to form a junction with that section of the main German forces which still clung to the Mahenge plateau.

To frustrate this scheme, as well as to complete his ever-tightening cordon round the bulk of Colonel von Lettow-Vorbeck's remaining forces, now sheltering on the Rufiji River and about

30 miles to the north of it, became the twofold object of the closing phases of General Smuts's strenuous campaign.

As the German western columns approached the great Ruaha River, other enemy forces in the Mahenge area—the only healthy part of the colony now left to them—assumed the offensive with the obvious intention of helping their comrades to join hands with the main German body. Severe fighting ensued at the various points of contact, with confused and varying results.

But for our transport hardships we should have had little difficulty in dealing with these troublesome units from the west. In his final dispatch, dated February 28, 1917, General Smuts makes it clear that "if we had been able to feed a larger number of troops at this stage, south of the Central Railway, in the western area, there is little doubt that we should have handled the enemy force from Tabora far more severely than we were able to in our difficult circumstances". Immense journeys had to be taken by troops sent to reinforce General Northey, who, at this period with his headquarters at Neu Langenburg, was often without means of communication with his detachments in the Iranga area. Thus one battalion of South African infantry had to travel by way of Chinde, the Zambesi, and Wiedhafen, on Lake Nyasa.

In order to deal with this threatening situation round Iranga, General Van Deventer pushed forward from the Central Railway the 7th South African Infantry and a cyclist battalion, under Lieutenant-Colonel J. M. Fairweather, D.S.O., but two days before these could reach their destination the larger portion of the enemy's Tabora force had broken through General Northey's line southwards, cutting all communication with him. Besides their concentrated portion it was discovered that many small parties had broken through in the darkness—"which, of course", writes General Smuts, "they were able to do without any fear of detection over a large front". The immediate result was that General Northey, whose troops on the Ruhuje now found themselves attacked by superior numbers, remained for some time without means of issuing orders to his detachments at Iranga. In these circumstances General Smuts placed General Van Deventer in charge of the situation at Iranga, where he temporarily assumed control of the portion of General Northey's force under Lieutenant-Colonel T. A. Rodger, D.S.O.

For three weeks the enemy's western troops, in small and scattered parties, continued their passage through our broken lines, the whole period being marked by much isolated fighting and patrol encounters. One small British detachment of Rhodesian Native Police, with which was Lieutenant-Colonel Baxendale, was ambushed, and suffered heavily in the course of difficult operations in the dense bush. Its casualties included Lieutenant-Colonel Baxendale himself, who was killed.

The tables were turned by a small detachment of the 4th South African Horse, who, two days later, encountered a strong force of the enemy some 12 miles north of Iranga and inflicted a heavy defeat on him. Besides losing many killed or captured the Germans abandoned all their sick and wounded, the commanding officer at the close of the action writing to ask for their protection by the victors. Needless to say, he did not write in vain.

On October 29 the small British post at Ngominji was forced to surrender after withstanding for five days over 200 killed and wounded and 81 prisoners, together with a 6-cm. gun, three machine-guns, and large quantities of ammunition and other material.

The enemy continued to harass our lines at every opportunity. One portion of General Wahle's western force proceeded to invest the British post at Lupembe, while another, flushed with its success at Ngominji, and mov-

An Affair of Outposts: British officers watching operations from the roof of a native house in German East Africa

the repeated attacks of a hostile detachment superior in number by eight to one. Captain Clerk, commanding the garrison, was killed in this gallant defence. Two naval 12-pounder guns, which were lost here, were retaken by us in the course of operations almost immediately afterwards. So the fortunes of war fluctuated for some time in this troublesome south-west region. A signal success was scored at dawn on the 29th by Lieutenant-Colonel Hawthorn, who caught a strong force of the enemy on the west bank of the Ruhuje, and defeated it with a loss of ing down General Northey's line of communication towards Neu Langenburg, struggled desperately to capture the similar post at Melangali. This time it failed, thanks to the stout resistance of the officer in command—Captain Tom Marriott, who was promptly awarded the Military Cross—and the arrival, after four days' fighting, of the relief force under Colonel Murray. Lupembe also held out, though manned by native troops less than half the strength of the attacking German column. This column, after an investment of six days, found itself in danger of being caught between converging British forces, and fled, abandoning a field-gun. A more conspicuous British success was the isolation of the remainder of General Wahle's force at Ilembule Mission Station, where it was forced to surrender on November 26, 1916, to the number of 7 officers, 47 other Europeans, and 449 seasoned and fully trained Askaris. A 10.5-cm. howitzer, with ammunition, and three machine-guns were included in the booty.

These and other rebuffs in November apparently caused the Germans to abandon any idea of further offensive action—for the time being at all events—and the situation on this front reverted to a minor degree of importance. When General Smuts visited it from his head-quarters at Morogoro towards the end of November, he proposed to clear up the situation by driving the enemy over the Ruhuje and Ulanga Rivers as a preliminary to his general plan for renewing his offensive against the main German force. Preparations were accordingly begun to create a great dump of supplies south of the Ruaha River, this being the only means of feeding any considerable force in this region during the wet season, when it was impossible to avoid vast swampy areas of which the passage appeared impossible. The question of supplies, however, proved an insurmountable difficulty.

"Continuous heavy rain in the west produced conditions under which every movement became a matter of extraordinary difficulty, and the supply situation was at times seriously insecure; and on the 19th December General van Deventer, whose head-quarters were now at Iringa, reported that he had been unable to build up the reserve which we had hoped we should have been able to collect at Iringa, and that he could not feed his whole division during the forward move which was then imminent. He further advised moving a considerable portion of his command back to the railway, and that a reduced force of three infantry battalions and a squadron of mounted troops should be kept at Iringa for the advance."

General Smuts agreed to this, and mentions in this connection, as an instance of the difficulties attendant upon military movements on a large scale in Central Africa, that of 1000 mounted men who had marched from Morogoro early that November more than 90 per cent had lost their horses from disease within the ensuing six weeks.

Meantime the Lake force under General Crewe, which, as we have seen, had followed the fugitive foe to Tabora from the north-west, had been abolished, save one battalion, which remained in possession of a portion of the Central Railway east of Tabora, that town itself being occupied by the Belgians.

Save for some sharp engagements in the hilly district round Kibata, which lies some 10 miles inland, between the Rufiji and the coastal town of Kilwa, there was little serious fighting in East Africa before the resumption of the general advance at the close of the year. Meantime, however, every effort was continued by General Smuts to strengthen the cordon which he was slowly but relentlessly drawing round the German Commander-in-Chief and the remnants of his army. A fresh move had taken place to cut off their retreat to the south, General Smuts ordering a strong British column to advance inland from the southern German port of Kilwa—the Quiloa of the Portuguese navigators of the sixteenth century—which had been occupied by the naval forces on September 7, and prepared as a base for these new operations. The first news that this column had landed was not published until December 7, 1916, when it had already penetrated 60 miles inland, but a force of some 2000 rifles under Brigadier-General Hannyngton had been conveyed there from Dar-es-Salaam early in October as the nucleus of a reorganized First Division under General Hoskins, intended to take part in a great encircling move south of the Rufiji. The Portuguese, in the meantime, had strengthened their strategic hold farther south, moving up from the Rovuma stations and Kionga, and establishing communication with the British forces at Mikindani.

With General Smuts in German East Africa: ox transport for the guns

General Smuts himself was not destined to witness the last act of the drama in German East Africa. Scarcely had the curtain been drawn up on the opening scene of the new year when it was announced that the Commander-in-Chief had been chosen to represent the Government of the Union of South Africa at the forthcoming Imperial War Conference in London. The choice inevitably rested between General Botha and General Smuts, and since insuperable difficulties at home prevented the Prime Minister from accepting the invitation of His Majesty's Government, his right-hand man was chosen in his stead. Happily the military situation in East Africa at this stage was such as to make a change of command and some reorganization comparatively simple. Indeed, it was officially declared that the change in any case would have taken place shortly. The campaign was practically over.

"In February, 1916, when General Smuts assumed command," declared the Secretary of State for War, "the whole of German East Africa and some portion of British territory was in enemy possession. At the present time, eleven months later, nothing of German East Africa remains to the enemy, except a comparatively small and unimportant area to the south and south-east, where his retiring forces are collecting. The enemy does not possess a single railway, town, or seaport. His forces, in consequence of casualties and desertion, are much reduced in strength and *moral*; his loss in artillery has been considerable; his food supply is dwindling, and he is compelled to remain where he has established magazines. . . . In these circumstances it has been possible to accede to the wish of the Union Government, and arrange for the release of General Smuts from the East Africa command."

This brief official summary speaks eloquently enough of General Smuts's achievement. Only the heavy rains prevented an earlier arrival of the absolute end of the campaign. With the end in sight, as well as another rainy season, the Commander-in-Chief had already sent a large proportion of the British and South Africans home. White troops, he soon found, could not long stand the climate. His advance to the unhealthy areas of the Rufiji and Great Ruaha Rivers had resulted not only in the loss of most of the animals of the mounted men, but also in an alarming rise of the sick rate among the troops themselves. "It was clear", he wrote, "that white troops who had had repeated attacks of malaria or dysentery would, in the further prosecution of the campaign in these extremely unhealthy areas, be more of an encumbrance than a help." The 3rd Division, under Major-General Brits, including the 2nd Mounted Brigade, under Brigadier-General Enslin, was, therefore, abolished, and their officers and staffs returned to South Africa. All fit men belonging to the 2nd Mounted Brigade were incorporated in the 1st Mounted Brigade, under Brigadier-General Nussey, and all white troops declared to be medically unfit by special medical boards were finally evacuated from East Africa. As a result of these steps some 12,000 white troops were sent home between the middle of October and the end of December, 1916. Their places were to some extent taken by the new battalions of the King's African Rifles, which General Smuts had formed and trained with the sanction of the War Office, as well as by the Nigerian Brigade, under Brigadier-General F. H. B. Cunliffe, C.B., C.M.G, which landed at Dar-es-Salaam towards the end of December. The natives, as General Smuts pointed out on arriving in London for the Imperial Conference, made splendid infantry, and had already done magnificent work. When the East African campaign was over, too, they would be available elsewhere.

In his dispatches, General Smuts paid a glowing tribute to the whole of the force under his command.

"The plain tale of their achievements bears the most convincing testimony to the spirit, determination, and prodigious efforts of all ranks. Their work has been done

Brigadier-General J. A. Hannyngton, C.M.G., D.S.O., who "proved his worth as a commander in the field" in East Africa
(From a photograph by Elliott & Fry)

under tropical conditions, which not only produce bodily weariness and unfitness, but which create mental languor and depression, and finally appal the stoutest hearts. To march day by day, and week by week, through the African jungle or high grass, in which vision is limited to a few yards, in which danger always lurks near but seldom becomes visible, even when experienced, supplies a test to human nature often in the long run beyond the limits of human endurance. And what is true of the fighting troops applies in one degree or another to all the subsidiary and administrative services. The efforts of all have been beyond praise, the strain on all has been overwhelming. May the end soon crown their labours!"

The Empire's indebtedness to General Smuts himself for his brilliant leadership throughout was acknowledged in the House of Commons by the Prime Minister, and in the War Honours List at the beginning of 1917, in which he was promoted from his temporary to full rank of honorary Lieutenant-General. From the King himself he received the following message:—

"As you are relinquishing the chief command in East Africa, I desire to congratulate you upon the effective manner in which you have so successfully conducted your operations, notwithstanding the unusually difficult conditions. I wish to thank you for the valuable service you have recently rendered to the Empire."

General Smuts handed over the command, on January 20, to Lieu-

Brigadier-General P. S. Beves, C.M.G., who "sustained his high soldierly record" in the East African Campaign
(From a photograph by Elliott & Fry)

Brigadier-General C. A. L. Berrangé, one of the South African leaders to whom General Smuts expressed himself as "particularly indebted"
(From a photograph by Elliott & Fry)

tenant-General A. R. Hoskins, C.M.G., D.S.O., who had been appointed to the 1st Division with the distinct knowledge on the part of the War Office that he would be required to succeed General Smuts if such a contingency arose. The new Commander-in-Chief—a brevet colonel in the Prince of Wales's (North Staffordshire) Regiment—had fought under Lord Kitchener in the Soudan and in the Boer War, and later took part in some minor operations in East Africa. In 1913 he became Inspector-General of the King's African Rifles. General Smuts, in his last dispatch, warmly acknowledged his indebtedness to General Hoskins for rendering him the greatest services while commanding the 1st Division, "by the ability and loyal manner in which he has carried out my orders".

Major-Generals Van Deventer and Brits, commanding the 2nd and 3rd Divisions respectively, were also mentioned for loyal and distinguished service throughout. Brigadier-General Sheppard received the Commander-in-Chief's acknowledgments not only for excellent work at the head of his brigade, but also for using his great engineering capabilities to the best advantage on many occasions, "thereby enabling our advance to proceed unchecked". Brigadier-General Hannyngton "proved his worth as a commander in the field, having been very largely employed in carrying out independent operations". Brigadier-General Beves "sustained his high soldierly record, and the 2nd South African Brigade under him has borne more than its due share of the labours and hardships of the campaign". Brigadier-Generals Berrangé, Enslin, Nussey, Sir C. P. Crewe, and Edwards were also included among the leaders to whom General Smuts expressed himself as "particularly indebted". In thanking the railway service, he mentions specially Lieutenant-Colonel C. W. Wilkinson and Major J. H. Dobson, of the South African Pioneers, who carried out the temporary repairs to the Central Railway, which enabled the troops in the interior to be supplied from Dar-es-Salaam practically within a month of its occupation. He further refers to his "very great debt" to his Chief of the General Staff, Brigadier-General J. J. Collier, C.M.G., and Brigadier-General R. H. Ewart, C.B., D.S.O., of the Administrative Staff, whose tireless energy and unfailing tact relieved the Commander-in-Chief of all detail work, and left him free to devote himself solely to the prosecution of the campaign.

A great reception awaited General Smuts on his return to Cape Town before leaving for the Imperial Conference in London. In his reply to the address presented to him in the City Hall, he emphasized the fact that South Africa, by the lion's share which she had taken in the colonial campaigns, had secured a permanent voice in the disposal of the African continent. As the only white community in Africa, the South Africans were more deeply interested in the fate of that continent than most other nations. Whatever happened in German East Africa, he added, they knew that they would have to be heard. "Future generations will never be able to say that we did not peg out our claims, and thus establish our rights regarding the future of this continent." They were fighting the Germans, he said in effect—obviously by way of answer to the Nationalists—because a Prussian victory would undoubtedly involve a grave menace to all liberty-loving peoples. The British connection, on the other hand, possessed no perils for South Africa. Finally, the soldier-statesman paid an emphatic tribute to the value of the British co-operation in the East African campaign, striking testimony being also reserved for

Lieutenant-General A. R. Hoskins, C.M.G., D.S.O., who succeeded to the command in East Africa after General Smuts's departure for the Imperial Conference
(From a photograph by Bassano)

the work of the Indians, General Smuts declaring that he had no more loyal or more devoted and braver troops than those heroes from Asia.

F. A. M.

# CHAPTER XI

## THE BATTLES OF THE ANCRE AND THE WINTER CAMPAIGN OF 1916–17

(October, 1916–February, 1917)

Rounding off the Somme Victory—Strategic Value of the Ancre Positions—Clearing the Slopes above Thiepval—Capture of Stuff and Regina Trenches—The Battle of November 13—Fall of St. Pierre Divion—Serre Attack abandoned—Capture of Beaumont-Hamel by the Scottish Troops—The Battle for Y Ravine—Royal Naval Division's Advance on Beaucourt-sur-Ancre—How Colonel Freyberg won the V.C.—King George's Congratulations to Sir Douglas Haig—Bitter Struggle for the Butte de Warlencourt—Closing Operations of 1916—Achievements of British Raiders—The Third Christmas in the Trenches—New Year's Day Celebrations—Sir Douglas Haig becomes a Field-Marshal—His Ceaseless Pressure on the Ancre Front—Successful Advance near Le Transloy—First Signs of German Retreat—Evacuation of Grandcourt—Fall of Miraumont, Puisieux, Gommecourt, and other German Strongholds above the Ancre—Capture of the Butte de Warlencourt and other Enemy Positions on the Road to Bapaume—The King's Congratulations on the "fitting sequel to the Battle of the Somme"—Other Winter Operations along the Western Front—Dashing Scottish Success—Londoners' "Record" Raid.

THOUGH condemned by the weather to cry "Halt!" to his main attack on the Somme in the autumn of 1916, just when he had reached the stage which promised successes for the Allied Armies more brilliant than any that had gone before, Sir Douglas Haig determined to press on with preparations for exploiting the favourable situation on his left flank. Here, accordingly, the Fifth Army, under General Gough, whose self-sacrificing rôle since the beginning of July had been to act as the pivot to the remainder of the fighting-line, began gradually to attack more as General Rawlinson's Fourth Army attacked less. As explained in our story of the Battle of the Somme, Gough's gallant troops had already prepared for the final conquest of the heights dominating this sector of the battle-field by the capture of Thiepval and Mouquet Farm on September 25, and the reduction of the Schwaben and Stuff Redoubts a few days later. Possession of these key positions on the downs north of Thiepval had carried with it observation over the gorge through which the upper waters of the Ancre ran between the German strongholds of St. Pierre Divion and Miraumont, including the slopes still held by the enemy on the scene of the Ulstermen and Newfoundlanders' heroic sacrifices on July 1, 1916.

Full well the Germans, as much as the British, knew the great strategic value of the lost positions, and made desperate efforts to recover them throughout the succeeding weeks. A thrilling chapter could be written round the fortunes of the twin redoubts—Schwaben and Stuff—alone. Portions of them changed hands repeatedly in the miniature battles which raged round them almost every day for several weeks after the fall of Thiepval. When that fortress fell into our hands they remained the most formidable obstacles barring our advance south of the Ancre. Both redoubts passed firmly into our possession on October 15 with an attack which brought in some 400 prisoners and carried our line well to the north. Nevertheless the enemy still persisted in disputing every foot of ground, and clinging to his remaining defences with a grim resolve. Six days later he made a supreme effort to win back Schwaben, a captured German Regimental Order, dated October 21, emphasizing the necessity of recovering this pivot of the German position. "The men", it proceeded, "are to be informed by their immediate superiors that this attack is not merely a matter of retaking a trench because it was formerly in German possession, but that the recapture of an extremely important position is involved." The new storm burst in the early morning of the 21st, when the enemy attacked in successive waves of infantry. At all points save two he was hurled back before reaching our trenches,. but at two points his waves succeeded in gaining a temporary footing in the advanced traverses of the redoubt. It was but a momentary success, for the intruders were immediately thrown out again, leaving five officers and seventy-nine other ranks prisoners in our hands, besides a large number of dead in front of our trenches. Another costly failure had been added to those German counter-attacks against the British, which, as General von Arnim protested in his Army Report, "cost much blood".

Mouquet Farm: general view—continued on the opposite page—of the ruins of the famous German stronghold after its final capture by the British on the Thiepval slopes

This assault came opportunely for us, as we had taken advantage of the same brief interval of fine, hard weather to plan a blow of our own on our right.

This blow we delivered in fine style shortly after noon along a front of about 5000 yards, extending from Schwaben Redoubt as far as the Courcelette-Pys road, passing above Courcelette at a distance of about three-quarters of a mile. The main object was to capture the Stuff Trench and the western portion of the Regina ber struggles for this elongated trench, but in the face of our vigorous assault of the 21st, when most of the prisoners were found to belong to the 28th Bavarian and 5th Ersatz Divisions, the whole defence along the front attacked fell to pieces. It was obvious that the Germans were taken by surprise. Before they could recover from the sudden

British Official Photograph

Mouquet Farm: general view—continued from the opposite page—of the ruins of the famous German stronghold after its final capture by the British on the Thiepval slopes

Trench—a recent addition to the German first-line defences, facing due south—and hurl the enemy farther down the slope towards the southern bank of the Ancre. Regina Trench in particular had hitherto been defended with great tenacity, the hard-pressed enemy having drawn on his Naval Division for reinforcements at this point—the first time that any of his naval units had fought so far inland as the Somme country. The sailors put up a stiff fight in the earlier Octo-

preliminary bombardment our infantry were among them at all points, not only capturing the Stuff and Regina Trenches, but also certain troublesome advance posts well to the north and north-east of Schwaben. Nearly 1100 prisoners—a number only slightly exceeded by our total casualties—were taken in this dashing affair. "The Canadians and the troops of the New Army, who conducted the operation" —to quote from Sir Douglas Haig's *communiqué* of November 1—"deserve great credit for a signal and most economical victory." Small wonder that the Commander-in-Chief, in his full dispatch of December 23, expressed himself as well content in October with the situation on his left flank. "I was quite confident of the ability of our troops," he wrote, "not only to repulse the enemy's attacks, but to clear him entirely from his last positions on the ridge whenever it should suit my plans to do so." Following upon their long, unbroken series of successes, our troops, now hardened and experienced, and sure of their individual superiority over the foe, were filled with the same quiet confidence. The unevenness in the quality of German discipline and *moral* became more marked with each new phase of the prolonged offensive. According to our ideas, as the *Times* special correspondent remarked in a sanguine message at the time from British Head-quarters, the German army had always relied too much on discipline, and the progress of the Somme offensive seemed to prove that our ideas were right.

"The new men—the men with whom Germany is making up her deficiencies now—have not been through the same grinding training as the old. We have proved in our army that the right kind of men can be made into magnificent soldiers with very short training; but with German material, under the German system, when discipline is inadequate there seems not to be the right stuff in the men to take its place. . . . It seems as if we had broken, as it were, through the hard crust of severely disciplined and trained men and were coming to a softer interior. We ought to find it easier work ploughing through that interior next year than it was breaking the crust this year."

It was only the weather which now caused any real anxiety in the British ranks. This had broken again, transforming once more the whole chalky soil between the Ancre and the Somme into a wilderness of glutinous mud. Doubts began to rise as to the possibility after all of clearing up the situation on the Ancre before the state of the ground rendered unavoidable a cessation in the British offensive on the left as well as on the right flank. Day after day, as the pitiless rain proceeded steadily to break all past weather records in that watery region, the one remaining big operation of the 1916 campaign was postponed. When, at last, on November 9, the weather took a turn for the better, and remained for some days dry and cold, with frosty nights and misty mornings, men anxiously wondered if the change had come too late. But Sir Douglas Haig's preparations soon showed that he at least thought there was still time to clear out the viper's nest at Beaumont-Hamel, and square accounts on the Ancre. It was necessary to do this in order to round off the conquests of the preceding four months.

Not only Beaumont-Hamel, but also the river-side village of Beaucourt-sur-Ancre, and the ruins of St. Pierre Divion on the opposite bank, were still facing us, surrounded by elaborate systems of German entrenchments and hidden refuges, each one protecting the next, and perfected with all the arts of defensive skill which the war had taught both friend and foe. The eastern half of Regina Trench also needed clearing out. It had become a greater nuisance than ever, as a hot-bed of snipers, since the western portion fell into our hands on October 21, and heavy toll was daily taken of our ranks holding the line in front of Courcelette and Le Sars. During the bombardment preliminary to the impending battle, this, the remaining stretch of Regina Trench, was accordingly carried—shortly after midnight of November 11–12—by a surprise attack which, though not so productive in the matter of prisoners, was as successful as the last. This was the final incident of note on Sir Douglas Haig's left flank before he launched his great assault astride the river.

British Official Photograph

The Flooded Battle-field: a scene on the Ancre in the closing months of 1916

When the British line south of the Ancre was pushed above Thiepval and the Stuff and Schwaben Redoubts it reached the crest of the ridge overlooking Grandcourt and Miraumont, and passed beyond the sinister stronghold of St. Pierre Divion, with its maze of trenches running up the valley slopes, leaving the main defences of that fortress sheltered in the elbow of the river. Immense dug-outs under the bank—some of them holding as many as 250 men apiece—afforded the Germans snug quarters from which to make their sallies up the slopes towards their old rabbit-warren approach to the Schwaben. They were not altogether isolated on the bank, for the road fringing the Ancre threw an arm across the wide reedy shallows and the trickling stream itself, thus linking up St. Pierre Divion with Beaucourt station on the other side. But it was a road well shelled by British gunners, and only comparatively safe at night.

Had the weather conditions been more favourable the new operations would have been on a proportionately larger scale. The ground was still so bad in places, however, that it was necessary, as Sir Douglas Haig explains, to limit the operations to what it would be reasonably possible to consolidate and hold under the existing conditions. Hence the battle which began on November 13, after two days' preliminary bombardment, only extended along a five-mile front east of Schwaben Redoubt to north of Serre, and rapidly resolved itself into a struggle for Beaumont-Hamel, Beaucourt-sur-Ancre, and St. Pierre Divion—all bastions of the enemy's continuous chain of fortresses, which had defied every effort of our troops on the left flank to break through on July 1. Powerful enough at the first onset, the enemy had spent the succeeding four months and more in improving and adding to his defences in the light of the experience gained in our successful attacks farther south. Sir Douglas Haig held the opinion that each of these positions, like the rest of the villages forming part of the enemy's front line in this district, was intended to form a permanent line of fortifications while he developed his offensive elsewhere. When he realized that his foothold had become precarious the enemy multiplied the number of his guns, and brought up an additional division of troops to guard his front from Grandcourt to Hébuterne.

Our preliminary bombardment, which began at 5 a.m. on November 11 and continued with bursts of great intensity for forty-eight hours, warned him that we were beginning again, just when his Higher Command had been openly rejoicing that our offensive was at an end; and he knew that he would need all his resources to withstand the inevitable shock. If the enemy had strengthened his defences and reinforced his troops, the British, as he well knew from months of bitter experience, had gained enormously in battle practice and leadership, as well as in increasing numbers and unlimited munitions. It was obvious that July 1 was to be avenged by another frontal attack on the old German line, this time with all the lessons learned from four months' unceasing conflict. As on July 1, though on a miniature scale, the battle resolved itself into two parts, with the Ancre as the dividing-line; but both sides of the river blazed up simultaneously, when, at 5.45 on the morning of November 13, the moment came for our infantry to attack all along the line, and our bombardment developed into its effective barrage, covering the assaulting troops. It was a damp, shivery morning, with a thick, clammy fog which hampered the operations, encouraging tactical blunders in places, and robbing our artillery of its eyes overhead. But, while the weather handicapped us in these and other ways, it also enabled us to take the enemy somewhat unawares. He was not prepared for a grand attack in a dense fog, even though several fine drying days and an unmistakable artillery preparation pointed to a new offensive at the first favourable opportunity.

On the right flank the battle-field, which began some 700 yards to the north of Stuff Redoubt and swept down to the river opposite Beaucourt-sur-Ancre, was not so misty as on the other side of the stream, and the advance here met with a success described by the Commander-in-Chief himself as "altogether remarkable for rapidity of execution and lightness of cost". Nearly 1400 prisoners were taken by a single British division in this area at the expense of fewer than 600 casualties. Descending the slippery slopes in the dim morning light, our infantry, admirably supported by our guns, which had the range of the enemy's only sources of supply and reinforcements to an inch, seized the whole of their objectives east of St. Pierre Divion by 7.20 a.m. Now hemmed in between our troops and the Ancre—every passage across which was commanded by our artillery—the Germans in and about that river-side fortress were forced to realize that they were at last cut off completely. They might have made a good fight for it, for at 9 a.m. the number of prisoners was actually greater than the attacking force; but there was little fight left in the German garrisons at this point on the Ancre, in spite of their formidable fortifications, including the underground labyrinth at St. Pierre Divion, known to our Intelligence Officers as "The Tunnel". This remarkable gallery, starting from sheltered recesses on the valley level, ran back into the hill for at least 300 yards, branching out at the ends like a T for another 200 yards on each side. Like the subterranean barracks at Thiepval, it possessed its own dressing-station for the wounded, and was furnished with officers' quarters and accommodation for whole companies of men. A mine of machine-guns and machine-gun am-

British Official Photograph

The Battle-fields of the Ancre: wrecked water-mill in the St. Pierre Divion area

munition, besides much other booty, was discovered by its captors on November 13.

The phenomenal haul of prisoners in this area was accounted for by the fact that at the moment of the attack the garrison was being relieved by one of Hindenburg's new "combed-out" divisions—the 223rd—and both were caught in our unexpected net. It was an inglorious "blooding" for this new formation, thus going into action for the first time. Among the regiments of the division which the 223rd was sent to relieve was the 95th, whose colonel, the Duke of Albany, was reported to be waiting to inspect it on its return from St. Pierre Divion. If the inspection ever took place it must have been in horribly attenuated form, for we took heavy toll of the 95th that morning.

The most serious opposition at St. Pierre Divion occurred where a dauntless Tank, wriggling ahead of our advancing infantry, found itself for a moment nonplussed on the edge of a shell-crater. It was making up its mind what to do when the Germans in the nearest entrenchments, jumping rashly to the conclusion that it had broken down, took their courage in both hands, and rushed to the attack. They paid dearly for their sudden hardihood. The Tank, well able to take care of itself, scattered death all round from its quick-firers, and the infantry, coming up at this moment,

British Official Photograph

After the Capture of St. Pierre Divion: German prisoners resting in their "cage" carried with a rush the trenches which the enemy had so rashly vacated. Many of the Germans were driven into their capacious dug-outs, and surrendered. St. Pierre Divion soon fell, and the rest of the forces operating south of the stream attained their objectives with equal completeness and success. The sequel was described as even more astonishing than the attack.

"Immediately after the trenches down to the river had been captured", wrote Mr. Beach Thomas,[1] "our men strolled about above ground as if they were out for an airing. They picked up relics. They shared out German cigars and sat on parapets smoking, and enjoyed to the hilt, for the little while that it lasted, the serenity of the battle-field."

There were neither German machine-gunners nor German snipers to fear now that they had all been smoked out of this malignant nest. Even the German artillery, apparently, decided to leave St. Pierre Divion to its fate. All this while, however, the struggle was raging furiously across the river, where the Royal Naval Division was fighting with superb gallantry against heavy odds, carrying the tide of battle from the northern bank to its junction with the Scottish Division, whose objective was Beaumont-Hamel itself. Thence the battle-front was carried farther north until it faced the grim stronghold of Serre—won and lost by Territorial heroes in the sanguinary struggle of July 1. Once more this sector proved the most difficult to win and hold. For the first half-mile beyond Beaumont-Hamel, on the left of the Scottish troops, the enemy's first-line system was soon in our hands; but opposite Serre, where another famous division was sacrificing itself with equal heroism, the ground was so heavy that it became necessary, as Sir Douglas Haig pointed out, to abandon the attack at an early stage—"although", he added, "our troops had in places reached the enemy's trenches in the course of their assault". They held up many reinforcements, too, whose weight would otherwise have been thrown into the scale against the triumphant advance of the Scotsmen, naval men, and English and Irish regiments fighting astride the river.

To the Scotsmen, as already mentioned, fell the honour of conquering Beaumont-Hamel, the core of the German defence against which our troops had dashed themselves in vain on July 1. The strength of the whole position, apart from its outlying strong points and its successive rows of entrenchments, planned and completed by the Germans with all their ingenuity of protective fortification, had been carried underground. The enemy regarded this subterranean fortress as more impregnable than Thiepval, which so long had guarded the other side of the Ancre.

Looking from behind the Scottish lines, on the eve of the new attack, there was nothing to be seen in the dip of the hill beyond of the village which once slept peacefully there, embowered in trees, save a horribly battered site, and a few remaining tree stumps.

[1] *With the British on the Somme.* W. Beach Thomas. Methuen, 1917.

"Before its nearest edge," wrote the *Times* correspondent on the spot, "down to and across the low ground before our lines, ran successive lines of trenches, with the rusted wire entanglements so thick that they looked like a belt of brown ploughed land. The entanglements in some places were as many as five tiers deep, and, behind these and the front trenches, the face of the slope beyond, round in the crease of the hills and down on the other side to the Upper Ancre, was pierced everywhere with the entrances to the barrack-like cellars and deep dug-outs, which made the whole place a veritable fortress."

Most formidable of all the flank defences of Beaumont-Hamel was a deep ravine, nearly 1000 yards long, facing the Scottish right, and branching out in their direction in the shape of a catapult. Hence it became known as the "Y" Ravine; and the fight for its possession on November 13 was as savage as any of the bitter struggles for the Gully Ravine, of evil memory, in Gallipoli. Its precipitous sides—so steep in places as actually to overhang—dropped 30 feet and more to the bottom, and every foot had been cunningly utilized by the Germans to strengthen its defences. The prongs running down to their first line, as well as the main stem which receded to the road to Beaumont station at its entrance to Beaumont-Hamel, were pierced in all directions with tunnels, dug-outs impervious to every kind of shell-fire, and devious alley-ways along which reinforcements could be rushed, two or three abreast, from the lines in the rear.

This was the fearsome wasps' nest which the Scottish troops had first to storm as they leapt from their trenches in the clammy darkness of early morning on November 13, with the Royal Naval Division keeping step on their right. Happily the preliminary work of the gunners supporting them had been as near to perfection as possible. "The lanes shorn through the quintuple tiers of wire", wrote the *Morning Post* correspondent, "were clean and complete; the shells had dropped with almost mathematical nicety along one trench after another, and there were fewer 'waste' craters than anyone had expected." The result was that the troops, following up the protective barrage into which the bombardment had now developed, carried the first two rows of German defences without a check along the whole of their front, save at the deadly mouths of the Y Ravine. Here occurred the sternest fighting of the day, but, while this isolated battle was in progress, other Scottish troops swept on above and below the ravine, right into Beaumont-Hamel itself. Nothing remained of the village above ground, but stout opposition came from the trenches, which ran in front of what had once been the High Street. Here the trenches became so choked with bodies that the survivors fought with increasing difficulty, and presently surrendered; so that by midday the whole surface of the village and the entrances to all the tunnels and dug-outs, which led to the caverns and chambers beneath, were in Scottish possession.

One by one these formidable underground fastnesses were effectually cleared, some 600 prisoners being collected from below the village to join those already captured above. Many of these "pockets", apart from their human occupants, were well worth clearing. One food dump, according to Mr. Beach Thomas, contained excellent butter, white bread, tinned hams, cigars, and other luxuries. Some of these proved too tempting to resist, and tales are told by the same correspondent of soldiers who stopped to taste the welcome delicacies, to light German cigars, and to don German helmets, wearing these hilariously for the rest of the day. The most amazing episodes occurred in the rounding-up of the prisoners. A solitary Scottish officer, for instance, after leading his bombers from one position to another, dropping men as guards on the way, found himself at length far back through the German lines with only two men left. Placing these to hold approaches, he himself investigated a dug-out which proved to be a battalion head-quarters, with the staff officers sheltering within. Nothing daunted, he called on them to surrender, which they promptly did. Incautiously, however, he was persuaded, on some pretext, to join them in an inner room, where, closing the door, they politely informed him that the position was reversed: he was now their prisoner instead. With equal politeness he bowed to the inevitable, each side anxiously awaiting the course of events outside. This could be followed by the German officers through a giant periscope, which reflected the ground above. Presently an unmistakable exclamation from them told the Scottish officer that his country-

The Triumph of a "Tank": Germans surrendering in a body from one of their strong points

man were coming to place the matter beyond dispute. With a dignity and courtesy which did him credit, the German commander informed his captive that, since the troops were now all round them, they had perhaps better revert to the original arrangement. So the tables were again turned, and the Scotsman marched his prisoners out in triumph.

Deep down in some of the subterranean labyrinths the cellars were so full of dead Germans—long left unburied by their comrades—that there was no course left for the victors but to cover them in quicklime, the entrances to the charnel-house then being blocked with earth and sandbags. Meantime a ceaseless battle was raging in Y Ravine, to which the enemy clung with the courage of despair. Here the bombardment had left him practically untouched in his abysmal hiding-places, and the two entrances to the chasm were so powerfully defended by his machine-guns, that the first frontal attack, as already mentioned, had been checked. The longer prong in particular was guarded by a machine-gun redoubt, dovetailed into a slope of the hill. Its withering fire raked the whole surrounding area with appalling precision. It was one of the strong points which had broken down our tragic assault on July 1. On the present occasion the attack flowed round on both sides of the ravine until some of the Scottish troops made a breach in its side, just behind the fork of the Y, and bombed and bayoneted their

Drawn by H. W. Koekkoek

The Scotsmen's Triumph at Beaumont-Hamel: the storming of "Y" ravine

The eye-witness who sent the sketch from which the above illustration was made mentions that the Scotsmen wore their goatskins as they attacked in the early morning mist of November 13, 1916. They carried their gas-helmets in small flat cases on their chests.

British Official Photograph

"An Abomination of Desolation": among the ruins of Beaumont-Hamel, captured by the Scottish troops on November 13, 1916

way to right and left. The tumult and confusion of the struggle which ensued beggars description. Germans were holding the tips of the prongs, Germans were sheltering in the bottom of the stem, and other Germans in isolated sections were grappling hand-to-hand with irresistible Scotsmen, who, in ever-increasing numbers, drove wider wedges into the doomed stronghold. Once they came to grips, however, the issue was never long in doubt. Almost invariably the Germans, as soon as they were really cornered, flung down their arms and surrendered, sometimes singly, sometimes in considerable blocks.

While the middle of the ravine was thus being cleared, foot by foot, a new frontal attack was delivered against the still unbroken sector of the front line towards which the prongs of the Y projected. The new danger distracted the attention of the defenders, and enabled our troops greatly to extend their hold both towards the front and the rear. Surrounded on all sides, the Germans were at length forced to confess defeat, the last considerable group—some 350 in all—surrendering early in the afternoon. Altogether the ravine and its immediate defences yielded that day a total of about 700 prisoners. The *coup de grâce* was reserved for one of the Tanks, which came up during the evening to take the measure of the machine-gun redoubt—still spitting forth death from its sloping roof of reinforced concrete, and apparently equipped with an inexhaustible supply of ammunition. The Tank, however, was too much for it. A leisurely approach to within easy firing distance—under a hail of bullets which fell upon it like water on a duck's back—a brief duel, and then the flag of surrender, followed by the appearance of the defeated garrison, who were promptly marched off across the old front line.

There had been plenty of other stern work for the Scotsmen in the ravine, even after its formal evacuation early in the afternoon. Countless dug-outs and caverns had to be cleared, as well as an unsuspected tunnel which ran back from the forward end of the ravine as far as the fourth German line in the rear, and had been used for reinforcing the garrison in the midst of the battle. Here, as elsewhere along the captured Beaumont-Hamel line, the situation remained more or less confused throughout the night, and led to many strange incidents.

It was during this period that a Scottish private, to whom a German officer surrendered, put his captive to excellent use instead of sending him back at once. The private—so the story runs—had lived in Germany, and could speak the language; so, leading the officer along the ravine to a suspected dug-out, he bade him put his head into its mouth and order the occupants up. One by one they obeyed their officer's thundering command, filing out into the ravine with their hands duly raised above their heads, until they stood, all told, in a dejected row of fifty men. The private, we are told, took their surrender from the officer "with the dignity of a field-marshal". Altogether over 1400 prisoners fell to the Scottish troops on that November 13, 1916, and captured machine-guns were gathered in by the score. It was a proud day for Scotland, and a crowning triumph for British arms.

We can now leave Beaumont-Hamel and its vast confusion of caves in the safe hands of its captors, and retrace our steps to the northern slopes of the Ancre, where the Royal Naval Division, on the Scottish right, was engaged in the fiercest and longest struggle of all in this battle astride the river. It was the Royal Naval Division's first opportunity in the Somme offensive, but it had long since proved its courage both in the hapless Antwerp expedition and the Gallipoli campaign, where it greatly distinguished itself. Subsequently it had taken its turn in the dreary round of trench warfare along comparatively uneventful sectors of the Western front, and all ranks had eagerly awaited the chance of sharing in the battle honours of the Somme and the Ancre. Their chief regret was that they were not pitted against the German Naval Division, which, as already mentioned, had lately been fighting not far away on the other side of the Ancre.

While the Scotsmen were hurling themselves upon Beaumont-Hamel and Y Ravine, in the early morning mist of November 13, these eager battalions of the Naval Division—each named after some illustrious old sea-captain—were launched along those northern slopes of the river bank whence had come the murderous machine-gun fire which had decimated the Ulster troops attacking up the southern bank on July 1. Beaucourt-sur-Ancre, their ultimate objective, was farther away than that of the Scotsmen. It lay in ruins some 2000 yards back, over a tangle of winding trenches, communicating-alleys, and cleverly concealed redoubts bristling with machine-guns. Practically the whole approach was thus honeycombed for defence, and swept by vicious redoubts, which, built almost flush with the ground, were impossible to see in the rising mist. The enemy's profusion of guns in these strong points, working on sliding platforms on beds of concrete, almost justified the German boast that no troops in the world could advance up the valley under their fire. But the Royal Naval Division, though these boasted defences cost it very dear, was not to be denied.

It was a blind rush in the darkness of early morning on November 13, when its first waves went over, keeping pace, as already said, with the Scotsmen on the left. The plan provided that as each naval battalion gained its first objective the first waves should wait for their second line to go through them towards the next objective, and so on; but it was not the day, according to Mr. Beach Thomas, who had it from the lips of those who took part, and the men were not the men, for precise and mathematical manœuvres.

"Like some of the heroes whose names they fought under, the Drakes, Hawkes, and the rest, they won more by their spirit than by their learning. 'They made tactical mistakes,' said a general, 'but did all, and more than, they had to do.'"[1]

It was hardly surprising that some units lost touch in the thick fog and the maze of trenches. One hidden redoubt in the enemy's centre literally mowed down their ranks as they poured over the captured first line towards their second objective. This unsuspected stronghold—concealed by the curve of the slope across which our troops were charging—was full of machine-guns, and these, firing almost level with the ground, swept the whole shell-pitted area in all directions with a driving sheet of bullets which made any considerable advance beneath it impossible. Troops on the flanks poured past and onwards, but the attack in the centre was hung up. For a time the situation was undoubtedly critical. It was gloriously saved, however, by the prowess of the battalions which had swept on under the leadership of an officer whose heroic achievement on this occasion will always be remembered among the outstanding deeds of the war.

The officer was Lieutenant-Colonel Bernard Cyril Freyberg, who had already distinguished himself with the Naval Division in the Gallipoli campaign, in which, besides being wounded, he had won the D.S.O. Gallipoli had been but the continuation of an adventurous career, not unconnected at one time, it is said, with gun-running exploits in Mexico. The Battle of the Ancre, however, brought him the great adventure of his life. He was commanding the Hood Battalion, and was wounded in the first moments of the attack while crossing No Man's Land. Taking no notice of this mishap, Colonel Freyberg carried the initial

[1] *With the British on the Somme.* By W. Beach Thomas. Methuen, 1917.

assault by his splendid personal bravery through the enemy's first series of trenches. He was holding the extreme right of the line, by the northern bank of the Ancre, and escaped the deadly directness of the machine-gun redoubt which was temporarily holding up the battalions on his left. Even so, owing to the fog and heavy fire of every description, his command became much disorganized after the capture of the first objective. Men from other units became intermixed with his own; but, though wounded a second time, he rallied and re-formed his ranks and inspired everyone with his own splendid spirit. Then, at the appointed time, he led his men to the successful assault of the second objective, on the outskirts of Beaucourt, taking many prisoners in the process. Here, under heavy artillery and machine-gun fire, Colonel Freyberg held on for the remainder of the day and night, with his left flank "in the air", and practically isolated from the rest of the attacking troops. This tenacity, as Sir Douglas Haig testified in his dispatch, "was of the utmost value, and contributed very largely to the success of the operations".

All that night Colonel Freyberg was collecting scattered remnants from other units, and reorganizing his command for a surprise attack on Beaucourt on the following morning. He meant the Naval Division to have that village at all costs. He had only some 500 or 600 men to spare for the task, after allowing for the necessary guards for the captured positions and prisoners. But he spent the night to such good purpose that at daybreak on November 14 he was again leading his troops to the attack, and carrying all before him. The victory was extraordinarily quick and complete. It was all over in less than half an hour, not only the whole of this strongly-fortified village, but also its garrison of 500 men, falling into his hands. While leading the

Lieutenant-Colonel Bernard C. Freyberg, V.C., D.S.O. the hero of the capture of Beaucourt by the Royal Naval Division

assault Colonel Freyberg received his third wound, and was wounded yet again—this time severely—later in the day, but refused to leave the line till he had issued final instructions. "The personality, valour, and utter contempt of danger on the part of this single officer", recorded the *London Gazette* in announcing that the Victoria Cross had been added to his D.S.O., "enabled the lodgment in the most advanced objective of the corps to be

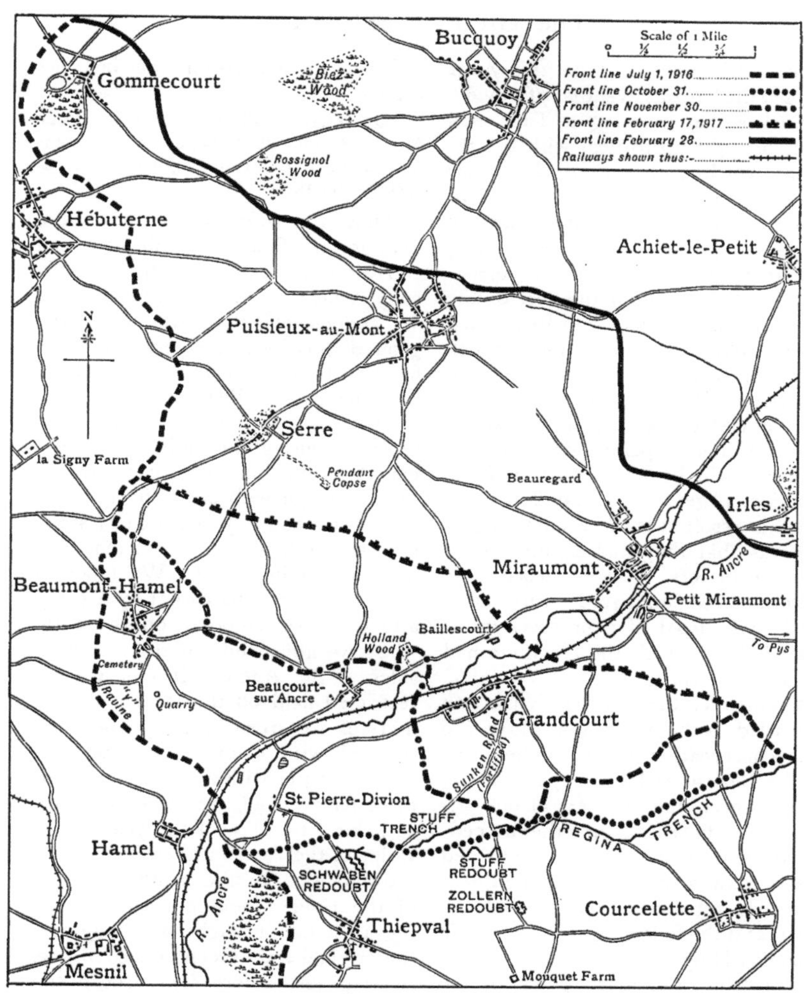


The Battles of the Ancre: map illustrating the successive British advances from October, 1916, to February 28, 1917

permanently held, and on this *point d'appui* the line was eventually formed".

Earlier that morning a Tank had been brought up to deal with the redoubt which had mowed down our ranks on the slopes of the ridge, and struck such terror into the hearts of the German machine-gunners holding it that at six o'clock they all surrendered. This brought the rest of the Naval Division in line with Beaucourt, where Colonel Freyberg was in touch with our triumphant troops south of the river. When some day the full story comes to be told of the sailors' share in this desperate Battle of the Ancre it will be found worthy of the proudest pages in our naval history. The net result of their two days' fighting was that they had captured over 1700 prisoners, besides much war material, and advanced some 2000 yards on a front of over 1000 yards, the whole of which the Germans had boasted as impregnable.

On their left the new British line now extended to the north-west along the Beaucourt road across the southern end of the Beaumont-Hamel spur. Here, as elsewhere, the numbers of our prisoners steadily rose during the succeeding days, while our front was extended eastwards and northwards up the Beaumont-Hamel slopes. On the 15th the King sent the following message to Sir Douglas Haig:—

"I heartily congratulate you upon the great success achieved by my gallant troops during the past three days in the advance on both sides of the Ancre. This further capture of the enemy's first-line trenches, under special difficulties owing to the recent wet weather, redounds to the credit of all ranks."

To which the Commander-in-Chief replied:—

"On behalf of all ranks, to whom Your Majesty's gracious message has been communicated, I return most grateful and respectful thanks".

That afternoon the enemy, who, save for his first frantic, ill-organized counter-attacks, which we had no difficulty in beating off, had hitherto made no serious effort to win back the ground thus lost, bombarded our new front north of the Ancre, especially in the vicinity of Beaucourt. Heavy shelling against the Somme area was repeated during the night of November 17th; but our own guns took up the challenge with such effect that if the enemy had any intention of striking back with his infantry at that time he changed his mind. We followed up our own bombardment by a sharp attack before daybreak on the 18th, when we advanced our front on both sides of the Ancre. It was a more restricted field on this occasion, on a front of not more than 2½ miles, and covered with snow; for winter was now setting in with a vengeance. For three days it had been freezing hard, and this final blow of the year in the valley of the Ancre was delivered in a snowstorm. On the southern slopes of the river, where our advance on the 13th had brought us up against the original main German second line, running just before Grandcourt, the assault was delivered by troops from the British Isles in conjunction with the Canadians on their right, holding the captured Regina Trench above Courcelette.

Plunging through the snow both

from Stuff and Regina Trenches the Home and Dominion troops bombed and bayoneted their way through the main German second line, which, with its serried rows of elaborate defence works, particularly in the sunken road along the southern approach to the river, winning here an average distance of 500 yards. The Canadians alone took nearly 500 unwounded prisoners on their front, where all their objectives were won and securely held, save for a short stretch on the right of the point at which the captured

Canadian Official Photograph

"Over the Top": Canadian troops leaving their trenches for an attack on the German positions

village, proved as strong at Grandcourt as the first system. The battle for its possession was of the most stubborn character. The snowstorm had added considerably to the difficulties of the attack, especially in the sunken road, where our advance was held up; but to left of it the troops won their way to the outlying ruins of Grandcourt, and to right over another stage of the descent from the ridge towards the trench crossed the Pys road, passing over a knoll exposed to a destructive fire from the enemy's batteries. This was left to be dealt with later, like a section of the Grandcourt Trench, captured by one of the Canadian battalions who pushed on beyond their objective to a distance of some 500 yards. Though this section of the trench was successfully consolidated the position formed too dangerous a salient in the line, the unit in possession being accordingly withdrawn.

On the other side of the Ancre the advance was brought as far as it was necessary to go to keep pace with the southern line. This was no great distance from Beaucourt, but it included the quadrilateral Holland Wood, above what was known as the River Trench. The capture of this copse was expected to involve a small repetition of the Battle of the Woods which had been so costly a feature of the earlier phase of the Somme offensive. Happily, however, the Germans had withdrawn their field-guns, and the remaining defence soon crumpled up before our advance, leaving the wood entirely in our hands. Further progress was also made higher up the northern slopes leading towards Miraumont, the largest of these river-side villages of the Ancre, but before the morning was over the weather broke so completely that continued advance was out of the question. Two inches of melted snow and rain did their very worst with a ground which for several precious days had remained as hard as iron. "The day", to quote from the *Times* correspondent's account from the battle-field, "closed on an earth all slime and slush and pools of standing water, with the air thick with a raw, wet November fog". On such a day it was no mean achievement to have added as many as 772 German prisoners to the total bag, including 20 officers. It was the closing phase of a victory which Sir Douglas Haig had snatched just in time. Bad weather, with rare and insufficient

British Official Photograph

One of Bapaume's Outer Defences: the Butte de Warlencourt, the scene of much of the hardest fighting in the British Advance

The men in the foreground are transporting ammunition and supplies over a light railway.

intervals for further operations on a large scale, now made inevitable the dreary stagnancy of winter warfare.

The Battle of the Ancre had brought the British campaign in the West in 1916 to a brilliant close. In prisoners alone it had added to the Somme total 7200 of all ranks, including 149 officers. What was of far greater consequence was that we had at length, without excessive cost to ourselves, secured the command of the Ancre valley on both banks where it entered the enemy's lines, thus paving the way for the early triumphs of the following spring, when the full measure of the Allies' hard-won victory on the Somme was at length revealed beyond dispute.

While the Battle of the Ancre was being won, with the naval men snatching Beaucourt from the enemy, and the Scotsmen consolidating their hold on Beaumont-Hamel, a secondary struggle was taking place on the sector of the Fourth Army, east of the infamous Butte de Warlencourt, one of the main defences of Bapaume on the road from Albert. The Butte itself—a sepulchral mound, which local tradition established as the burial-place of ancient captains or kings—had been converted by the Germans into a hive of machine-gunners, with power to sweep with deadly effect every attack across the open uplands which gave this area its strategic importance. Before the Great War dragged it into the full glare of history, the tumulus was a grass-covered slope, some 50 feet high and several hundred yards at its base, with a path climbing up its gentle slopes, and a sheltered resting-place on its summit. By November, 1916, it was no longer symmetrical and smooth, and tempting to the eye. A *Times* correspondent who climbed its dreadful sides in the spring of the following year, when the fall of Bapaume and the new British advance had left it well in the wake of war, described it as "beaten out of shape till it looks like some huge lump of

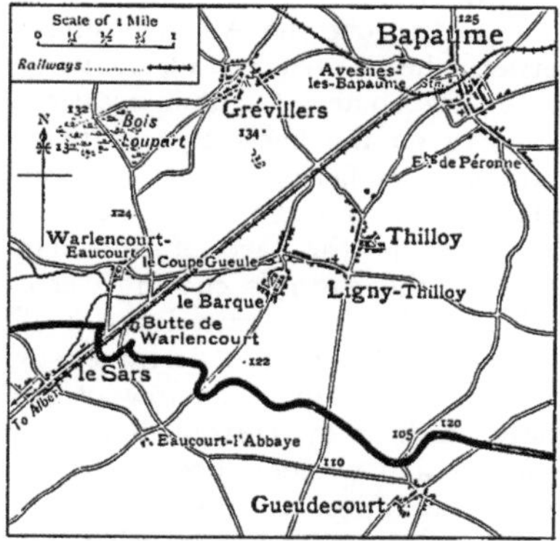


The Butte de Warlencourt and the approximate Position of the British Line before Bapaume at the end of November, 1916

dough kneaded by clumsy fingers. The whole surface", he added, "is so ploughed and sifted, that nowhere is there a yard of stable footing, but it is all crumbled up, like a plum-pudding mixture before it is boiled, and your feet slide and slither in it as you climb." Beneath the Butte were vaults of pre-war construction—perhaps dating from prehistoric times. The Germans had converted these into dug-outs, in which the garrison could shelter more or less comfortably in the midst of our artillery fire.

Though pounded by successive bombardments in the October fighting, the Butte remained, at the beginning of November, among the most formidable bulwarks of Bapaume's defences, and the most conspicuous landmark between that threatened town and the British lines. A great effort to seize and hold it was made on November 5, when, in conjunction with the French, a local attack was made to improve the Allied positions between the two trunk roads converging on Bapaume. On that occasion, following on the heels of an intense barrage, our infantry fought their way before noon through the mud and shell-holes in the face of appalling fire from the enemy's cunningly-concealed machine-gun batteries, not all of which had yet been destroyed by our guns. Reaching the foot of the Butte itself, they cleared both the southern and western faces, inflicting heavy casualties on the garrison—caught apparently while a relief was in progress—rooting out all the enemy positions within reach, and establishing posts by 1 p.m. in the shell-holes running south-east from the south-eastern corner. One young officer gained a foothold on the summit itself, and remained there, transmitting messages, for several hours. The enemy's guns, however, swept the lost ground with a searching, devastating fire, and one of the sunken roads of the country leading back to his supporting positions enabled him to pour down reinforcements under cover. Late in the afternoon, word reached the men holding the captured slopes of the Butte that the advanced posts had been driven in. Then, with the early shades of night, came massed counter-attacks, against which our thinned ranks, to which it was impossible at the time to send up supporting troops—the enemy's machine-gun batteries in the still unconquered parts of the Butte, and the larger guns behind, completely dominating the approach—were forced to fall back to a line to the south. Though they had failed to hold their objective, they had put up a magnificent fight, leaving behind them irreparable damage to one of the enemy's strongest positions, inflicting upon him fearful loses in killed and wounded, and bringing away their prisoners.

The whole of this region was indescribably muddy—worse even than most of the ground about the Ancre, where it was bad enough. Progress became possible only by easy stages at a time. The next local "push" at this point was the operation already referred to, in the midst of the Battle of the Ancre, when Beaumont-Hamel and Beaucourt fell into our possession. This time our object was to break through some 400 or 500 yards of the Gird Trench—the name being a corruption of the first syllable of Gueudecourt—which ran in strongly fortified double lines right up to the Butte de Warlencourt, and just behind it. Home and Dominion troops co-operated on this occasion, and, after a sharp, sanguinary struggle, advanced our front some distance east of the Butte, incidentally capturing another eighty prisoners. Two days later, however—on November 16, to be exact—the Prussian Guard were brought up in strength with orders to win back the lost positions at all costs. This counter-attack was launched with such strength, and pressed home with such reckless determination, that we were compelled, after fierce hand-to-hand fighting against overwhelming odds, to relinquish part of the ground won two days before.

Winter Campaigning on the Western Front: hard going to the trenches British Official Photograph

Winter now stepped in, effectually stopping the savage fighting for this hideous expanse of mud and shell-holes. Two more months were to pass before the whole of it fell finally into our hands. When, not long afterwards, the *Times* correspondent crossed the shattered slopes of the mound which had been its storm-centre, he found on the summit a monument already erected to the officers and men of the Durham Light Infantry who had fallen in the gallant attack on the Butte on November 5: *Dulce et decorum est pro patriâ mori.* "It is a noble site for a monument", writes the correspondent, "and the Durhams deserve it. When the present cross is replaced by permanent marble or granite, there should be grouped around it also memorials to all the other troops who took part in the desperate fighting here."

For the rest of the year 1916 the Western campaign resolved itself largely into a war of the elements—a bitter time for the men in the trenches, but rather more bearable when hard frost succeeded the dismal rains and foul floods of October and November. The official *communiqués* from British Head-quarters dropped to one a day, instead of the two which had served to allay the anxiety of those at home during the progress of the great offensive; and, save for an occasional raid and "the usual artillery activity", or news of much successful fighting and reconnaissance work by our air-craft, there were few incidents of importance to record on the British front throughout the month of December.

In this and the preceding chapter on the Battle of the Somme it has not

British Official Photograph
A Captured German Trench Mortar

been possible to chronicle all the minor happenings since the Allied Offensive began on July 1, 1916. Throughout that period, as Sir Douglas Haig points out in his dispatch of December 23, the rôle of the other armies holding our fighting-line from the northern limits of the battle front to beyond Ypres was necessarily of a secondary nature, but their task was neither light nor unimportant.

"While required to give precedence in all respects to the needs of the Somme battle," he adds, "they were responsible for the security of the line held by them and for keeping the enemy on their front constantly on the alert. The *rôle* was a very trying one, entailing heavy work on the troops and constant vigilance on the part of commanders and staffs. It was carried out to my entire satisfaction, and in an unfailing spirit of unselfish and broad-minded devotion to the general good, which is deserving of the highest commendation."

As affording some idea of the thoroughness with which these subsidiary duties were performed, the Commander-in-Chief mentions that between the beginning of July, when the Battle of the Somme began, to the middle of November, no fewer than 360 raids were carried out on the enemy's trenches. This meant an average of between two and three raids every day throughout that period, the sum total of which resulted in a steady stream of prisoners to the barbed-wire "cages", continual smashing up of hostile trenches and defence works, and a constant strain on the enemy's nerves from one end of the line to the other.

Towards the middle of December, 1916, Germany made her first hollow peace proposals—exactly a year after Sir Douglas Haig's appointment to command the British army in France and Flanders. The first answer came readily and emphatically enough from France in the shape of the great victory at Verdun on December 15, when General Nivelle, who had just taken over the command in the field on the Western front, in succession to General—now Marshal—Joffre, flung the Germans back from the chief strategic strongholds for which they had sacrificed so many thousand lives in the earlier months of the year. It was the crowning triumph in 1916 of the Battle of the Somme, proving that that victory had not only saved "the inviolate citadel", but had also enabled the French to gather fresh strength for a new offensive, thus enabling them to push forward their own line again. and, much as they longed for peace, they saw at once that the German proposals were sham proposals, lacking, as the Allies' reply said, all substance and precision, and being less an offer of peace than a war manœuvre. So, while Parliament was prorogued on December 22, with the King's message proclaiming that "the vigorous prosecution of the war must be our sole endeavour", the troops were doing their best to convince the foe that peace proposals would bring no respite until they were made in a properly chastened spirit. Our guns were still far busier than those of the enemy, and, somewhere along the line, were never silent, day or night. Somewhere along the line, too, the grim business of trench-raiding was continued with ever-increasing enter-

British Official Photograph

Ready for a Further Advance: British troops awaiting the order to attack

Among the British armies there was only one opinion regarding the German peace proposals—that they were due to the long series of shattering blows rained on the enemy during the past five months, and the consciousness of the War Lords that the odds against them were steadily increasing. British soldiers knew that the enemy's real strength was being tested on the Western front, not in the spectacular fields of Roumania or anywhere else;

prise, amounting in the aggregate to operations on a very considerable scale.

One of the most successful affairs of the kind fell to the credit of the Canadians north of Arras about a week before Christmas—a "flying matinée", as those raids were called, carried out in the afternoon in broad daylight. Carefully planned in every detail, it was so successful that the Canadians remained in possession of two lines of enemy trenches on a 400-yard front for something like two hours, spreading death and destruction on all sides, and bringing back nearly sixty prisoners. All the German dug-outs were methodically searched and blown in before the raiders returned. Two nights later the New Zealanders followed suit with a dashing raid, from which they brought back another bunch of prisoners, besides leaving many killed and wounded in the entrenchments, and destroying a section of tramway behind the German lines. They also blew up the pumping apparatus used by the enemy for draining his trenches.

British Official Photograph

Yule-tide on the Western Front: "Tommy's" Christmas dinner in a shell-hole

The Germans retaliated by similar raids, but never possessed the real initiative or true spirit for this kind of fighting. One such attempt was made to celebrate Christmas in the neighbourhood of Lesbœufs, when some fifty Germans crept towards our lines at night-time. Our men and machine-guns, however, were ready for them. Many were killed or wounded, and eighteen remained in our hands as prisoners. Nor did we call a truce in the trenches on this Christmas of 1916. Successful raids were recorded by Sir Douglas Haig, both on Christmas Eve—south-west of Lens and east of Armentières—and the night of Christmas itself, when we repeated the dose in the neighbourhood of Armentières, besides raiding the German positions east of Ploegsteert. Christmas Day north of the Somme, too, was spent by our gunners in systematically shelling the hostile defences and head-quarters. "Elsewhere", to repeat the familiar phrase in the day's laconic *communiqué*, "the usual artillery activity has continued."

Yet the spirit of Christmas was not to be denied, even in the front line. The guns, in festive places, were decked with holly and mistletoe; the very shells often bore legends conveying the season's greetings from the unquenchable spirits behind the guns. And the men who blackened their faces for the raids at night did so with the same irrepressible humour, as though merely the chief actors in some Christmas extravaganza. Behind the lines the Christmas mood had freer scope, and reigned supreme in thousands of billets and camps, where extra rations included a generous helping of plum-pudding for every man. There was another helping on New Year's Day, after the Scots, for the third year in succession, had celebrated Hogmanay within sound of the guns, turning as readily to the amenities of peace as to the barbaric business of war. This year, as before, the colonels of the Scottish battalions paid their little ceremonial visits to the men in their billets, drinking their health and making their New Year speeches. That night, as Mr. Philip Gibbs records in one of his dispatches in the *Daily Telegraph*, there was "sword-dancing by kilted men as

Canadian Official Photograph

A Canadian Message to the Enemy

nimble as Nijinski in their stockinged feet, and old songs of Scotland, which are blown down the wind of France in this strange nightmare of a war, where men from all the Empire are crowded along the fighting-lines, waiting for the bloody battles that will come, as sure as fate, while the new year is yet young". The high hopes inspired by the coming of another year were reflected by the King himself in the following message to President Poincaré and the French nation:—

Canadian Official Photograph

Happy Warriors: Canadians returning from a successful attack

"Once more, Monsieur le Président, the opening of a new year finds our two countries fighting in close alliance for the independence of Europe and justice to the smaller nations. Confident as ever in a victorious issue to the struggle, I pray, Monsieur le Président, that you may continue to be endowed with health and strength to bear the responsibilities of your high office, and that the noble French nation, whose sons have recently, in so striking a manner, given fresh proof of their will to victory, may, by the triumph of the Allied arms, re-enter the path of peaceful progress, secured against aggression and bound to my own people by enduring ties of friendship, cemented by comradeship in arms.

"GEORGE R.I."

Some striking figures came from the French authorities at the beginning of the new year, giving the totals of prisoners taken by the Allied armies on the various European fronts during 1916. These amounted in all to close upon 600,000, made up as follows:—

French: 78,500 Germans, including 26,660 at Verdun.

British: 40,500 Germans.

Italians: 52,250 Austrians.

Russians: some 400,000, mostly Austrians.

Army of the Orient: 11,173 Bulgarians, Turks, and Germans.

This formidable total of 582,423 would be considerably increased if we included the prisoners taken by the British in Egypt and German East

Africa, and by the Roumanians before their country was overrun by the enemy.

The year 1917 was only a week or so old when, a spell of fair weather having somewhat hardened the ground, Sir Douglas Haig, now raised to the rank of field-marshal, set about improving the front on the obstinate slopes to the north of the Ancre. Throughout the intervening period our guns had done their best to frustrate the enemy's efforts to elaborate new lines of defence on his threatened front, while minor engagements, raids, and patrol actions had relieved the monotony of the campaign at the turn of the year so effectively that the Commander-in-Chief was able to report, on January 6, that as many as 240 further prisoners had fallen into our hands since Christmas. Some fifty or sixty were captured in a particularly neat little enterprise on January 5, when we seized and held two hostile posts north of Beaumont-Hamel, dominating a German support trench running up towards Serre, and known to be full of garrisoned dug-outs. Another nibble east of Beaumont-Hamel four nights later gave us a section of enemy trench and 140 additional prisoners, including 3 officers. In the early morning of the 11th both these advantages were pushed home by the capture of the crest of the ridge just south of Serre, bringing the doom of that famous fortress within measurable distance. This larger operation followed a successful raid south

Canadian Official Photograph

The Land-ship in Action: front view of a "Tank" advancing across No-Man's Land of the Ancre, when we entered the enemy's trenches at two places in the neighbourhood of Grandcourt, and secured a number of prisoners.

On the 17th another line of enemy posts was seized on the opposite slopes of the Ancre valley, north of Beaucourt, when our troops, following a

British Official Photograph

In the Midst of an Attack: shell-holes as field-gun pits

whirlwind bombardment by our guns, advanced in a snowstorm and carried the whole of their objectives. The fresh gain, on a frontage of some 600 yards, considerably improved our observation in this area, just as a somewhat similar attack in the neighbourhood of Le Transloy, in the early morning of the 27th, gave us a commanding portion of the German position on the road from Peronne to Bapaume. This latest affair—"The Kaiser's Birthday Show", as our men described it—was a noteworthy success, involving the capture of 6 officers and 352 men of crack regiments, chiefly Würtembergers of the redoubtable Königin Olga Division—all picked men. The attack was launched without warning, save the barrage of fire for the infantry at half-past five, which the enemy, to his cost, regarded as the usual "morning hate". Retiring to his dug-outs until, as he thought, it would be safe to venture out again, he was caught there, wholly unprepared, by our assaulting troops, and faced with no alternative but surrender or death. Most of the Germans yielded at once, and were quickly bundled into a number of motor omnibuses which the organizers of the affair—so confident were they of success—had thoughtfully provided for the purpose. Thus, as Reuter's correspondent expressed it, "358 stout Boches had a free ride —on the Kaiser's birthday". The enemy made several furious attempts to recover their lost ground, but failed completely. Our bold stroke had helped to swell the total number of Germans caught by the British forces in France during the month of January, 1917, to 1228, including 27 officers. In his *communiqué* of February 1 Sir Douglas Haig mentioned the following regiments as having specially distinguished themselves in the capture of these prisoners:—

2nd Royal Scots.
8th E. Kent Regiment.
12th Royal Fusiliers.
1st King's Own Scottish Borderers.
1st Royal Inniskilling Fusiliers.
1st Border Regiment.
2nd Border Regiment.
1st South Staffordshire Regiment.
10th Loyal North Lancashire Regiment.
21st and 22nd Manchester Regiment.
8–10th Gordon Highlanders.
2nd Leinster Regiment.
2nd Monmouthshire Regiment.
20th, 21st, and 49th Canadian Battalion.
Newfoundland Battalion.
2nd Battalion 3rd New Zealand Rifle Brigade.

The German losses since the beginning of the war, according to the casualties announced in German official lists, and summarized by the British authorities, now reached the total of 4,087,692, the figures for January, compared with the totals, being as follows:—

| | Jan., 1917. | Totals. |
|---|---|---|
| Killed and died of wounds ... | 14,192 | 929,116 |
| Died of sickness... | 1,714 | 59,213 |
| Prisoners ... | 1,645 | 247,991 |
| Missing ... ... | 11,872 | 276,278 |
| Severely wounded | 10,577 | 539,655 |
| Wounded ... | 4,621 | 299,907 |
| Slightly wounded | 26,778 | 1,512,271 |
| Wounded remaining with units... | 6,133 | 223,261 |
| | 77,532 | 4,087,692 |

It should be borne in mind that though these are the official German figures it does not follow that they are reliable.

With the beginning of February the swing of the pendulum carried the centre of activity back to the Ancre, where our hard and unceasing pressure on the enemy's weakening line was about to tell with startling effect. Besides further improving our positions north of Beaumont-Hamel, we pushed forward our line some 500 yards on a front of about three-quarters of a mile east of Beaucourt, surprising the enemy in his dug-outs shortly before midnight on February 3–4, and sending back, all told, nearly 200 prisoners, as well as a number of machine-guns. Four costly counter-attacks during the ensuing twenty-four hours failed to rob us of our new advantage, which was succeeded on the 6th by a dashing advance on the opposite slopes of the river, where we occupied about 1000 yards of hostile trench in the neighbourhood of Grandcourt without opposition.

This last surprising fact marked the

Drawn by F. Matania

Through Clouds of Poison Gas: British troops raiding the German lines

The Germans wore smoke-helmets containing round chemical filters much larger than the nozzles of the British helmets. On both sides bombs and bayonets were used as the principal weapons. The bombs were carried in bags round the waist and hurled at the advancing foe.

beginning of the end of the enemy's remaining foothold in the valley of the Ancre. It was the prelude to the surrender of the final links in that northern chain of fortress positions, attacked by us in vain on July 1, 1916, which he had boasted that no troops in the world would ever succeed in conquering. Though we did not realize its full significance at the time, the evacuation of Grandcourt meant the opening of a fresh page in the history of the war, and convincing proof of the thorough defeat of the Germans in the Battle of the Somme. A year before, the pride of the German Higher Command would have prevented this retreat without a struggle. But, just as the enemy had abandoned Combles, because he knew there was no help for it, so he had now crept away from Grandcourt, well aware that our inexorable pincers were closing round the second stronghold as they had closed round the first.

The advance of our men north of Beaucourt on the opposite side of the Ancre had given them a line of ground which dominated Grandcourt on the north-west, and during the last two days of his occupation the enemy had suffered heavy losses in the neighbourhood. The final assault on the afternoon of February 7 was made beneath a protecting curtain of our shells, but apart from a few Germans left as rear-guards, who surrendered without a fuss, no opposition was encountered beyond the heavy fire from German guns, which failed to check the advance. The village itself was, of course, a mere heap of ruins, but it had been most elaborately fortified, and deep dug-outs were stored with rations which our men were not slow to enjoy as a change of diet. They were all unfeignedly glad to have turned out the foe from this villainous spot. Grandcourt, as Mr. Philip Gibbs wrote from British Head-quarters at the time, "was an evil-sounding name to soldiers on the Somme, because here for many months the enemy had massed his guns which fired down to Contalmaison, and flung high-explosives over the country below the Pozières ridge". Now he had been obliged to draw his artillery farther back, and the dominating ground was entirely in our hands.

Pursuing this advantage without delay, Sir Douglas Haig pushed up his troops vigorously on both sides of the Ancre. During the night they attacked and captured Baillescourt Farm on the Beaucourt-Miraumont road, while south of the river they carried another hostile trench lying between Grandcourt and our old front line. On the night of Saturday, the 10th, came a further move in the prolonged Battle of the Ancre; this time by Scottish regiments against a formidable section of the German trenches lying at the foot of the Serre Hill. This was stormed in the darkness, and held on a front of more than three-quarters of a mile. Some 215 prisoners were taken in this surprise attack, a "bag" considerably exceeding the number of our total casualties. Most of our losses were incurred in the ravine which the centre and left of the assaulting troops had to cross on their way to their objective on the opposite slope: a gully which the Ger-

British Official Photograph

Photographed under Fire: British patrol crawling up to the German trenches

mans, as usual, had converted into a rabbit-warren of fortified dug-outs. The place had been used by them as an ammunition dump while they still held Beaumont-Hamel, and was protected at its bottle-neck end by the machine-gun posts which were our chief source of trouble on the right of the attack. But the Scotsmen knew how to deal with these, as well as with the attempted counter-attack in the early Sunday morning, planned as soon as the German generals realized that our new line had now been advanced almost immediately under Pendant Copse.

South of the Ancre, on the same night, another line of trenches was entered in the neighbourhood of Pys, many casualties being inflicted on the enemy, and all his dug-outs destroyed. He was given no rest, indeed, on either side of the river, and though these local attacks did not sound very impressive at the time, as they were read day by day in the brief *communiqués* from British Head-quarters, their cumulative results were about to be seen with dramatic effect. There was a further nibble on the northern slopes on the Sunday night, when some 600 yards of hostile trench were occupied without much difficulty in the neighbourhood of the Beaucourt-Puisieux road. The Germans, who were finding it increasingly difficult to explain away this incessant wearing process on their line, and had made no mention at all in their war bulletins of their flight from Grandcourt, referred to this last withdrawal as the evacuation of useless trenches according to plan, the truth being, of course, that Sir Douglas Haig was threatening the whole of their strongest positions, and that their days on the Ancre were numbered. Incidentally the German war bulletin mentioned on this occasion that the British storming troops "frequently wore snow shirts" to reduce visibility as far as possible over the white slopes of the snow-clad ground. On the 12th the enemy made repeated attacks upon our new positions south of Serre, but were beaten back every time.

Five days later Sir Douglas Haig forced the pace on both sides of the Ancre, where Southerners, Londoners, and Midlanders won the heights dominating the ruined villages of Miraumont and Petit Miraumont, thus bringing both places within our power, just as the Scotsmen a week before had sealed the fate of Serre. The action was fought several hours before daybreak, along a 2-mile front, astride the tiny stream which already had been the scene of so many fierce encounters. Long after sunrise the battle was continued in the dense fog accompanying a general thaw, so that without consummate skill and indomitable resolution the attack must have failed lamentably. As it was, it proved a brilliant success, though the enemy, knowing that after the fall of Grandcourt we were certain to make this one of our next points of attack, had greatly strengthened his positions in the neighbourhood, all of which were garrisoned by Prussian troops ordered to hold the ground at all costs.

"To counteract the fog, which gave the enemy many chances," wrote Mr. Philip

Drawn by C. Clark

Fighting the Weather on the Western Front: British troops bringing up an 18-pounder through the mud in support of an infantry attack

Gibbs from the front, "one of our artillery officers risked his life for many hours by crawling close to the German lines and lying in a shell-hole with a field-telephone, from which he sent back messages directing the fire of our batteries. There was only a narrow margin of chance between his shell-house and the barrage beyond him, but luck rewarded his courage. Many other men took high risks, so that the attack should not fail, and its success is due to many individual acts of self-sacrifice and leadership."[1]

As a result, we penetrated over 1000 yards into the hostile defences on the south side of the river, and advanced our line to within a few hundred yards of the village of Petit Miraumont; while on the northern bank we reached a commanding position south of Miraumont itself by a most gallant charge on the upper slopes of the spur north of Baillescourt Farm. This last foothold was stubbornly contested all day, and on the following morning a great effort was made to hurl us back. Advancing along the spur in three waves, with masses of supporting troops in the rear, the Prussian infantry came under the concentrated fire of our artillery, and were driven back with heavy losses. In addition to this and the gains on the southern bank, we had captured during the previous day's battle in the fog 12 officers and 761 other ranks, together with a number of machine-guns and trench mortars.

The counter-attack that failed was the last offensive effort of the German war machine in the valley of the Ancre. Our heavy and unceasing strain upon

[1] *The Daily Telegraph.*

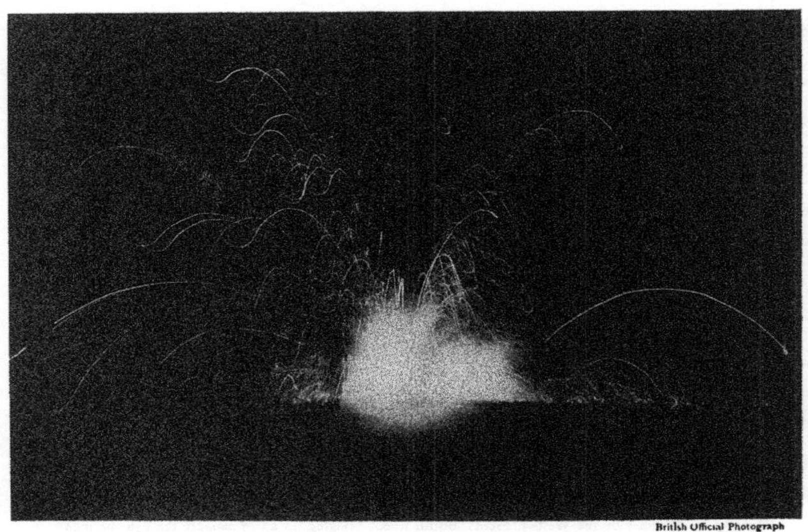

British Official Photograph

War's Pyrotechnics on the Western Front: German star-shell bursting at night near the British lines

Trench Architecture on the British Front: a row of dug-outs British Official Photograph

every part of the mechanism south of Gommecourt to Le Transloy had at length become unbearable. There was nothing for it but to withdraw and reassemble on a new alignment. This had long since been prepared for such a contingency, but was never intended for use unless the Allies forced the Germans back from a point of such immense strategic significance as the battle-fields of the Ancre and the Somme. For some time past they had been stealthily removing their guns, using those left to the last to get rid of the ammunition dumped near the front line. This accounted for much erratic firing and sudden outbursts of activity here and there without apparent reason. Then came the thick mist from the earth when the thaw set in, hiding the enemy's movements from the prying eyes of our airmen, and giving him the best opportunity to retreat that he was ever likely to get before we launched our spring campaign in conjunction with the armies of France. It was "now or never", and the German Higher Command chose their time well in withdrawing when they did.

The new chapter in the history of the war began when, suspecting what had happened, bodies of our troops were pushed forward cautiously, while patrols kept in touch with the retreating foe. The need to move warily was emphasized at Miraumont, where a mine was blown up in the main street after our entry—otherwise practically unopposed. It was uncanny work at first hunting in the mist among deserted craters and dug-outs for lurking Huns. Not many, however, were left behind to keep up the pretence of force as long as possible. The first hint of the general retreat appeared in Sir Douglas Haig's *communiqué* of February 24, in which he announced that "as a result of the unceasing pressure of our troops, the enemy to-day vacated further important positions on both banks of the Ancre", adding that, besides entering Petit Miraumont, we had made considerable progress south and south-east of Miraumont itself, and had also advanced our line on a front of over 1½ miles south and south-east of Serre.

British Official Photograph

Captured Intact by the Royal Irish: artillery examining a German gun prior to firing into the German lines with it

On the following day, Sunday, February 25, Serre, which had cost us so many lives, and, with its powerful fortifications, might still have exacted a heavy price to take, fell into our hands without any resistance worthy of the name. No single wall was left standing in this pulverized village, but some sniping took place from the ruins at the far end of the village before the last of the foe retreated. One or two scattered "pockets" of Germans were gathered up in the neighbourhood, but for the rest, the garrison and its guns had gone, after destroying everything of value in the dug-outs, and burning all supplies which could not be taken away.

Though the enemy evaded our infantry, he did not escape our guns, which had the range of all his roads to a nicety, and must have taken heavy toll as they swept them night and day with shells. With the prevailing mist and the treacherous sludge of the thawing ground, the pursuit of our troops and guns was extraordinarily difficult, made additionally so by the obstructive tactics adopted by the Germans to avoid any rear-guard actions. Barriers were flung across the roads in the shape of huge trees, and vast mine-craters opened beyond them when the last retreating column had passed. Machine-gun posts and picked snipers were stationed along the line of our pursuit, and here and there the German rear-guards stiffened their resistance; but in every case the enemy was compelled to continue his retreat. Pys, lying in ruins between Grandcourt and Warlencourt, and long known for its evil reputation as a place where the enemy used to keep his guns, was taken as easily as Serre.

British Official Photograph

In the abandoned German Lines: examining captured machine-guns

Astonishing things were happening, indeed, all along the front from Gommecourt to Warlencourt, where our troops moved up without opposition to the Butte, which had so long defied our farther advance along that road to Bapaume.

On February 26, when we also occupied the village of Warlencourt, we pushed on in the same direction and captured Le Barque during the night, occupying Ligny, east of that village, on the following day, and Thilloy—only $1\frac{1}{2}$ miles south-west of Bapaume—on the 28th. While these easy captures were being made to the south of the Ancre, similar progress was taking place to the north, with intervals of hard fighting between the historic park and château of Gommecourt and the considerable village of Puisieux, as though the Germans were loath to give up these long-held strongholds without something of a struggle.

Puisieux was stubbornly defended by isolated detachments of machine-gunners and snipers, and with its barbed-wire defences and elaborate fortifications would have been no easy place to take had it been held in force. A thrilling hunt among the ruins for the last defenders finally routed them all out, and our new line was extended beyond it, with the left resting on Gommecourt, which we occupied about the same time.

There was no stranger contrast in all these sensational episodes than this bloodless triumph at Gommecourt on the night of February 27, 1917, on the scene of the tragic assault of July 1, 1916, when so many of London's bravest and best laid down their lives in an heroic attempt to hold what they had won against annihilating odds. Now the enemy had scuttled away in the mist and darkness, putting up no rear-guard fights, but defending his retreat on either side by machine-gun posts in Rossignal and Biaz Woods. The little garrisons in these connected posts held on to the last with undeniable grit and determination, and much crafty fighting from tree to tree took place before they were finally exterminated or forced to surrender.

Savage and bitter as it was, the struggle was more suited to the British temperament than the deadly monotony of trench warfare. It was worth any risk to get into new country, and fight in the open again; and the knowledge that they had the Germans really on the run at last, if only for a time, inspired the whole British army with supreme confidence in the prospects of the spring campaign. All the sacrifices on the Ancre and the Somme had clearly been justified, King George himself in the following message correctly interpreting the German retreat as a fitting sequel to the prolonged battle of the preceding year:—

"*1st March*, 1917.

"I wish to express my admiration for the splendid work of all ranks under your command in forcing the enemy by a steady and persistent pressure to quit carefully prepared and strongly fortified positions. These successes are a fitting sequel to the fine achievements of my army last year in the Battle of the Somme, and reflect great credit on those responsible for drawing up the plans of this campaign.

"GEORGE R.I."

Sir Douglas Haig replied as follows:

"*2nd March*, 1917.

"His Majesty the King,

"On behalf of all ranks I beg leave to express our very respectful thanks for Your Majesty's most gracious message of approval of what has been recently accomplished by the forces under my command as a sequel to the Somme battle. It is a deep satisfaction to those responsible for drawing up the plans of this campaign to know that their work has been so generously commended by Your Gracious Majesty.

"SIR DOUGLAS HAIG."

Elsewhere along the British front in France and Flanders during the first two months of 1917, apart from the ever-swelling volume of artillery-fire and aerial activity, there was little to record save a repetition of raids and counter-raids, to enumerate all of which would be merely to repeat much that has been written before. Two outstanding performances of the kind, however, call for special mention, partly to illustrate the perplexing weakness of certain sections of the German front at the beginning of the new year, partly to demonstrate that our superiority in thus harassing the enemy remained as marked as ever. The first instance occurred on January 6, on the east side of Arras, where, over a front of some 2000 yards, English and Scottish troops joined forces in a daylight raid which led to results which were more astonishing then than six weeks or so later, when the possibility of a great German retreat became an accomplished fact. On January 6, when our troops advanced to the attack, following an exceptionally severe bombardment of the enemy's lines, and protected by a dense barrage of smoke, they were amazed to find that they could walk into the German positions with little or no opposition. Our guns had cut the wire to pieces; the trenches were in ruins; but instead of German machine-gunners swarming out of dug-outs that had escaped the bombardment, there was neither hostile gun nor hostile soldier in sight—save some German dead lying among the rubbish heaps. A little bombing here and there on the flanks, a few shots from snipers, and some erratic shelling from the enemy's guns at Tilloy offered such a mild reception compared with the ordinary canons of Teutonic frightfulness that the raiders naturally scented a trap, suspecting that behind all this local weakness lay hidden strength ready to overwhelm them if they ventured too far. One English and one Scottish detachment penetrated as far as the third German line in a vain search for the vanished foe, but, since they were not sent to hold the position, there was nothing for it, when all the dug-outs had been blown in and all evidence collected of military value, but to return with the news to the British lines. The Scottish officer who led his party to the farthest of the sectors at his part of the German system afterwards related to Mr. Philip Gibbs how, from first to last, he saw no living German. Having blown up the remaining undamaged dug-outs in the first and second lines, he had advanced with four men to the

With the "Heavies" on the Western Front: a big British howitzer

British Official Photograph

third line, where two more dug-outs awaited destruction. Since there was nothing more to do, he climbed up on the parados of the third German trench and smoked a cigarette while peacefully observing the surrounding country.

"The enemy was firing from Tilloy, but not heavily. The five-point-nine was at work, and a few field-guns. Somewhere out in the shell-craters German snipers lay, firing a shot or two now and then. The officer saw no use in staying longer. The raid was not for the capture of ground. The cigarette finished, he strolled back to the second line, chatted with a brother officer, and said: 'Better get back'. The men were prowling about the shell-craters, searching for Germans, and finding some dead ones, but not many living. The Scottish officer had brought a French hunting-horn with him—a queer thing to take into a fight, but quite useful. He blew on it—'tantara, tantara!'—and called off the chase. The wolf-hounds slouched back to the master of the hunt. So the raid ended, and there was no retaliation."[1]

Colonel Campbell, of the Coldstreams, had proved the value of the hunting-horn in the fighting-line when he won his V.C. in the advance of the Guards on the Somme four months before. Its usefulness was again demonstrated in the Londoners' "record" raid in the Ypres salient on February 21, 1917, when the "Tally Ho!" and "Hark For'ard!" played no inconspicuous part in one of the smartest feats of the kind in the history of the war. The heroes of the affair belonged to a Cockney Territorial Battalion which already boasted a proud record of service on the Western front, but most of the men on this occasion

British Official Photograph

An Interval of Peace: British bomb-gun section enjoying a hand at cards while the sentries keep watch through the periscopes

[1] *The Daily Telegraph.*

were new-comers, and had never been "over the top" before. The whole thing was a triumph of initiative, organization, and nerve. The Germans attacked were holding a troublesome minor salient some 500 feet wide, lying between Hill 60 and the Bluff, and denting our line in a way that decided the colonel commanding these London Territorials to make a clean sweep of it. The raid was so planned that, when the preliminary bombardment broke out on the evening of February 21, before it was dark, the Germans were at a loss to know exactly where the expected blow would fall. The shelling suggested a raid on Hill 60, and frantic preparations were accordingly made to repel an attack there. When the Londoners advanced to the south of this, amid all the surrounding confusion of guns, they did so under their own barrage of "Stokes"—a variety of bombs which is not only highly destructive but particularly awe-inspiring in appearance—and carried out their individual instructions like clockwork. Some prisoners were taken in the first line, and promptly escorted home. Others bolted up side alleys, little dreaming that we knew every inch of their German trench system, and that our flankers were shepherding them along converging lines, so that presently, as a *Times* correspondent wrote at the time from British Headquarters, everybody would meet.

"Suspicion took the Germans, however, for they heard behind them horns calling 'Tally-Ho!' and 'Hark For'ard!' and they waited at the rendezvous with their hands up—a gesture which our leading files ignored for the moment. Coming from different directions, and meeting as arranged, our men rushed at each other and shook hands over it, while the Prussians still looked on, in the passive attitude of submission. That was at the third German line. Very fine going, indeed! The men were told to give the enemy every chance to surrender. But those in some dug-outs were obstinate, or frightened. Not so a German officer seen down below at a telephone. He stoutly refused to come out—'So—er—I had to switch him off, sir', said a corporal, blushing."

The day's record bag included about 120 prisoners, belonging to the 185th Regiment, and Prussians. In one brief, crowded hour—just before the Germans, now fully alive to the situation, began pounding their own front at this point with concentrated hate from artillery and trench mortars—the Londoners had also succeeded in wrecking the whole area, including mine shafts, stores of grenades, and every machine-gun that could not be carried back.

This was one of many striking proofs during the winter of 1916–17 that not only our officers, but also our men were learning their business thoroughly.

"The fact is," to quote Mr. Bonar Law's reference to the subject at the time, "that this army, composed of men who three years ago were engaged in peaceful occupations, who loved peace and never dreamt they would be called upon to use weapons of destruction, these men are showing themselves the equal—and one can give them no higher praise—of the regular troops who in the early days of the war did so much to save the situation."

By this time the British front in France had again been considerably

The Last Footbridge before the German Lines: Belgian sentinel on the flooded Yser, which barred the road to Calais

extended. The lengthening process had begun on the right towards the end of 1916, the whole of the ground won by the French during the Somme offensive being gradually taken over by Sir Douglas Haig. By the end of February, 1917, at which point our present survey comes to an end, the British front, stretching from a point near Ypres on the left to the neighbourhood of Roye on the right, reached a total length of nearly 120 miles. This expansion not only served to facilitate the Allies' plans for the ensuing campaign, but also lessened the increasing strain on the resources of France.

Towards the middle of February, before the German retreat became general in the valley of the Ancre, French correspondents, eager to learn Sir Douglas Haig's views on the next phase of the conflict in the West, found him confident that the war of trenches must make way for a war of movement. Only thus, as he pointed out, could we hope to win the great advantages upon which we counted. The British Commander-in-Chief was equally confident of the Allies' power eventually to break the German front. Justified as he was in this by the achievements and unflinching spirits of his troops, as well as by the inexorable resolve of the nation behind them, he was not blind, however, to the magnitude of the task ahead. If Germany, which, numerically, was a great nation, could not be conquered in 1917, let us, he said in effect, continue the struggle until in the military sense she is finally and decisively beaten. Let us beware of a lame and premature peace, which would leave German militarism still in power, stealthily preparing a terrible revenge in the none-too-distant future. F. A. M.

Lightning Source UK Ltd.
Milton Keynes UK
UKHW020756060119
335045UK00011B/770/P

9 781333 926694